The Finance Curse

Also by Nicholas Shaxson

Poisoned Wells: The Dirty Politics of African Oil
Treasure Islands: Tax Havens and the Men who Stole the World

The Finance Curse

How Global Finance Is Making Us All Poorer

Nicholas Shaxson

THE BODLEY HEAD
LONDON

1 3 5 7 9 10 8 6 4 2

The Bodley Head, an imprint of Vintage,
20 Vauxhall Bridge Road,
London SW1V 2SA

The Bodley Head is part of the Penguin Random House group of companies
whose addresses can be found at global.penguinrandomhouse.com

Copyright © Nicholas Shaxson 2018

Nicholas Shaxson has asserted his right to be identified as the author of this
Work in accordance with the Copyright, Designs and Patents Act 1988

First published by The Bodley Head in 2018

www.penguin.co.uk/vintage

A CIP catalogue record for this book is available from the British Library

Hardback ISBN 9781847925381
Trade Paperback ISBN 9781847924216

Typeset in 11.5/14 pt Dante MT
by Integra Software Services Pvt. Ltd, Pondicherry

Printed and bound in Great Britain by Clays Ltd, Elcograf S.p.A.

Penguin Random House is committed to a sustainable future for our
business, our readers and our planet. This book is made from Forest
Stewardship Council® certified paper.

MIX
Paper from
responsible sources
FSC® C018179

For Emma, Oscar and George.

Contents

Introduction

If you've recently bought a ticket through Trainline, the digital rail ticket seller, you may have paid a small booking fee, perhaps 75p. Your rail journey may have been straightforward, but the journey taken by that little booking fee after it left your bank account would have been more extraordinary.

Trainline.com Limited, the London-based company that runs the service, is owned by another company called Trainline Holdings Limited. That company is owned by another, which is owned by another, and so on. Five companies above Trainline.com, your little booking fee would skip out across the English Channel to the tax haven of Jersey, then back again to London, where it would pass through five more companies, then hop back out to Jersey once more, before migrating over to the European mainland where it would enter the accounts of two companies in Luxembourg, another tax haven.

Along the way, all sorts of other rivulets join in and leave the tinkling, rustling flows of money, as different companies in this hierarchy borrow money from banks, or from each other, or inject and lend cash back and forth, sometimes at eye-wateringly high interest rates. Once it has reached Luxembourg, our brave little 75p enters a financial tunnel where it becomes a little harder to track. But it soon pops up again, this time in the Caribbean, where it dances upwards through three or four more mysterious and impenetrable Cayman Islands companies. There, having already passed through twenty or so companies after leaving your bank account, it joins a multitude of other financial streams and rivers from around the world, which come together and flow into the United States and into the maw of KKR, a giant US investment firm.

The river of money doesn't even stop there, though. It then flows onwards into the accounts of KKR's shareholders: the world's biggest banks, investment funds and wealthy individuals – including KKR's two surviving founders, the billionaires George Roberts and Henry Kravis. Since it did its first deal in 1977, KKR has bought full or partial stakes in nearly 300 real, solid companies including Safeway, Toys R Us, Alliance Boots, Del Monte foods, the makers of the Sonos wireless hi-fi system, Boots the chemist, and Trainline. KKR makes most of its money by re-engineering companies for profit, and if they haven't gone bankrupt, selling them off. At the last count, it still owned over 180 real companies. I say 'real' because KKR actually owns or controls well over 4,000 corporate entities, including over twenty in Jersey, over 200 in Luxembourg, and over 800 in the Cayman Islands, most of which are detached from the lives of real people and exist only in the accountants' virtual reality world. Each solid underlying company in the KKR empire, like Boots or Trainline, has one of these convoluted corporate structures perched on top of it, snaking chains of entities often with peculiar names drawn from finance's arcane lingo, like (in Trainline's case) 'Trainline Junior Mezz Limited' or 'Victoria Investments Intermediate Holdco Limited'.[1]

None of what I have described so far is remotely illegal: in fact, this is increasingly the way business is done. But the example of Trainline's corporate architecture does raise some big questions.

Question one is this: what is it all for?

To answer this, it is necessary to understand financialisation, a phenomenon that first properly emerged in the 1970s and has slowly, silently, crept up on us all. Financialisation has involved a massive growth in the size and power of the financial, insurance and real estate (FIRE) sectors, and it has also seen financial markets, techniques, motives and ways of thinking penetrate ever deeper into our economies, our societies and even our culture. Trainline's corporate structure is an example of this second aspect of financialisation, where the bosses of companies that create real wealth in the economy – by making widgets and sprockets, finding cures for malaria, selling toys or package holidays, or creating efficient platforms for selling rail tickets – are increasingly encouraged to turn their attentions away from the hard slog of trying to boost productivity and genuine entrepreneurship, and towards the more profitable sugar rush of financial engineering to tease out more profits for the owners.

Half a century ago it was widely accepted that the purpose of corporations was not just to make profits, but also to serve employees, communities and wider society. In the era of financialisation of the last few decades, our businesses have undergone a massive transformation. The purpose of business has been whittled down to little more than a single-minded focus on maximising the wealth of shareholders, the owners of those companies. Trainline's convoluted corporate structure is actually a *financial* structure sitting on top of the real, genuinely useful work going on underneath, and it siphons money upwards in whizzy and sophisticated new ways. It is just one example of the financialisation at work, all around us, almost everywhere we turn.

There is a second big question about this corporate complexity. The Trainline group of companies earned around £148 million in revenue from UK customers in 2017: that's a lot of 75p booking fees. Trainline has provided you with a useful service: a train ticket, with minimal hassle. But should it have levied £148 million or so on Britain's rail commuters in 2017 for providing this service?[2] Could it have provided just as good a service for half this cost? How much of this £148 million represents genuine added value, plus a reasonable reward for any risk-taking, and how much represents unwarranted wealth extraction by this company with a rather privileged position in rail ticket sales? It isn't easy to answer this question, not least because a lot of the financial pipework is hidden in Jersey, Luxembourg and the Cayman Islands, but also because it is partly a philosophical question: where do we as a society want to draw the line, and judge profits to be excessive? What we do know is that Britain's beleaguered rail travellers are paying a lot of money to Trainline – and that KKR and its investors are making a lot of money. Whatever we judge the size of the excess profits to be, that is a hidden tax on British rail travellers.

In the era of financialisation, the corporate bosses and their advisers, and the financial sector, have moved away from creating wealth *for* the economy, and towards extracting wealth *from* the economy, using financial techniques. Financialisation has unleashed gushers of profits for the owners and bosses of these firms, while the underlying economy – the place where most of us live and work – has stagnated.

The profits, and the stagnation, are two sides of the same coin: wealth extraction.

This is a central part of what I call the finance curse. The concept of the finance curse is simple: it's the idea that once a financial sector grows above an optimal size and beyond its useful roles, it begins to harm the country that hosts it. Finance turns away from its traditional role serving society and creating wealth, and towards often more profitable activities to extract wealth from other parts of the economy. It also becomes politically powerful, shaping laws and rules and even society to suit it. The results include lower economic growth, steeper inequality, inefficient markets, damage to public services, worse corruption, the hollowing-out of alternative economic sectors, and widespread damage to democracy and to society.

To unpack the idea of the finance curse we'll go on a century-long journey that spans the globe; from the era of American robber barons in the early twentieth century, through the 1950s to explore the rebirth of the City of London as a global financial centre after the fall of the British empire, to the birth of modern British tax havens in the Caribbean in the 1960s, then to explore the early roots of Ireland's Celtic Tiger economy in the 1970s and 80s, and then on to uncover some surprising truths about London's outsized role in generating the global financial crisis. After the crisis, we enter the peculiar world of wealth managers, examine the billionaire-friendly subterfuges and immense powers of the accounting giants, and follow the twisting corporate trails leading from care workers in northern England up to the glittering offices of private equity moguls in Mayfair. And we will see how, all along the way, evidence has been beaten, twisted and abused to perpetrate a great hoax upon the public, persuading us that all this activity is normal, necessary and even a good thing. It is anything but.

The finance curse concept has a long history. It began in the early to mid-1990s when I was working as a correspondent for Reuters in oil-rich and diamond-rich Angola, which the United Nations at the time said was suffering the worst war in the world. Every Western visitor I met asked me a version of the same question: how could the people of a country with such vast mineral wealth be so shockingly, appallingly destitute? Corruption was one answer, of course: a venal leadership was getting extremely rich from the oil money, eating lobsters and drinking champagne on the beach in the capital Luanda while their ragged and malnourished compatriots slaughtered each other out in the dusty provinces. But something else was going on too.

I didn't know it then, but I was getting a front-line view of a grand new thesis that academics were just starting to put together, known as the resource curse.[3] Academics had worked out that for many mineral-rich countries like Angola, their natural resource abundance seemed to result in slower economic growth, more corruption, more conflict, more authoritarian politics and greater poverty than their resource-poor peers. If you remember just one thing about the resource curse, then remember this: it's not just that mineral-rich countries don't harness their mineral riches to benefit their people, or that powerful crooks snaffle the wealth and stash it offshore, though that is also true. The big point is that all this money flowing from their natural resource endowments can make their populations *even worse off* than if the riches had never been discovered. In short, more money can make a country poorer. That's why the resource curse is also some-times known as the Paradox of Poverty from Plenty. It affects different countries in different ways – some countries, like Norway, even seem to have benefited from their minerals – but few people in Angola back then doubted that the minerals that were feeding the war had cursed their country in deep and long-lasting ways.

As I wrote about the resource curse in Angola, John Christensen was reading my articles, and noticing more and more parallels between what I was describing in Angola, and what he was seeing in the British tax haven of Jersey, where he was the official economic adviser. 'I was fascinated by this counter-intuitive concept that too much oil and gas wealth could make you poorer,' he recalled. 'The more I read about it, the more I thought "But this is Jersey!" The parallels with Jersey were uncanny.' And he understood a bigger point: it wasn't just finance-dependent Jersey that was suffering something like Angola's resource curse. It was Britain too. (Christensen, horrified by the venality he had seen in Jersey's tax haven sector, left, and in 2003 and helped set up the Tax Justice Network, an organisation to fight against tax havens.)

The parallels between Britain and Angola start with the basic fact that each country is dominated by a large economic sector: oil, in Angola's case, and finance, in Britain's. As a measure of this, UK banking assets stood at the equivalent of around 50 per cent of annual national income (or GDP) for a century or so before 1970, then suddenly roared upwards as the era of financialisation got under way. By 2006, just ahead of the global financial crisis, UK banking assets had reached 500 per cent (or five times) GDP, a ratio that hasn't since changed very much. This is twice the European average, and four to five times that of the United States. If you widen this beyond banking to include assets held by insurance companies and other financial institutions, it is well over ten times GDP.[4]

In Angola and in other countries up and down Africa's oil-soaked western coastline, I'd watched the oil sector draining the life out of other parts of the economy. All the best-educated people were being sucked out of industry, agriculture, government, civil society and the media, and were instead flocking towards the high-salaried oil jobs.

Those clever people who *did* stay in Angola's government soon lost interest in the difficult challenges of national development, whose prospects oil had savaged anyway, and politics became little more than a corrupting, conflict-ridden game of jostling to get access to the flows of oil money. The City of London has achieved something remarkably similar with Britain's best and brightest. 'Finance literally bids rocket scientists away from the satellite industry,' wrote the authors of a well-known academic study on the rise of finance and economic growth. 'The result is that people who might have become scientists, who in another age dreamt of curing cancer and of flying people to Mars, today dream of becoming hedge fund managers.' Among other important things, the financial brain drain out of politics and into highly paid finance is a big reason why Britain has had such poor prime ministers recently.[5] Many excellent possible candidates have been diverted into hedge funds, their talents washed away in a deluge of money. With this giant shift of political focus, balanced national development takes a second hit.

In Angola the cascading inflows of oil wealth raised the local price levels of goods and services, from housing to haircuts. This high-price environment caused a third wave of destruction to local industry and agriculture, which found it ever harder to compete with imported goods. Likewise, inflows of money into the City of London (and money created in the City of London) have had a similar effect on house prices and on local price levels, making it harder for British exporters to compete with foreign competitors.[6]

Oil booms and busts also had a disastrous effect in Angola. Cranes would festoon the Luanda skyline in good times, then would leave a residue of half-finished concrete hulks when the bust came. Massive borrowing in the good times and a build-up of debt arrears in the bad times magnified the problem. In Britain's case, the booms and busts of finance are differently timed and mostly caused by different things, but as with oil booms, it has a ratchet effect. In good times the dominant sector damages alternative economic sectors, but when the bust comes, the destroyed sectors aren't easily rebuilt. And bankers – who famously are the sort of people who will lend you an umbrella when it's dry but want it back once it rains – reinforce it all by turning on the credit taps during booms, amplifying their effects, then whipping away the goodies when things go bad, worsening the slump.

In a more 'normal' economy like France's, wealth is created at the bottom by many people working in diverse fields: in factories, construction, banking, fishing or catering. The government contributes by paying for the police, roads, schools, the rule of law, the sewers, and so on. Governments must then bargain with voting citizens and their businesses to raise the taxes from them, and this bargaining develops healthy lines of accountability. But when you have oil money sluicing in at the top of the political system, you don't need to bargain with your citizens any more. Oil money washes away checks and balances and institutions, leaving rulers with a crude political formula: they allocate wealth, or permissions to access wealth, in exchange for loyalty. If your citizens complain, the oil money pays for paramilitary police to keep them in their place. (For this reason, oil economies are often authoritarian.) I sometimes picture an oil-dominated economy like Angola's as a river, with flotillas of boats loaded with treasure – the oil wealth – gliding downstream. Along the way there are gatekeepers exacting tolls from the passing boats. The big diversions occur far upstream, and as it flows downwards and splits into ever more rivulets, there is steadily less to go around. Most people live far out at the end of the river delta, where there is almost nothing left.

Something similar is happening in Britain. Britain has a far more diversified economy than Angola's, so plenty of wealth is being generated at the bottom – but there is also a gusher of wealth flowing in at the top, not from pipes inserted into the ground but instead engineered by the financial sector, much of it siphoned out from other parts of the economy. These top-down wealth flows from the financial sector haven't exactly turned Britain into an authoritarian state (though this has certainly happened to a fair degree in some of the smaller tax havens where financial dominance is much greater), but what *has* happened is that finance is often in conflict with other parts of the economy, and in these battles finance always seems to win out.

All these factors have conspired to damage the non-oil economies of both Angola and Britain. Britain's industrial decline hasn't been nearly so calamitous – but Angola's past carries big lessons for our future. Excessive prosperity in the dominant sector can strangle other sectors. And those thrilling flows of money flooding into your country are likely to stunt economic growth over the long term, and damage your country in many ways.

It is no coincidence that the decline of British manufacturing since the 1970s has been so much faster than in other industrial economies, at the same time as Britain's financial sector assets have grown so much larger as a share of the economy than in comparable Western nations. It is no coincidence, either, that – for all the trillions of dollars that sluice through the City of London and the glitzy oligarchs who populate our restaurants and theatres – the United Kingdom as a whole is no better off than its peers: if anything, it's worse off. Britain's GDP per capita is lower than that of its northern European peers, but it is also a much more unequal place, and with poorer overall scores on health and well-being.[7]

You'd expect the enormous growth in our financial sector to have generated a fountain of investment capital for other sectors in our economy, but the exact opposite has happened. A century ago, 80 per cent of bank lending went to finance business. Now, banks are lending mostly to each other and into housing and commercial real estate: little more than 10 per cent of UK bank lending goes to businesses outside the financial sector.[8] Investment in the non-financial parts of the UK economy has been less than that of Italy. In fact it is the lowest of any G7 economy. And this is a long-term trend: since 1997 this investment share has been the lowest in the OECD, a club of thirty-four rich countries which includes Mexico, Chile and Turkey. Many British people take pride in our supposedly 'competitive' low-tax, high-finance economy – but on an income-per-person basis, Britain's economy is smaller than that of nearly all its northern European peers, and its productivity is a full 25 per cent lower than high-tax France. Outside of London, British productivity is lower still, and has been for a very long time.[9] To compensate for this sluggishness, and to escape from politically difficult choices, successive governments have filled the holes with policies of financial loosening, which has allowed bank credit to grow three times as fast as the underlying economy since the 1960s.[10] And yet most of this credit has been circulating in the financial sector, unmoored, disconnected from the real economy and from the people it is supposed to serve. The transformation that has happened in the era of financialisation has had little to do with the needs of ordinary business and ordinary people.

The same question emerges here again, but on a bigger scale: *what is it all for?* John Kay, one of Britain's best-known financial commentators, poses this question himself, and adds this observation: 'If a closed circle of people keep exchanging bits of paper with each other, common sense suggests that the overall value of these bits of paper won't change much. If some members of that closed circle make extraordinary profits, these profits can only be made at the expense of other members of the same circle.'[11]

But the finance curse analysis shows that it seems to be even worse than that: all this money swirling around our oversized financial sector seems to be making us collectively poorer. The mainstream narrative in Britain is that the City of London is the goose that lays the golden eggs. But the finance curse reveals the City to be a different bird: a cuckoo in the nest that is crowding out other sectors.

We all need finance. We need it to pay our bills, to help us save for retirement, to redirect our savings to businesses so they can invest, to insure us against unforeseen calamities, and also sometimes for speculators to sniff out new investment opportunities in our economy. We need finance – but this tells us nothing about how big our financial centre should be, or what roles it should serve. The measure of finance's contribution to our economy is whether it provides useful services to us at a reasonable cost – not whether it produces large profits and high salaries. Imagine if telephone companies suddenly became insanely profitable and began churning out lots of billionaires, and telephony grew to dwarf every other economic sector – but our phone calls were still crackly and expensive and the service unreliable. It would be obvious that something strange was going on.

The rise of finance and financialisation has not been a zero-sum game that transfers wealth from poorer majorities to a relatively small number of players in the financial sector. It is a long-term, negative-sum game. A lot of evidence and research is now emerging to show that once the financial sector in a country grows beyond a certain size it starts to turn away from its critically useful functions and towards more lucrative and more destructive goals. Further expansion beyond this optimal size tends to make the economy that hosts it grow more slowly and generate a range of other harms. Britain's financial sector passed its optimal size long ago. And this raises more big questions. First, where is the tipping point? Second, how big is the damage?

On the first question, I will take a more historical and political approach and through this book I will describe how the first seeds of trouble were sown in the 1950s, an era when Britain lost its empire and when the City of London faced powerful democratic forces at home which curbed its profits and its power, and which delivered unprecedented growth to other parts of the economy. The City then began to construct a new globalised financial model, which was so successful for the City that some have described its rebirth as the dawn of a second British empire. After these early beginnings, this new model began to emerge in the 1970s, and the damage began to mount in earnest.

On the second question, we can take a more data-orientated approach. In 2016 two US finance academics, Professor Gerald Epstein of the University of Massachusetts, one of the US's best-known authorities on financialisation, and Juan Montecino of Columbia University, published a document called *Overcharged: The High Costs of High Finance*. It was a kind of finance curse analysis for the United States, and it sought to use established methods to create an estimate of the overall damage created by an outsized financial sector in the US. Their conclusion? That the US financial system will impose an excess cost of between $12.9 trillion and $22.7 trillion on the US economy between 1990 and 2023, thereby 'making finance in its current form a net drag on the American economy'. This calculation of the benefits of the financial sector to the US economy, minus the costs imposed by the financial sector on the US economy, is equivalent to a net $105,000–$184,000 for the average American family: without this loss, the typical US household would have doubled its wealth at retirement. The US economy would have been stronger today if the US government had simply paid its highest-paying financiers their full salaries, then sent them off to live in luxurious gated communities to play golf all day.

In 2017 John Christensen and I discussed with Epstein and Montecino the possibility of producing a similar calculation for Britain. They did so, and I can now reveal the results. Overall, they estimate the costs of the damage to the UK economy from having an oversized finance sector at £4.5 trillion, plus some. To put that in perspective, that is equivalent to two and a half years' economic output, or £170,000 per household. That gives an idea of how much more the average family might have saved, had the UK financial sector been the optimal (much smaller) size, and serving society as it should.[12]

These are conservative numbers, in purely numerical terms. But there is also a large range of unmeasurable costs to add to the numbers. One is that the finance curse has powerful racial, gender, geographical and generational effects. Pretty much every time, as I will show, financialisation and the rise of finance tends to mean wealth and power are extracted from the more disadvantaged groups, and delivered up to those least in need of it, worsening inequalities of wealth and power across many dimensions. Another potential cost that cannot be measured is that excess finance, by worsening these inequalities, will have added to a pervasive sense of injustice among many British people, and contributed significantly towards the Brexit vote.

A further unmeasurable cost is the rise in organised crime and other abusive activities that happen in the City of London. It's impossible to convey here the sheer scale of this. A good indication though can be found in a list entitled 'Robert Jenkins' partial list of bank misdeeds'. This list is a kind of running score published and updated by a group called Finance Watch. Jenkins is a former member of the Bank of England's Financial Policy Committee and a former Citigroup and Credit Suisse banker, who has seen it all. His list enumerates the multitude of ways in which banks do wrong. It begins, for example, with '1. Mis-selling of payment protection insurance' ('mis-selling' is usually a euphemism for fraud). And it goes on like this, for a long time.

Each element is a shocker. Coming in at number 11, there's 'Abusive small business lending practices', a hallmark of modern finance. At number 16, there is the humble 'Aiding and abetting tax evasion' – a sport that has cost treasuries around the world hundreds of billions. Number 17 is 'Aiding and abetting money laundering for violent drugs cartels', a reference to, among other things, the role played by HSBC in washing hundreds of millions of dollars for Russian gangsters and for Mexico's Sinaloa cartel. Number 19 is 'Manipulation of Libor', referring to the numbers used to calculate payments in the $800 trillion derivatives market, and a whole lot more besides. Number 61 is the less weighty 'Offers to procure prostitutes to curry favour with Sovereign Wealth Fund clients'. Tucked away at number 109, there's 'Facilitating African money laundering on a grand scale'.

At the time of writing, this list contained 144 items – and counting. Each represents a large can of villainous worms. And this is only a *partial* list of the misdeeds – and even then, this only refers to *banks*. Trying to get your arms around all this feels a bit like trying to convey to a child the distances between galaxies in the known universe. Many of the costs these activities impose on society lie outside the scope of our estimate of £4.5 trillion in damages.

It is certainly possible to raise all sorts of objections to this gigantic £4.5 trillion number – and defenders of the City of London will doubtless shoot plenty of arrows at it. But this is a *better* estimate than the standard dominant narrative that has emerged from the City, which involves simply totting up the total number of jobs, tax revenues, or the financial services export surplus, thereby discreetly stripping out all the costs, and then calling this the 'contribution' of finance to the economy and flogging it to the media. Without including the costs of oversized finance alongside the benefits, the City's numbers are meaningless. Theirs is a gross figure, this new research provides a net figure – which turns out to be large and negative. As ever, more research is needed here.[13] But for now it is the best numerical estimate of how far the City has outgrown its useful role. And it is a good starting point for understanding the scale of the finance curse.

By now, a new question emerges: why have we put up with an overgrown sector that is making us worse off? A large part of the reason lies in a narrative we're fed by politicians and by the many players in the City of London: that the City is indispensable, full of brilliant wealth creators, and must be pampered. This narrative is underpinned by the ubiquitous idea of 'national competitiveness' which has emerged in a particular and malign form in Britain and in many other countries: a form I call the Competitiveness Agenda. This narrative has pervaded all aspects of British political and economic life for decades.

The basic proposition that 'Britain must be competitive' is immensely appealing. But the Competitiveness Agenda which rests on this idea turns out to be one of the most confused economic narratives of all time. It has bamboozled many people in Britain, persuading them that they must deliver a constant stream of financial subsidies, deregulation and other gifts to the City, for fear that all the bankers will run away to more 'competitive' places like Singapore or Geneva. These constant calls to support the 'competitiveness' of the City have been used as a cosh to bludgeon away opposition to corporate tax cuts, financial deregulation, or Britain's soft-touch approach to policing dirty money and financial crime. It is the financial sector's strongest ideological weapon, enabling it to capture Britain's policymaking apparatus and large parts of the media. This capture is mostly a subtle, networked thing, backed up by dollops of well-aimed sponsorship as banks, insurance firms and hedge funds hurl funding at opinion-forming think tanks, throw banquets for visiting dignitaries, or organise drunken grouse-hunting expeditions for politicians or distinguished members of the metropolitan punditry. I call it 'country capture' because it goes far beyond the political system, penetrating deep into our economy, our culture and our society. This widely accepted story about the pressing need to preserve the City's 'competitiveness' goes a long way towards explaining why our banks are too big to fail and our bankers too important to jail, why our hospitals aren't getting funded, why your favourite local bookshop closed down, and why tax havens seem to be so hard to tackle.

The concept of 'national competitiveness' is a complex, tricky area, whose history and meaning I will explore throughout this book. Many people have been tricked into believing that Britain can be compared to a giant corporation, as if there is something called 'UK PLC' competing in the world marketplace, pitted against Germany or China or Luxembourg in a global race. These claims are nonsense, and this book will expose the deep fallacies and misunderstandings that form the basis of this pervasive narrative that underpins the finance curse.

The finance curse turns the dominant story decisively on its head. The purpose of having a 'competitive' financial sector, under the prevailing logic, is to keep the City as big and strong as possible. But if more finance is bad for Britain, then logically the City must *shrink* if we want our country to prosper. So pursuing this kind of 'competitiveness' is a fool's errand: we should do exactly the opposite. Understand this, and democracy gets a wholesale new lease of life. If Britain and its financial sector don't need to 'compete' in a 'global race' on this stuff, then it can *unilaterally* tax and regulate its financial sector in the interests of society – and be better off overall. As I will show, this will generally tend to preserve the good stuff and get rid of the stuff that's harming us. That is quite a prize.

And this book contains a tremendous piece of good news: that prize is well within our grasp.

1

Sabotage

Some economists behave like aliens who sit in spaceships high above the earth, watching us through powerful telescopes. They record all the scurrying back and forth, then build theories and mathematical models about what we're up to, without accounting for folly, cruelty, sex, friendship, credulity and the general rough and tumble of our crazy lives.

The renegade economist and thinker Thorstein Veblen was an extraterrestrial of a different kind. He too perched himself outside the normal range of human experience, but this enabled him to sit far enough back from humanity to be able to observe our foibles clearly, so as to use them as a starting point for properly understanding the world of money and business. He rebelled against conventional wisdom in many ways, but particularly so in his attitude towards economics. Veblen has been called an American Karl Marx or the Charles Darwin of economics, but in truth his varied output is too diverse and weird to categorise. Yet his messy understanding of human behaviour is exactly what makes his ideas so remarkable. By linking economics with uglier truths about how we as humans really behave and think, he summarised many of the deepest principles that underpin the finance curse.

Veblen was a Norwegian-American economist, sociologist, woman-iser and misfit. He made his own furniture, didn't make his bed, and he would let his dishes pile up in tottering heaps before washing them all in a barrel with a hosepipe. It is said he once borrowed a sack from a neighbour just so that he could return it with a hornets' nest inside. In his florid, peculiar writing style he described religion as 'the fabrication of vendible imponderables in the nth dimension', the main Churches as 'chain stores' and their individual churches as 'retail outlets'. At the fiercely religious Carleton College Academy in Minnesota he asked a student to calculate the value of her Church to her in kegs of beer, and provoked uproar with a speech entitled 'A Plea for Cannibalism'. A lank-haired weirdo genius, he observed society unencumbered by strictures of religion, economic conventions, or the petty airs and graces of the early twentieth century that kept the grubby workers down and the landed gentry in their rightful place. His apartness let him see things others couldn't, and helped him say the unsayable.

Born to Norwegian immigrant parents in rural Wisconsin in 1857, Veblen was the sixth and the cleverest of twelve children. The farmstead where he grew up was so isolated that when he left he was, as one historian put it, 'emigrating to America'. His brilliance took him from these humble beginnings to Yale, where he got a PhD in 1884, before going to ground and mooching around listlessly for several years. 'He read and loafed,' his brother remembered, 'and the next day he loafed and read.' Some said he was unemployable because he hated Christianity, or that he had a prejudice against Norwegians. His oddball, sardonic wit surely didn't help, nor did his open contempt for economists and other academics. He clashed repeatedly with university authorities but also relished scholarly cut and thrust, calling himself 'a disturber of the intellectual peace' and 'a wanderer in the intellectual no-man's land'.

It wasn't all solitude, though. He was later ejected from the University of Chicago for marital infidelities with colleagues and students. As one story goes, the dean summoned Veblen into his office in 1905 for a chat.

DEAN: We have a problem with the faculty wives.
VEBLEN: Oh yes, I know. They're terrible. I've had them all.[1]

His womanising prowess wasn't down to his appearance. Longish hair plastered down either side of a centre parting, bushy eyebrows and a roughly cut moustache and beard combined to suggest he hadn't tried very hard to discard his Norwegian peasant-farmer upbringing. One lover apparently described him as a chimpanzee. Others remembered a strange domestic charisma. 'Lounging about in his loose dressing gown and looking not nearly as anaemic and fragile as in his street clothes, he reminded one, with his drooping moustaches and Nordic features, of nothing so much as a hospitable Viking taking his ease at his own fireside,' a visitor attested. 'At such times, he was at his best, doling out curious information, throwing off a little malicious gossip which, in view of his seclusiveness, he must have picked miraculously out of the air, mixing picturesque slang with brilliant phrases of his own coinage, solicitously watching out for his guests' comfort.'[2]

This charisma extended to the realm of ideas and gained him a following which has endured more than a century after his death. He vivisected capitalism, impaling the complacent orthodoxy of Victorian and neoclassical economists, who regarded humanity as a set of identical perfectly informed 'utility-maximising' individuals and firms pursuing their own self-interest, to be treated as data inputs for their mathematical sausage-making machines. In these economists' hands, he acidly observed, a human became 'a lightning calculator of pleasures and pains, who oscillates like a homogenous globule of desire of happiness under the impulse of stimuli'. Such economists, he jeered, would take 'a gang of Aleutian Islanders, slashing about in the wrack and surf with rakes and magical incantations for the capture of shellfish', and shovel them all into equations about rent, wages and interest. Bring back history, he lamented. Bring back politics. Bring back real life. He had a point then, and he would still have a point today.

Veblen's best-known book, *The Theory of the Leisure Class*, published in 1899, is a vicious exposé of a world where productive workers toiled long hours, and parasitic elites fed off the fruits of their labours. The wealthy also engaged in 'conspicuous consumption' and 'conspicuous leisure' – wasteful activities to show others they were so rich they didn't need to work. Plutocrats always wanted more wealth and power, he noted, and worse, their petulance and excesses generally provoked not anger but reverence! The oppressed masses didn't try to overthrow their social betters; they wanted to copy them. (The popularity of shows like *Made in Chelsea* and *Keeping up with the Kardashians* might be the modern equivalents.) In short, he concluded, twentieth-century man wasn't that far removed from his barbarian ancestors.

Veblen's next big book, *The Theory of Business Enterprise*, published in 1904, was less well known but more radical and more important, and contained glimpses of the finance curse.[3] In this he contrasted industry and the 'machine process' – the productive engineers and entrepreneurs who rolled their sleeves up and made useful stuff – with what he called the 'business' of making profits. Above the foundation of production rose a financial superstructure of credit, loans, ownership, bets and markets, to be controlled and milked. While Karl Marx had focused on tensions between workers and factory owners, Veblen concentrated on a different but related struggle: between wealth *creators* and wealth *extractors*. Makers versus takers; producers versus predators. Imagine a group of old men in top hats, manipulating a Heath-Robinson-like contraption of spindly pipework perched on top of the economy, hoovering up coins and notes and IOUs from the pockets of the workers and consumers toiling away underneath.[4]

Generations of economic thinkers had known about this distinction, at least as far back as Adam Smith's *Wealth of Nations* in 1776.[5] The main problem, though, was that people disagreed about who the wealth creators were. A conservative tradition holds that they are the rich, the owners of money and capital, who build the factories, then get taxed by government, which redistributes their wealth to the poor and to the recipients of handouts. In this view of history, it's the poor and disadvantaged who are the leeches, preying on the capitalists.

Veblen, however, was having none of it. He compared the rich wealth extractor to a self-satisfied toad which 'has found his appointed place along some frequented run where many flies and spiders pass and repass', and then went a whole step further into more controversial terrain. Many businessmen get rich, Veblen went on, not just through extraction, like the lazy toad catching passing flies, but through active sabotage – or, as he put it in his spiky language, 'the conscientious withdrawing of efficiency'. These players, he said, interrupt the regular flow of outputs, shaking the tree so they can more easily make off with the fruit.

Nonsense, the critics sneered. Who'd do such a rotten, foolish thing?

Everyone, it turns out. Veblen had brutally exposed one of capitalism's great open secrets: big capitalists don't like efficient competition, and they don't like free markets. They *say* they do, but genuine competition drives down prices and drives up wages – and so reduces profits. What they really like is markets rigged in their favour – against workers, against consumers and against taxpayers. That's where the big money is. 'Instead of competing against one another to their mutual defeat, the absentee owners now turn their undivided competition efforts against the consumers,' Veblen wrote. 'It became a competition not within the business but between the business as a whole and the rest of the community.' This conflict is at the heart of the finance curse.

The Theory of Business Enterprise came out in the wake of what was then, and may still be, the most impressive feat of investigative journalism in world history. This was an exposé of John D. Rockefeller's Standard Oil monopoly by the journalist Ida Tarbell, who uncovered a conspiracy and cartel the likes of which the world had never seen. Rockefeller, she revealed, was a master of Veblenite sabotage, rigging markets in the production and distribution of oil and its refined products, buying or elbowing out rivals in a ruthless and sometimes violent quest to build an America-wide monopoly. Her articles, serialised in *McClure's* magazine from 1902 to 1904, opened with a picture of rugged young men carving out new frontier towns in the Pennsylvania oilfields.

Life ran swift and ruddy and joyous in these men. They were still young, most of them under forty, and they looked forward with all the eagerness of the young who have just learned their powers, to years of struggle and development. They would make their towns the most beautiful in the world.

But suddenly, at the very heyday of this confidence, a big hand reached out from nobody knew where, to steal their conquest and throttle their future. The suddenness and the blackness of the assault on their business stirred to the bottom their manhood and their sense of fair play.[6]

In one Rockefeller operation a hundred ruffians descended on Hancock in Delaware County in 1892 to prevent a competing pipe being laid. As another account put it, 'Dynamite was part of their armament, and they were equipped with grappling irons, cant-hooks, and other tools to pull the pipe up if laid. Cannon ... are used to perforate tanks in which the oil takes fire. To let the 'independents' know what they were to expect the cannon was fired at ten o'clock at night with a report that shook the people and the windows for miles about.'⁷ The independents abandoned Hancock. A more overt act of business sabotage is hard to imagine.

Tarbell's explosive articles were an obsessive labour of love and loathing. She had watched her own father, a small-time oilman named Franklin Tarbell, transmogrified by Rockefeller's ruthless tactics from genial, loving father into a grim-faced, humourless shell. 'Take Standard Oil stock, and your family will never know want,' Rockefeller crooned to the victims of his semi-legal practices. He would offer to swap their degraded business interests for Standard Oil stock, offering the equivalent of pennies on the dollar while assuring them that they would be much better off with him because 'I have ways of making money you know nothing of.' Franklin Tarbell held out and paid a heavy price, so much so that his business partner killed himself. Ida's father 'no longer told of the funny things he had seen and heard during the day,' she remembered. 'He no longer played his Jew's harp, nor sang to my little sister on the arm of his chair.'⁸

Rockefeller paid bribes and kickbacks; he eliminated rivals by spying, smear tactics, thuggery and buyouts with menaces. He sabotaged producers of oil barrels, hoarded oil and squashed middlemen. He secretly financed politicians and haughtily dismissed requests to appear at official inquiries. He covered his tracks, delegating questionable tasks to juniors and avoiding compromising language on internal documents. He expanded overseas, dodging regulations and gaming gaps in the global tax system to become, as one biographer put it, 'a sovereign power, endowed with resources rivalling those of governments'.⁹

It takes time, Tarbell noted, to crush men who are pursuing legitimate trade. 'But one of Mr Rockefeller's most impressive characteristics is patience. He was like a general who, besieging a city surrounded by forti- fied hills, views from a balloon the whole great field, and sees how, this point taken, that must fall; this hill reached, that fort is commanded. And nothing was too small: the corner grocery in Browntown, the humble refining still on Oil Creek, the shortest private pipe line. Nothing, for little things grow.'

In the early days of Rockefeller's business operations corporations weren't allowed to do business across state lines, but he had found a loophole. He brought all his different state corporations together under the ownership of a trust, a flexible and powerful mechanism of central control which could operate at a national level and in great secrecy. (This is why anti-monopoly laws and actions have been known as antitrust measures ever since.) Through his trust mechanism, Rockefeller got to control over 90 per cent of the oil refined in the United States, extracting vast amounts from consumers and generating fountains of profit, which were funnelled beyond the core business into railroads, banking, steel, copper, and more.[10] If this reminds you of today's Amazon, you're on the right track. It is no coincidence that Rockefeller was America's biggest monopolist and also its first billionaire. Monopoly was, and still is, where the big money is.

But Rockefeller was in fact just one of several robber barons dominating the American economic landscape in Veblen's day. There were monopolies in beef, sugar, whiskey, shipping, railroads, steel, cotton, textiles and furs, and the rulers of these fiefdoms amassed fortunes so great that their names (Rockefeller, Carnegie, Vanderbilt) still resonate today. But one force eclipsed them all, a financial monopoly.

In 1913, nearly a decade after Veblen published *Business Enterprise*, a US Congressional committee produced its now-famous 'Money Trust Investigation', a report exposing a grand conspiracy of American business leaders to rig half the national economy. Rockefeller was implicated, but it was bigger than him or Standard Oil. The Money Trust was a monstrous interlocking lattice of at least eighteen major financial corporations and over 300 cross-cutting directorships and lines of control which directed much of industrial America and manipulated the financial clearing houses and the New York Stock Exchange.[11] It was based on a secret rogues' charter known insidiously as 'banking ethics' by which they agreed not to compete with each other. Atop it all sat a banker, John Pierpoint Morgan.

The report warned chillingly that there were forces more dangerous than monopoly in industry: the greater danger was monopoly control of the means by which credit is allocated to industry and across the economy. If you controlled credit, it warned, you controlled the economy. 'The arteries of credit [are] now clogged well-nigh to choking by the obstructions created through the control of these groups,' it said. 'The acts of this inner group [have] been more destructive of competition than anything accomplished by the trusts, for they strike at the very vitals of potential competition in every industry that is under their protection.'

When the report went public, national fury ensued. Political cartoonists drew octopuses with tentacles wrapped around buildings, men in top hats grasping the world, bankers sitting on sacks of money while the poor queued up to hand them their savings. Devils with pitchforks pranced with bags of cash. A scowling eight-armed J. P. Morgan cranked eight handles turning machinery inside eight banks; or he was a giant Pied Piper, leading great crowds on a merry dance into the wilderness. Louis Brandeis, the best-known lawyer of Veblen's era, summarised the report's findings: 'The goose that lays the golden eggs has been considered a most valuable possession. But even more profitable is the privilege of taking the golden eggs laid by someone else's goose. The investment bankers now enjoy that privilege ... The dominant element in our financial oligarchy is the investment banker.'

Brandeis pointed to something else too: a lesson that recurs again and again in the story of the finance curse. At the heart of all the extraction and predation there usually lies a genuinely useful function. The central problem isn't finance, but *too much* finance, finance that is *too powerful*, and the *wrong kind* of finance, unchecked by democracy.

Although monopolies are one of the most important methods of sabotage, there were many other varieties around in Veblen's time. One of the biggest, which wasn't mentioned in the 'Money Trust Investigation', also involved Morgan's bank. This saga began in 1899 when William Cromwell, Morgan's legal counsel, incorporated a new company, the Panama Canal Company of America. At the time, Panama was a province of Colombia and had a profitable railroad running across the narrow isthmus connecting North and South America. In league with J. P. Morgan, President Roosevelt armed and supported separatists who wanted to wrest Panama away from Colombia and get their hands on those lucrative rail transhipment fees. And if they could build a canal, why, the profits would multiply. To cut a long conspiracy short, Panama won independence from Colombia, but only under effective US control. The new country's first official fiscal agent was J. P. Morgan, and the Panama Canal opened in 1914. 'Wall Street planned, financed and executed the entire independence of Panama,' summarised Ovidio Diaz Espino, a former Morgan lawyer who wrote a book about the affair entitled *How Wall*

Street Created a Nation. This episode 'brought down the Colombian government, created a new republic, shook the political foundations in Washington with corruption and gave birth to American imperialism in Latin America'.

Essentially, Wall Street interests had harnessed their government's military resources to build and operate a mighty tollbooth at the choke point of one of the world's great trade arteries. Soon whole communities of American financial toads were ensconced happily here, with the flies and spiders of Veblen's imagination replaced by some of the world's largest ships. In 1919, as Panama was taking its first steps setting up its ask-no-questions ship registry, Veblen summarised how the game worked: 'In this international competition the machinery and policy of the state are in a peculiar degree drawn into the service of the larger business interests; so that, both in commerce and industrial enterprise, the business men of one nation are pitted against those of another and swing the forces of the state, legislative, diplomatic, and military, against one another in the strategic game of pecuniary advantage.'

These are 'channels of sabotage', he said, wrapped up in the flag. To help the national champions 'compete' on a global stage, the common man must shoulder the burden. The idea of national champions is a recurring theme in economic history. When Mark Zuckerberg of Facebook was grilled by the US Senate in April 2018 over privacy violations, photos of his crib notes revealed this: 'US tech companies key asset for America; break up strengthens Chinese companies.' This kind of nonsense – an apparent call to leave his monopoly alone to profitably harvest and sell valuable and sensitive data about American users in the interests of national security – was summarised by Veblen in his usual style. Armies and navies, he said, were used 'to enforce or defend the businesslike right of particular vested interests to get something for nothing in some particular place and in some particular way – and the common man pays the cost and swells with pride'. Veblen had identified what was then and remains today one of the greatest and most misunderstood themes of international finance and business, the 'competitiveness' of nations.

But sabotage wasn't and isn't only about monopoly. The creation of Panama's shipping registry, as it happened, was that country's first big step towards the creation of a tax haven. And tax havens are another widely used modern tool for sabotage. There's no general agreement as to what a tax haven is, though the concept can usefully be boiled down to 'escape' and 'elsewhere'. You take your money or your business elsewhere – offshore – to escape the rules and laws at home that you don't like. These laws may involve taxes, disclosure, financial or labour regulations, shipping requirements or whatever, so 'tax haven' is a misnomer; these places are about so much more than tax.

But let's take tax, and a classic tax haven trick which began to emerge in Veblen's day called transfer pricing. Imagine it costs a multinational $1000 to produce a container of bananas in Ecuador, and a supermarket in Wales will buy that container for $3000. Somewhere in this system lies $2000 profit. The question is: who gets to tax that profit? The multinational now sets up three subsidiaries: EcuadorCo, which produces the bananas, WalesCo, which sells the bananas to the supermarket, and a third shell company with no employees, PanamaCo, in a tax haven. These companies sell the container to each other inside the multinational: first, EcuadorCo sells it to PanamaCo for $1000, then PanamaCo sells it to WalesCo for $3000.

Where does the $2000 profit end up? It cost EcuadorCo $1000 to produce the container, but it sold the container for $1000 to PanamaCo, so there's zero profit – hence no tax – in Ecuador. Similarly, WalesCo bought from PanamaCo for $3000 but sold to the supermarket for $3000, so again no profit or tax in Britain. PanamaCo, though, bought the container for $1000 and sold it for $3000, making $2000 profit. But because it's in a tax haven, the tax is zero. Hey presto! No tax anywhere!

In the real world it's obviously much more complicated than this, but this is the basic idea, and it's clear that nobody anywhere in this financial game has produced a better, more efficient way to grow, transport or sell bananas. This is simply wealth extraction: a shift of wealth away from taxpayers in both rich and poor countries towards the businesses. But it's also sabotage because it rigs markets in favour of the large multinationals who can afford to set up these expensive international schemes, at the expense of their smaller domestic competitors, who can't.

Two brothers who became pioneers of this kind of multinational tax strategy were Edmund and William Vestey, who founded the Union Cold Storage company in Liverpool in 1897. Meat monopolists extraordinaire, the Vesteys ran cattle operations in South America at one end, where they crushed the unions on their extensive holdings. At the other end, in Britain, they crushed rival meat traders – including one of my great-great-uncles[12] – and monopolised the retail trade. In between they dominated certain shipping lines and rigged the international tax system in their favour. 'If I kill a beast in the Argentine and sell the product of that beast in Spain,' William Vestey taunted a British royal commission in 1920, 'this country can get no tax on that business. You may do what you like, but you cannot have it.'

From those early beginnings in the 1920s, tax havens would grow to offer a wider ecosystem of market-cornering possibilities. And with the growth of mobile global finance, particularly after the 1970s, the possibilities for sabotage would multiply.

As the twentieth century progressed, Veblen's views would be vindicated again and again. Take, for instance, the great American streetcar scandal, when a consortium of oil companies, bus, car and tyre companies came together in a loose arrangement to buy up streetcars and electric mass-transit rail systems in forty-five major US cities, then kill them off. Antitrust lawyers argued that the ensuing destruction of rail-based urban transport was part of a 'deliberate concerted action' to push America into dependency on cars, buses, tyres and oil. It seems to have worked, helping pave the way for, among other things, massive climate change.

Or, for a more recent example of sabotage, take the now-notorious activities of the Royal Bank of Scotland's Global Restructuring Group – nicknamed the Vampire Unit. RBS described the GRG as an 'intensive care unit' for ailing firms, which restructured their loan agreements to 'help them back to health', but following the global financial crisis, the GRG hit thousands of fragile small businesses with crippling, unexpected fees, fines and interest-rate hikes. Under what bank staff called Project Dash for Cash, they engineered financial terms that made it more likely the businesses would fail so that RBS could get hold of their assets on the cheap. Hundreds of small UK businesses have sued RBS, accusing the bank of having preyed on them. 'Rope: sometimes you need to let customers hang themselves,' a widely circulated internal bank memo said. 'Leverage upsides with high initial monthly fees … just hit budget.' A leaked report for the Financial Conduct Authority, which City regulators tried to suppress, even cited a memo to twenty-four staff inviting GRG staff to grab goodies from a shop that had gone under: 'Go in and add your name and what you want ... keep things to staff only and don't take the p**s ... GRG only!'

An earlier report found that over 90 per cent of viable firms the GRG dealt with suffered 'inappropriate action' by the group during 2009–13. And it wasn't just RBS: an independent report by Lawrence Tomlinson, a government adviser, described 'profiteering and abhorrent behaviour' all across retail banking in the UK. 'Some of the banks,' he wrote, 'are harming their customers through their decisions and causing their financial downfall.' This kind of sabotage crushed small businesses and led to family breakdowns, heart attacks and suicides.[13]

Veblen made an observation about such behaviour which remains relevant today. The fountains of profit that can ensue from this kind of rapacity and market rigging underpin what he sneeringly called business sagacity. We hear 'business sagacity' every day from the leaders of politics, industry and finance. We hear it when the BBC wheels out know-nothing bankers or City pundits to applaud the latest merger-driven rise in the stock market, or the latest deregulatory or tax-cutting gift to the City of London, or a surge in banker bonuses or private equity activity, as if these things benefit Britain.[14] To the extent that these profits are extracted from the veins of our economy, these soaring profits are all signs of economic malaise, not health. As Veblen famously put it, 'business sagacity reduces itself in the last analysis to the judicious use of sabotage'.

Veblen and Tarbell were often pilloried by their contemporaries, yet they have both been repeatedly proved correct. After her exposé of Standard Oil, Ida Tarbell was vilified by sections of the media. 'The dear girl's efforts ... are pathetic,' wrote one academic. She and her followers were 'sentimental sob sisters', wrote another. Rockefeller called her Miss Tar Barrel, a socialist and 'that misguided woman'. She pretended to be fair, he said, but 'like some women, she distorts facts ... and utterly disregards reason'. The vilification made her long to 'escape into the safe retreat of a library' and be liberated from 'harrowing human beings confronting me, tearing me'.[15] But in 1911 her investigations bore fruit. Standard Oil was broken up into thirty-four different companies, to become the forerunners of today's oil giants ExxonMobil and Chevron, and even a part of BP. Although it didn't last: at a meeting in 1928 at Achnacarry Castle in Inverness-shire the heads of some of the biggest fragments of Standard Oil got together with some foreign rivals and hammered out a secret criminal deal to carve up the world's oil industry into profitably collaborating fiefdoms.

Veblen died in 1929, a few weeks before the great financial crash vindicated his big ideas. The crash, and the ensuing turmoil, fed dark forces which eventually plunged the world into bloody global warfare again, still in the lifetime of Tarbell, who died in 1944. Their work and history contain great warnings: these great malignancies of capitalism must be tackled.

2

Neoliberalism Across Borders

Some time in the mid-1950s a disagreement took place in the cafeteria of Northwestern University, in Chicago's northern suburbs, between Meyer Burstein, a conservative economist, and his colleague Charles Tiebout, a high-spirited left-winger who was teaching microeconomics at the faculty there. The argument when it started was simply about high rents, but by the end it had developed into something bigger: a grand and influential new theory about how states and nations 'compete' with each other. The two colleagues got on well enough as friends, but Tiebout was irritated that Burstein had become one of the fast-growing band of what he called Friedmaniacs, a group that blindly followed Milton Friedman, the Chicago School economist who was then on his way to becoming America's financial godfather of the right.

Tiebout was 'one of the funniest guys I have ever known', said Lee Hansen, one of his only surviving close friends. Tiebout would imitate academic bigwigs in his classes, give them silly nicknames and turn up to meetings in dungarees despite the university's suit and tie convention. When a student's father complained about a 'socialist' book Tiebout had set his son as part of his coursework, Tiebout impishly got the dean to send a letter back stating, 'This is to inform you that Professor Tiebout is not a socialist; he is a communist.'[1]

Tiebout was not in fact a communist: he was simply a mischief-maker. It was, however, a risky thing to even joke about; America was then in the late stages of McCarthyism. Senator Joseph McCarthy had been conducting anti-communist witch-hunts in Hollywood, government, academia and other parts of American society. He had even accused George Marshall – originator of the Marshall Plan to block global communist expansion by providing aid to Europe after the Second World War – of having communist leanings.[2]

Behind the fun, though, Tiebout did believe that government could do good. And at that lunch in the Northwestern cafeteria he felt the need to defend this belief when Burstein started griping about the high rents in the part of Chicago where he lived, reflecting high property taxes that were earmarked for local schools when he didn't have children. 'But Meyer,' Tiebout said, 'you don't have to pay those high rents! Why don't you just move to Rogers Park?'[3]

Later that day Tiebout was chatting to an undergraduate student, Charles Leven. 'You know, Chas,' Tiebout said, 'I was absolutely right. People do have a choice over their local public goods and a way of showing it through their revealed preference simply by moving. In fact, that's a damn good idea. I should stick to my guns and write it up!' In less than a week he had written a first draft, and he submitted it to the conservative *Journal of Political Economy*, which published it in October 1956 under the dull title 'A Pure Theory of Local Expenditures'. Tiebout could not know it then, but his hastily drafted article would eventually become one of the most widely cited articles in economics.[4]

A phrase in that conversation with Leven – 'revealed preference' – ought to twitch the antennae of any mainstream economist. Tiebout was referring to Revealed Preference Theory, which the US economist Paul Samuelson had created in 1938. The basic idea was that while you can't insert psychological probes directly into people's minds to figure out their consumer preferences, you can have the next best thing: if you study their buying habits you can reveal their preferences and plug this data into the Chicago School's elegant mathematical models and graphs. This data will allow you to study the effects of government policies, and subject it all to the penetrating analyses of market economics.

By the 1950s the theory was already quite widely used for understanding consumer behaviour. But when you switched away from consumers and markets and tried to apply the model to public services like schools, roads or hospitals there was a snag, which Samuelson himself had laid out in a paper in 1954. And it was a biggy: the so-called free-rider problem. People will happily consume public services, Samuelson explained, but they like to dodge the taxes that pay for these things. The free-rider problem means that you can't get people to reveal their preferences regarding taxes and public services, so you can't shoehorn this stuff into the Chicago School's elegant mathematical models to determine optimal levels of taxes and public spending. Government and democratic politics had to step in and deal with this one, and the economists wouldn't get a look-in. Ouch.

Tiebout's 1956 paper claimed to have found the riposte.[5] There *was* a way to envisage a market for public services and taxes after all, he explained, and here's how. Samuelson might be right that you couldn't apply market analysis to the US *federal* government, Tiebout reasoned, but you could do so with *local* governments. Each US state offers a different package combining a particular bundle of taxes with a particular bundle of public services, and people can move between these jurisdictions according to which mix of taxes and public goods works best for them. (Burstein, as it happens, did move to Rogers Park. He paid less rent and was 'was happy as a clam and stayed there'.) Shopping for better public services like this was, Tiebout wrote, like shopping in a mall: public services are analogous to consumer goods, while taxes are akin to the prices of those consumer goods. Communities will 'compete' to provide the best mixes of tax and public services, as in a private market.

If people can vote with their feet, he went on, then not only could economists reveal Americans' preferences for the right mix of public goods and taxes and fit this data into their mathematical models, but you'd also get a 'competitive sorting' of people into optimal communities, thus bringing the efficiency of private markets into the government sphere. With a little mathematics, governments could discover the ideal equilibrium, balancing taxes against public services.

Countering the rising tide of anti-government Friedmaniacs, Tiebout felt he had shown how government could be efficient after all. Tax cuts weren't the magic elixir to entice productive companies and people to move across borders; those firms and people also needed good tax-financed public services too. It was a trade-off, and when people moved across borders to make this trade-off work best for them, it improved overall welfare. All this amounted to a rather progressive agenda – or so he thought.[6]

Tiebout himself never really pursued his idea; it was certainly elegant, but for him it was 'just another paper'.[7] And for a long time it didn't take off. Political centralisation was in vogue so nobody cared much for theories about local politics, and the media usually only brought up local government in the context of desegregation, incompetence or corruption. The story might well have ended there – and for Charlie Tiebout it did: he died of a heart attack in January 1968, aged forty-three.

When the world finally started to wake up to Tiebout's paper, the year after his death, it would kick off a debate about one of the most important questions in the modern global economy: what happens when rich people, banks, multinational firms or profits shift across borders in response to different incentives like corporate tax cuts, financial deregulation and so on? This debate goes to the heart of questions around what has been called the competitiveness of nations, and whether competing on things like corporate tax cuts or environmental standards is a good thing or an unhealthy race to the bottom. In the end, Tiebout's ideas would end up magnified, then distorted and used as ideological underpinning for a wide range of policies that generate the finance curse. Which is not what the leftist Charlie Tiebout would have wanted at all.

History shows that inequality usually only gets properly upended after large, violent shocks.[8] For Tiebout's generation, it was the Second World War that provided the shock. The financial crisis and Great Depression of the 1930s had discredited the old certainties of free trade, financial deregulation and laissez-faire economics which had given the market saboteurs like Rockefeller or the Vesteys such freedom to operate. Workers who had spilled their blood on the battlefields of France were in no mood to pander to moneyed elites any more; they wanted their countries to give something back to them. The end of the war in 1945 provided a unique political opening to put into practice the progressive, revolutionary ideas of the British economist and polymath John Maynard Keynes.

Keynes knew that finance had its uses, but he knew that it could also be dangerous, especially when it was allowed to slosh around the world at will, unchecked by democratic controls. If your economy is open to tides of global hot money – rootless money not tied to any particular real project or nation, that is – then it is harder to pursue desirable policies like full employment. This is because if you try, for instance, to boost industry by lowering interest rates in a country that is open to flows of financial capital, then money will simply sluice out, looking for better returns elsewhere. Capital will become scarcer; the value of the currency will tend to fall; and interest rates will be forced up again. If governments wanted to act in the interests of their citizens, Keynes knew, there was no alternative but to curb those wild, speculative flows. 'Let goods be homespun whenever it is reasonably and conveniently possible,' he famously said. 'Above all, let finance be primarily national.' Keynes carefully distinguished between cross-border *trade*, which was often beneficial, and speculative cross-border *finance*, which he knew was far more dangerous. It wasn't just governments at risk; the Great Crash of 1929 had exposed how cross-border speculative flows could wreak havoc with the private sector too. 'Experience is accumulating,' he said, 'that remoteness between ownership and operation is an evil in the relations among men, likely or certain in the long run to set up strains and enmities which will bring to nought the financial calculation.' If distant foreign financiers control your business, he was saying, the damage is likely to outweigh whatever profits might emerge.[9]

Keynes's ideas about the dangers of cross-border finance carried such intellectual force that by the time the Second World War got under way they had become mainstream wisdom. Governments and general public opinion accepted that if countries were to avoid a repeat of the economic and military horrors that had occurred in recent years they were going to have to transform the global financial system. So in 1944, under the intellectual guidance of Keynes and in the dominating presence of his US counterpart Harry Dexter White, the world's most advanced countries got together at Bretton Woods in New Hampshire and hammered out an agreement to set up a global system of negotiated cooperation, to curb flows of financial capital across borders and to protect countries from these destabilising tides of hot money. The system had a shaky start: from 1945 to 1947 Wall Street interests forced through a brief financial liberalisation which caused huge waves of capital flight from war-shattered Europe, as rich Europeans sent their wealth overseas to escape having to pay for reconstruction. But fears of a communist takeover in Europe soon focused policymakers' minds, and the Bretton Woods system was at last given teeth.

Bretton Woods was a remarkable system and almost unimaginable today. Cross-border finance was heavily constrained, while trade remained fairly free. So cross-border financial flows were permitted if they were to finance trade or real investment or other specified priorities, but cross-border speculation was not. Exchange rates were more or less fixed against the dollar, which in turn was anchored to gold. So if you wanted to import, say, some agricultural machinery or go on holiday to France, you could take your pounds and the relevant import or travel documents to your bank or central bank, and if the bank was satisfied that it was a bona fide purchase or trip it would take your pounds then arrange for the equivalent amount of dollars or French francs to be paid to the appropriate accounts overseas or paid to you in cash. But if you took a million pounds to the Bank of England and asked it to provide you with the equivalent in Deutschmarks because you thought you could get a better interest rate in a German bank, you would be told to get lost. The overall aim of this vast international administrative machinery was, as US Treasury Secretary Henry Morgenthau declared, to 'drive the usurious moneylenders from the temple of international finance'.

The Bretton Woods system was leaky and troublesome but it held together for roughly a quarter-century after the Second World War. With finance bottled up, governments felt free to act in their countries' best interests, without fear that all the money would flee overseas. Taxes for the wealthy were high, sometimes very high: average top income tax rates fluctuated around 70–80 per cent in the United States between the 1950s and 1970s, and in the UK they even reached 99.25 per cent during the Second World War, then stood at 97.5 per cent for most of the 1950s before falling to 80 per cent in 1959. Domestic financial regulations were amazingly robust too: the New Deal in the United States, combined with vibrant anti-monopoly laws, split up mega-banks and hedged bankers with all kinds of restrictions. Massive government-led technological developments during the war were also unleashing waves of industrialisation, and governments continued to invest aggressively in research considered too risky for the private sector.[10]

Amid all this massive, coordinated government intervention and in some cases astonishingly high tax rates, economic growth in both rich and poor countries was collectively higher – much, much higher – during this period than in any other age of human history, before or since. Western Europe for instance grew at an average 4.1 per cent a year during 1950–73. Trade flourished, even as speculative capital flows were repressed. The era is now often known as the Golden Age of Capitalism.[11] As growth powered ahead, economic inequalities fell, inflation was tamed, debts shrank, and financial crises were small and infrequent. This was the American Dream, but on a global scale.

'Most of our people have never had it so good,' declared British Prime Minister Harold Macmillan. 'Go around the country, go to the industrial towns, go to the farms and you will see a state of prosperity such as we have never had in my lifetime – nor indeed in the history of this country.' Health services and government-funded welfare provision blossomed across the Western world; labour unions were mighty; and developing countries successfully nurtured infant industries behind trade barriers. It is hard to imagine now, but investment bankers weren't paid outrageously more than teachers.[12] The Bank of England was nationalised in 1946, as Britain's chancellor declared that the government 'must be on the side of the active producer as against the passive rentier'. All this was a vast, explicit, brassy administrative and political antidote to the curse of overweening finance and to the freewheeling policies of the earlier robber-baron age. Finance would be society's servant, not its master. And it worked.

Keynes never got to see his ideas so thoroughly vindicated – he died in 1946 – but neither would his ideas go uncontested for long. A counter-revolution determined to shackle governments and unleash the full power of money and finance again was already well under way.

While the controls lasted, the bankers loathed the Bretton Woods system. A letter from Lord Harlech, a board member of the Midland Bank, shows the mood. It denounced Sir Stafford Cripps, President of the Board of Trade, and the Chancellor of the Exchequer the 'swine' Hugh Dalton, as being driven by 'political and personal ambition & venom against the interests of the Empire, commerce, industry & all fair play' and he complained of how these 'enemies of all we stand for at the Midland Bank are the two worst elements in this bloody government.'[13]

This fightback from the banks was organised around a simple idea which had come in a 'sudden illumination' in 1936 to a mediocre Austrian economist called Friedrich Hayek. Within a couple of years this idea had a name: neoliberalism. For many people, neoliberalism isn't a serious term but a political swearword brandished by people on the left against anyone to their right whom they don't like. It often is, but it also has a particular history and meaning, which in terms of its practical effects has meant financial deregulation, privatisation and globalisation actively promoted and protected by governments.

Neoliberalism is an outgrowth of eighteenth-century classic liberalism. There's political liberalism, which is all about citizens having equal democratic rights in a system of sovereign law, and then there's economic liberalism, which starts from Adam Smith's 'invisible hand', by which free exchanges or trade in properly functioning markets are supposed to make society better off overall. The more liberal (or free) the exchange, in this view, the better for society as a whole; government's role is to provide basic functions like defence, to enforce property rights, and to keep a watchful eye out for monopolies, but otherwise to get out of the way. Political and economic liberalism are fairly separate realms, but in each case freedom is to the fore. And neoclassical economics is heavily invested in these ideas. This is basically a set of techniques for analysing markets, and one of its core conclusions is that competition in (unsabotaged) markets is collectively efficient and a good thing for society.

Neoliberalism put these ideas on steroids. Its starting point was that government inevitably amasses ever more power and heads towards tyranny. This fear was understandable at the time. The Nazis had almost conquered Europe; Soviet totalitarianism loomed, and the Thought Police from George Orwell's hit novel *Nineteen Eighty-Four*, published in 1949, hung like a leering spectre over Western culture. Hayek, now recognised as the founder of neoliberalism, began with the neoclassical notion that competition in markets delivered efficiency and collective benefits for all. Then he took a giant leap of faith, and argued that this conclusion could be, and even should be, true not just of markets and commercial exchange, but of all sorts of other aspects of life. What if you could re-engineer society and laws into a giant market or set of markets, he wondered, using government scissors to cut the social fabric into separate fragments, then pitching these fragments into competition with each other? The simplest example of this is privatisation, where you sell off state assets to the private sector in the hope that they will compete and become more efficient. If you can achieve this, Hayek argued, then the market can become a tool for finally taming government, the handmaiden of tyranny. (If this has got you thinking about today's NHS, you're on the right track.)

Hayek's most famous book, *The Road to Serfdom*, laid this all out. Competition and the price system were the *only* legitimate arbiters of what was good and true, he said. And this soon became a neoliberal mantra. Cut taxes, deregulate, privatise and launch all these pieces into competition with each other, then let it all rip. Not just banks or companies, but also health services, universities, school playing fields, environmental protection bodies, sexual abuse referral services, regulators, lawyers, shell companies and the kitchen sink: all of it could be, should be, *must be*, shoehorned into the same competitive framework, to be sorted and judged by the one true test of virtue: the test of the market.

Within this framework, explains Stephen Metcalf, humans are transformed from being 'bearers of grace, or of inalienable rights and duties' into ruthless profit-and-loss calculators, sorted into winners and losers. Society is no longer a space for political debate or collective action but a kind of universal market which harnesses the benefits of competition to work as a kind of giant, all-knowing mind, a sort of organically emerging intelligence in which the market constantly figures out the best way to distribute scarce resources among competing priorities and deliver the greatest good for all. Government is re-engineered as an agent for making markets penetrate as deep into society as possible. Things like citizenship and traditional notions of justice and even the rule of law are swept aside and replaced with technocratic questions like productivity, risk and returns on capital. Neoliberalism is 'the disenchantment of politics by economics', as the British political thinker Will Davies put it: 'an attempt to replace political judgement with economic evaluation ... through processes of competition it becomes possible to discern who and what is valuable. Competition, competitiveness and, ultimately, inequality, are rendered justifiable and acceptable.'[14]

This was a wholly new notion of justice. A more revolutionary idea is hard to imagine.

The neoliberal revolution was born in earnest at a historic meeting of American and European intellectuals at Mont Pèlerin near Geneva in 1947, just a few years after the Bretton Woods summit. The meeting was attended by Hayek and by many other famous economists and thinkers, including Milton Friedman, Ludwig von Mises, George Stigler, Frank Knight, Karl Popper and Lionel Robbins. The meeting was financed by Switzerland's three largest banks, its two largest insurance companies, the Swiss central bank, the Bank of England and City of London interests. Hayek himself, after leaving the London School of Economics in 1950, 'never held a permanent appointment that was not paid for by corporate sponsors'.

The ambition of the Mont Pèlerin Society, born at that meeting, was utopian, even messianic, envisaging private-sector heroes overturning the dark forces of authoritarian state control. 'We must raise and train an army of fighters for freedom,' declared Hayek, 'to work out, in continuous effort, a philosophy of freedom.' Economic freedom would deliver political freedom. A tide of corporate money began to flow into a new network of radical think tanks, which pushed these ideas. The network would form the cradle of neoliberalism, and of the fightback against the Keynesian consensus.

This took authority away from politicians and handed it to economists and money interests. At the apex of this new form of authority sit the financial players who buy and sell global companies, with a kind of veto power over governments that have drunk the neoliberal elixir. Perhaps the most pervasive and insidious outcome of this ideology is the broad-based phenomenon known as financialisation, a central element of the finance curse, which involves not just the growth in size of the financial sector but also the injection of financial techniques and competition into pretty much anything that can't be nailed down – and a lot that can be.

Hayek's thrilling ideas enraptured growing numbers of people, including Margaret Roberts, the president of the Oxford University Conservative Association. Half a century later, long after she had married, taken the surname Thatcher and become Britain's first female prime minister, she would call Hayek's *Road to Serfdom* the book 'to which I have returned so often'.[15] And many other politicians have come to love neoliberalism because the 'verdict of the market' absolves them of responsibility for making hard choices, helping them sidestep troublesome notions like fairness or justice. They can simply sit back, watching as the laissez-faire machinery of the market sorts out all that noisy, sweaty, difficult kerfuffle. And this has proved popular: after all, who doesn't like competition? To borrow a few words from Keynes, 'nothing except copulation is so enthralling'. When BBC presenters take the government policies of the day and say, 'Let's see if the City thinks this is a good idea,' they aren't just promoting what Veblen sneeringly called business sagacity, they're embracing neoliberalism and its *political* judgements.

Yet neoliberals did not want to stop at shoehorning people and companies and fragments of our societies into the great sausage machine of the price system, this utopian, all-knowing, all-for-the-best market-mind; they wanted to shovel in whole countries too. And it was the work of Charlie Tiebout which opened up this wonderland for them. Like two powerful attracting magnets brought into close proximity, the two bodies of thought – one arguing that parts of government or society should be pitched into efficient competition with each other, and the other arguing that states and jurisdictions could compete efficiently with each other – were inevitably going to come together.

The full merger happened when a Princeton economist called Wallace Oates wrote a paper in 1969 with some measurements that seemed to confirm Tiebout's thesis.[16] Oates looked at fifty-three communities in New Jersey and studied their property taxes, along with local authority spending on schools. Then he looked at how this related to house prices. And his results were just as Tiebout had predicted: higher local property taxes seemed to mean lower house prices, while more school spending meant higher house prices. People did 'vote with their feet' after all, moving in and out of communities in response to taxation and spending packages. Tiebout was right!

Oates's results may not seem so surprising today, but it was radically new then. As the scholar William Fischel put it, 'everyone knew that Americans were mobile, but no economist had previously connected mobility with demand for the services of local government'. The model grew and grew in stature and has now become, according to Fischel, 'pretty much the touchstone for local public economics in the United States ... its influence has expanded beyond economics and beyond the public sector'.[17] Those arguing for greater taxation and spending powers for Scotland, Northern Ireland or even London often draw support from this model born out of Tiebout's and Oates's work. Behind the scenes, Tiebout's big idea is everywhere.

For the neoliberals, the idea of states 'efficiently sorting' was thrilling: a mechanism for shovelling districts, states and even whole countries into their competitive models at last, enabling them to declare the whole process a good thing. Even better, it could justify the view that public services and tax systems and even laws were just another commodity to be bought and sold in the marketplace. 'Law became one of many "assets" through which a nation can compete,' wrote Will Davies; tax 'becomes nothing but a "cost" for the national PLC to minimise'.

It's not hard to see how subversive this was: the rule of law has a monetary price, and so does your corporate tax system. After these ideas began to enter mainstream politics in the late 1970s the inevitable results included corruption, oligarchy, bank bail-outs and the growth of international organised crime.[18]

As these intellectual and political changes unfolded, a series of events was starting to play out on the ground in the US which would expose Tiebout's ideas in ways he would never have intended. Rather than demonstrating how governments could 'compete' with each other and thus be efficient, as he had once thought, the emerging 'competition' between the states was revealing itself to be a powerful tool for big financial and corporate interests to get what they wanted from states and nations by playing them off against each other in a vicious race to the bottom. (For the rest of this book, I will call this latter form 'competition' – in inverted commas – as opposed to competition in private markets).

In 1973, just four years after Oates published his paper, Idaho's Democrat governor Cecil Andrus had a meeting with David Packard, the boss of the fast-growing computer company Hewlett-Packard. The company was looking to build a major new computer plant, and had narrowed its options down to Idaho or Oregon. Andrus described in his autobiography how he pitched his state's attractions in the face of an attractive counter-offer from Oregon. 'Packard listened politely,' Andrus remembered, 'then asked in a level voice, "What type of tax concessions is the state willing to give?"' Andrus's answer would seem quaint today.

I took a deep breath and set out to sell him on a difficult argument. 'We don't believe in existing businesses subsidising new businesses,' I told him. 'When you come to Idaho you become a citizen, and we all play by the same rules. A few years down the line and you'll be an old-timer. Do you want to subsidise the next guy who comes along?' It was a nervous moment. After a brief pause, Packard grunted: 'Makes sense. That's the way to go.' He moved on to other questions. We captured the computer plant and gained a top-notch corporate citizen.[19]

At that time the old consensus was still alive which held that corporations were not just machines for creating profit but had a wider purpose: they were stable social institutions which created good jobs, wonderful goods and services, tax payments and thriving communities. That consensus was about to come under threat, and eventually change beyond all recognition.

One of the least well-known instruments of change was a new industry that was already stirring in America by the time Andrus spoke. This industry had first emerged in 1934 when a businessman called Leonard Yaseen created the Fantus Factory Location Service in New York. The company set out to provide expert local guidance for companies that wanted to relocate or expand into unfamiliar parts of the country. This was in itself a perfectly reasonable idea. The problems began, however, when companies went beyond looking for the good stuff that benefits everyone in a locality, such as strong infrastructure or a healthy and educated workforce, and into searching for wealth-extracting free rides such as special tax treatment, exemptions from pro-union laws, lax environmental standards or outright financial inducements from local taxpayers.

By the time Oates popularised Tiebout's paper in the late 1960s, the relocation industry was already maturing, with secretive consultants playing local areas off against each other and constantly pushing states to get the 'business climate' right – which meant extracting maximum subsidies from local taxpayers. In the words of Greg LeRoy of the US nonprofit group Good Jobs First, a veteran observer of these change, these consultants are now:

the rock stars in expensive suits at economic development conferences: the speaker-bait that brings in hundreds of public officials who hang on their every word. They are the shock troops of the corporate-orchestrated 'economic war among the states' that is slashing corporate tax rates and manipulating state and local governments everywhere ... Cities and states are 'whipsawed' against each other to maximise subsidies ... they have played our state-eat-state system like a fiddle.[20]

LeRoy outlines fourteen free-riding scams the site consultants deploy, including 'Job blackmail: how to get paid to do what you were going to do anyway'; 'Create a bogus competitor'; 'Payoffs for layoffs' and 'Pay poverty wages; stick taxpayers with hidden costs'. Since the 1970s this race between the US states has been getting faster and faster, and today the system has run amok.

One of the best Petri dishes for studying this at close quarters is Kansas City, where the state border between Kansas and Missouri runs through the middle of town. Companies here can relocate across the state line simply by crossing the street, and this has sparked especially fierce local border wars on incentives, even calls for 'ceasefires'.

On a visit to Kansas City one icy December morning in late 2016 I met Blake Schreck, president of the Chamber of Commerce in Lenexa, a municipality in Johnson County on the Kansas side of the border. Soft-spoken and genial, Schreck reminded me of Apple's founder, Steve Jobs: tall and silver-haired, wearing a polo neck and wire-framed glasses. He operates out of an office in a beautiful white-painted former farmhouse with Harrods-green shutters, set among lush clipped lawns, and his job is to persuade businesses to move to the area: first Lenexa, then Johnson County, then Kansas State. He seems to have been effective. Lenexa is a haven of high-end business parks, sprawling low-rise office buildings and industrial centres, nestled among pretty suburban developments chock full of architects, engineers and bioscientists living comfortably behind white picket fences. Employment in Johnson County has been growing by over 4,000 a year through good and bad times, and the unemployment rate, at 3.3 per cent in 2016, has nearly always been lower than the national average.[21]

When I met him Schreck outlined a number of old-school reasons why so many businesses come to the area. 'We have had good elected officials who are not afraid to get infrastructure out ahead of growth: streets and roads and sewers and all these kinds of non-sexy things. Over the years it has paid off,' he told me. But the excellent local public school system is key, he said. 'The hard right come here and say all that matters is the lowest possible taxes. But here in Johnson County we are the antithesis of that. It is about total community development. Here they are paying for excellence in a safe neighbourhood. We have proven that that is the model that works. Honestly and truly,' he continued, 'in thirty years of doing this I have never had anyone telling me the taxes in Kansas are too high. It has never been an issue. When I started here, we looked down our noses at anyone who even dared ask for an abatement or incentive: we thought, *If you want to be in our community you pay your way and join the community.*' Idaho's governor Cecil Andrus would have approved.

But the conversation then turned darker. Certainly by the 1990s, Schreck said, he had noticed direct contact with potential businesses being replaced by a more aggressive brand of consultant, who rudely and ruthlessly changed the calculations.

Instead of 'Hey, come on in and have a beer and a steak and let's get to know each other and see if you like our community' the whole process is more cold and clinical now. You're put in a matrix on some consultant's spreadsheet, and you want to get into their top ten. You have to be ready to respond to these data-heavy requests: they want information overnight on a five- and ten-mile demographic slice and study. Everything is now driven by the consultants. That is the big change in the industry. Incentives coalesced around and became part of this whole culture when the consultants started driving the relocation train.

A culture of secrecy has crept in along with the consultants, and in their hands it is a deadly weapon for jimmying more corporate subsidies from the public purse. Secrecy helps the consultants exaggerate and lie about what rival places are offering while preventing you from checking, so they can squeeze the last drops out of your desperate state or city. Schreck pulled out some files and riffled through them, reading out project names like Bigfoot, Redwood and Maple, each with iron confidentiality clauses attached. 'We've had big deals here where six to ten people come in from a company, and we're not even allowed to know their *first* names,' he said. On one visit, Schreck and his colleagues gave them names from the Quentin Tarantino movie *Reservoir Dogs*: Mr Pink, Mr Orange and so on. 'These are the extremes we've been driven to.'

Companies nearly always decide where they want to relocate to before they start playing the states against each other, but the consultants, who earn up to 30 per cent of the value of the subsidy package, have every incentive to deceive and exert undue pressure. Not only that, but the tax incentive game is notorious for exploitation, with juicy deals having been given to corporations that have provided campaign financing, and endless revolving doors for public officials.[22] The Missouri-controlled part of Kansas City, for instance, has set up an arm's-length Economic Development Corporation whose avowed goal is 'a competitive, vibrant and self-sustaining economy', but its staff rotate in and out of the big law firms negotiating the handouts. The EDC also gets a cut of each deal, while tax abatements come out of someone else's budget: the classic free-rider problem.

Johnson County, Schreck said, now typically gives a 50–55 per cent property tax abatement for incoming businesses, but aggressive companies have squeezed out more: the restaurant chain Applebee's got 90 per cent for ten years, by playing the we'll-move-to-Missouri card. The Missouri Port Authority gives up to 100 per cent. Even more remarkably, the Promoting Employment Across Kansas programme peels off – get this – as much as 95 per cent of the withholding taxes levied on employees' payrolls and, instead of handing those taxes over to the hard-pressed state, funnels these sums instead to the companies employing them for up to ten years. Such deals are common. Other deals allow companies to get their hands on sales taxes paid in their projects. This is becoming increasingly common across the US, and it's got a nickname: 'paying taxes to the boss'. There are other goodies, such as zero-interest loans or outright grants from states. 'We are now at a point where there is an expectation pretty much from every company that comes along that there is going to be some financing,' Schreck said. 'There are other states that blatantly pay you – we aren't close to that point.' Yet the race seems to be speeding up, and different tax jurisdictions are increasingly at each other's throats.

'We've traditionally been great partners, but it's put us at odds with each other. Put a bunch of rats in a box and if there's plenty of cheese, no problem. But take away the cheese, and they start biting each other.'

Just a few miles east of Schreck's offices, immediately across the state line, is Jackson County, Missouri, where I met Bruce Eddy, executive director of the Community Mental Health Fund. This is a public sub-fund that channels a little over $10 million per year into charities serving some 15,000 victims of domestic and sexual violence and people with mental health needs.[23] Most of its revenues come from a single stream, local property taxes. This is different from most tax systems around the world, where different taxes flow into the maw of a general public budget then get mixed up and spat out in different spending allocations, so you can't see the direct effects of any given tax cut. But here property taxes railroad straight through to particular spending lines, such as this fund. So competitive tax abatements have direct victims.

Eddy's work is intensely political and he reports to elected officials, so he was guarded talking to me, but it was soon clear how badly the property tax abatements slice into his budget. 'It's like a hydra,' he said. 'There are many tax abatements, and I have to fight for revenue to serve mentally ill people. This is not a sport.' 'Competitive' tax-cutting has become like a mania. 'There's a circular discussion going on here. Cutting taxes is good. Why? Because it's "competitive". Why is "competitive" good? Because it means lower taxes!' That plays into the neoliberal agenda that doesn't like the common good. The notion of being a human that merits some reasonable standard has been totally dismantled. And it's getting worse.'

This game is spreading across the United States. One of the bleakest recent stories concerns Amazon, which in 2017 announced plans to build a second headquarters and asked cities to submit bids with incentive packages. At the time of writing a total of 238 locations had bid for the 'HQ2' project, and the highest offer was from Maryland, which offered $8.5 billion in tax credits and other benefits – for a project which Amazon itself has said would only cost $5 billion to build. Maryland is a small state: if it wins, many Amazon staff will come from the surrounding states.

The Amazon example highlights two more crucial points about the race to the bottom. First, the race does not stop at zero. Once corporate tax payments are down to nothing, it keeps going: you start getting into grants, peeled-off sales and payroll taxes and other financial chicanery: an ever-growing pile of wealth extracted from taxpayers and handed to ever-larger corporations. There is literally no limit to the extent to which large, cross-border corporate players and the wealthy wish to free-ride off the taxes paid by the rest of us. Cut their taxes, give them subsidies, appease them, and they will demand even more, like the playground bully. Why wouldn't they?

A second point is the winner's curse, an idea well understood by economists. This is a common phenomenon in auctions, where winning bidders often overpay substantially. This is because they don't understand the value of what they are bidding for, because they don't understand what they're giving away, because they're cajoled or bullied or enticed into overpaying or they're playing with other people's money and just don't care about the cost. A detailed study in 2016 found that the pursuit of corporate mega-deals such as Amazon's HQ2 – known as buffalo hunting in economic development circles – was costing US states an average of $658,000 per job directly created: an overall loss for the states that do this. For technology data centres the average cost was $2 million per job. By contrast, US states spent less than $600 per worker on training schemes, which are known to be vastly more effective in creating jobs.[24]

This chapter poses three big questions for policymakers. The first is: do tax cuts and other goodies attract out-of-town business investment to my area? The answer is a pretty clear and obvious yes, sometimes. Since Oates's 1969 paper came out, this question has been measured and confirmed over and again.[25] It doesn't just happen with US states; it happens with countries too.

The second question is: when states or countries compete to attract businesses or citizens, is this good for the world at large, or is it a harmful race to the bottom between the participating states?[26] As I've explained, the neoliberals used Tiebout's big idea to argue that such 'competition' is healthy and efficient. And if you look for this argument, as I do, you'll find it everywhere. For example, in 2013 Switzerland's president Ueli Maurer told the World Economic Forum at Davos, 'Locational competition exists within our own borders. Diversity stimulates competition: that is not only the case in business, but also in politics. This leads to good infrastructure, to restraint in creating red tape and to low taxes.' These arguments can be boiled down to an appealing sound bite: competition is good; if it works for companies, then it works for countries. It was Tiebout, Oates and the Chicago School that lent academic credibility to the idea that states and countries can compete as if they were businesses, generating prosperity. This idea has been massively, world-changingly influential.

But there is one snag with Tiebout's argument: it's hogwash. Utter nonsense. Even Tiebout said his model was unrealistic. Indeed people who were at the seminar where Tiebout first presented his theory to the academic community said he offered it as an inside joke on the conservative economics establishment. He certainly found it delicious to have his paper accepted by the right-wing *Journal of Political Economy*. Tiebout reportedly said, 'I don't think those fuckers know I'm a liberal and they'll feel compelled to publish it!'[27]

And the paper itself is clear about its limits. 'Those who are tempted to compare this model with the competitive private model,' he wrote, 'may be disappointed.' Each of the major flaws in the model are fatal, collectively they are a catastrophe. For starters, a moment's thought reveals that 'competition' between countries or tax systems bears no resemblance *whatsoever* to competition between companies in a market. To get a taste of this, ponder the difference between a failed company like Carillion or Enron and a failed state like Somalia a few years back. When a company fails it is sad, but hopefully its employees will get new jobs, and the creative destruction involved when companies compete in markets can be a source of dynamism for capitalism. A failed state, involving warlords and murder and nuclear trafficking, is an utterly different beast. They only thing they really have in common is a shared word in the English language: competition. Even if you believe, as I do, that competition between private actors in unsabotaged markets can be a great thing, this says nothing about the state-versus-state kind.

Not only that, but the Tiebout model requires eye-wateringly crazy assumptions to make his 'efficient sorting' work, and Tiebout himself laid most of these out in black and white. For one thing, it assumes that hordes of citizen-consumers will flit back and forth from state to state or country to country at the drop of a tax inspector's hat, selling and buying their homes costlessly and ripping their kids in and out of local schools when tax rates change. It also assumes that tax havens don't exist, that corporations don't use them to shift profits around the world, or even threaten to shift them in order to terrify politicians into giving them unwarranted tax cuts and other goodies. In Tiebout's model rich people don't dodge tax or free-ride off public services. Crime, pollution and other bad things don't spill across borders. There is only one kind of tax – property taxes – and everyone lives off dividend income alone, while infinitely wise community leaders, in harmony with all other political forces, guide infinitely wise citizens. Company executives pondering where to relocate are never swayed in their decisions by free hookers sent up to their hotel rooms or cash-filled brown envelopes stuffed under doors on their location scouting trips, and corruption is absent from local politics.

To avoid the free-rider problem, everyone must go to school and college or university in one place, then work, live, pay taxes and grow old in the same locality, exclusively, for their whole life; otherwise jurisdictions will free-ride off each other's education or pensions systems – so people can't vote with their feet after all. There's no room in this model for people like former UK chancellor Nigel Lawson, who spent his working life railing against and cutting 'high' and 'uncompetitive' British taxes then moved to retire in high-tax France, with all its fine public services.[28] Tiebout's assumptions, in turn, rest on another entire layer of assumptions required to make the general 'efficient markets' theories work. In a nutshell, humans must be rational, wise and self-interested and markets are infallible.

In a world of rising inequality this kind of 'competition' is always and generically harmful, for it rewards the big multinationals, global banks, wealthy individuals and owners of flighty capital, who can easily shift profits or themselves across borders, shop for the best deal, the lowest taxes, the least-unionised workers, the greatest secrecy for their financial affairs or the most lax financial regulations and threaten to go elsewhere if they don't get state handouts. Your local car wash, your barber, your last surviving family fruit and veg merchant or your average worker can't jump (or credibly threaten to jump) to Geneva if they don't like their tax rates or fruit hygiene regulations. So the big players get the handouts, and the small fry are forced to pay the full price of civilisation – plus a surcharge to cover the roaming members of the billionaire classes who won't pay. This 'competition' systematically shifts wealth upwards from poor to rich, distorting our economies and undermining our communities and democracies. The free-rider problem is 'one of those things you hear about in your first term of economics, then never hear about it again', says John Christensen, who co-founded the finance curse concept with me. 'It is one of the biggest dark continents in economics.' The answer to the second of my three questions for policymakers then is clear: 'competition' between states on corporate taxes is indeed a race to the bottom which increases inequality and harms the world at large.

The third question is bigger, in fact it is one of the great economic questions of all time. It is this: whether or not 'competition' is a harmful race to the bottom that hurts the world at large, does it make sense for *my* country or state to 'compete' from the perspective of local self-interest?

Schreck used to think not, at least for his area, but now he seems less certain. 'In Lenexa we used to just say no,' he said. 'But you have to get in the game, and once you're in the game, it's hard to get back out, the argument being that half of something is better than all of nothing. There are states, especially in the deep south, which are much more aggressive, with amazing incentive packages. It's a little whirlpool sucking on all of us. If you tried to swim out of it, you know, could you make it?'

There is a deep and pervasive belief which holds firm to the idea that yes, the giveaways are necessary and that we should play beggar-my-neighbour. The notion that countries have no choice but to be 'competitive' in areas such as corporate tax or financial regulation sounds reasonable to many people; in fact it has been the basis of Britain's main national economic strategy for the past few decades. As former UK Prime Minister David Cameron put it, 'We are in a global race today. And that means an hour of reckoning for countries like ours. Sink or swim. Do or decline.'

This belief system is, however, flat wrong. Like Tiebout's theory, it is underpinned by elementary economic fallacies and schoolboy howlers. In general terms countries can opt out of this race unilaterally, with no economic penalty, in fact with a net national benefit. Beggar-my-neighbour is in reality beggar-myself. Let others play the game.

To see why this is so, it is necessary to leave the relatively calm waters of individual US states and venture into rougher, wilder, more perilous global seas. Here we will find that of the major economies Britain decided to play this game harder, faster and more ruthlessly than the others, partly to compensate for the loss of its empire after the Second World War. In the process Britain has caused devastating damage to the international economy, but it has also beggared itself.

3

Britain's Second Empire

For centuries the City of London, the cash-pumping heart of the British empire, ran the greatest system of wealth extraction ever devised. Royal Navy gunships had long supported the predations of City-based groups like the East India Company, which began as an officially sanctioned trading company in 1600 but evolved into a bloodthirsty and unregulated operation with a private army which in the eighteenth century looted the Indian subcontinent. At the battle of Plassey in 1757 the company defeated the nawab of Bengal; it then loaded the Bengal treasury's gold and silver into a fleet of over a hundred boats and sailed off with it.

The City's core principle underpinning these imperial adventures was freedom – specifically, freedom for finance and trade to flow unmolested across borders. The City's devotion to this principle was so extreme it became the unofficial religion of empire. 'Free trade is Jesus Christ, and Jesus Christ is free trade,' declared Sir John Bowring, a former City trader who became governor of the British territory of Hong Kong as Britain sought to bludgeon open the mouth-wateringly large Chinese market for its goods and services. Britain provoked and won the First Opium War in 1839 when the Chinese tried to stop it exporting industrial quantities of opium into China. When China objected again in 1856, Bowring ordered the Royal Navy to shell Canton, unleashing the Second Opium War. This cracked China wide open, enabling Britain and other European powers to impose on it their system of free trade.

As with everything in finance, the City's imperial role was not a simple tale of good and evil. Alongside all the militarised predation the City financed railways, roads and many other life-changing projects and services around the world; it also provided loans to France, Russia, Prussia, Greece and the new South American republics, as well as to Britain's formal empire. London was, as the financier Nathan Rothschild put it, 'the bank for the whole world'. Its relentlessly international outlook was also the bedrock of Britain's relatively tolerant multiculturalism, which has for centuries made London one of the most diverse and exciting cities on the planet. 'There the Jew, the Mahometan, and the Christian transact together,' Voltaire declared in 1733, 'as though they all professed the same religion, and give the name of infidel to none but bankrupts.'

Yet the riches flowing into the City of London didn't benefit Britain; they benefited certain interest groups in Britain, often at the expense of others. Clashes and tensions between finance and the other parts of economies have happened in myriad ways over the centuries. For instance, large inflows of foreign exchange from overseas can push up the value of the domestic currency, making local manufactures more expensive in international terms, thereby hurting exporters and their ability to create jobs – in Britain often in areas away from London. Or take free trade: it benefits City interests that profit from servicing both imports and exports but potentially harms local industrialists, who often benefit from protective barriers against cheaper foreign imports; and for all the free-trade rhetoric, protectionism has been a centrepiece of the successful industrialising strategies of Britain, the United States, Japan, South Korea and many others.[1]

More surprisingly, the outward-focused City has for long periods failed to provide much finance for Britain's own domestic industrialists and businesses, especially those outside London. British regional players have tended to get investment money from local and regional channels or from their own retained profits. And the City's dominance has airbrushed this from public consciousness, explains the historian Peter Cain. When an MP from an industrial region stands up and talks about his locality, he is seen to be representing his constituents' interests, but 'if the MP for the City of London gets up on his pins in the House of Commons, he is often assumed to be speaking for the nation', says Cain. 'This is thinking that you can see running on and on and on. It is very difficult to break.'[2]

The sinews of empire – British cunning, diplomacy, money and violence – were finally broken by the Second World War, as Britain spent its national strength and treasure defending itself against Nazi Germany. So when the world's leading nations put together the Bretton Woods architecture at the end of the war, power had shifted decisively across the Atlantic to Washington, and Keynes and the British establishment failed in their attempts to fashion the new system in a way that would restore Britain to its self-appointed place at the centre of world economic affairs. The empire staggered on for a few years but by then it was an empty shell, ready to crack.

It may seem counter-intuitive, but Britain entered its greatest period of broad-based prosperity and economic growth at precisely the moment the City of London was at its lowest ebb. This was no coincidence, for it was a reflection of the age-old clash between finance and other parts of the economy. The Bretton Woods restrictions, preventing speculative financial flows across borders, brought this clash into the sharpest possible relief.

By the 1950s, members of the City of London could only look with envy at the giant, fragmented yet fast-growing global marketplace which the Bretton Woods controls had now mostly placed out of their reach. Bottling up City activities inside Britain's war-shattered domestic economy plus the remaining British territories and outposts that still used the pound sterling was bad enough for City profits, but the Bretton Woods system also gave the British government the freedom to impose high taxes on the rich, and strong financial regulations. Heavily constrained, the City became suffused with lethargy. 'I fear that the various ancient businesses of London have practically come to an end, or continue more as shadows,' a British official wrote in 1947.[3] Oliver Franks, the chairman of Lloyds Bank, lamented that his daily job was 'like dragging a sleeping elephant to its feet with your own two hands'.

In the depths of this torpor, in 1951, three senior British officials hatched a top-secret plot to bust the City of London out of the Bretton Woods straitjacket, in order to restore the City to its former glory and dominance. The plot was named Operation Robot after its three top conspirators: Sir Leslie Rowan at the Treasury, Sir George Bolton at the Bank of England and Otto Clarke also at the Treasury. Their idea was suddenly to float sterling, which was then fixed at around four dollars to the pound, and make it freely convertible against other currencies. Had this taken place, Operation Robot would have thrown a grenade into the entire Bretton Woods architecture and might have changed the course of world economic history. Robot was one of those classic skirmishes between finance and manufacturing – and one of the last in the modern era where the financiers lost.

Even Robot's authors conceded that it would lead to economic chaos in Britain, higher interests rates, steeper food prices and hefty unemployment. Knowing how unpalatable their plan was, they tried to bounce it suddenly through an unbriefed Cabinet, having already won over the Bank of England and the Conservative prime minister Winston Churchill, who knew little of economics but 'felt in his bones' that it was the right thing to do. Robot, Bolton wrote, was the 'only international policy which guaranteed the nation's survival in worthwhile form'. Yet word soon got out, and once the implications of the plan had sunk in, people reacted with horror. It was denounced as a 'bankers' ramp' – which it was. Lord Cherwell, head of the civil service, predicted massively higher bread prices and two million more unemployed people, and he feared the situation would be so dire that it could keep the Conservative Party out of government for a generation. The economy, he added sarcastically, 'would be taken out of the hands of politicians and planners and handed over to financiers and bankers who alone understand these things'.

By the middle of 1952 the plot was dead. The Bretton Woods system held together, and the City of London and the pound sterling had lost their global leadership position to New York and the dollar. And for the next couple of decades Britain and the countries participating in the Bretton Woods system would collectively enjoy the strongest, most broad-based and most crisis-free economic expansion in history, with growth running at nearly 4 per cent in the advanced economies and 3 per cent in developing nations, more than twice the rate that had been attained in a thousand years of history.[4]

Despite the remarkable prosperity now flowering across the country, the City of London and its backers didn't give up trying to overthrow the system. A letter to Sir George Bolton in 1952 from Britain's then housing minister, Harold Macmillan, another Conservative, captures the mood. Iran had nationalised British oil assets in March 1951, which, he wrote, had 'struck a blow at British credit', which in itself may have cost Britain as much as the value of the lost oil. He urged robust military action to defend British oil interests and the empire, so as to restore confidence in sterling and return it to its glorious place at the forefront of world affairs. 'This is the choice,' Macmillan wrote: 'to slide into a shoddy and slushy socialism, or the march to the third British Empire.'[5] Macmillan didn't seem to grasp that Britain's imperial magnificence had already, inexorably, begun to crumble. India had gained its independence in 1947, and others would soon follow.

The trigger for the near-total collapse of the British empire was the decision by Egypt's feisty president, Gamal Abdel Nasser, to take over the Suez Canal in 1956. Britain and France joined Israel in an invasion of the canal zone, but the United States, which had lost patience with European imperialism and fretted that the escapade would inflame pro-Soviet passions in the Arab world, forced the invaders to withdraw. The weakness of war-shattered Britain had been exposed, and in colony after colony people realised that it was possible to break free. Decolonisation happened slowly at first, then in a rush: Ghana in 1957, Nigeria in 1960; then Uganda, Kenya, Tanganyika, Northern and Southern Rhodesia, Bechuanaland, Nyasaland, Basutoland and a few others all secured their independence in the early 1960s.[6] To the members of the City-focused British establishment, this was a grievous psychological blow. Streams of easy profit from the colonies, enforced by Britain's imperial armies, had seemingly dried up for ever. It seemed like a calamitous end to past glories.

Yet it was not, for in 1956, the year of Britain's great imperial humiliation at Nasser's hands, a new financial market was born in London which would nurture itself on the City's religion of freedom and would reinvent the City as a global financial centre armed with an amazing array of sophisticated new tools for extracting wealth from other parts of the world – and from other parts of Britain. Nobody imagined it then, but this market would grow so spectacularly that it would come to replace and even surpass the empire as a source of wealth and prestige for the City establishment.

The new market first came to the notice of officials at the Bank of England a few months before the Suez crisis, when they saw that the Midland Bank (now part of HSBC), one of the City's more adventurous institutions, was taking US dollar deposits unrelated to any commercial or trade deals. Under Bretton Woods this was classified as speculative activity, which wasn't allowed. The City of London in those days was an old boys' network of elaborate rituals and agreement by gentleman's handshake. Financial regulation was achieved, often quite effectively, by the Bank of England governor inviting in the relevant members of the banking establishment for tea and using discreet cultural signals to let them know they were stepping out of line. The Midland's chief foreign manager was called in, and whether or not throats were cleared in his direction, a subsequent Bank of England memo noted that the Midland 'appreciates that a warning light has been shown'. Yet the Midland was finding its new cross-border business unusually profitable, so it pressed quietly on.

One of the key problems facing any central bank trying to implement the Bretton Woods system was that it needed to have enough foreign exchange or gold reserves on hand to defend its currency at the fixed level. The Bank of England was constantly anxious about those reserves running out, making it impossible for the country to source essential foreign goods if things came to a crunch. Midland's dodgy activities were generating healthy dollar fees, which bolstered Britain's dollar reserves, so the Bank of England decided to look the other way. And as more dollar profits tumbled in, this temporary indulgence solidified into a permanent tolerance. In effect, the Bank of England had decided to host but not regulate a new market for dollars in London, yet this new business wasn't regulated or taxed by the United States either, so who *was* regulating or taxing it? The answer was nobody.

Ironically, some of the first users of this uber-capitalist market were Soviet and communist Chinese banks, whose bosses were delighted not to have their transactions overseen by Western governments during the Cold War. But their funds were soon swamped by far bigger tides, as American banks realised they could come to London and do things they weren't allowed to do at home, bypassing both the Bretton Woods straitjacket, and tight New Deal financial regulations at home.[7] In short, these bankers could take their business elsewhere to escape the rules they didn't like at home. Amid high anxiety about the loss of empire, the City establishment had quietly turned Britain into an offshore tax and financial haven.

As word got out, more and more banks, especially American ones, got in on the action. Switzerland and Luxembourg, two long-standing

European tax havens, also joined the party. The Americans gave this business an appropriate name, the Eurodollar markets or the Euromarkets. This wasn't anything to do with today's euro currency; a Eurodollar was simply a dollar that had escaped Bretton Woods controls and was being traded in these new libertarian markets, mostly located in Europe. Eurodollars were a new form of stateless money and, as a London banker put it, 'completely isolated from the monetary mass' of the rest of the UK. Bankers in London would simply keep two sets of books: one for offshore Eurodollar deals in foreign currencies, where (mostly) dollars got borrowed and re-lent around the world, and a second book for deals in sterling hooked into the British economy.

So Eurodollars were in one sense dollars like any other, but in another sense they were different because they had escaped into a market outside government control, where they could behave freely. It's a bit like taking someone from their family home in the suburbs to a wild part of town and offering them whisky and cocaine. They are the same person but also different – more fun but also more irresponsible.

A Bank of England memo in those early days explained the Euromarkets' attractions: freedom from local supervisory controls such as banking regulations to stop excessive risk-taking; freedom from macroeconomic controls such as foreign exchange restrictions; low or zero taxes for the players and for their customers; secrecy and 'very liberal company legislation'. Though the Euromarkets were mostly disconnected from mainstream economies, the unrestricted interconnections between the emerging centres were intense, effectively creating a single rootless nowhere zone of finance – think of it as being a bit like cloud computing. It was an unaccountable, profitable, seamless global financial adventure playground, overseen by nobody and growing like the clappers.[8]

One of the main reasons the Euromarkets grew so fast was that their lack of controls made them a paradise for tax cheats, scammers and criminals. Another reason was that they allowed banks to create new money out of thin air without any official restraint. The banking system in any country constantly creates new money when banks make new loans to customers. As the US economist J. K. Galbraith put it, 'the process by which money is created is so simple that the mind is repelled'. To stop banks running amok, governments put brakes on money creation by enforcing reserve requirements, which restrict how much they can lend out in relation to their deposits. But the Euromarkets had none of these brakes. Eurodollar lending, a Bank of England memo noted, 'is not controlled, as regards amount, nature or tenor: reliance is placed on the commercial prudence of the lenders'. Prudent bankers won't indulge in an orgy of reckless lending, whatever the official constraints are, but the Bank of England was assuming that everyone operating in the Euromarkets was prudent.

To start with, the US authorities didn't seem too worried about these ripples across the Atlantic. Benjamin J. Cohen, who worked at the Federal Reserve Bank of New York at the time, remembers being asked to look into Eurodollars in 1962. 'It was in the manner of, "There's this development over in London we want to understand better,"' Cohen recalled, '"go over there and find out about it."' But pretty quickly it became obvious to the Americans that this interconnected system was serving as a global amplifier of financial shocks, relayed by rising tides of financial capital sluicing back and forth across the world in the Euromarkets. Worried US officials were soon calling the markets 'disruptive forces' and a dangerous 'transnational reservoir' of rootless money. By 1963 messages were flying between Washington and New York as higher interest rates in the Euromarkets drew dollars out of the US to London and beyond. A memo from the time lamented 'the undercutting of New York as a financial center' and slammed the Euromarkets for generating the same kinds of risks that caused the crash of 1929. The Federal Reserve Bank of New York and the US Treasury complained that the markets were making 'the pursuit of an independent monetary policy in any one country far more difficult' and aggravating a 'world payments disequilibrium'. Robert Roosa, a top US Treasury official, told the American banking community using the markets that they should 'ask themselves whether they are serving the national interest'.[9]

By the beginning of the 1960s Euromarket deposits already amounted to $1 billion, the equivalent of perhaps $50 billion in today's money. Then things went crazy. Just between 1963 and 1969, US bank deposits in London rose twentyfold. Late in that decade Roosa raised the alarm about speculative global capital flows moving around the globe 'in magnitudes much larger than anything experienced in the past, massive movements'. Then, from 1970 to 1980, volumes expanded tenfold *again*.[10]

The Vietnam War, which heated up in the early 1970s, added to the flames, as the US was sending more dollars overseas for military spending than it was receiving back in foreign earnings. The result was a growing overhang of dollars in the global system, feeding the Euromarkets further. The twin oil price shocks of the 1970s accelerated the flows, generating giant new surges of petrodollars – more accurately, petro-Eurodollars – which the large banks recycled out of the oil-producing countries via the giant turntable in the City of London back into disastrous, criminalised cycles of Third World lending. Those loans would often be looted by national elites through bogus development schemes or outright theft, and sent back for safekeeping into the Euromarkets, where nobody would ask questions about the money's origins, and then re-lent *again* back into those looted countries. With each turn of this whirligig, the bankers took a profitable cut.

When Mexico's Harvard-educated president Miguel de la Madrid took power in 1982, he lectured his fellow citizens about 'belt-tightening' while starting to accumulate tens of millions in foreign bank accounts – $162 million in 1983 alone, according to US intelligence reports. Most of this was first obtained by snaffling the proceeds from official Mexican loans via the Euromarkets, and pretty much all of it was then stashed offshore via the Euromarkets in Geneva, London and elsewhere. 'You have many friends here, not least in the City of London,' gushed Margaret Thatcher at a luncheon for him in London 1985. 'We shall continue to offer the widest possible trade opportunities to you.'

Leaders such as the murderous Jean-Claude 'Baby Doc' Duvalier of Haiti and the grasping Ferdinand Marcos of the Philippines became famous for looting their treasuries, and the phenomenon was far more widespread than these cases. It has been estimated that more than half the money borrowed by Mexico, Venezuela and Argentina in the late 1970s and early 1980s 'effectively flowed right back out the door, often the same year or even month it flowed in'. In Venezuela it was nearly dollar-for-dollar. In the Euromarkets there was nobody to stop it.[11] A few people noticed, but at the time almost nobody asked where the money had gone. Meanwhile the ordinary citizens of these countries had to shoulder the burden of crushing debt repayments. From their perspective this was another giant looting machine run out of the City of London long after the formal trappings of empire had been discarded. And this looting machine needed no British soldiers and was predicated on tight secrecy. It was all but invisible.

Fuelled by murky money, the Euromarkets just kept growing. The Bank of England routinely rebuffed American requests for ideas on how to tackle the problem. 'However much we dislike hot money we cannot be international bankers and refuse to accept money,' a Bank of England memo said. 'We shall do lasting damage.'[12] The Americans pressed further, and the British screw-you became more explicit. 'It doesn't matter to me whether Citibank is evading American regulations in London,' said James Keogh, a top Bank official. 'I wouldn't particularly want to know.'[13]

Like a slow-motion nuclear explosion, the Euromarkets began to give financial globalisation a life force of its own. They metastasised beyond Britain, beyond dollars and beyond anyone's control to become a frenzied financial battering ram, which would combine with Hayek and Friedman's ideological fightback against government intervention to smash holes in exchange controls and the cooperative international infrastructure. By 1973 the pressures had become too great. Major currencies were allowed to float against each other. The Bretton Woods architecture was rubble. The collapse coincided with a massive oil price surge and the beginning of a new period of slower global growth, rising inequality and more frequent financial crises across the Western world.[14] It was exactly what Keynes had warned about.

And as this mayhem unfurled across the world another set of darker developments, umbilically linked to the City of London and to the Euromarkets, was gathering pace.

Tucked away in the UK's National Archives there's a long memo from a Bank of England official to a colleague at the Treasury, dated 11 April 1969. It is marked SECRET, and it radiates alarm. The memo describes some outrageous developments that a Bank of England monitoring mission had discovered on a visit to some British overseas territories in the Caribbean.

The overseas territories were, and still are, the last fragments of the British empire: fourteen territories including seven important tax havens – Anguilla, Bermuda, the British Virgin Islands, the Cayman

Islands, Gibraltar, Montserrat and the Turks and Caicos Islands. Alongside the tax havens of Jersey, Guernsey and the Isle of Man around the British mainland, known as the Crown Dependencies, these colonies did not cut all their ties with Britain when the empire collapsed. Many already had long pedigrees as pirate refuges or dens of nefarious activities, out of the reach of the law-enforcement authorities of nearby mainland economies.[15]

These territories were either part of the Sterling Zone – whose members used the British pound – or had currencies fixed to it. Under Bretton Woods sterling could be transferred fairly freely to British territories, but if you tried to transfer money outside the Sterling Zone you hit controls on cross-border finance. This was tricky because several of these places, including the Caymans and the British Virgin Islands, used regional currencies or the US dollar as their money, so banking in these territories was routinely conducted in both dollars and pounds and also other currencies, and banks were supposed to keep different sets of books and implement exchange controls carefully between them. This was not only hard to do – even more so after they had all plunged into the super-profitable Euromarkets as well – but also created great temptations.

The author of that 1969 Bank of England memo, Stanley Payton, had noticed that these little British territories had punched holes in the Bretton Woods fence, and all sorts of curious creatures were scurrying through. The best-known and among the earliest of these were the Beatles, whose film *Help!* was shot in 1965 in the Bahamas, which was then a British colony, because they had to live there for a while in order to make it work as a tax shelter. Back in those days escaping tax was a rebellious and cool thing to do: other celebrities such as the Rolling Stones joined in, as did (later on) Richard Branson, who would state many years later that if he hadn't moved his businesses offshore, his company would be 'half the size.' (He now vigorously waves the British flag from his home in the British Virgin Islands.)

Payton's memo noted anxiously:

Events, however, seem to be moving rather faster. The potential gaps in the Exchange Control hedge can no longer be contained by occasional visits. The smaller, less sophisticated and remote Islands are receiving almost constant attention and blandishments from expatriate operators who aspire to turn them into their own private empires. The administrations in these places find it difficult to understand what is involved and to resist tempting offers ... Tax haven proposals by a US resident are leading them to have second thoughts about the need for Exchange Control at all. We might need to station a man somewhere in the area.[16]

This is ferocious by crusty British civil service standards. It describes a game of whack-a-mole in this outgrowth of the Euromarkets, which is getting faster and faster, and foreign criminals and shady characters are the chief beneficiaries. But which interest groups in Britain benefited and who were the losers? Undoubtedly spurred by Payton's memo, different government departments in London, each representing different interests, bickered over what to do. In one corner was a fellow called Rednall from the Overseas Development Ministry, who seemed gung-ho for secret banking and seedy shell company business: it 'attracts entrepreneurs and financiers', he said, arguing that this was a fine way for these Caribbean microstates to develop their economies – without apparently sparing a thought for the hundreds of millions of Latin Americans, North Americans, Africans and others paying a murderous price for Britain helping their elites, drugs gangs and kleptocrats to ransack their national coffers.

Then there was the Bank of England, which has historically tended to take the side of the City of London.[17] Bank of England correspondence fretted about shoring up exchange controls and the risks that the overseas territories posed to them, but it also quietly liked the idea of foreigners stashing money in the territories, which generated foreign currency fees for handling it. As one Bank memo put it, 'We need, therefore, to be quite sure that the possible proliferation of trust companies, banks, etc. which in most cases would be no more than brass plates manipulating assets outside the Islands, does not get out of hand.' As long as sterling does not leak out of the Sterling Zone, it said, 'there is of course no objection to their providing bolt holes for non-residents'. That last sentence is, of course, code language for welcoming shady money.

But the Bank wasn't entirely gung-ho; the archives reveal a conflicted and confused institution. Other correspondence opposed a proposed 'financial pirates' nest' for the British Virgin Islands, which it suspected were to be used for drugs and gun-running. It expressed shock at a scheme proposed for the Turks and Caicos by an American, Clovis McAlpin, amounting to an 'annual tribute in return for exclusive rights, which would virtually turn him into the uncrowned king of the islands'. (The scheme came to nothing.) It fretted that the Caymans had been 'literally raided by an expatriate tax council, who overnight persuaded them to enact trust legislation which goes beyond anything yet attempted elsewhere'. This council still exists today, and plays a central role in writing the Caymans' tax haven laws.[18]

The Inland Revenue, Britain's tax authorities, had a different, clearer view. Their correspondence described the Cayman Trust Law of 1967 as 'quite uncivilised … it is deplorable that we should encounter it in territories which still derive a considerable measure of assistance from the UK'. These brass-plate entities, the Revenue argued, provided few local benefits beyond modest lawyers' fees, since nearly all the activity took place elsewhere, and island treasuries, one official estimated, 'have only received £1 for every £20 that we have lost: this is hardly an economic form of aid'. The Revenue was also anxious that the United States would be infuriated by British Virgin Islands laws to promote secret shell companies, whose users would be 'immune for at least 20 years from all enquiries from any source'. Both the Bank and the Revenue lamented the role of the accounting firm Price Waterhouse, which the correspondence claimed had been urging nearby Montserrat to set up an 'objectionable' brass-plate business.

The wrangling continued, but slowly those supporting the offshore tax haven model began to gain the upper hand. Payton at the Bank of England increasingly backed Rednall at Overseas Development, musing that this stuff might just provide the 'take-off' the islands needed. Talk shifted away from a crackdown towards using aid as a lever to nudge the territories into behaving slightly better.[19] Yet even then nothing was done, and the merry-go-round was allowed to continue, getting ever faster and more interconnected with the Euromarkets. More and more private operators flocked to the territories, urging each place to compete fiercely with its rivals by putting in place ever more devious and criminal-friendly secrecy facilities, trust laws and financial regulatory loopholes.

This era, from the mid-1950s to the early 1980s, was the great watershed between the two ages of the global system of tax havens, as the slow, discreet system of secret offshore banking dominated by the Swiss ceded ground to a more hyperactive, aggressive Anglo-Saxon strain, operating first out of the London-centred Euromarkets, then rippling out into the unpoliced and heavily criminalised British offshore network that still exists today.

This network acts like a spider's web, linking the City of London at the centre to satellite havens like the Caymans or Gibraltar.[20] A spider's web is a sinister analogy, but it's an apt one. Fees or assets captured in the web, typically from jurisdictions near the British haven in question, get fed upwards to the City of London. So for example a Colombian criminal might set up a shell company or bank in the Cayman Islands; or a French bank or energy company will establish a special purpose vehicle in Jersey to hide assets from shareholders or from government regulators; or a Russian oligarch wants to set up a dodgy bank in Gibraltar. Sometimes illegal activity is involved, sometimes not. Each step needs lawyers, accountants and banking services, which the British network is only too happy to provide. Much of the most profitable heavy lifting happens in London, but it is often the haven that snared the business in the first place. Overall, as one far-sighted UK tax lawyer put it, 'the UK uses the Cayman Islands and similar jurisdictions to create a tax-free space for rich people from everywhere else in the world to place their assets under UK-based management.' Although the UK did not tax those foreigners or foreign assets directly, it could tax many of those London-based managers receiving fat fees for managing those 'swollen sacs of undertaxed capital' sitting offshore. Thus the UK takes a cut of the tax dodged elsewhere.

The link with London is crucial for the British territories, because it provides the reassuring legal bedrock that other fly-speck havens can't match. If there's a dispute over a Cayman-incorporated structure, for instance, British courts and British judges will rule on the case and have the final say. Who would deposit their money in a banana republic bank when you can go to the Cayman Islands and have your stash protected by the British legal system? This highlights the fact that tax havens turn two faces to the world. On the one hand they need to appear clean, trustworthy and efficient, to reassure flighty money that they're not dodgy. On the other hand, they want to get their hands on as much dirty money as they can. They square this apparent contradiction with a simple offering to the world's stateless hot money which goes roughly like this: 'You can trust us not to steal your money, but if you want to steal someone else's money, then you can also trust us to turn a blind eye.'

British people are admired the world over for fair play, and British judges for their incorruptibility, yet at the same time we find Roberto Saviano, Italy's most celebrated anti-Mafia journalist, calling Britain 'the most corrupt place on earth' because of all the City's dirty money. This contrast between apparently clean officials and dirty money is no coincidence; it is the heart of the offshore model.

With the collapse of the British empire in the second half of the twentieth century, the City temporarily lost its ability to use gunboats and government officials to extract riches from foreign countries, but the overseas territories tax havens, plugged into the Euromarkets, enabled the City to regain its wealth-extracting mojo. Professor Ronen Palan of City University, one of the first academics to take tax havens seriously, describes this spider's web as 'a second British empire which is at the very core of global financial markets today'.

This second financial empire, with London at the centre of a globe-spanning web of loose money, has many characteristics in common with Britain's lost territorial empire. First, the libertarian character of these escape routes strongly echoes the old empire's evangelical devotion to freedom. It was, and is, freedom from oversight that makes these offshore places such a haven for nefarious activity. Criminals inevitably flock to libertarian, unpoliced spaces for dealing in money, just as wasps will mysteriously turn up when you open a pot of strawberry jam at a summer picnic. Laws were carefully drafted to achieve maximum secrecy, and when packing crates full of drugs money flew into the Caymans or Panama, the police would be on hand to escort it safely from the airport to the local banks.

This laissez-faire approach to money in the British tax havens has extended far beyond handling the proceeds of drugs deals and organised crime, and into high finance. These territories were also zones of great freedom for banking activities, and they incubated outgrowths of the Euromarkets which posed new and fast-mutating risks for financial stability in the mainstream economies like Britain or the United States. The veteran US crime-fighting lawyer Jack Blum remembers first understanding the links between crime and financial deregulation on a trip to Cayman in the 1980s. 'I began to see that drugs were only a fraction of the thing,' he told me. 'Then there was the [other] criminal money. Then the tax evasion money. And then I realised: *Oh my God, It's all about off the books – off balance sheet.*' By 1989 the Cayman Islands, with just 25,000 inhabitants, would be on paper the world's fifth-biggest banking centre, a position it more or less holds today.

The spider's web has enabled certain people connected to the City of London to make immense profits from illegal or immoral activities while using the overseas territories like bargepoles – to hold the stink at arm's length. And in this game the British government has generally been a willing accomplice. Whenever a bad smell emerges, British officials will tell the newspapers, 'Look, chaps, these places are largely independent from us; there's really not much we can do.' Yet this claim of powerlessness is false. Her Majesty the Queen appoints the governors of British overseas territories; all their laws were and still are sent to London for approval, and Britain has always had complete power to revoke these laws. Yet it almost never does.[21]

The problem with the Janus-faced offshore business model – from the point of view of a country like Britain that hosts and encourages this kind of activity – is that it assumes one can ring-fence the dirt and the criminality safely away from the rest of your economy, from your democracy and from society. This, however, is impossible, for it is precisely in the most dangerous part of your political system that the two things are most likely to meet and become intertwined: among the richest and most powerful members of society, who are of course the biggest users of tax havens.

Fish, as the saying goes, rot from the head. Crafting a national economic strategy that relies on offshore finance creates inevitable blowback, which has criminalised Britain's own elites in four main ways: it brings the wealthiest and most powerful into close proximity with criminals; it offers the elites permanent temptations to criminality; it makes criminals rich, enabling them to join the ranks of the elites; and by making it easy to escape rules and laws, it creates a culture of impunity and a real sense of being above the law.

And all this in turn helps answer a question that bothers many people about tax havens: why don't governments just close these financial brothels down? Lee Sheppard, a leading US tax expert, summarises the answer to this question as well as any: 'We fuss about them, we howl that the activity is illegal, but we don't shut them down because the town fathers are in there, with their pants around their ankles.'

And this brings us to a second major characteristic of these offshore territories: they are all, in the words of the British tax haven expert Prem Sikka, 'legislatures for hire'. Like the old colonies, their political and economic development is mainly dictated not by local democracy but by foreign interests, and in the case of tax havens this means rootless foreign money. A memo in Britain's national archives from 1969 illustrates how quickly this characteristic developed in the British territories. It described

a flow of propositions involving Crown lands put daily and endlessly to the government by private developers. These propositions are inevitably propounded in an atmosphere of geniality, lavish hospitality, implied generosity and overwhelming urgency. They are usually backed by glossy lay-outs, and declaimed by a team of businessmen supported by consultants of all sorts. They are invariably staged against an impossibly tight deadline, with an implicit threat of jam today or none tomorrow. On the other side of the table – the Administrator and his civil servants. No business expertise, no consultants, no economists, no statisticians, no specialists in any of the vital fields. Gentlemen vs Players – with the Gentlemen unskilled in the game and unversed in its rules. It is hardly surprising that the professionals are winning, hands-down.[22]

This has always been the pattern, especially in small island tax havens, where administrations staffed by former fisherfolk or owners or employees of bed-and-breakfast hotels are asked to scrutinise complex laws on special-purpose vehicles or offshore trusts. Even in those rare cases where administrators do possess the technical knowledge to understand such laws, there is a wall of money pressuring them not to oppose any proposal. With Cayman-registered banks holding US$ 1 trillion in assets, equivalent to 100,000 per cent of that microstate's gross national product, it is clear where the power lies. As a result, local administrators can usually do little more than rubber-stamp laws devised for the owners of the world's hot money. For instance, the Panama Papers leaks in 2015 revealed how Mossack Fonseca, the Panamanian firm at the centre of the scandal, effectively wrote the tax haven laws of Niue, a tiny Pacific island of 1,500 people.

Mossack Fonseca got an exclusive agreement to register offshore companies there, and this operation was soon generating 80 per cent of that territory's government revenue. The logic, as described by the firm's co-founder Ramón Fonseca, was that 'if we had a jurisdiction that was small, and we had it from the beginning, we could offer people a stable environment, a stable price'. They certainly had Niue.[23]

In fact the business model of these places is deliberately anti-democratic. A tax haven's purposefully constructed loopholes are not designed to help locals escape laws and rules, but to help foreigners do so, elsewhere, offshore – and they carefully write their laws to ensure that any resulting damage is inflicted elsewhere, ring-fencing the tax haven against self-harm. This 'offshore' element means that the people who make the tax haven laws are always separated from those people, elsewhere, who are affected by those laws. So there is never democratic consultation between lawmakers in tax havens and the people elsewhere affected by their laws. That is the whole point of offshore. And it means that offshore is, almost by definition, the equivalent of the smoke-filled room, where business always gets done outside of, and indeed in opposition to, the democratic process. They operate according to the Golden Rule: whoever has the gold, makes the rules.

In such places deference to offshore financial interests becomes reinforced by a ferocious social consensus to make sure everyone does the right thing to keep bringing in the money. The wealthy high-society folk who run these places rarely do anything as crude as to throw opponents of offshore finance in jail. The threat usually lies in more discreet mechanisms, such as the knowledge that if you rock the boat, your employment opportunities will dry up or you will be ostracised. In the goldfish bowl of small-island life, where opportunities are often scant, that is usually enough to silence even the reddest of radicals. John Christensen remembers this pressure from his days when he was the official economic adviser to the tax haven of Jersey. He recalls choking with anger during meetings yet feeling immense pressure to conform to what offshore finance wanted from the island. 'It took real strength to stand up and say, "I'm sorry, I don't agree with this." I felt like the little boy farting in church.' Many years after leaving Jersey and setting up the Tax Justice Network to combat tax havens, he says he is still a hate figure in Jersey financial circles. In such places the capture of the tax haven by offshore financial interests – or financial capture – often extends into family life itself. A few years ago in one tiny tax haven I spoke to a woman who had once spoken out publicly against her country's financial laws. Subsequently, she said, her own sister would cross to the other side of the street rather than talk to her.

Financial capture is contagious too. In the 1990s the accountancy firm Price Waterhouse (now PwC), the London law firm Slaughter and May, and a Jersey-based law firm Mourant du Feu & Jeune persuaded the Jersey establishment to write a new law on limited liability partnerships which would make partners in such firms less accountable for auditing failures. Objectors to the new law were denounced as 'enemies of the state' and 'traitors', and the legislation went through. Next the large accounting firms threatened that if the UK didn't put in place a similar LLP law they would decamp to Jersey. They were bluffing, but as the *Financial Times* noted astutely at the time, 'they want to keep the threat of moving "off-shore" as a cosh with which to threaten the government'. Britain nevertheless passed its own 'competitive' LLP law. The long-term effect has been to transfer large sums of wealth away from the victims of bad audits and bank errors – most British taxpayers – to partners in the so-called Big Four accounting firms.

The capture and contagion is so virulent that since the birth of the Euromarkets offshore practices have steadily spread to onshore economies, as countries like Britain have operated under the assumption that they need to 'compete' to attract the world's hot money. There has been no larger arena for this game than the Euromarkets, which, as one analysis put it, created a giant 'translatlantic regulatory feedback loop that stimulated deregulation on both sides of the Atlantic … eroding the regulatory architecture of the postwar Keynesian state in Britain and destabilising American New Deal regulations'.[24]

This great global deregulation, via the Euromarkets and the world's tax havens, marked the proper start of the era of financialisation, another grand theme of the finance curse. Financialisation involves a gravitational shift inside capitalism towards the needs of the finance sector, which has steadily grown in size and power. A growing global 'wall of money' is constantly seeking and finding new ways to burrow into the many nooks and crannies of our economies and our political systems, injecting debt into corporate Britain and into the housing market, and in the process delivering a payload of financial techniques and methods that have transformed the way we think about businesses, our homes, our public services and even our cultural values.[25] This global transformation has been accompanied by its ideological cousin, neoliberalism, which has encouraged governments to wrench large parts of what had been regarded as the public sector from government control and feed them to an increasingly financialised private sector.

Meanwhile another set of changes was under way in the United States which would turn out to be just as powerful as the Euromarkets in terms of undoing the progressive reforms that had generated such widespread prosperity during the Golden Age of Capitalism. These would deliver a knockout blow not to the Bretton Woods system but to an older but no less powerful democratic tradition: antitrust. And these changes would help create the wealthiest robber barons in world history.

4

The Invisible Fist

In September 2017 James Murdoch, the chairman of Sky, said an odd thing. The Murdoch family, owners of 21st Century Fox, had been trying for some time to win full control of Sky in an £11.7 billion takeover, but the British authorities had referred the move to the Competition and Markets Authority, the monopolies regulator. Murdoch complained that this decision was sending a terrible signal to the world's investors amid swirling Brexit anxiety: 'If the UK is truly open for business post-Brexit, we look forward to moving through the regulatory process.'

It was the sort of thing big businessmen say all the time, and nobody got too worked up about it. But it was a weird statement if you stop to think about it. This was an example of what I call the competitiveness agenda: the notion that you must dangle endless goodies in front of multinationals and large global investors in case they run away to somewhere like Geneva or Singapore. Murdoch had uttered a phrase that any connoisseur of the competitiveness agenda would recognise – 'open for business', which in practice means being willing to do what big banks or multinationals want, at the cost of other parts of your economy if need be. Britain, he argued, should strive to be more 'competitive' by approving a deal that would strengthen an already dominant firm, thereby restricting competition in the market. For Britain to be more 'competitive', it should reduce competition. This is obviously an odd argument, yet big businesses make it all the time.

There has been plenty of pushback against Fox's attempts to take over Sky, mostly over questions about whether the Murdochs are 'fit and proper' persons to run a media empire in Britain, and fears that Sky would be 'Foxified' to create a virulent British version of Fox News. But what's surprising is that there has been almost no effective pushback against this deal on the grounds of monopolies, competition or market dominance. It was down to Karen Bradley, the Conservative Party's own culture secretary, to refer the deal to the regulators (which she did), while across British civil society and the media there was very little resistance from the left or the right. Nobody seemed to be questioning the notion of improving 'competitiveness' by restricting competition.

How can these remarkable blind spots have come to exist? The perils of monopoly power have been clearly understood since long before Rockefeller built Standard Oil, and the New Deal programme put in place in the United States after the crash of 1929 had antitrust measures – a large and varied body of anti-monopoly laws to tackle great concentrations of economic power – at its centre. Yet this has all been swept away on both sides of the Atlantic. A silent revolution has occurred.

Who killed anti-monopoly?

In fact, there is a clear answer to this question. We can trace the shift back to an ideological insurgency in the 1960s and 1970s that would transform the way the world thinks about monopolies. This revolution, which was led by a group of Chicago School economists, would, like a magician's trick of misdirection, shift attention away from the all-important question of whether corporations have too much economic and political power towards an obsession with a far narrower issue: whether the price is right. If the merger of two large companies doesn't lead to higher prices, the argument now goes, what's the problem? The services of Facebook and Google are free, apparently, so move along, folks, there's nothing to see here. This narrowing of attention and focus has blinded us to deeper issues, which are among the biggest drivers of financialisation and the finance curse.

The spark of this revolution can be pinned down to a moment at a dinner party in 1960 at the Chicago home of Aaron Director, an American economist. Sporting a small moustache, horn-rimmed glasses and a boxer's wiry frame, Director was a contrarian, pugnacious anti-government fanatic, a former radical leftist union organiser who had crossed over and now seemed hell-bent on smashing the consensus that had once fed his idealism. Director's politics were 'completely pure free market', explains Matthew Watson, professor of political economy at Warwick University. He was even to the right of Milton Friedman, the American godfather of libertarian free-market economics, who was married to Director's sister Rose. Director would persistently tease Friedman about the fact that he had previously worked in government. 'Family dinners at the Friedmans' house must have been a bundle of laughs,' says Watson. 'There can't have been many house guests where Milton would have been accused of being too pro-government and too left wing.'

That particular night Director hosted twenty dinner guests, largely conservative thinkers, including not just Friedman but George Stigler, who would go on to make a name for himself attacking government regulation, the British economist Ronald Coase and a fire-breathing conservative lawyer called Robert Bork.[1]

The University of Chicago in those days was a bear pit, an arena of intense macho intellectual combat where academics were constantly struggling to outdo each other with clever theories about efficient markets – theories that often perched on toe-curling assumptions – to adopt unconventional, even anti-social positions usually supporting big business and attacking big government. Mathematical and logical elegance trumped the messy reality of life and the world. Director himself was one of the truest of true believers in neoliberalism: that pretty much anything worthwhile could and should be shoehorned into the price mechanism in the interests of 'efficiency'. His messianic zeal mesmerised many of his students. One was Bork, who commented, 'Aaron gradually destroyed my dreams of socialism with price theory,' adding that many of his colleagues 'underwent what can only be called a religious conversion'.[2]

The guests that evening were there to listen to Ronald Coase present a draft paper, *The Problem of Social Cost*. At the start of the evening Coase summarised his argument and a vote was taken. All twenty guests opposed him, and Stigler remembered wondering 'how so fine an economist could make such an obvious mistake'.

Coase deployed a novel argument. Corporations in those days were supposed to be subject to the law – or at least the law came first. If a corporation was pumping illegal pollutants into a river, you went out and found the pipe or some incriminating documents, then went to the law. Pollution is an externality: a consequence that affects other parties who aren't involved in the relevant transactions or businesses. Markets can't generally solve externalities; it had long been accepted that governments and the law need to step in to stop such failures in market mechanisms. But Coase wasn't having this.

Imagine, he said, that a farmer's cattle ravaged his neighbour's wheat crop. If the law held the cattle farmer liable, he would have to pay for a fence or negotiate compensation with his neighbour. If the law didn't hold him liable, the wheat farmer would pay for the fence. But from an overall efficiency perspective it didn't matter which farmer paid for the fence, since the cost was the same. So the law itself didn't really matter. Laws, Coase went on, should be subject to a sort of cost–benefit analysis, where the harm to others caused by the polluter or the careless farmer or the tax cheat should be weighed against the benefits derived by those actors who gain. It was enough to show that overall 'welfare' was maximised to let this happen. (This was not so different from the Tiebout model of welfare-maximising states 'competing' to produce a socially 'efficient' world.)

You could extend this logic. If there was a large banking monopoly, for instance, any losses to consumers or workers could be balanced out by gains to the bank and its shareholders, and there might be no net loss overall. Bring in other net gains, such as economies of scale reaped by larger corporations, and large monopolies might just turn out to be a good thing! Monopolies were the natural way markets wanted to go, and it wasn't the job of judges to interfere. Once you took into account the apparent costs of regulation to the monopolisers, he said, it became hard to justify doing anything at all about them.

The guests were stunned. Until then antitrust – the large body of established law and theory that said monopolies were harmful and that governments should regulate them – was supported both on the left of the political spectrum, where people fretted about powerful bankers and industrialists oppressing workers and customers, and on the right too, where people were keen to protect and promote competition and the integrity of markets. Coase had just lobbed a bomb into this whole edifice – and into a few other edifices too.

The dinner progressed. The arguments mounted. 'As usual, Milton [Friedman] did most of the talking,' Stigler remembered. 'My recollection is that Ronald didn't persuade us. But he refused to yield to all our erroneous arguments. Milton would hit him from one side, then from another, then from another.' But then, like the plot of *Twelve Angry Men*, the mood began to change. 'To our horror,' Stigler said, 'Milton missed him and hit us.' By the end of the evening they took another vote: all were for Coase. 'I have never really forgiven Aaron for not having brought a tape recorder,' Stigler said. 'It was one of the most exciting intellectual events of my life.'[3]

This violent attack on the foundations of legal authority – that laws should be subjected to economic cost–benefit calculations and rejected if they fail to pass muster – was a classic example of economics imperialism – a power grab by economics professors with ambitions to colonise as many areas of social and political life as they could get their hands on. It was also an extension of red-blooded neoliberalism, which argued that lawyers and laws should bow down to economists and economics, and everything had a price.

The scale and success of this insurrection was made clear when in 1983 a group of Chicago-school economists was reminiscing about – one might even say gloating over – this power grab. There was a short exchange between Robert Bork, Richard Posner, an influential pro-monopoly jurist and economist, and Henry Manne, another influential (and corporate-funded) economist. Manne was an associate of the libertarian theorist James Buchanan, and they had joined with the conservative tycoon Charles Koch to penetrate academia by setting up think tanks to spread anti-government ideas. They pushed the anti-Veblen idea that wealthy property owners were the 'makers', while the poor and middle classes were the 'takers', out to fleece them. As one account put it, 'the Holy Grail was the Constitution: alter it and you could increase and secure the power of the wealthy in a way that no politician could ever challenge.' This is exemplified by the exchange below:

BORK: As far as I know, the economists have not yet done any damage to constitutional law.
POSNER: We are working on that.
MANNE: We'll chase you out of that too. [*laughter*][4]

It doesn't take a genius to see how elevating easy-to-massage numbers above the rule of law was likely to boost lawbreaking everywhere, not least in the financial sector.

Such revolutionary ideas percolated slowly at first, but cheerleaders and corporate funders weren't hard to find. One of the earliest enthusiasts was a partner at a Wall Street consulting firm who was already a manic devotee of the anti-government novelist and libertarian guru Ayn Rand. His name was Alan Greenspan, and he would later become chairman of the US Federal Reserve. 'The entire structure of antitrust statutes in this country is a jumble of economic irrationality and ignorance ... confusion, contradictions and legalistic hairsplitting,' he thundered in 1961. 'The world of antitrust is reminiscent of *Alice in Wonderland.*' The problem wasn't big business, Greenspan said; it was big antitrust and big government.[5]

The United States is the historical home of anti-monopoly, and trends around the world have been led by what happens there. Anti-monopoly has been hard-wired into the American psyche since the country's founding. America's rugged individualism emerged not only as a bulwark against oversized government, but also against overwhelming business and financial power too. It was well understood from the outset that concentrations of financial and commercial power weren't just economic problems, they were fundamental threats to liberty and democracy. The Boston Tea Party of 1773, which helped trigger the War of Independence from Britain, was a protest against the monopolising East India Company. Anti-monopoly measures usually prioritised political and democratic goals above monetary ones, and Louis Brandeis, the most famous antitrust lawyer in the early part of the twentieth century, explained why economic efficiency was not the important goal. The whole point of antitrust laws, he said, 'was not to avoid friction, but by means of the inevitable friction incident to the distribution of the government powers among three departments, to save the people from autocracy'.

Anti-monopoly zeal and lawmaking in the United States have ebbed and flowed for centuries alongside shifting political tides. President Jackson launched a titanic struggle in the years 1829–37 against what he called a 'hydra of corruption' – a net of interlinked monopolies centred on the Second Bank of the United States – and his victory preceded a period of strong defences against business predation and tremendous economic dynamism. 'The stranger is constantly amazed by the immense public works executed by a nation which contains, so to speak, no rich men,' wrote the French writer Alexis de Tocqueville in 1840. 'What astonishes me is not so much the marvellous grandeur of some undertakings, as the innumerable multitude of small ones.' Then, after the American Civil War ended in 1865, America moved into the 'age of Caesarism', the era of the Rockefellers, Carnegies, and J. P. Morgan, who justified their power as necessary to 'rationalise' their industries in more 'efficient' ways.[6]

The democratic fightback that emerged to confront these concentrations of economic and political power had strong geographical roots that are eerily similar to what we see today. Communities across America saw the conglomerates as sucking wealth and control away from their regions to benefit elites in mostly coastal cities like New York. The Sherman Antitrust Act of 1890, which empowered the government finally to break up Standard Oil in 1911, was partly inspired by such geographical iniquities. 'If we would not submit to an emperor,' declared Senator John Sherman, after whom the act was named, 'we should not submit to an autocrat of trade.'[7] The Sherman Act had fairly blunt teeth, but these were sharpened with new laws in 1914, and then again in the 1930s with Franklin D. Roosevelt's New Deal, a sweeping package of progressive political reforms in response to the First World War and the great crash of 1929 which shifted economic and political power away from finance and large corporations towards ordinary folk. The New Dealers created a carefully calibrated system of government checks and balances to mediate between competing social and national priorities, regionally and nationally, breaking up concentrations of power wherever they found it. Their flagship legislation was the Glass-Steagall Act of 1933, which forced banks to separate their commercial banking activities from the more speculative investment banking, thereby breaking up the banking behemoths.

At every stage it was understood that this was not so much about economics as political power and protecting democracy. While Hayek and the neoliberals saw government as the agent of tyranny, and the Soviet Union as the prime bogey, the anti-monopoly crusaders saw the threat as coming from large concentrations of private power, which also led to tyrannical forms of government, especially fascism. For them Nazi Germany was the prime exhibit. 'The liberty of a democracy is not safe if the people tolerate the growth of private power to a point where it becomes stronger than their democratic state itself,'

Roosevelt said in a landmark address to Congress in 1938, as war loomed in Europe. 'That, in its essence, is Fascism – ownership of Government by an individual, by a group, or by any other controlling private power.' The Nazi state, the corporatist Fascist Italian state and the imperial Japanese economic system were all heavily cartelised; in fact the Nazis in 1933 had actively encouraged the formation of big industrial cartels as a way of enforcing top–down control, eliminating foreign competitors and juicing up profits for big firms backing the war effort. As trust-busting US Congressman Emmanuel Celler summarised, 'The monopolies soon got control of Germany, brought Hitler to power and forced virtually the whole world into war.'[8]

When the war ended, a victorious America began to spread its doctrine of benevolent antitrust around the globe like a democratising shock wave. The US inserted anti-monopoly principles into the constitutions of the defeated aggressor countries as one of its 'four Ds' for postwar governance: Denazification, Deconcentration, Democratisation, and Decartelisation.

For a while Britain took all this rather seriously too, though in its own way. For Britain's financial sector, run by an old boys' network which had grown fat off the profits of empire and protected from international competition, the problem was less about monopolising giants like J. P. Morgan or Standard Oil, and more about gentlemen's agreements to carve up turf, restrict competition and trouser the resulting profits.[9] But after the war Britain's bloodied workers were in no mood for compromise, and Clement Attlee's Labour Party ran in the 1945 election with a manifesto that brassily declared, 'The Labour Party is a Socialist Party, and proud of it.' It won with a thumping majority, and on their first day in parliament the new MPs lustily sang that workers' favourite the 'Red Flag'. Labour's approach wasn't so much about breaking up giant corporations, but full-scale nationalisation, bringing the energy industries, the railways, the coalmines, and iron and steel under government control. On the European continent, American antitrust principles also had a strong influence. The Treaty of Rome in 1957, which laid the foundations for the European Economic Community, contained strong antitrust provisions modelled on the Sherman Act.[10]

But as the Euromarkets and Britain's offshore empire began to expand, and as Britain entered a long period of dominance by the business-friendly Conservative Party in 1951, the pendulum swung back again. US regulators began to notice British intransigence. 'There was always a lot of trouble across borders,' said Jack Blum, a veteran US antitrust lawyer active from the 1960s. US laws in this area were supposed to apply internationally, but 'the British fought us tooth and nail on that proposition', Blum said. 'That was with regularity. There were any number of cartels that the British defended, and the US fought. This was a real source of acrimony. The UK passed laws to prevent the US investigating.' Big business was attacking antitrust in the United States too, said Blum; it was 'an area where pure political power was exercised to prevent prosecutions'." Yet British hostility was a minor difficulty when compared to the devastating blows that were to come from inside America itself, from Aaron Director's students and dinner guests and above all Robert Bork.

Bork was a cantankerous lawyer who had been growing steadily more agitated about impending moral collapse. He blamed feminists, multiculturalists, gays, pornographers and most especially leftist professors. He once asserted that 'homosexuals, American Indians, blacks, Hispanics, women, and so on *allegedly* have been subjected to oppression'. The answer to modern moral turpitude, he said, was censorship, adding that the US Constitution should not be interpreted according to prevailing democratic spirits but instead should be taken literally, just as the founding fathers had originally intended, however much the country had moved on since their day.

   With eyes alternately hooded and bulging, and sometimes both at the same time, if you can picture that, Bork was beefy and physically imposing. He terrified his opponents, one television critic saying he 'looked and talked like a man who would throw the book at you – and maybe the whole country'. As US solicitor general, Bork sacked the courageous special prosecutor in the Watergate scandal that would eventually bring down President Nixon in 1974, a dismissal that was later ruled illegal. Years later Senator Edward Kennedy would denounce him in these terms:

Robert Bork's America is a land in which women would be forced into back-alley abortions, blacks would sit at segregated lunch counters, rogue police could break down citizens' doors in midnight raids, schoolchildren could not be taught about evolution, writers and artists would be censored at the whim of government, and the doors of the federal courts would be shut on the fingers of millions of citizens for whom the judiciary is often the only protector of the individual rights that are the heart of our democracy.[12]

Bork denied these charges and his record was more nuanced than Kennedy's picture suggests, but there is no doubting it: Robert Bork was a scary piece of work.

Bork's singular – and colossal – contribution to the game at hand was a little firecracker of a book published in 1978 called *The Antitrust Paradox*. This built on work by Richard Posner and went even further than Coase, decisively shifting the focus of antitrust law beyond Coase's focus on 'efficiency' to something simpler to understand: prices for consumers. 'The only legitimate goal of American antitrust law,' he said, 'is the maximisation of consumer welfare.' Channelling his guru Aaron Director, he made some astonishing arguments based on the assumption that markets behave efficiently. Predatory pricing – in which players in a market collude to extract profits by restricting competition – was 'a phenomenon that probably does not exist', he said, because monopolists making large profits would be instantly undercut by 'entrants who would arrive in sky-darkening swarms for the profitable alternatives'. It was 'all but impossible' for predators to corner markets by buying up competitors. (Try telling that to anyone these days who has attempted to compete head to head with Amazon.) If monopolies did persist, Bork said, it was only because they were more efficient, and if monopolists did raise prices, this was just fine because monopolists were consumers too![13] Traditional antitrust concerns, he argued, were 'nonsense ... mechanisms the law has imagined' and a conspiracy by dangerous leftists.

What mattered to Bork was not reality, but elegant models of reality. Boil everything down to price, ignore all this claptrap about laws and rights and power, and efficiency will follow. The book was, as the US antitrust expert Gerald Berk put it, 'vehemently anti-constitutional democracy'.[14] Instead of regulating pre-emptively by focusing on the structure of markets and whether any players have too much power in those markets, regulation should happen only after the event, once an alleged monopoly had been established and you could measure its effects. Those monopolies staring people in the face could simply be assumed out of existence because they just couldn't exist, and if they did, they might just be brilliant. Bork's book was so influential, says the leading anti-monopoly group in the US, the Open Markets Institute, it 'has become the main guide to more than a generation of policymakers and enforcers'.

These ideas were boosted by heavy tailwinds. The high inflation of the 1970s and early 1980s was obviously going to promote a world view focused on lowering prices. Big business and big banks loved Bork too. More and more allies emerged, and Borkist attitudes spread. It wasn't so much that Bork's and Posner's ideas transformed antitrust laws; it was more that judges began interpreting them in new ways and allowed business to steer around them.

When Republican Ronald Reagan became president in 1980, Borkist lobbyists increasingly used another odd argument – similar to the one that James Murdoch would use to try and bamboozle Britain many years later – that antitrust laws had to be diluted in the name of building up American national economic champions in order to defend 'America's international competitiveness'.[15] Let them exploit American consumers and workers, they were saying, to boost their profits so they can better compete on the world stage. Similar arguments were being made in Europe, where since the 1960s policymakers had fretted about high-tech US multinationals running rampant in their recovering markets.

Many US firms were then large vertically integrated companies guided by Fordism – a one-stop-shop production model named after the Ford Motor Company, which brought coal, iron ore and other raw materials into one side of its vast River Rouge Complex, finished cars emerging from the other. US antitrust authorities recognised that in industries such as vehicle manufacture it was necessary to operate on a large scale, so they tolerated these behemoths, but they tried to ensure there were several competing against one another in any market. Europe wanted its own champions to take on the Americans and was setting up the projects that would create today's giants, such as Airbus and the Ariane rocket programme. European financial and market integration, it was calculated, would provide the expanded base for launching these cross-border Eurochampions into the world economy, going head to head with the Americans and Japanese.

As the 1970s became the 1980s and the focus of American antitrust law narrowed down from concerns about power to the simpler question of price, the authorities stopped writing detailed analyses of the industries and markets they regulated, and came to understand less and less about how markets worked and what made economies tick. Some of the growing band of anti-antitrust academics also realised that there was a lot of money to be made by selling consultancy services to big corporations and increasingly 'seemed like paid apologists for wealthy corporate interests', says Kenneth Davidson, a veteran US antitrust expert and former regulator. The consulting firms the academics founded made millions in the Wall Street-led feeding frenzy of monopolising mergers and acquisitions in the 1980s that the revolution in antitrust had helped unleash. During the period 1981–97 there were over 7,000 bank mergers in the United States alone, and these days economics professors can earn over $1,000 per hour defending mega-mergers.[16]

To understand how badly things went from here and why this matters so much to us now, it is necessary to delve further into the madness of the real world, and look at how monopolies work.

Walk into a shopping mall today and you'll see the progeny of Bork and his allies all around you. That brightly coloured cornucopia of goods on your supermarket shelves, packaged under myriad different brands – most are made by a few goliaths like Unilever or Kraft Heinz. (Note the double-barrelled name of that last behemoth, the product of a gigantic merger – and there's been talk of it merging with Unilever.)[17] Via the chocolates we buy, the phones we chatter into, the sunglasses or shoes we wear, the water we drink, the airlines we fly with, the railways we suffer from or the social media platforms we're addicted to, we pay hidden 'monopoly taxes' almost every time we open our wallets. Bork said predatory pricing wouldn't – couldn't – happen, but we are enslaved by it, as businesses leverage their market power to screw us over in endless hard-to-see ways.

Countless situations and strategies exist: monopoly (a single seller), oligopoly (a few sellers), monopsony (a single buyer), oligopsony (a few buyers), predatory pricing and wage-setting, patents and plenty more. These structures operate across all sorts of markets, market niches and micro-niches, locally, nationally and globally. Here, to avoid needless complication, I'll generally lump these all together, a bit inaccurately, as monopolies, their defining characteristic being that someone is exerting power in markets – usually in order to extract supersized profits.

The simplest and best-known version is the horizontal monopoly, in which companies buy out rivals making or doing similar stuff, or use superior financial reserves to sell below cost, undercutting their competitors and driving them to the wall. (The deaths of most high-street family businesses at the hands of the large supermarkets, and more recently Amazon, is one example.) Slightly more complex are vertical monopolies. In these a big manufacturer buys up the distributors and retailers of its products, then refuses to sell rival manufacturers' products.

Take, for instance, the Italian eyewear giant Luxottica, which has integrated the optical business with the fashion industry to generate enormous wealth for its owners. Luxottica controls large parts of the spectacles industry, from design and product development to manufacturing, logistics, distribution and retail. It owns the iconic Ray-Ban, Oakley, Vogue Eyewear, Persol and Arnette brands, and has exclusive agreements with Giorgio Armani, Emporio Armani, Bulgari, Chanel, Dolce & Gabbana, Prada Eyewear, Paul Smith, Polo, Ralph Lauren, Valentino, Versace and several others. At the same time it owns the major UK retail outlets Sunglass Hut and David Clulow, plus around 9,000 other retail stores around the world. In the early 2000s Luxottica stopped selling Oakley products in its stores, crashing Oakley's stock price, then buying it cheaply.

Luxottica specialises in frames, while the French multinational Essilor controls nearly half the world's prescription lens business and says it supplies 300,000–400,000 retail stores around the world. I paid over £500 for my last pair of glasses; in a more competitive market I would have paid far less.[18] A few weeks before writing this, US and European regulators approved a merger to create EssilorLuxottica. 'Forgive me,' a longtime entrepreneur in the optical sector said. 'But it is nothing short of control of the industry.' I expect my next pair of glasses to be even more expensive. Businesses supplying this behemoth should also expect to be rewarded less for their hard work.

Different but also familiar are too-big-to-fail monopolies. Large institutions, usually banks, become so systemically important that a collapse would trigger mayhem, which is what happened in the global financial crisis of 2007–8. They milk markets by making profits from risky business, then get taxpayers to bail them out when the risks crystallise in a crisis. There is actually an official list of these monsters published by the Financial Stability Board, an international body based in Switzerland. There were thirty too-big-to-fail banks at the last count in 2017, plus nine too-big-to-fail insurers, including Barclays, HSBC, Deutsche Bank, Prudential, JP Morgan Chase and Citigroup.[19] This is not just a matter for financial regulators; it is an antitrust issue, but in Britain, Europe and the United States the antitrust regulators are asleep.

Another version is the home-base monopoly. Walmart, for instance, grew by focusing on towns too small to support two supermarkets, extracting supersized profits from customers in those towns, growing profits further by imposing crushing terms on its local suppliers, then using those profits to open in other towns and finance other monopolising strategies. The game of regional or local monopoly has also been popular with banks, and arch-monopoliser Warren Buffett has made large sums playing this version of monopoly with local media organisations. 'If you've got a good enough business, if you have a monopoly newspaper or if you have a network television station, your idiot nephew could run it,' says Buffett.

Take the leapfrog monopoly, where you innovate so fast or repackage an old business in new technology so well that flat-footed antitrust regulators can't keep up. Many technology firms, and some private equity firms, specialise in this.

Monopolies are contagious too. This is the case with defensive monopolies, where the only response to bigger players squeezing you out of your markets is to merge with others, to acquire the clout to be able to push back. For instance, Sainsbury's planned merger with Asda, announced in May 2018, was billed by analysts as a strategy to create an 'Amazon crusher'. Martin Gilbert, co-chief executive of Standard Life Aberdeen – product of the merger of asset managers Standard Life and Aberdeen Asset Management in 2017 – has described a race between asset management firms to get bigger. 'Size matters now,' he says.

There are many other varieties of financial monopoly run by banks or hedge funds or private equity firms, where the aim is to influence or control several players in a particular market, or to buy up competitors.

J. P. Morgan's uber-monopoly a century ago, controlling various industries, is the most obvious of these. Today financiers are building up stakes across economies. Just three financial firms, Blackrock, State Street and Capital Group, own 10–20 per cent of most major American companies, including many that compete with each other. They also own many in Britain. Large financial institutions in the City of London and Wall Street are not just assembling market power by owning strategic stakes in markets, but they are also the financialising machines that assemble mergers and build monopolies. Mergers and acquisitions are among the most lucrative sports in the City of London and Wall Street.[20] Pick up any copy of the *Financial Times*, and there's a good chance that the top headline involves a mega-merger.

There are natural monopolies where so-called network effects permanently prevent competitors from breaking in. Facebook is one: you want to be on the platform where your friends are, not searching for them on five different platforms. The UK financial payments system, dominated by just four banks, is another example. Then there is the hydra monopoly, where if you control one part of a supply chain, you can hold the whole industry to ransom. When a minor earthquake off Niigata in Japan crippled a monopolising car parts producer making piston rings, it all but shut down Japan's automobile industry; Toyota alone produced 120,000 fewer cars in the following weeks. These monopolies can generate instability, with a limited failure at one monopolised node rippling out.[21]

Or try the offshore secrets monopoly. Here commonly owned or closely collaborating financial interests pretend to compete by hiding their ownership of companies behind secretive shell companies in tax havens, while really controlling them all. The beauty of this strategy is that you can give government regulators secret personal stakes in its success. Who knows who might be using this mechanism to amass financial power over our economies? Monopolies are about power. Allowing opaque foreign interests to obtain monopolising locks over parts of an economy can threaten national security, and such interests even venture out into the open. Russia's Gazprom and Chinese state enterprises are acutely alive to the advantages of controlling bottle-necks in energy and technology markets; the European Commission is currently grappling with Gazprom over gas supplies in a case that has been called 'the antitrust clash of the decade'.[22]

There are also what might be called corrupt monopolies. A trader/manager at a major US bank in London told me how the bank would bribe clients. He had seen this at work in the tax haven of Singapore, where oil traders would buy 'masses of hookers' for their clients. 'We'd go to the Orchard Shopping Centre – they called it the Four Floors of Whores – where $200 gets you Russians, Chinese – whatever you want.' Collaboration in markets depends on trust, he said, but of the honour-among-thieves variety. 'If you want someone to trust you, you'd better be sleeping with a hooker at least – to get in as deep as they are.' The money is made from having advance information, enabling you to trade ahead of clients' moves; for example buying jet fuel just before BA, KLM and Easyjet come stumbling into the market, pushing prices up. 'You talk to everyone, you know all that information, so you can move first. It's easy money if you have the size.' A much bigger example is the famous London Inter-Bank Offered Rate (LIBOR) scandal. This involved trillions of dollars' worth of financial transactions and was another cartel-like arrangement.[23] Who pays the cost of these supersized profits? You, ultimately, when you buy your airline tickets, or when the next financial crisis hits.

Another massive source of market power comes through the ownership of patents, trademarks and copyrights. The original intent of these was to carve out limited exceptions to antitrust laws in order to encourage firms to innovate, guaranteeing that for a fixed period of time only they could profit from something they had invested in. But they have become blanket licences to profiteer and now often stifle innovation. The song 'Happy Birthday', originally created by a US kindergarten teacher in 1893, was under copyright until a judge overturned it in 2016 after a long legal battle. Until then you were supposed to pay the copyright holders royalties every time you sang it in public.[24] And patents are often combined with other wealth-extraction techniques. Remember those transfer pricing games I described in Chapter 1, where the banana company shifted all its profits from Ecuador and Wales into a tax haven? Multinationals also shovel bucketloads of patents into shell companies in tax havens, not just slashing their tax bills, but also turbocharging the incentives to keep prices high.

American biopharmaceutical company Gilead's hepatitis-C drug Sovaldi, for instance, which is priced at $84,000 in the US and £35,000 in the UK for a twelve-week treatment versus a manufacturing cost as low as $68, has been parked in the corporate tax haven of Ireland. Despite sales of Sovaldi and a related drug, Harvoni, booming in 2015, the company's tax bill plummeted as it 'engaged in a massive shift of American profits offshore', according to research by the advocacy group Americans for Tax Fairness. By the end of 2015 Gilead was sitting on $28.5 billion in accumulated offshore profits. In 2016 the NHS decided to prescribe the drugs but, because of the price, only to 10,000 hepatitis-C sufferers, even though the deadly disease has infected over 200,000 in the UK. Breaking such monopolies can have dramatic results. When South Africa broke a patent stranglehold and managed to cut the cost of anti-retroviral drugs for Aids sufferers from $15,000 per patient per year down to less than a hundredth of that figure, the country's average life expectancy surged from 53.4 years in 2004 to 62.5 in 2015. South Africa's statistician general, Pali Lehohla, believes the change was largely down to increased access to these drugs.[25] With a thousand-dollar patent-protected pill, explains Matt Stoller, a US monopolies expert, 'you aren't paying for health care. You are paying for yachts.' And those are killer yachts.

In the light of all this complexity, it is clear that the popular view – tackling monopolies is just about breaking up cartels or big firms – is wrong-headed. Monopolies need to be tackled using varied and comprehensive economy-wide strategies: empowering labour unions, reforming banking rules, addressing billionaire and financial control over the media, focusing on conflicts of interest among large audit firms, cracking down on tax havens that prioritise banks and large multinationals over small businesses, and plenty more. Break-up is just one tool in the kit.

One of the first people to understand properly the potential of the relaxation of antitrust rules after Bork's vandalism was Jack Welch, the CEO of the American conglomerate General Electric. In the early 1980s outfits like GE – large corporations involved in a wide variety of different and often unrelated activities, each contributing to overall profits – were common. GE, for example, produced televisions, electric trains, lights, motors, X-ray machines, washing machines, hospital equipment, aircraft and plenty more. The clue was in its name. But in 1981, three years after Bork's book came out, Welch inaugurated a new company strategy: GE would aim to be the number one or number two in every business line it was involved in.

He set about reshaping GE, and in the process boosting its market power where possible. The company bought out competitors in related market sectors, created economies of scale to make it harder for competitors to break in, and sold off or closed business units that did not pass muster. In the pre-Bork era antitrust laws would have stopped much of this, but no longer. Welch's strategy caught on, helping fuel the great Wall Street merger boom of the 1980s, and spurred by Bork's beefy message the administration of President Ronald Reagan took the brakes off.[26] 'The general modus operandi was to break apart the old conglomerates that had been assembled in the 1950s and 1960s,' says Barry Lynn, a US antitrust expert, 'and then reassemble the parts in ways that better linked like to like ... [the] goal was to reduce competition as much as possible.'

This was profitable enough, but the transformation had a second stage: outsourcing, particularly the outsourcing of labour-intensive production facilities to cheap-labour countries like China or Bangladesh. This was driven especially hard by financial players and activist share-holders. And at the same time, also driven by financial players, bigger firms were aggressively expanding their use of tax havens to cut tax bills. These two related forms of offshoring – each involving taking money or operations elsewhere to escape paying out at home – gave large firms a killer cost advantage over their smaller, more domestically focused rivals, boosting their market power further. Old nurseries of jobs, skills and technologies were being smashed open in cash raids, and big firms often began to look less like industrial manufacturers rooted in communities, and more like trading companies: loosely connected, cross-border conglomerations of monopolies and near-monopolies focused on financial returns rather than building up in-house strength and expertise. You might call these firms middleman monopolies, inserting themselves at the choke points linking many different actors in a market, just as the giant supermarket chains position themselves between producers and consumers then use this position to extract more profit from both sides.

This can be especially scary for the small producers who supply these giants and who sometimes have nowhere else to turn. For example, Alicia Harvie of Farm Aid, a group that represents US family farmers, said in 2017, 'We can't overstate the level of fear and intimidation felt by poultry growers that contact us or our partner organisations. If they choose to speak up, they risk everything – their contract, their land, their homes.'[27] James Bloodworth, a British journalist who went undercover as a worker at an Amazon warehouse at Rugeley in Staffordshire in 2016, said he saw a similar problem affecting workers: he claimed conditions were so bad that it was 'like a prison'.[28]

These changes in the landscape of economic power have most often been driven by investment funds, activist shareholders and other financial interests, which have forced firms to channel their growing profits not into research and development but into paying bumper dividends. 'The pressure from financiers to increase profits has resulted in an ever swifter monopolisation of the industrial systems upon which we depend,' wrote Lynn, and the new model of antitrust 'builds vandalism right into the system'. This process has been part of the financialisation of large corporations in country after country.

But this isn't just about industrial processes; far from it. At every turn it has been about corporate power and its relationship with democracy and society. The monopolisation of news has been especially dangerous because it eliminates ideological competition, leading to 'a mushy liberal sameness in every market', as the US economic historian Bruce Bartlett once put it. Haughty and distant from large parts of the population, large news organisations based in London or New York peddle what often feels, to rural communities and the poor, like fake news. As Facebook, Google and other monopolising Internet behemoths slaughter newspapers' advertising revenues, only the strongest news giants prosper, reinforcing these dangerous trends and fuelling the furious new politics now convulsing large parts of the world. In 2017 and 2018 the Trump administration rolled back protections against monopolies in local broadcast news, allowing a slew of stations to come under the control of the arch-conservative and pro-Trump Sinclair Broadcast Group. These stations quickly began parroting the centrally dictated line, so much so that a video overlaying the voices of a multitude of different local news anchors all saying precisely the same thing – attacking the mainstream media and Trump's critics – went viral.[29]

The power now being amassed is staggering. Amazon, the 'Everything Store', thrills consumers with its convenience and low prices. It owns and sells books, toys, patents, cloud computing space and endless other stuff, but it also owns much of the infrastructure for selling these things. Imagine a single trucking company owning most of Britain's roads and being allowed to charge drivers to use them. This is a vertical, horizontal, everything monopoly. Amazon once had a Gazelle Project to approach and buy competitors, 'the way a cheetah would a sickly gazelle' as Amazon's boss Jeff Bezos described it. Amazon's policy isn't so much buying its competitors as eating them whole. It is massacring competing bookshops, replacing good jobs with smaller numbers of poorer, more menial, windowless shelf-stacking ones, as it spreads relentlessly into new markets. Its prices seem low, but it has such power that it can also influence its competitors' prices, in the process weakening them so it can then pick them off.[30] But prices aren't the real killer. The real action lies underneath, where through its sophisticated control of markets Amazon can extract monopolistic prices from publishers, from bookstores, from Amazon workers, from tax authorities, and ultimately from consumers as its market power grows and grows.

The behemoths have certainly eked out efficiencies from economies of scale. But whether the owners have passed these gains on to consumers, or taken them for themselves is another matter. When a large supermarket moves into a town, shoppers value the convenience and the apparently lower prices. But this is only part of the picture. The supermarket may sell sausages cheaper than the butcher did – although it may not, if it has a tight enough lock on the local sausage market. The combination of cheaper sausages with a bankrupt butcher might be justifiable overall, if this left more money in the pockets of local consumers, who could then support other high street businesses. But much, often most, of the wealth that the monopolisers generate is shipped out of local communities to mostly wealthy shareholders in places like London, New York or Geneva, while the butcher's employees, and those of some local suppliers and distributors, lose their jobs. All this is like picking someone's pocket, then opening their wallet and giving them a few dollars back, telling them with a smile what a good deal they've got.

And monopolising trends have hit workers hard, in countries around the world. Since the 1970s workers' wages have fallen by a whopping 10–15 per cent of national income in rich countries. As a result, our economies may have grown overall but workers, and especially low-skilled workers, aren't seeing the fruits of this growth. It has been estimated for the US that if wages hadn't fallen by this much, then (all other things being equal) net corporate profits would have been two-thirds lower. Slicing this another way, if British workers' share of national income were at 1975 levels, then (again all other things being equal) the average British employee would be £6000–£9,000 better off *each year*.[31]

There are other reasons for these changes – technology, outsourcing, tax cuts for billionaires, weaker unions, the extractive financialisation of our economies and the long hangover from the global financial crisis – but some studies suggest that monopolisation, which overlaps with all of the above factors, has played a starring role. The big corporate cause of inequality these days, it seems, isn't so much soaring CEO pay as the rise of super-wealthy monopolising firms which have left their competitors choking in their dust.[32] And something telling and unexpected has been happening in poorer countries too. Trade theorists used to think that as companies in rich countries outsourced lower-skilled jobs to poorer countries, workers' share of income in those poorer countries would rise. But this hasn't happened.

This puzzle can be explained in large part by the growth of monopolising international 'lead companies' sitting (usually offshore) at choke points on long international supply chains for goods and services, using their global market power to extract the profits, replacing workers with robots where possible, and keeping workers' wages low in all countries, rich and poor. In all countries this game isn't just about the big players taking a bigger share of the pie; the pie has actually shrunk as workers have lost purchasing power and thus found themselves less able to buy goods, sapping demand for corporate output. This in turn has refocused the attention of corporate managers – away from investment and towards more financial engineering (and even more monopolisation) to improve profits.

In the process we've traded balanced economies with plentiful, stable well-paying jobs and thriving communities for unbalanced economies, zero-hour contracts, atomised communities and cheap televisions – and they probably aren't much cheaper, either. We've traded Adam Smith's invisible hand of the well-functioning market for the invisible fist of monopoly power. These changes have joined with other developments such as financial deregulation, independent central banking and the rise of the Euromarkets to create the typhoon-force winds filling the sails of large banks and multinational firms, nearly always to the detriment of smaller domestic competitors and taxpayers.

This sabotage of the tools that underpinned the prosperity of the Golden Age of Capitalism also created unprecedented challenges for the political parties of the left. Infused with these new ideas, they now began to look for new paths forward less hostile to finance and big business. 'We have moved past the sterile debate between those who say government is the enemy and those who say government is the answer,' said US President Bill Clinton, who, along with his wife Hillary, had studied under Bork at Yale Law School in the 1970s. 'My fellow Americans, we have found a third way.'

5

The Third Way

In 1972, as the Golden Age was coming to an end, a fashionably dressed Pakistani banker called Agha Hasan Abedi confessed to a couple of colleagues a dream to set up 'a world bank: a global bank for the Third World'. Within ten years, he grandly promised, 'you'll see: we will all be millionaires'. That year Abedi got start-up funding from the president of the United Arab Emirates, incorporated a new banking institution in the tiny European tax haven of Luxembourg, formed an international alliance with the Bank of America and began opening up branches and hoovering up deposits from around the world. Within five years the Bank of Credit and Commerce International (BCCI) had 146 branches in 32 countries and a shiny new headquarters just a few minutes' walk from the Bank of England in the City of London.

BCCI would do anything, for anyone, anywhere, using any methods. It trafficked in nuclear materials and secrets, and in Chinese Silkworm anti-ship missiles. It financed and co-ran transnational cocaine and heroin operations, and procured hookers, mercenaries and assassins for clients. Alongside normal deposit-taking services for expatriates, it worked with Saddam Hussein, Manuel Noriega, Colombia's Medellín and Calí drugs cartels, Hezbollah, assorted warlords, the Afghan muja-hideen and the North Koreans. Bribes flowed like champagne in every place where it did business. 'I would go to 101 Leadenhall Street [in the City of London] and see a man called —,' recalled a former employee who delivered bribes and payments. 'He would smile at me and say, "Sign this piece of paper." I would write "Mickey Mouse" on a piece of tissue paper, which was then thrown away. He handed me a bag of money, which I would then take back and distribute.' (To whom the payments were distributed, he did not say.)

BCCI infested US politics too: when Jack Blum, one of the lawyers who eventually helped bring the bank down, started investigating it he soon came up against the CIA and 'an army of people working in Washington on all sides'. BCCI wasn't just a global octopus of murder and organised crime; it was also a giant Ponzi scheme for ripping off its depositors and investors, and turned out to be the biggest banking fraud of the twentieth century.[1] It bamboozled everyone by splitting its main operations three ways: between two separate holding companies in Luxembourg and Cayman, and its headquarters in London.

By this stage of the book it should be obvious why Abedi chose Cayman and London. Less well understood, however, is the role of Luxembourg, a small tax haven nestled at the geographical meeting point of France, Germany and Belgium. It is often useful to look at globalisation through the lens of small tax havens because in such places the checks and balances and the messy kerfuffle that you find in large democracies generally get swept aside, revealing some of the processes at play in purer, more distilled forms.

Luxembourg has a long history of welcoming the world's criminal money with few questions asked and barely enforcing even its own laws when it gets there. BCCI was just one case among several global scandals implicating the grand duchy. It was here, and in Switzerland, that the bearded American hustler and fraudster Bernie Cornfeld chose to build up his now-notorious Investors Overseas Services (IOS) in the 1960s. Cornfeld surrounded himself with purring cheetahs, leather-clad female chauffeurs and beautiful women who included the actress Victoria Principal and the famed 'Hollywood madam', Heidi Fleiss. He operated IOS out of a castle in Geneva that had been built by Napoleon. Like BCCI, IOS – before it collapsed in accounting scandals and fell into the hands of violent gangsters in 1971 – hoovered up shady money from rich and poor countries and fed it into US securities via the Eurodollar market. Luxembourg was also home to the thoroughly rotten Banco Ambrosiano Holdings SA, the subsidiary at the centre of the giant Banco Ambrosiano bank scandal, which involved the Italian Mafia, the Vatican, Masonic lodges, and famously the hanging of 'God's Banker' Roberto Calvi under Blackfriars Bridge in London.

Luxembourg was key to the Elf Affair, Europe's biggest corruption scandal since the Second World War, which involved the French state oil company Elf Aquitaine serving as a giant offshore slush fund pumping secret finance to all the main French political parties and to the intelligence services, and supplying bribes on behalf of French businesses all around the world, from Venezuela to Germany to Taiwan. The global fraudster Bernie Madoff ran some of his largest scams out of Luxembourg. In fact, almost any large-scale financial and political scandal in western Europe since the 1960s has had a colourful Luxembourg chapter. And things haven't changed that much: as a *Financial Times* analysis put it in 2017, 'Luxembourg sometimes resembles a criminal enterprise with a country attached.'[2]

If anyone can be called the architect of the modern tax haven of Luxembourg, it's the man who served as finance minister from 1989, then prime minister from 1995 to 2013 and now president of the European Commission, Jean-Claude Juncker. The son of a steelworker and trade unionist, Juncker is an ebullient, charismatic, chain-smoking, larger-than-life master manipulator. A short video from a summit of European leaders in Latvia in May 2015 points to his public appeal; Juncker stands, swaying and tittering, as a succession of heads of state and government walk past. As they greet him he slaps them in the face, grabs ties, manhandles them and lovingly kisses bald patches. At the approach of Viktor Orbán, Hungary's hardline right-wing prime minister, Juncker greets him with a half raised-hand salute then gives him a gangster handshake and the greeting, 'Dictator!' Then, beaming broadly, he slaps the stony-faced Orbán on the cheek. Juncker has denied rumours that he is an alcoholic, telling a French newspaper in 2016 that his occasional lurches and staggers are due to a leg injury he got in a car crash in 1989. (He chugged four glasses of champagne during that interview.) His outbreaks of irrational honesty are legendary. 'When it becomes serious, you have to lie,' he once said with a shrug in 2011, on live television.

Though Juncker built his career in the centre-right CSV party, he was always a bit of a lefty. He splashed state subsidies widely, including handsome pensions and unemployment benefits; he promoted very strict employment-protection laws and progressive wage policies, and a Euro-style tripartite social dialogue between workers, company owners and the state, softening globalisation's hard edges. This formula made him astonishingly popular in Luxembourg, where his approval ratings while in office sometimes exceeded 80 per cent.[3]

On Juncker's watch, Luxembourg multiplied its tax-haven offerings. Since the 1980s it has run devastatingly successful campaigns in partnership with Switzerland (and sometimes Britain and Austria) to sabotage European efforts to crack down on tax havens, secret banking, shell companies and other secrecy services. Juncker also oversaw Luxembourg during a dramatic flowering of its role helping global multinationals to escape tax. This was finally exposed in the Luxleaks scandal of 2014, when two whistle-blowers leaked tens of thousands of confidential documents showing how Luxembourg had rubber-stamped schemes created by PwC to help the world's biggest multinationals cut their tax bills: Walt Disney, Koch Brothers, Pepsi, Ikea, FedEx, Deutsche Bank, Blackstone, JP Morgan Chase and over 300 others.[4] Marius Kohl, head of one Luxembourg tax agency, would receive applications for tax rulings every Wednesday in batches of thirty or forty, on a USB memory stick. When he started losing them and forgetting passwords, PwC gave him direct access to their system; they even had his agency's letterhead paper in their offices so they could draft his acceptance notices themselves. When a journalist asked Kohl how he judged a complex scheme's legality, he simply licked his thumb and held it in the air. According to Richard Brooks, a Luxleaks journalist and former UK tax inspector, these tax schemes may have involved 'mass tax crimes' by some of the world's largest multinationals,[5] yet the only people prosecuted were the two whistle-blowers. Juncker denied all knowledge of these games, but leaked diplomatic cables show that he fought tenaciously and successfully in Brussels to prevent proper crackdowns.[6]

Dissent against the financial consensus in Luxembourg is hard. The place is suffused by an attitude that characterises every tax haven I've visited or studied: don't rock the boat, don't ask questions, and don't do anything to threaten the offshore financial sector. Bend over backwards, bend the law, look the other way, and do everything possible to keep your financial centre 'competitive'. Meanwhile, tell outsiders that it is clean, responsible and well regulated – and that it is not a tax haven. This consensus pervades Luxembourg; all the main newspapers follow it, and most Luxembourgers believe it.[7]

Usually the mechanisms to control financial dissidents in a tax haven are subtle: an invisible melting away of job chances, a bias in the courts, family disapproval or social scorn. People who protest publicly against offshore finance in Luxembourg are sometimes called *Nestbeschmützer* – nest polluters, the dirtiest kind of traitor. Ahead of a trip to Luxembourg City in October 2011, I got an email from a local businessman who was in conflict with a Luxembourg bank. I should be aware, he wrote, of 'the absolutely scandalous discrepancy' between Luxembourg's laws and their application by its judges. He continued:

The people involved fear retaliation from Luxembourg authorities when going public. I know by personal experience how bad this may turn out. You just don't make it in this country unless you've proven your absolute loyalty to the system in place, including being OK if not more with all of its malpractices. I also know by personal experience how difficult it is for foreigners to get a firm grasp of the Mafia-like functioning of Luxembourg. No foreigner can imagine how bad it really is. But if you're really willing to find out, you'd better be ready for some surprises.

Luxembourg has the world's second-largest mutual funds sector after the United States, but a courts system 'the size of a small provincial town' as one lawyer put it. They can't possibly police the financial oceans that roil through here – and they don't want to; competitive policing of finance is after all, part of the point.[8] Many of the funds that channelled European investors' savings into Bernie Madoff's giant Ponzi scheme were run out of Luxembourg, and 'the whole set-up violated European law,' said Erik Bomans, a partner in Deminor, a financial recovery firm representing some 3,000 defrauded Madoff investors. 'There were no control mechanisms, no yearly due diligence, nothing, nothing, nothing,' Bomans told me. 'He could basically do what he wanted.' The Big Four accounting firms didn't raise any objections, and the captured regulator, riddled with conflicts of interest, didn't blink at Madoff's outrageous schemes. And when the victims tried to get their money back from the banks responsible, Luxembourg took the banks' side every time. 'It is unbelievable, it is a scandal,' Bomans continued. 'We have no access to justice, thanks to the Luxembourg judicial system.'[9] Luxembourg is the classic tax haven, captured wholesale, laws and all, by offshore finance.

With one hand Juncker nurtured a huge expansion in this Euro-beacon of offshore finance, neoliberal deregulation, laxity in policing financial crime and national 'competitiveness'. With the other he used the wealth thus acquired to shower Luxembourgers with highly progressive spending and social policies. This seemingly contradictory behaviour should be familiar to many of us, for it has formed the economic heart of an agenda that has enraptured a generation of Western politicians and underpinned the main economic strategies of many countries for more than a quarter of a century. From the 1990s many politicians adopted the recipe: it brought Bill Clinton's New Democrats to power in 1993, Tony Blair's New Labour to power in 1997, and a host of other leaders including in Australia, France, Germany, Italy, the Netherlands, Portugal and Sweden. Those who adopted the formula often found themselves winning elections with large majorities. And it made tremendous fortunes in the City of London. They called it the Third Way.

The Third Way was a pretty simple idea: it was an attempt by the parties of the left to stake out a new middle ground in politics. Globalisation was inevitable, its proponents argued, so countries should embrace it and adapt to it, hitching a ride on the growth of global financial markets, then shaving off globalisation's raw edges with progressive social policies and dollops of good old-fashioned redistribution. As Tony Blair and Germany's Gerhard Schröder summarised it in a joint declaration in 1998, the Third Way 'stands not only for social justice but also for economic dynamism and the unleashing of creativity and innovation'.

But the Third Way was always an offshore model, a recipe for countries effectively to turn themselves into tax havens in order to prosper in rough, globalising seas. This model was, in turn, driven by the competitiveness agenda, the idea or ideology that countries must be 'open for business', constantly dangling enticements to large multinationals and banks and to rootless global money – tax cuts, financial deregulation, turning a blind eye to crime – for fear that they will decamp to more hospitable or 'competitive' places like Dubai or Singapore or Geneva.[10]

However, the competitiveness agenda – and by extension the Third Way – has not turned out to be a recipe for national prosperity for the countries like Britain that have embraced it; quite the opposite, in fact.

There's no single genius or jarring event that brought about the Third Way. It was probably going to happen anyway. As financial globalisation caught fire, left-leaning politicians found themselves, like passengers on a sinking ship, looking for a way out. And they were delighted to see a retinue of white-gloved stewards beckoning them towards a glamorous exit route and life rafts. Luxembourg was already happily afloat and had grabbed itself a bottle of champagne.

In fact you can find the roots of the thinking behind the Third Way as far back in history as you care to look. When William Pitt introduced income tax in 1799 at 10 per cent, the City of London called it a 'galling, oppressive and hateful inquisition' and wheeled out the 'competitiveness' argument: that the tax would scare the rich away and encourage 'a spirit of migration'. (It didn't happen.) In the modern era it's possible to see clear outlines of this agenda stretching back to the early days of the project that became today's European Union. The general idea of European integration was noble and progressive – to create economic entanglements so that Europe's bloodied nations would never want to go to war with each other again – yet if you look at the Treaty of Rome of 1957, which established the European Economic Community, it is possible to discern anxiety about inter-national competition and a desire to promote large pan-European firms to take on American giants. The treaty called for 'a high degree of competitiveness' alongside 'a high level of employment and of social protection'. Things were looking a little Third-Wayish already.

Meanwhile, in the United States, Chicago School ideas about efficient markets were beginning to percolate through the Democratic Party, the traditional party of the left. By the mid-1970s a new breed of liberal northern Democrat was emerging in the party, vowing to clean up Washington after the Watergate scandal. Anti-banker sentiment had faded along with memories of the Great Depression; crusaders against big banks and monopolies, crusaders like Wright Patman, a tough, bespectacled old Texas Democrat populist who had been known as the Bane of the Banks before the Second World War, fell out of favour.

In with the new blood came Tony Coelho, a Portuguese-American who had a gift for fundraising and a related fondness for large firms. Coelho became a leading defender of large agribusiness interests against small farmers, and got elected to Congress in 1978, the same year that Bork wrote his bestselling book, *The Antitrust Paradox*. At the

Democrats' annual party dinner Coelho raised fifty times the normal amount, and as a result was soon appointed to chair the Democratic Congressional Campaign Committee. 'Money is part of politics, and always will be,' he declared as he cranked up a new Democratic corporate fundraising machine. His key insight was that big business and rich folks weren't only interested in supporting Republicans with their low-tax, free-market ideology; what the moneybags really wanted was special favours, tax breaks and loopholes, nods and winks to mergers, and juicy government contracts. Rigged markets, in other words. And the Democrats were just as able to offer these as the Republicans.

Coelho opened the gates to a flood of new money into the Democratic Party. Some came from Don Dixon, a deal maker who later went to prison for fraud after a lurid six-week trial with testimony describing call girls, hot tubs, yachts and the gift of a $40,000 painting to the Vatican, which got him an audience with the pope. After the Democrats' devastating loss to Ronald Reagan in 1980 Coelho became even more single-minded about pursuing the big money – in effect, corrupting the party – as the route to power.[11]

At the same time the new Democrats shifted their attention away from working-class whites and labour issues towards civil rights and social tolerance. In 1982 the Democratic National Committee officially recognised seven new caucuses: women, blacks, Hispanics, Asians, gays, liberals and business professionals. Behind this move lay a less salubrious calculation: if they could get enough of these cultural groups on board, they might then be able to dispense with their traditional role as the guardians of workers against big banks and monopolising big corporations, and do what many influential and ambitious people in the party *really* wanted to do – cosy up to big business. And the tactic worked for a while: they boasted of a reliably Democrat 'blue wall' of Midwestern and upper Midwestern states, which mostly held together until the global financial crisis.[12]

The overall result of this sea change from progressive economics towards identity politics created a paradox, explained Matt Stoller of the Open Markets Institute in a landmark article in *The Atlantic* in 2016 entitled 'How the Democrats Killed their Populist Soul'. 'At the same time that the nation has achieved perhaps the most tolerant culture in US history, the destruction of the anti-monopoly and anti-bank tradition in the Democratic Party has also cleared the way for the greatest concentration of economic power in a century.' This 'is part of the larger story of how the Democratic Party helped to create today's shockingly disillusioned and sullen public, a large chunk of whom is now marching for Donald Trump'.[13] And this shift paved the path for the Third Way. Hillary Clinton even crystallised the shift in an election rally speech in 2016.

'If we broke up the big banks tomorrow,' she shouted, 'would that end racism?'

'No!' her audience replied.

'Would that end sexism?'

'No!'

And on she went, razzing the crowd up with a pro-big bank message couched as something very different.

In Europe the big money was extending its influence in other ways. One of the most influential vehicles was a group called the European Round Table of Industrialists (ERT), set up in 1983, its declared aim to push Europe to 'upgrade its competitiveness'. The ERT was and is a club of the bosses of Europe's biggest companies, and served for years as a corporate beachhead inside Europe's top decision-making bodies. The ERT has pushed steadily for a more seamless, deregulated, de-tarriffed single internal European market for giant cross-border banks and multinationals, and its influence has been so immense that Jacques Delors, a former European Commission chief, has described it as 'one of the main driving forces behind the European Single Market'. The ERT has pushed the competitiveness agenda hard and used Bork's antitrust revolution to help gut Europe's anti-monopoly safeguards, so that its guiding documents in this area are now suffused by a tolerance for giant monopolies and a Borkish obsession with consumer welfare and prices.[14]

And don't be fooled by those large European fines you might have read about in the papers; they are relative pinpricks.[15] The €10 billion euros in total European cartel-related fines in the five years to 2017 may sound grand, but at €2 billion per year represented just 0.03 per cent, or about one three-thousandth, of European corporate profits over the period, which is astonishing, given how extensively monopolies now pervade our economies.

As with all changes that favour the big money, there were academics on hand to support the changes. The best-known was

Harvard Business School guru Michael Porter, author of several influential books and articles about corporate strategy, including one in the *Harvard Business Review* in 1979 arguing that the best business strategy is to avoid competition by finding monopolising niches where others can't compete.[16] Porter scaled up his insights about corporations to the level of the nation state in an 850-page doorstop in 1990 called *The Competitive Advantage of Nations*, which was a bestseller. The book wasn't straightforwardly neoliberal. Countries should play to their strengths, Porter said. They should create clusters of knowledge and innovation, avoid short-termism and many other mostly unobjectionable things. But it also rested solidly on the idea that 'competitive' countries and cities must look after business, and especially big business, to prosper. The emphasis, for instance, was not so much on education – the stuff that creates rounded, knowledgeable, social, politically engaged and honest human beings – but skills, the part of education that business needs.[17] And by framing public policy strategies in corporate terms, Porter helped political leaders of the left develop a common language and empathy with big banks and multinationals, while at the same time making the parties of the left seem less scary to big business.

This globalising quasi-leftist love-in was reinvigorated each year in the Swiss ski resort of Davos at the annual jamboree of the World Economic Forum (WEF), an organisation which was set up in 1971 originally as a discussion forum for the world's biggest multinationals, but which has expanded every year. Through the 1990s it became increasingly important for world leaders to come to Davos and discuss the state of the world with financial and business bosses, think-tank glitterati and prominent journalists – incidentally providing Swiss bankers with fabulous opportunities to market their anti-tax, criminalised wealth management services and offshore attitudes to the assembled global elites. The WEF, with Porter's help, began to issue annual competitiveness rankings and scores for countries, generating anxiety among policymakers about whether their country was keeping up in the global race. The answer was always no, even for top-ranked countries, because the pack was always there, snapping at their heels. Adding fuel to the fire, President Clinton chimed in with a declaration in 1993 that each nation was 'like a big corporation competing in the marketplace'.

In Britain we were constantly told by voices in the City that we were at a 'tipping point' and unless we did something now capital would lose confidence in Britain and flee, and jobs would disappear down the plug hole. A global economic race was on, and by now everyone knew it. 'The fate of nations became entangled with the fate of enterprises, and vice versa,' wrote the British political economist Will Davies of the new Davos era. 'A new vision of political authority was invented, in which the nation or city or region was comparable to a corporation, of which the political leader was the CEO and the citizens were employees.'[18]

As the 1990s progressed, world leaders steadily tuned in to the competitiveness agenda and to Third-Wayish ideas: embrace globalisation, 'compete' and redistribute what you can. There was Australia's blokeish Bob Hawke, who could have given Juncker a run for his money: Hawke once held the world speed record for drinking a yard of ale. There was Italy's Romano Prodi, Sweden's Göran Persson, Dutch prime minister Wim Kok and Germany's Gerhard Schröder with his project for *Die Neue Mitte* — the New Middle. The political philosopher Francis Fukuyama had famously summed up the changes in 1989, as the movement was gathering steam, with the declaration that the victory of market capitalism was 'the end of history as such: the end point of mankind's ideological evolution and the universalisation of Western liberal democracy as the final form of human government'. For the left, the Third Way was the only way.

This was the spirit of the age in 1997 when Britain, parched by eighteen hard years of Conservative rule, was offered the chance to elect a rock-star politician at the head of a renewed Labour Party. Tony Blair promised reform, renewal, modernisation, enterprise and innovation – with a generous dose of redistribution and a new social agenda that mirrored the US Democrats' switch away from their working-class base towards a new multicultural one. He won the election, and once in office his approval ratings surged: at one point in 1997, after the death of Princess Diana, he had a Juncker-like 93 per cent popularity rating. For a while Tony Blair dazzled me too.

Even before he became prime minister, Blair was wielding the C-word to devastating effect, and to a much greater degree than his Conservative predecessors.[19] 'With foreign businesspeople and

foreign journalists, he'd talk about all the opportunities of globalisation: to attract overseas businesses to act as role models in the
UK, to lift the competitiveness levels of the economy. He managed
their expectations upwards: "invest in Britain, come to Britain",'
explains Warwick University's Matthew Watson. But with domestic
audiences it was a different message. It wasn't about opportunities
but about imperatives and restraints on policy: how limited the
opportunities would be to redistribute, tax and spend, and do the
things that Labour was traditionally associated with. For the home
audience 'it was all about managing expectations downwards. There
was a functional necessity for business interests to win out. It was
an opportunity – or a threat. A chance for national renewal – or an
imperative to follow blindly.'

One of Blair's most uncompromising speeches on this subject
came in 2005, in a signature address to the Labour Party conference.
The changing world, he told the room, was 'indifferent to tradition.
Unforgiving of frailty ... replete with opportunities, but they only go
to those swift to adapt, slow to complain. I hear people say we have
to stop and debate globalisation. You might as well debate whether
autumn should follow summer.' The headline of an article in the
London Review of Books summed up the attitude: DEFEATISM, DEFEATISM,
DEFEATISM. 'New Labour capitulated,' wrote Ross McKibbin. 'And it
capitulated because it believed that, apart from the occasional fudge,
it could do little else.' Bow down to foreign hot money, degrade
the taxes and the laws and the oversight, was the message, and the
money will come. Blair's Third Way was a replica of the Jean-Claude
Juncker tax haven model: a selfish doctrine of dog-eat-dog national
self-interest, a well-padded boxing glove of social solidarity covering
a neoliberal fist, a technique for papering over the ugly truths of the
finance curse.

Blair and his many followers didn't see it as a surrender though
because they had hitched their wagons to exciting new powerhouses:
the shiny modernity of private equity titans, profit-gushing global
banks and private finance initiatives. New Labour politicians were
bored by old-school 'smokestack' industries, stood back from the
hard graft of regional industrial development and watched benignly
as British manufacturing retreated faster than in other industrialised
nations. Instead they courted glamorous Irish musicians like U2

who posed for photos in African villages, urging taxpayers to fund more foreign aid while dodging their own taxes and all but ignoring the rising rivers of wealth looted and sucked out of Africa through Britain's tax haven rackets. Blair sugar-coated his financial medicine with the restorative of his personal-responsibility agenda and the feel-good tonics of U2, Oasis, the Spice Girls, Cool Britannia and the Mayfair hedge fund set. Even Margaret Thatcher, who had crushed the unions and built on the Eurodollar mayhem with the Big Bang of financial deregulation in the City, was no longer the Labour Party's sworn enemy, but a moderniser, to be treated with grudging respect.[20]

The new attitudes were captured in a spoof letter circulating in the UK tax authorities' Large Business Office, whose job was to tax multinational companies. Amid allegations of fake intelligence used to justify invading Iraq in 2002, the letter pretended to be from Hans Blix, the UN's chief weapons inspector. 'Dear Saddam,' it began. 'We are trialling a new weapons inspection regime modelled on the Inland Revenue's approach to large corporate taxation. All you have to do is tell us you don't have any and we'll go away. Yours, Hans Blix.'[21] The satire followed the sale of over 600 government tax office buildings to a company based in the tax haven of Bermuda, in the name of 'efficiency', the latest of a series of humiliations that had transformed some tax inspectors' careers from a source of pride into bitterness, even despair, as they were rebranded 'customer relationship managers'. If they tried too hard to do their job, one tax inspector wearily told me, a superior 'reaches down and gets involved in cases no one like that should ever get involved in. We used to have a priority to collect tax. Now we have a priority to have a good relationship.' It was an approach to taxing multinationals that Jean-Claude Juncker would have been proud of.

Blair also mounted an attack on Britain's financial regulators, as big banks based in London gorged on frauds on their customers and trillion-dollar risk-taking at taxpayers' expense. The Financial Services Authority, Blair said, 'is seen as hugely inhibiting of efficient business by perfectly respectable companies that have never defrauded anyone'. He chided regulators' tendency 'to regulate to eliminate risk: to restrict rather than enable. We pay a price if we react like this. We lose out in business to India and China, who are prepared to accept the risks.'

This was the leader of the *Labour* Party effectively urging Britain to degrade its laws, and even to degrade its labour force to the level of developing-country sweatshops.[22]

A few spoilsports had, to be fair, called out the Third Way from the beginning. 'The "Third Way" has been hyped as "a new kind of politics",' carped Stuart Hall in *Marxism Today* in 1998. 'Its central claim is the discovery of a mysterious middle course on every question between all the existing extremes. However, the closer one examines this via media, the more it looks, not like a way through the problems, but a soft-headed way around them.' From the right, *The Economist* printed a bitchy piece making the same basic point. Its target was a book called *The Third Way* by Anthony Giddens of the London School of Economics, Blair's academic guru. The book, *The Economist* wrote, is 'a list of conventional appeals to civic virtue, in which every bet is hedged and every hard choice ducked'.

Yet these analyses only scratched the surface of the issue, because they missed the intellectual fallacies and practical hogwash that constitute the very foundations of the Third Way and the competitiveness agenda.

In 1994, the year Blair became Labour Party leader, US economist Paul Krugman wrote an essay entitled 'Competitiveness: A Dangerous Obsession'. In it he declared, 'The growing obsession in most advanced nations with national competitiveness should be seen, not as a well-founded concern, but as a view held in the face of overwhelming contrary evidence. And yet it is clearly a view that people very much want to hold.' Krugman raked through various things 'national competitiveness' might possibly mean: trade surplus, terms of trade, labour costs, David Ricardo's (very different) concept of comparative advantage, or simply the question of national power and global economic heft. He concluded that – being as charitable as possible – the concept boiled down to 'a funny way of talking about productivity'. Not relative to other countries, mind, just plain old productivity. 'If we can teach undergraduates to wince when they hear someone talk about "competitiveness", we will have done our nation a great service,' he continued. 'A government wedded to the ideology of competitiveness is as unlikely to make good economic policy as a government committed to creationism is to make good science policy.'[23]

The confusions at the heart of the competitiveness agenda stack up, one after another. Economies or tax systems or cities are nothing like companies and don't 'compete' in any meaningful way. The most coherent meaning of the term is a military one, when one country 'out-competes' another by becoming strong enough to conquer it. But this isn't how economics works. Companies pursue profits, which then get taxed. What is the equivalent of profits for a nation? A budget surplus? A trade surplus? These can be signs of diseased economic policies such as unnecessary austerity, or of underconsumption. (And how would you tax a budget surplus?) The simplest way for a country to make cheaper exports is to devalue its currency. Companies don't have their own currencies to devalue. If a company shapes up and produces better, slicker products, it can put its rivals out of business, but if Britain improves its technology or education, that won't put Germany out of business. It could well make Germans richer. You improve education to make Britain's people more productive, more equal, wealthier and other good things, but not because you're in a race with Germany. 'It is one of those things that sounds good – "Make Britain competitive!"' said Jonathan Portes, a former chief economist at the Cabinet Office. 'I tend to take the view that this is meaningless fluff … a distraction from what is really going on.'[24]

Now this is, admittedly, a tricky area. You can take any term in the English language, in this case 'national competitiveness', and make it mean whatever you want it to mean. You can argue, for instance, that the best way to support something you call 'national competitiveness' is to upgrade education, build strong social protections, or control dangerous capital flows across borders. You could argue that it means adopting protectionism and carefully targeted industrial policies of nurturing productive domestic economic ecosystems. You could insist that 'national competitiveness' must meet the test of productivity, good jobs and a broad-based rise in living standards. There are strong, respectable arguments along all these lines.[25] But Blair wasn't making these arguments at all; he was pushing the competitiveness agenda, which was all about pursuing rootless capital in a globalised world. Give big banks and multinationals what they ask for, look the other way when they behave badly, then watch the wealth spring up and trickle down.

Another core confusion of the agenda is the idea that globalisation is unstoppable and implacable, like the weather, and the best you can do is adapt your societies to the needs and whims of big banks and corporations and mobile rich people, then compensate the losers as best you can. This self-abasing belief, that we must bow down to global markets and run as fast as we can in some sort of a race to the bottom, is widely held, both on the right – whose members see benefi-cent global markets reining in and disciplining grasping, incompetent governments – and also on the left, which fears that governments are powerless to shield their people from nasty global forces. 'Both agree that impotent politicians must now bow before omnipotent markets,' explained Martin Wolf, chief economic commentator for the *Financial Times*. 'This has become one of the clichés of the age. But it is (almost) total nonsense.'[26]

People believe this nonsense because of other confusions. One is that they fail to see how the pro-finance changes that have happened with globalisation have generally required active intervention, or deliberate non-intervention, by governments. Central banks have been actively freed from direct democratic controls, and their objec-tives have been purposefully changed from goals such as promoting full employment to targeting inflation. Financial deregulation has involved actively de-fanging laws to protect societies. Trade and invest-ment treaties, consciously negotiated and signed, tie the hands of governments and prevent them from intervening to protect domestic industries. Governments have knowingly privatised huge swathes of public assets, and carefully fed them into competitive, financialised frameworks. They have chosen to cut taxes on capital, and to reduce workers' rights. Financial globalisation isn't just about mobile capital inevitably flowing effortlessly through the surly bonds of the state; it requires intergovernmental agreements to guarantee that creditors will be paid back and endless decisions to remove impediments to these flows. All these are solid policy choices, made deliberately by states – and they are reversible.[27]

Yet there's a still deeper confusion at the heart of the competi-tiveness agenda. This one hinges on a concept called the 'fallacy of composition', which is where you think that the fortunes of your big businesses and big banks are identical to the fortunes of the economy as a whole. If government policy can make HSBC more globally competitive, the argument goes, this makes Britain as a whole more 'competitive'. Few people get beyond this simple, beguiling formula. Yet improving the fortunes of HSBC won't necessarily improve the fortunes of Britain as a whole, and this is especially true if a big chunk of HSBC's profits are extracted from other parts of the economy. Large banks, multinationals or hedge funds, the biggest beneficiaries of this agenda, are not just competing in global markets; they are also competing against and killing their smaller domestic rivals, not just in markets where they sell stuff, but also in terms of the people they can hire. High wages in the City of London suck talented, educated people out of often more genuinely productive areas of the economy. Instead of finding a cure for malaria, our best and brightest are getting rich as high-frequency traders. This is where the finance curse concept comes back into play: if *too much* finance reduces economic growth and causes other damage to your country, then the pursuit of *more* finance through policies that follow that agenda will most likely make things worse.

Language has proved a fabulous tool for bamboozlement here. One is the standard confusion that conflates the market competitiveness of firms and the 'competitiveness' of nations: two very different things. Others think it is something to do with the nineteenth-century British economist David Ricardo's similar-sounding, but very different, concept of 'comparative advantage' – a concept that suggests that a country should focus on nurturing its most productive strengths and trade with other nations to import the goods and services in sectors where it is relatively weaker. Or take the very British idea of 'UK plc' – a term that reimagines the whole economy as a business. This is wielded to tremendous rhetorical effect to show that there is a 'need' to make 'tough choices' and cut back health, education and disability benefits, in order to free up the resources to help 'our' giants compete on a world stage. Yet we feel no corresponding need to lend such support to our local handyman or photocopy shop, which aren't competing globally. Large parts of our political classes *need* this global competitive bogey to frighten the masses into accepting policies that benefit their friends in big business, Wall Street and the City. In 2017 Donald Trump wielded this fear-mongering tactic to great effect, praising China and 'highly competitive' countries with 'unbelievably low tax rates', who are 'taking us, frankly, to the cleaners, so we must – we have no choice – we must lower our taxes'. His administration went on to give US multinationals and billionaires the biggest collective tax cut in world history.

'National competitiveness' means, under the Third Way and its associated competitiveness agenda, extracting wealth from poorer, smaller, less mobile elements of the economy, and handing it to bigger, more mobile global players, so that they may compete on a world stage. It is, from first principles, an inequality machine. It is also a machine for generating crime and abusive behaviour. Dig behind pretty much any large modern economic scandal – the LIBOR affair, Luxleaks, the Panama Papers, Apple's $250-odd billion untaxed offshore cash pile, the global financial crisis, you name it – and the competitiveness agenda lurks behind the headline, deregulating, de-policing and de-taxing global financial markets. It is globalisation's most potent battering ram, cowing governments and populations.

There's something else that risks embedding this false idea of 'competitiveness' even more deeply into the British psyche: the event that now overshadows everything in British politics, paralyses the main political parties and polarises the public – Brexit.

Many embattled Remainers romanticise Europe as a progressive social-democratic bulwark restraining the worst excesses of Britain's oligarchic City-centred establishment. There's a lot to be said for that: inequality in European countries is generally less extreme than in Britain or America, and many member states have welfare states that are the envy of the world. Brexiteers, for their part, attack everything European, pointing to the EU's sprawling and undemocratic bureaucracies and its partial capture by corporate and financial interests.[28] They have some good arguments too. But it is important for Remainers to understand how thoroughly the European project is suffused with Third Way ideas and the competitiveness agenda, and therefore underpinned by the same intellectual fallacies. This means that the European Union in its current form is an unstable, fragile project. Without a revolutionary reappraisal of what Europe is for, the whole project seems destined eventually to collapse.

Europe's grand Lisbon Agenda, unleashed in 2000, declared as its aim to make Europe 'the most dynamic and competitive knowledge-based economy in the world by 2010 ... the easiest and cheapest place to do business in the world'. What could this mean? Well, the details show that it is substantially about the competitiveness agenda, typically leavened with (admittedly large) 'cohesion funds' and other shock absorbers. And it contains some remarkable Euro-confusions.

To get a sense of some of these confusions, consider a speech in 2007 given by Neelie Kroes, then Europe's commissioner for competition. 'The merger tsunami is a good sign,' was one of the things she said; mergers 'must be allowed to run their course without undue political interference'. This was the commissioner whose job was to rein in and regulate monopolies welcoming a 'merger tsunami', slamming 'unjustified obstacles in the way of cross-border mergers' and declaring openly for the price-obsessed Chicago School approach. (The *Wall Street Journal* reported EU officials saying they had 'never dealt with a commission candidate with such extensive business ties – and potential conflicts' as Kroes.) She wasn't exaggerating about mergers; by the turn of the millennium, on one measure, over 80 per cent of all measured global flows of foreign direct investment involved mergers as opposed to productive new 'greenfield' investment, as the former Soviet Union spewed forth a treasure train of fresh assets ready for weaving into monopolising, labour-crushing, tax-escaping giants and investment funds. For rich countries, almost *100 per cent* of investment flows happened through mergers.[29]

Kroes's second statement was shorter, but seems even odder: 'Competition is the main driver for competitiveness.' Her thinking went like this: if you free up Europe's internal single market for multinationals, then finance, trade and investment will flow more freely across seamless European borders, forcing European firms to compete more intensely with one another, creating efficiencies which would then help these firms compete more effectively on a global stage. This, in a nutshell, is Europe's rickety bridge between market competition and Europe's 'global competitiveness'.

But this raises new questions and confusions. How do firms create these efficiencies to become more globally competitive? Well, one way is to tolerate and even encourage the growth of monopolies. This means letting large European firms exploit their European customers in order to help them go head to head with the Americans and the Chinese. Or, once again, making Europe more 'competitive' by allowing less competition in Europe. These ideas are not just confused; history shows us that they can be dangerous. When Germany's monopolies commission warned in 2004 that plans to nurture a national banking champion (Deutsche Bank, in other words) would lead to 'too big to fail' banks and a financial crisis, and that a similar policy in 1931 had contributed to the conditions that fed the rise of the Nazi Party, the government told it to get lost. Bank regulation was excellent, they said.[30] Deutsche Bank's shaky finances remain a source of concern to Germany and to the European economy today.

Another way for firms to create efficiencies and become more competitive on the global stage is to strip out costs. But what are those costs? Why, wages, pensions, corporate taxes, financial regulations, social and environmental protections, and more – the lifeblood of European democracies and societies. This is, again, about shifting wealth and capital upwards, away from workers and taxpayers into the hands of big business. Angela Wigger, a Dutch expert on monopolies, summarises the whole Euro-competitiveness approach as 'a massive assault on labour and democracy ... it is unbelievable what is going on'.

The Lisbon Agenda is now widely regarded as having failed, not least because it delivered anaemic economic growth, with no sign of a European industrial resurgence either.[31] In response, EU leaders have doubled down, trying to make the internal market still more seamless, intensifying competition while promoting 'solidarity mechanisms' to deaden the pain. They floated a Convergence and Competitiveness Instrument, which sounds like (and is) a tool for torture. When Jean-Claude Juncker took over as head of the European Commission in 2014, he started pushing for a 'Euro area system of Competitiveness Authorities' to ram it all home, country after country, with 'competitiveness boards' to bypass opposition by circumventing normal European procedures.[32]

Juncker, of course, is an especially ardent fan of the competitiveness agenda, thanks to his background in Luxembourg. And this brings me back to a tricky question I asked near the start of this chapter: if Luxembourg is so rich, then how come it isn't a model to emulate? Luxembourg's affluence – its GDP per capita is 260 per cent of the European average – might seem like the perfect counter-example to the idea of a finance curse. So it is vital to explain why Luxembourg is no model for other countries like Britain.

Some leading Brexiteers fantasise about creating a prosperous free-trading Luxembourg model or 'Singapore on the Thames' tax haven model outside Europe. In 2017 British chancellor Phillip Hammond turned this fantasy into a threat, telling EU officials that if Britain was offered a bad deal in Brexit negotiations, 'we will have to change our model to regain competitiveness ... we will come back and we will be competitively engaged'. Give us what we want, Europe, he was saying, or we'll double down on our offshore tax haven model and undercut you.

This threat was empty; more like, 'Give us what we want, or we'll shoot ourselves in the foot.' For one thing, well over two-thirds of Luxembourg's workers are foreign, cross-border commuters into Luxembourg from France, Germany or Belgium, or foreign residents. Other countries educate these people when they are young, then Luxembourg benefits from their most productive years as employees. And when these workers retire or get sick they usually go back home and fall back on those other countries' health and benefits systems. Britain couldn't possibly replicate that.[33]

Luxembourg also plays several other games that couldn't be matched, such as profitably printing disproportionate mountains of euro banknotes and slashing fuel taxes so that every car or truck driver coming anywhere near the border chooses to fill up in Luxembourg, contributing to its revenues.[34] Also, GDP is a terrible measure for tax havens because it includes all the corporate profit-shuffling via Luxembourg letterbox companies, which hardly benefit locals. Gross national income, a better measure which strips out this stuff, cuts Luxembourg's 230 per cent to 170 per cent.

Yet a bigger reason why Luxembourg is no model is that its formula of spreading wealth from the Eurozone's biggest financial centre around a tiny population of half a million or so couldn't be scaled up to match Britain. To pull off a similar trick for Britain's 65 million people would need a financial centre servicing all of planet Earth plus several other economically successful planets. Citizens would then have to fight against massively increased financial lobbying power to ensure that wealth was redistributed back to the people – and even then, no matter how 'competitive' the secrecy dodge or tax loophole you put in place to lure the hot money, there would always be nimble little Luxembourg, with its fingers on the levers of European power, ready to undercut you. Not only that, but Luxembourg's other main attraction for financial sector players is its position at the heart of Europe, giving it preferential access to huge European capital markets that almost no other tax haven can match. Brexit may well sabotage that access for Britain. Singapore-on-Thames won't fly.

On the internet you can easily find a short video produced by a group called the Intruders, who in 2012 donned black-tie outfits and gatecrashed a gala dinner at a tax conference at New College, Oxford to honour Dave Hartnett, Britain's outgoing boss of HMRC, the tax authorities. Earlier, *Private Eye* had revealed how Hartnett had stopped a court case over a potential £6 billion tax bill for Vodafone without properly consulting HMRC's lawyers or tax specialists.[35] Hartnett had also publicly chided his own tax inspectors for being 'too tough' on multinationals, saying, 'we are sometimes too black and white about the law'.

In the YouTube video the Intruders present Hartnett with an ironic Lifetime Achievement Award for Services to Corporate Tax Planning, and the dignitaries begin to clap – that is until Robert Venables QC stands up and announces, 'These people are trespassers and intruders!' He begins to usher them out towards the door, with 'You will depart immediately, before we set the dogs on you.' The retreating activists sing, 'For he's a jolly good fellow / And so say Goldman Sachs!' Venables sees them off with a parting shot: 'You are trespassing scum! Go!'

But to the horror of grouse-shooting City tax accountants, the trespassing scum, along with groups like the Tax Justice Network (with whom I have worked) have carried the nation, gaining support across the political spectrum from left to right with campaigns for tax justice. There was by 2010 a second three-letter word ending in 'x' which filled newspaper headlines in the popular press. Even the right-wing *Daily Mail* took a breather from fulminating about benefit cheats and ran a series expressing outrage at much larger corporate giveaways. 'If you won't pay our taxes, we won't eat your cheese, Kraft!' ran one *Mail* campaign, after the US food giant bought up Cadbury's and shifted its ownership to a holding company in Zurich. (The *Mail* overlooked the offshore tax-escaping shenanigans of its controlling shareholder, Lord Rothermere.) The activists won over the public with a simple trick: shifting the debate away from the thorny question of whether corporate tax cheating was legal or not, towards basic questions of economics, democracy, level playing fields and the integrity of markets. In profoundly important ways the media and the general public understood tax better than many tax accountants did.

But despite the huge public fury that followed the global financial crisis and its after-effects, meaningful change did not come. Exactly the opposite happened, in fact: successive governments after 2010 entered into opaque special partnerships with global multinationals to design Britain's corporate tax policies. They slashed corporate tax rates again and again, and effectively legalised many of the loopholes that Vodafone and other corporations had been using to escape tax, thus actively and deliberately encouraging multinational affiliates based in Britain to shift their profits into tax havens, under the delusion that this would encourage multinationals to set up new affiliates in the UK. A KPMG director told an undercover reporter from *Private Eye* that under the new laws, 'you'd actually be left with a net sort of minus 15 [per cent tax rate]' on some transactions, and that some multinationals could eliminate their UK profits entirely. On the government's own figures, the changes that encourage multinational affiliates located in the UK to use tax havens are costing around £1 billion in taxes per year, while the ongoing corporate tax cuts since 2010 are now giving away ten to fifteen times as much.[36] None of these 'competitive' policies have moved the needle on Britain's 'great productivity puzzle', the fact that British workers are now around 25–30 per cent less productive than their French, American, Dutch, Swedish or German counterparts. And the gap is growing.[37]

The government and its allies sold these kinds of pro-multinational moves by throwing the concept of 'competitiveness' into the public's eyes, helping to generate a mindset that underpins every tax haven in the world. It wasn't Tony Blair or even Bill Clinton who invented the Third Way; Jean-Claude Juncker had blazed the trail long before. However there was another English-speaking politician with a similar outlook, who had been there too, operating in the fast-growing corporate tax haven of Ireland – the indefatigable, irrepressible Charles Haughey. He was also an evangelist for the need to 'unleash the wealth creators' with a 'competitive' economy, and to spend the bountiful proceeds – but with a difference. While Blair and Clinton waited until they had left office to take on lucrative consultancies, Haughey was happy to enrich himself while still in office. And the Celtic Tiger economy that he helped usher in would be the shining poster child for them all.

6

The Celtic Tiger

The tale of the Celtic Tiger, the Irish economic growth miracle of the 1990s and early 2000s, has become one of the most influential morality tales in the economic history of the modern world. The Irish model of low corporate taxes offered the ultimate free lunch: painless tax cuts leading to economic growth and, ultimately, larger tax revenues from the flood of new investment generated by those cuts. 'The Irish formula [became] the new universal truth of economics, society and development,' wrote Fintan O'Toole, a commentator for the *Irish Times* and author of *Ship of Fools*, a firecracker of a book about the Celtic Tiger. 'It transcended history and geography and worked irrespective of time and place.'[1]

And though the boom contained a lot of froth, and the global financial crisis mauled Ireland worse than most countries, the tiger was no illusion, and the beast remains alive today: foreign investment remains strong; cranes decorate the skyline again; cafés groan with banker-talk, and there is a palpable sense of life and purpose in Dublin. The story of the Celtic Tiger seems like a thunderbolt of evidence aimed squarely at one of the central arguments of this book: that if you want to build a prosperous and inclusive economy, you don't need to 'compete' on things like cutting corporate tax rates or relaxing financial regulations.

To understand why this widespread belief is wrong, it's necessary to tell a different story. This one goes back to the 1940s, when DC-3s and other propeller aircraft crossing the Atlantic needed to refuel at Shannon Airport on Ireland's west coast, near Europe's most westward landfall. To sugar the pill for aviators, in 1947 Shannon carved out from Ireland's tax system the world's first duty-free shop. But within five years commercial airlines began using jets, and their planes could now fly direct to New York from London or Paris without having to refuel at Shannon. Brendan O'Regan, an ebullient local entrepreneur, warned that Shannon would have to 'pull aircraft out of the sky' if it wasn't to sink back into green-pastured obscurity. He proposed a new tax-free zone just outside the airport, modelled on an emerging zone in Puerto Rico, where foreign investors could escape normal Irish taxes and regulations. The zone was established in 1959 and grew rapidly. (Happily for O'Regan, he was able to use his position as the airport's comptroller of catering and services to give the key contracts to a company he controlled.)

In the Shannon archives there's a photo from 1980 of a Chinese delegation sent to report on this Irish experiment, just as new president Deng Xiaoping was setting China on a big modernisation drive. In the line-up you can see a junior Chinese customs official with thick black spectacles standing in a heavy coat. After a tour of the tax-free zone the delegation was treated to a sing-song at Durty Nelly's pub – a fact that perhaps helps explain the remarkable warmth with which Bertie Ahern, the Irish Taoiseach (prime minister), was received in Beijing in 1998 by the same bespectacled official, who by then had risen to become President Jiang Zemin. Shannon had inspired China to set up the special economic zones that would prove key to propelling its own subsequent economic growth miracle,[2] and it is now regarded with such historical veneration that Xi Jinping and a succession of other top Chinese officials have made the pilgrimage to Shannon since then. 'The Chinese embassy in London was constantly bringing guys to Shannon, it was a kind of Lourdes to them,' said Tom Kelleher, a veteran consultant for the Shannon zone. 'Visit Shannon and you get an indulgence.'

This backstory illuminates the supposed magic trick that Ireland hit upon: corporate tax-cutting and financial deregulation as the magic potion of economic growth. But there is a wrinkle in this happy tale, and it is a big one. Ireland's economic growth under the Celtic Tiger shows no correlation – no correlation *at all* – to its long history as a corporate tax haven. In fact, Ireland's population may well have been better off without its corporate tax cuts and its wild-west financial centre. The real story of the Celtic Tiger lies elsewhere.

Ireland's tax haven strategy was never about secrecy, as in some tax havens, but about corporate tax cuts. The strategy properly began in 1956 with a facility called Export Profits Tax Relief – an aggressive corporate tax haven strategy by the standards of the day which, once tweaked and embedded, meant zero taxes on export sales of manufactured goods. There was a bit of a pick-up in exports and growth soon after that, and this has led many to conclude that it was the corporate tax cuts that did it. But the truth is, these growth rates were no higher than what was happening across western Europe amid the Golden Age. Employment in manufacturing in Ireland would rise at 1 per cent a year for the foreseeable future, and by the early 1970s less than 3 per cent of the Irish workforce were employed in foreign-owned industry, mostly in low-wage employment.[3]

Then, in the early 1970s, an odd thing happened. Foreign direct investment (FDI) into Ireland suddenly exploded: a *fifteenfold* jump in just seven years from $25 million in 1971 to $375 million by 1978.[4] Many economists regard FDI as the great elixir of growth for countries playing catch-up; not only do those foreign investors build factories and pay taxes and create jobs, but they also deliver a world of know-how and skills into the countries that receive it.

Irish corporate tax policies were being constantly mildly tweaked over this period, but there was only one event that could explain this sudden FDI explosion: Ireland's accession to the European Economic Community in 1973. Previously, a firm based in Ireland could sell freely to the tiny Irish market and to a certain degree into Britain, but faced tariffs and difficulties if they wanted to sell further afield. Accession to the EEC, two years before Britain joined, transformed investors' calculations. And a more convenient, friendly, English-speaking platform for American investors – especially those firms whose CEOs had Irish ancestry – was hard to imagine. 'Multinational firms locating here could use the country as a platform for exports to a European market of 250 million people,' wrote Ray MacSharry, a former deputy prime minister, and Padraic White, a former head of the Irish Industrial Development Authority, in their jointly authored book *The Making of the Celtic Tiger*. 'Above all, joining the EEC allowed Ireland to step out of the shadow of British influence.'[5]

Europe's impact went far beyond market access. It helped usher in deep-rooted social reforms, not least a remarkable emancipation of women. Until 1973, would you believe it, female civil servants and other public employees in Ireland had to resign their jobs when they got married on the grounds that they were taking jobs from men. 'Marital rape' was in law a contradiction, because Irish husbands were assumed to have the right to have sex with their wives whenever they felt so inclined. Women had almost no access to contraceptives; child benefits could only be collected by the father, and women couldn't own their homes outright. Many pubs wouldn't admit women unless accompanied by a man. Europe forced Ireland to get rid of these archaic forms of discrimination, and in fairly short order. In the words of Irish journalist Justine McCarthy, joining Europe 'rescued us from slavery'.[6]

But Europe also didn't like the 'discriminatory' rules of the fledgling Irish corporate tax haven. The EU cut the poverty-stricken country, which wasn't much more than half as rich as the European average, some slack for a while, but by 1980 Ireland had to phase out its zero per cent rate for manufacturing and replace it with a 10 per cent tax on profits for 'manufacturing and internationally traded services'. By then, the new foreign investment surge had created 70,000 jobs, a decent but still only modest 5 per cent of the workforce. Yet something was still amiss.

For an economy trying to develop, foreign investment is only a means to an end. What matters ultimately is how the economy as a whole performs. For one thing, if you have to take wealth or skilled workers out of other parts of the economy to subsidise FDI, that may not necessarily increase growth overall. The best measure of Irish economic performance for our purposes is to look at gross national income (GNI) per person compared to the European average. On this measure, Irish incomes had flatlined at 60 per cent of the European average since 1956, and had dipped slightly during the early 1970s even amid the rising tide of foreign investment. By the end of the 1980s Irish GNI per capita still hadn't budged above around 60 per cent of the European average; unemployment was well over 15 per cent, and one in every hundred Irish people was emigrating each year. For well over a quarter of a century Ireland's aggressive corporate tax haven strategy had worked for a minority, but not for the country as a whole.[7]

Then suddenly, in about 1992, something new happened. Economic growth exploded. The Celtic Tiger had been born.

To understand the nature of the beast that had been unleashed, it's necessary first to understand the man who had dominated Irish politics in the previous decade or more, Charles Haughey.

Haughey was a practitioner of Vatican-level crookery who on his death in 2006 had amassed a mansion and a 280-acre estate near Dublin, a string of racehorses, a yacht, an island retreat off the south coast, lavish gifts from Saudi princes and a complex financial web of personal accounts and assets scattered across several tax havens. Staff at the exclusive Charvet outfitters in Paris, where Haughey paid thousands for bespoke silk shirts and dressing gowns, called him 'Your Excellency', but to close associates he was simply 'the Boss'. Born in rural County Mayo in 1925 to a captain in the Irish Free State Army, Haughey qualified as an accountant and trained as a lawyer but was always destined for politics. In 1951 he married the daughter of a grandee in the mainstream Fianna Fáil party, a centrist, populist but conservative grouping which, alongside the more right-wing Fine Gael, had dominated Irish politics for half a century.

Haughey's thirst for influence was something to behold. 'Friends and enemies alike were mesmerised by his relentless pursuit of power,' explained Joe Joyce and Peter Murtaugh in their 1983 biography *The Boss*. 'He was living proof of the dictum that, in politics, one should never resign.'[8] By 1961, aged thirty-six, he was minister of justice; five years later he was made finance minister, and eventually he would become Ireland's Taoiseach, winning power three times, in 1979, 1982 and 1987. He introduced, among other things, the 1968 Finance Act, which would for the rest of his life essentially exempt his riches and that of many of his friends from tax. In 1970, a year after getting caught taking a lucky punt on 100 million Deutschmarks with public funds, he was finally dismissed from government after being found to have helped gunrunners for the Irish Republican Army fighting the British army in Northern Ireland (he was also arrested and tried, but found not guilty).[9]

Ireland's economy in the 1970s was still dominated by the Church, big agricultural interests and a loose group of high-society bankers and accountants in a system still economically subservient to London and rigged against the rural poor in favour of wealthy middlemen who collected and exported the fruits of their labours, mostly to Britain. Haughey wore his shaky working-class roots as a badge of honour, and positioned himself as the anti-establishment candidate. But this ducking-and-diving interloper, dogged by endless rumours about his profitable shenanigans in Irish real estate, was about as welcome to the establishment as flatulence in a packed hotel lift. They'd call Haughey and his associates 'men in mohair suits' or 'gombeen men'. The nearest English equivalent is perhaps 'shyster', explained the political historian Conor McCabe. 'The fucking gombeens, you know? The spivs.'[10]

This seems to have inspired terrible insecurity in Haughey. He designed a family coat of arms to bolster his fake claim to being a direct descendant of the ancient high kings of Ireland. Amid applause from guests at a luncheon in Washington DC in 1982 he turned plaintively to Irish journalists: 'Listen. They love me.' This insecurity 'would eat at him all his life', wrote the journalist Colm Keena in his book *Haughey's Millions*. 'And he would never gain acceptance.'

Subsequent public tribunals, long after he left power for the last time in 1992, found that the biggest flows of dubious money into Haughey's personal accounts had tended to come within days of his assuming his ministerial posts. And this was a long, steady pattern throughout his political life. 'When Haughey was in power the money tended to flow in,' says Keena, 'and when he was out of power the money tended to dry up.' After his sacking in 1970 he simply went overdrawn on the correct assumption that the banks would write off his debts once he got back into power.[11]

Haughey also seems to have had no shame about getting rich from his political connections and activities. 'Haughey would have had the attitude that he was completely entitled to the money,' says O'Toole, 'as in "I ought to have a stud farm and fly around in a helicopter. It's important if I'm representing the nation, to be on the same level as these wealth creators."' And this attitude gives a clue to the deep connections between Haughey's corruption, the corporate tax haven which Ireland aspired to become and the Third Way attitude of cutting corporate taxes and letting the financial sector rip, not looking too closely under the hood and redistributing the proceeds.[12]

The basic ideological assumption, O'Toole explains, is to separate out the creation of wealth from its distribution. 'So you don't have to ask questions about what kind of wealth is being created, or if it has any corruption at its heart. The moral side happens at the distributional level.' That analysis could be applied to Juncker, Blair, Clinton and any of the other Third Way leaders and hangers-on. Bono, when asked to justify U2's decision to shift a chunk of its business affairs from low-tax Ireland to the Netherlands, another corporate tax haven, enabling them to pay even less tax, described this as 'smart' business and slammed the critics as non-Irish people who 'wouldn't understand' that the country got rich by being a corporate tax haven.[13]

It's a funny thing, but a taint of corruption can sometimes help politicians. To the man in the pub Haughey was either a crook or the workers' saviour. Centuries of British domination had fixed the Irish state in people's minds as something alien and British, explains Elaine Byrne, author of *Political Corruption in Ireland 1922–2010: A Crooked Harp?* 'There is a sense that Dublin is a different country. When Haughey was taking money out, people didn't make the connection – "That's my money."' In a wider context this helps to explain, among other things, voters' remarkable willingness in many countries to support ethically challenged candidates like Silvio Berlusconi or Donald Trump. 'As a reaction to the idea of faceless, fluid forces shaping one's destiny, an extreme of local loyalty and of personal intimacy,' says O'Toole, 'is an act of defiance against Them – whoever They are. Doing the last thing you're supposed to do may be the final assertion of power against a feeling of powerlessness … The real wonder was not that fraudsters got elected but that more politicians did not claim to be crooks in order to get elected.'[14]

Prioritising the local, the family and the personal at the expense of the wider nation is a basis for corruption the world over – heroic corruption, you might call it. And this can be expanded to a global level. It wasn't a stretch for Haughey and his successors to harness this mentality to gain support for Ireland's tax haven policies, prioritising the interests of Ireland – or to be more exact, a section of Irish society – at the expense of large taxpaying populations in other countries whose multinationals used Ireland as a financial brothel to cut their taxes and other regulations.

Haughey finally left office in February 1992, just as Ireland was about to enjoy its astonishing surge of economic growth and foreign investment. Irish gross national income per person would rise from

60 per cent of the European average in 1990 to parity by the year 2000, and to a fabulous, undreamed-of 130 per cent by 2007. This explosion, which became known as the Celtic Tiger economy, was made up of two booms. There was a real one based on job-creating foreign investment, which soared from 2.2 per cent of GDP in 1990 to an astonishing 25 per cent by 2000.[15] Then, in 2001, when a global recession hit and global FDI flows fell back sharply, the foreign investment machine gave way to a fake boom led by financial services and what O'Toole has called 'a demented property cult' mixed with 'a lethal cocktail of global ideology and Irish habits'. This second boom would bring the tearaway tiger back to earth with a teeth-cracking crunch. But despite all the excesses this was still one of the biggest growth spurts in world economic history. And herein lies the big question. What was the secret ingredient that generated this sudden burst of growth?

The corporate tax-cut story doesn't seem convincing: all those tax haven facilities since 1956 had failed to ignite the economic growth engine, as Ireland barely kept pace with the rest of Europe for the next thirty-five years. The first sudden surge of foreign investment in the early 1970s was triggered above all by Ireland's accession to the European Economic Community. In fact, Ireland's iconic 12.5 per cent corporate tax rate was first applied in 2003, long after the sudden growth explosion began – and that involved a tax rate *increase* from 10 per cent, which was itself an increase on the previous 0 per cent rate for exporting firms. The comparable French and British corporate tax rates in the 1990s were between 30 and 35 per cent, and had been at that level or higher for years. And in any case, the main tax attraction for multinationals wasn't so much the corporate tax rate; it was the tax loopholes, which enabled multinationals to end up paying close to zero in Ireland. One of Apple's Irish subsidiaries, for example, typically paid less than 0.1 per cent. Irish loopholes for multinationals had been available since the 1950s too.[16]

If it wasn't corporate tax that fathered the tiger, then what was it? The shortest answer to this big question really does come down to the luck of the Irish. A perfect storm of seven or eight extraordinary factors came together all at once to propel Ireland's explosive growth. As will become clear, no country has a hope of replicating even a fraction of this. Ireland is no growth model for anyone.

The biggest factor by far, once again, came from Europe, and Ireland's accession to the European single market in 1992. The EEC had already created a spike in foreign investment into Ireland, but countries still had in place endless hurdles to protect their national businesses.[17] The single market washed that all away. Ireland's accession was described by Padraic Fallon, the chair of *Euromoney*, as being akin to 'Guderian's tanks breaking through the Maginot Line'. Peter Sutherland, Irish former director general of the World Trade Organisation and the EU's competition commissioner ahead of the single market opening, summarised the importance of accession by saying, 'The completion of the single market was the vital moment for us. Suddenly, Ireland became as good a location for access to the French market as was France.'

This event coincided with a remarkable trend: at exactly the same time a stupendous global investment boom was getting under way. Foreign direct investment flowing from rich countries nearly *quintupled* from 1991 to 1999 – from $230 billion to $1 trillion – and from the United States, which was by far the largest investor into Ireland, the global total rose nearly sevenfold.[18] And this investment explosion was bolstered and channelled into Ireland by another crucial actor: Ireland's heroic, indefatigable Industrial Development Authority, a body that was so successful in enticing foreign investors that it's probably fair to say the world has seen nothing quite like it.

Long before the 1990s IDA teams had fanned out across the developed world. In 1973 alone, the year when Ireland became an EEC member, the IDA made an astonishing 2,600 presentations to companies around the world, mostly tailored to each client. The logic, explained Padraic White, a former IDA head, 'was to target with rifle-shot precision individual companies that met specific criteria, then go directly to them and make the case for locating in Ireland'. They dangled low corporate taxes of course and more – a *lot* more. They paid for advertising blitzes in the global business press. They invited journalists for all-expenses trips to Ireland to meet the Great and the Good. They carefully planned routes from the airport to avoid eyesores and traffic snarls. They organised networks of top-notch hotels, restaurants and entertainment for visitors. 'From sheer necessity, [we] carved out another Ireland,' says White. But, he adds, there was no doubt about the trump card. 'Ireland's membership of the EEC, with access to its large market, was the bedrock business rationale for investing in Ireland.'

The IDA used 'flagship marketing', aggressively targeting the big global names, whose vote of confidence would then make it easier to attract others. They got Apple to invest in 1980, then leveraged that to persuade Intel to move in. Next they went for Microsoft. It worked every time. 'I'm normally the sales guy,' says Steve Ballmer, the CEO of Microsoft, recalling the extraordinary job the IDA did on him. 'That is the first lunch I've been to where the government was selling to me!'

The IDA chiselled Ireland's quirky international image into appealing new forms. The traditional American view of Ireland was 'a romantic misty isle peopled by characters straight out of *The Quiet Man* and full of bog roads and stray donkeys', says White. But the new message tilted Ireland's charms in new directions. It still made plenty of Ireland's unspoiled rolling scenery, clean air and open spaces, its multiple attractions for family life and its disproportionately large share of the world's history, literature, song, humour and general cultural charm. But it successfully harnessed these as offering a haven away from London's high-cost urban-commuter rat race, Cayman's ghastly palm-fringed zero-tax soullessness or Luxembourg's and Geneva's creepy, foreign-language Euro-sterility. Here was a genuinely new offering for the world's corporate bosses.

They did surveys that found one of the biggest attractions for companies was highly qualified graduate staff, so they harnessed the product of the next element feeding the boom: massive education reforms and investment in the 1960s, which by the 1980s were sluicing waves of bright, well-educated Irish school- and college-leavers and graduates into the jobs market. Simultaneously, the European-led emancipation of Irish women was boosting female participation in the workforce, smartly boosting Irish productivity and growth. Over a quarter of the Irish women who worked within the home in 1994 – activity that generally isn't measured in economic growth figures – had taken outside jobs by 1999, just six years later. The economic benefits were immense.[19] Adding further to the workforce was a flood of Irish jobseekers who had fled the country in previous bad economic times, been educated and trained at other countries' schools and universities, and were now returning home to join the boom. All this helped transform the Irish economy from a position where in 1986 every ten workers supported twenty-two people too young, old or sick to work, to a ratio of ten workers to just five dependants by 2005. This was a revolutionary demographic dividend.[20]

The IDA designed a dazzling new marketing campaign to capitalise on this shift, with the slogan 'Ireland – We're the Young Europeans.' They ran splashes in *The Economist*, the *Wall Street Journal* and *Business Week*. 'People are to Ireland as oil is to Texas,' one advertisement went, accompanied by a photo of smiling male and female graduates on campus. Another image showed a mixed group of optimistic-looking young students, representing the flower of Irish youth, ranged up a Trinity College, Dublin stairway, against the simple caption 'Hire them – before they hire you.'[21] Top US executives still remember those campaigns. 'Advertising provides the air cover,' explained Irish advertising executive John Fanning, 'while IDA troops on the ground engage in the combat, fighting for investment.'

The IDA's approach was not to embrace the pure laissez-faire free-market orthodoxy of cutting taxes and waiting for the investors to come; rather it pursued an unashamed and aggressive strategy of government intervention, surgically targeting sectors and businesses, then going after them, howitzers and all.[22] The particular choices they made – especially pharmaceuticals and information and medical technologies – were well researched and exquisitely timed: the Celtic Tiger coincided with a golden era of productivity for Big Pharma in the 1980s and 1990s and with the dot-com boom of the 1990s. A splurge of government spending on modern telecommunications infrastructure for Ireland iced the cake.

But this is still not everything.

The peace process in Northern Ireland was bearing fruit, culminating in a ceasefire by the Irish Republican Army in 1994. 'For the first time in decades,' says Olivia O'Leary, a prominent Irish political analyst, 'you had Ireland as a good news story just at the time when the IDA was trying to get American investment into Ireland … This helped the IDA enormously [just as] a whole generation of Irish-American business people were beginning to surface in corporate America.' Everyone wanted a piece of Ireland. There was also an outbreak of industrial peace, the result of a set of social partnerships negotiated between employers, unions and farmers from 1987, an initiative considered so successful that the government of Sweden, itself a pioneer in social partnership, later turned to Ireland for advice. These deals, says former deputy prime minister Ray MacSharry 'laid secure foundations for ... the Irish economic miracle of the 1990s'.

Yet more factors contributed to the perfect storm. Not only was Ireland becoming a sales platform into Europe, but by the late 1980s it was also receiving large European agricultural transfers and billions in European structural funds, which doubled in 1988 and then doubled again in 1993. 'The funds helped finance a major investment in infra-structure that, in turn, has facilitated rapid economic expansion,' explains White. 'The foreign investment benefits to Ireland of EU membership are incalculable and enduring.' A country that had just one stretch of dual carriageway in 1972 was soon transformed into a modern investment hub, criss-crossed with shiny new roads, railways, ports and airports.[23]

With all this falling into place within just a few years, nothing short of putting the heads of Bill Gates and Steve Jobs on spikes at Dublin airport would have stopped a surge in US multinational investment, whatever the corporate tax incentives. And yet all this raises a question. The bosses of multinationals, the big accounting firms and many others all say that corporate tax-cutting was Ireland's secret ingredient, but how so? The simple answer is that they *would* say that, wouldn't they? There's nothing quite like Irish tax loopholes to boost stock options and partner income. And talk is cheap.

Yet in survey after survey around the world, tax rates typically come fifth or sixth in genuine investors' lists of priorities. What they consistently want is the rule of law, a healthy and educated workforce, access to markets, good infrastructure and ideally an English-speaking environment. 'I never made an investment decision based on the tax code,' said Paul O'Neill, chair of the US aluminium giant Alcoa and subsequently US Treasury secretary under George W. Bush. 'If you are giving money away I will take it. If you want to give me induce-ments for something I am going to do anyway, I will take it. But good business people do not do things because of inducements.'[24]

It wasn't corporate taxes but all these other factors *plus* the powerful natural tailwind of catch-up growth that was inevitably going to happen some day; that is the real story of the Celtic Tiger. Corporate tax-cutting contributed to the Irish investment boom for sure, but whether it boosted the Irish economic boom is quite another matter. Had Ireland had a more normal corporate tax system, most of this investment would have happened anyway; in fact Ireland would quite likely have earned higher tax revenues from the investment surge, helping support other parts of the economy such as an even better-educated workforce or infrastructure, which may have made the boom even boomier, and with stronger tax-financed foundations, making it more sustainable too.

Yet this isn't the full story, for alongside the corporate tax tale there's another, more financial and less salubrious, that is often credited with having fed the tiger.

On Custom House Quay on the north bank of the River Liffey in Dublin stands a group of yellowing rusty-bronze statues, a moving testament to the ships that sailed from here during the great Irish potato famine of 1845-9, when Ireland was part of the United Kingdom and an economic vassal of London. Irish peasants toiled on tiny precarious farms while a mostly Protestant Anglo-Irish hereditary ruling class of landlords and middlemen gathered the peasants' produce to send for processing or slaughter in Britain. When the blight struck, London provided little assistance, believing that Ireland should rely on its own resources and the free market. Crop failure led to mass farm evictions then a great hunger, which killed over a million people, an eighth of the Irish population. Over a million more emigrated.[25]

Next to the monument stands IFSC House, a hulking modernist seven-storey building fronted by greenish-blue glass.[26] The contrast with the commemoration of Irish historical misery could not be greater. IFSC stands for International Financial Services Centre, a reference to Ireland's low-tax, low-regulation offshore financial industry, whose futuristic buildings now straddle the Liffey up and down this part of Custom House Quay and beyond. The IFSC is, to an extent, a shadow-banking centre: the stuff that goes on outside the walls of traditionally regulated banks, involving hedge funds and other exotic financial creatures and activities with names that will be familiar to connoisseurs of the global financial crisis: conduits, special purpose vehicles, securitisation, credit default swaps and more.

The IFSC represents the second, smaller component of the Celtic Tiger. The offering wasn't corporate tax cuts this time but lax financial regulation and oversight for the entities that have accumulated there. Yet though the activities are different the myth making has essentially been the same: Ireland relaxed its financial laws, persuaded global financial players to relocate there, and in a run-down smokestack wasteland carved out a shiny new financial centre, creating tens of thousands of jobs in the process. And if you go to Dublin, you will struggle not to be impressed by the scale of what has been built there.

The origins of the IFSC go back to 1985, to a meeting of business people and public officials at the Shelbourne Hotel, a grand old red-brick Renaissance building in central Dublin just down the road from the Oireachtas, the Irish parliament. At the time, living standards were falling, unemployment and inflation were high, and young Irish were emigrating. Finance Secretary Maurice Doyle bitterly recalled writing to *The Times* in London to challenge a suggestion that 'international bankers were about to pull the shutters down on Ireland'.[27] At the meeting at the Shelbourne Hotel everyone was looking for new ideas. A flamboyant former Citibank and PriceWaterhouse official, Dermot Desmond, spoke up: how about setting up a financial centre?

Desmond had seen the world: he had worked for a time in Kabul for the World Bank but left when Soviet forces invaded in 1979. A natural charmer with the personality of a steam locomotive, he had become the first outsider in living memory to break successfully into the sniffy, incestuous world of Irish stockbroking, setting up National City Brokers at the age of just thirty-one.[28] The idea of setting up a financial centre in Dublin wasn't new. In the 1970s a Wall Street lawyer and expert on offshore banking, Bob Slater, had written a brief for the IDA urging Ireland to set up an offshore banking centre modelled on the secrecy haven of Bermuda, and had even got a couple of Wall Street banks interested. But the Central Bank of Ireland had blocked it. 'The project smacked of a banana republic,'[29] as the IDA's Padraic White puts it. A similar offshore proposal was floated in 1984 but also never took off.

But at the Shelbourne meeting Desmond at last detected a flicker of interest. As he recalled, he quickly wrote a short concept note, presented it to the government and agreed that his stockbroking firm would pay half the costs of a £150,000 feasibility study by PriceWaterhouse. It took a bit of time, but by 1987 he had garnered heavyweight political support, most notably from Haughey, who had long ago emerged from gunrunning disgrace and was now facing elections as leader of the opposition. Haughey gave Desmond forty-eight hours to write a brief to put into his election manifesto. Desmond and a couple of colleagues wrote the policy section overnight – a plan to create a financial centre with Irish characteristics. Haughey inserted the 'big hairy idea', as one of his manifesto writers put it, almost verbatim into a glossy party document launched at a pre-election press conference. This was all about Ireland joining in a 'competition' with other countries, Haughey declared. 'Let them off and let the best horse win.'

Though the proposal had been inspired most directly by the tax havens of Luxembourg, Singapore and Hong Kong, London was at the back of everyone's minds. 'We are certainly seeking to draw business away from London,' White said, 'but we want a satellite relationship, rather than try to take London on in a head-on conflict that we cannot win.' How the bankers in London must have chuckled at the idea of a success story rising out of Dublin's beaten-up docklands, yet Haughey was determined to push the project forward.[30] He was elected Taoiseach for the third time in March 1987, and on his first day in office set his chief political fixer, a bulldog of a man called Pádraig Ó hUigínn, onto the case.

Between them they conjured up a legally charmed zone at the Custom House Docks, inside which qualifying financial firms would be taken out of the normal Irish regulatory system and guaranteed a 10 per cent corporate tax rate, and they set up an all-powerful committee of financiers and civil servants to bulldoze the project forward. 'No one is going to stop us,' Haughey declared at the inaugural meeting. When objections arose or egos clashed, Ó hUigínn muscled everyone onto the true path. The Clearing House Group, as the committee became known, evolved into a fearsome, unaccountable and secretive body, a classic tool of the financially captured offshore state. Far from public scrutiny, the world's shadow bankers could sit down with Irish lawmakers and present their deregulatory wish lists, ring-fenced against such irritants as local democracy. A parliamentarian called Nessa Childers who got hold of the minutes of Clearing House Group meetings in the wake of the global financial crisis, described lobbying 'in secret, behind closed doors … The bankers and hedge fund industry got virtually everything they asked for while the public got hit with a number of austerity measures.' Any critics of the project were pilloried as traitors to the national interest, and everyone in Ireland was urged to get behind the patriotic green jersey agenda.

The Finance Act of 1987 that ushered in the IFSC explicitly targeted global money managers, dealers in foreign currencies, futures, options, bonds, equities, insurance, clearing, information storage and miscellaneous trading. Its provisions were drafted broadly because no one was quite sure who might turn up. In the words of Brendan Logue, a top IDA official: 'We engaged in dynamic research – which is another way of saying we made it up as we went along.' The special corporate tax rates available to companies located in the IFSC were attractive, but the major juice was light-touch financial regulation. This wasn't quite a brass-plate operation; there was usually some requirement that market entrants provided at least a bit of substance, generally meaning local jobs, but this wasn't onerous.

Two themes in the legislation stand out, which for those familiar with offshore marked it down as it an all-guns-blazing tax haven model. First, it specified that the IFSC's players should be 'persons not ordinarily resident in the State', an unambiguous bid for 'elsewhere' tax haven status. They didn't want Irish residents playing the game because they knew that this stuff harms countries whose residents use the facilities. (If the IFSC undermined the tax systems and regulatory regimes of other countries, well, that was just fine.) Second, regulators were required by law to promote the IFSC. That is a quintessentially offshore rule, because the standard way to promote and develop a financial sector based on non-resident business is to lure foreign money by creating loopholes, relaxing regulations and removing standard democratic controls on business; in other words, to not regulate foreign-owned businesses setting up shop there. That is a classic tax haven strategy.[31]

Cheerleaders among the Irish media served up helpful dog-whistle terms like 'stifling businesses with burdensome regulations', 'bonfire of red tape', 'tax efficiency,' a 'pro-business' (and the obligatory 'internationally competitive') regulatory environment. And under this unholy umbrella the world's banks, shadow banks and accountancy firms began to show up: first a trickle, and then in strength. By 1993 the IFSC had created a thousand jobs or so, and already foreign regulators were getting worried. The Swedes began an investigation, and

German officials said angrily that their banks were using the IFSC to escape paying their share of reunifiction costs.[32] But creating escape routes for large banks that would annoy other countries was kind of the point all along, as it always is with the tax haven model, so nothing was done.

The overall benefits to Ireland were never obvious, however. Over half of those arriving inside the charmed IFSC perimeter were simply shifting their existing non-resident operations into the IFSC to get the special treatment. 'Irish Life across the road have their filing cabinets lined up to move fifty yards across to the site,' a Labour Party official complained, 'to go from a 50 per cent tax regime down to 10 per cent.' Multinational companies already in Ireland dived in too, as the IFSC's low-regulation, blind-eyed, low-tax offering turned out to be a great place to put the operations managing their global cash flows.

Billions, then trillions started wheeling in and out of Dublin, barely touching the sides. This offshore turntable lured fly-by-night operators and many big names too, allowing Ireland to cream off some fees and taxes. By 2001, 'investment' in the IFSC was officially equivalent to six times the size of the Irish economy – and by 2005 bank assets in Ireland had nearly trebled again.[33] Charlie McCreevy, an Irish former EU commissioner, gushed about the 'great entrepreneurial energies that a "light touch" regulatory system can unleash', yet jobs and tax revenues were a whisper – less than 1 per cent of the Irish labour force was employed – compared to the frightening sums involved.

Access to Europe had also provoked an influx of credit into Ireland, spreading warm tingly feelings into places that the foreign direct investment boom hadn't yet reached, puffing up house prices, helping the middle classes to feel rich and encouraging them to spend, borrow, spend, borrow and build. Through the early 2000s this property-fed growth bubble kept growing. By 2006 Bertie Ahern, then Taoiseach, was exulting that 'the boom times are getting even more boomier', and by the following year Ireland was building half as many houses as property-crazed Britain, despite having a fourteenth of its population.

Caught up in this insane urban construction frenzy, hardly anyone noticed that manufacturing was actually shrinking, a classic symptom of the crowding-out effect of the finance curse.[34] Credit was roaring ahead, pumping up prices and eroding the cost competitiveness advantages that companies had found so attractive in Ireland. And now a volcano was beginning to tremble under everyone's feet.

When the global financial crisis hit, it turned out that the IFSC had been a key node in the global mischief. The collapse of four German banks – Landesbank Sachsen, IKB, WestLB and HypoVereinsbank – can all be traced to activities in the IFSC. Under the benign eye of Irish regulators, Hypo's Dublin-based subsidiary Depfa had been operating profitably under an insanely risky leverage ratio of 80:1, meaning that a decline in the value of their assets by a couple of per cent could have bankrupted the whole operation. The crisis quickly tipped it into insolvency; the German government had to put up €134 billion in an emergency bail-out, and Germany's leading business daily *Handelsblatt* called Depfa 'the source of all evil'. Sachsen LB also fell apart after meddling in US sub-prime mortgages through its IFSC vehicle Ormond Quay (named after a section of the northern bank of the Liffey, just along from Custom House Quay). The Irish financial regulator had stated in the boom times, 'it is not required to police the activities of vehicles such as Ormond Quay … internationally the approach therefore has been that these vehicles do not require close regulatory oversight'. You could submit your hundreds of pages of documents in a funds prospectus at 3 p.m. and have the authorisation to start business the next day. Nobody in Ireland, it seemed, had been checking anything.

When the US investment banking giant Bear Stearns collapsed in 2008, it turned out to have had several dodgy investment vehicles listed on the Irish Stock Exchange and three subsidiaries located in the IFSC owned by an Irish holding company, Bear Stearns Ireland Limited. Professor Jim Stewart of Trinity College, Dublin, among the only people in Ireland to have exposed the IFSC's shenanigans, found that by 2007 Bear Stearns Ireland Limited. was operating with gargantuan leverage, where each dollar of equity was propping up $119 of gross assets. A deterioration in value of those assets of less than 1 per cent could wipe it out. And it did.[35]

The Bear Stearns case illustrates a profound truth about offshore race-to-the-bottom finance and regulation. The trick is so often to drape your company across several jurisdictions and then to get each place to say, 'This thing is regulated elsewhere.' US company accounts said Bear Stearns Ireland Limited and its subsidiaries were regulated by the Irish regulator, yet the Irish regulator said its remit extended only to banks *headquartered* in Ireland. So this ultra-high-risk entity was regulated elsewhere – which effectively meant nowhere.[36] And the 'elsewhere, nowhere' concept has close parallels in tax. Apple Operations International (AOI), the subsidiary of the technology giant which owns most of Apple's offshore subsidiaries, played this game too. Under US law, AOI is incorporated in Ireland, so isn't tax resident in the United States. But Ireland uses a different test for tax residence: what matters is where the company is 'functionally managed and controlled from', which in AOI's case is the United States. This was, as US Senator Carl Levin put it, a 'ghost company ... magically, it is neither here nor there'. So AOI was taxed by nobody, and this helped Apple generate a mighty chunk of the $215 billion that it was estimated to have stashed offshore by the end of 2017 – out of reach, effectively nowhere.[37]

Has the IFSC benefited Ireland? On the face of it, yes. Visitors to Dublin can marvel at the acres of shiny glass, chrome and concrete, the expensive coats and tea shops, the up-market beer festivals and the general bustle that you'll find these days along the banks of the River Liffey where the IFSC sprawls. At the last count, firms in the IFSC had paid over 500 million euros a year in tax to Ireland since the global financial crisis, and it hosted over 38,000 jobs, according to official figures. Ireland deregulated – the story goes – it slashed red tape, and a new economic engine was born.

Yet this simple tale doesn't add up either. Those 38,000 jobs amount to less than 2 per cent of Irish jobs and tax revenues, and those revenues are equivalent to just 0.2 per cent of gross national income. That's not nothing, but it's not so special. And since the government won't publish a breakdown of employment in the IFSC, there's no way to know if those job figures are accurate or not. Two people I spoke to in Ireland said they believed the true numbers were significantly smaller. The IFSC certainly creates few jobs when the trillions of dollars and euros that come reeling through it each year are considered. In 2013 Jim Stewart studied a sample of eighty-two special purpose vehicles – companies owned and controlled from other large financial centres but incorporated in Ireland. These exotic, unregulated vehicles held assets averaging $350 million each and were perched on a tiny, rickety capital base averaging just $40,000 – a leverage ratio of one dollar of capital to a staggering $8,200 of assets. And, as Stewart stated, median corporate tax payments were zero for all years: 'SPVs pay more in tax advice than in tax payments.' The big banks may not be much better. It is expected, for instance, that Allied Irish, one of Ireland's biggest banks, will pay no corporation tax for the next twenty years because of tax losses generated during the crisis.[38]

Did the IFSC create jobs in Ireland overall? All those factors mentioned above – the European single market, European subsidies, the IDA's efforts, the education reforms bringing in waves of skilled graduates, the emancipation of women, the social partnership, the peace process and more – helped the IFSC to grow. Amid this golden environment, those highly educated Irish graduates who went to work in the IFSC would have in its absence gone instead into other professions that would surely have been more socially useful, and probably more genuinely productive. But the IFSC, by boosting Ireland's reckless banking system, helped inflict much larger damage. The European Commission's 2012 official investigation into the global financial crisis, known as the Liikanen Report, shows how much state aid each country provided to its banking system during the crisis. Eight member states gave no support. France provided the equivalent of 4 per cent of its gross domestic product, while Germany provided 10 per cent, and the UK nearly 20 per cent. For Ireland, the figure was 269 per cent. Those economic, democratic and social costs utterly swamp any tax or employment benefits. It's hard to accept that the IFSC has created jobs or tax revenues for Ireland; the opposite is surely true.

On top of this damage to Ireland, consider the unquantifiable global damage caused by the IFSC's role in undermining other countries' tax and regulatory systems, and its role in helping transmit giant global pulses of risk and fear out into the mayhem of international markets during the crisis, while collapsing Irish banks wreaked similar carnage at home. Then there is the question of the international damage from tax losses facilitated by Ireland's corporate tax system. It's hard to put numbers on this, because so many of these tax games involve multiple countries, but the figure is in the tens of billions each year.[39] The story of Ireland's role in the global financial crisis and its aftermath is a truly blood-curdling tale of greed, corruption, hubris, ignorance, arrogance, austerity, secrecy and competitiveness fetishism, the finance curse at its finest and most loathsome.

Until his death in 2006 Haughey, like many wealthy Irish people, used the libel courts to keep his scandalous acts hidden. But in December 2006, six months after he died, the Moriarty Tribunal, a government probe into political corruption in Ireland, produced a staggering array of damning facts. Not only was Haughey an Olympic-level tax evader, but he and his associates had built an enormous financial empire offshore. The Moriarty report mentions the Cayman Islands over 400 times and the Isle of Man over 130 times, plus several honourable mentions for Jersey, Zurich and Geneva.[40] There was, for instance, the Ansbacher scam, involving a bank within a bank set up in the Caymans by Haughey's friend, bagman and fundraiser, Dennis Traynor. The Central Bank of Ireland knew all about it but did nothing. 'In view of the delicate nature of these matters we did not pursue the matter further,' a bank memorandum states. 'The bank would be placed in a very embarrassing position should the Revenue Authorities ever become aware of the situation.' A Central Bank director took large loans from Ansbacher, and chaired a secret Haughey committee. The Bank even doctored its own records, changing 'evasion', which is illegal, to 'avoidance', which is not.

There was a scheme called DIRT – Deposit Interest Retention Tax. Non-residents didn't have to pay the tax, and anyone could walk into a bank and declare themselves non-resident. Even Irish farmers, who are about as locally rooted as you can get, were hard at it. 'Half the non-resident accounts are thought to be bogus,' said one official memo. 'We were broadly aware ... everybody agreed it was wrong. "For God's sake, don't rock the boat" ... that was the culture; that was the necessity that drove us all forward.'[41]

Moriarty reckoned Haughey had pocketed at least €45 million in 2006 money – 171 times his gross salary from 1979 to 1996. He even diverted money raised for his best friend's liver transplant for his personal use. He ran his lavish lifestyle out of an account flush with political donations, and built an incestuous network of complicity across the political spectrum and an intelligence-gathering operation that gave him material for blackmail and useful dirt on a hefty chunk of Ireland's political and business class. There was, as Byrne puts it, 'an extraordinary degree of deference by regulatory authorities towards the Irish banking system and, similarly, absolute deference by banking authorities towards politicians'.

Visiting Ireland and talking to public figures, I am struck by the level of nervousness – although for some there seems no word quite as appropriate as fear – that greets any mention of Ireland's financial set-up. Two particular taboos stand out: calling the country a tax haven and doubting the importance of the corporate tax rate in Ireland's success. Ireland offers the usual theatre of probity that all tax havens engage in, which involves endlessly repeating the same message – 'We are not a tax haven but a clean, well-regulated, transparent and co-operative jurisdiction' – burnished with cherry-picked statistics and violently out-of-context statements from august international bodies like the IMF.

There's a comical report by PwC, which claims to show that the effective corporate tax rate is higher in Ireland, at 12.3 per cent, than in France, at just 8.3 per cent. This statistic has been all over the Irish media. What the articles usually fail to add is that these numbers come from a PwC model of a company in Ireland that makes ceramic flowerpots, has no foreign owners and does not trade overseas.[42] Anyone who talks of messing with the corporate tax regime is shouted down by a chorus of voices from across Irish politics, society and the media. When the troika of the IMF, the European Commission and European Central Bank imposed savage spending cuts and outrageous conditions on Ireland in a bail-out deal in 2010, the corporate tax was the one thing that could not be put on the table, costing Ireland enormous negotiating capital. 'They are wedded to it, like a spiritual totem pole,' said Andrew Baker of Sheffield University, who worked in Northern Ireland for many years and closely analysed the tax policies of north and south. 'It has become part of the national psyche.'

Across the border certain tax-raising powers are being devolved to the Northern Irish Assembly, and there has been a clamour for a corporate tax cut to Ireland's 12.5 per cent, something that also chimes with nationalist politicians' aspirations for a united Ireland, according to Baker. Yet behind this push, if you look closely enough, are other interest groups. Delving into the nearly 200-page UK legislation devolving powers to Northern Ireland, Baker encountered a minefield: 'impenetrable legalese, with qualifications and sub-points all over the place, specifying who would qualify to pay 12.5 per cent, what they would have to do to qualify' and so on. Who would benefit most from all this complexity? Why, the large corporate law and accounting firms, the same firms that have been the most vocal cheerleaders for Ireland's corporate tax offering.[43]

The reality behind the Celtic Tiger is not corporate tax cuts or financial deregulation as tonics for growth; they have produced short-term bubbles at best, with deadly hangovers. In the words of Kenneth Thomas, a US economist who has studied Ireland's experience extensively, 'low taxes are not what makes the Irish economy tick'.[44] I'd bet that if Ireland's corporate tax rate had been twice the 12.5 per cent rate it would still have got a huge investment boom – with a less violent upswing perhaps, but a more sustainable one, with less focus on wealth extraction, stronger labour protection and smaller inequalities of wealth and power. People do sometimes point to other low-tax countries instead of Ireland (or Luxembourg) as their poster children to demonstrate the virtues of corporate tax cuts: Hong Kong, the eastern European countries which enjoyed high growth rates after being released from the Soviet orbit, or China's economic zones, modelled on Shannon. But their stories are, like Ireland's, unique and impossible for others to replicate, and not based on low corporate taxes.[45]

Ireland used to be one of those very few countries that everyone condescended to love: the ancestral home, the cheeky impoverished urchin in ragged trousers who livened up the world with music, whiskey, green fields, leprechauns and the *craic*, never hurting anyone. Now, as Ireland swings wrecking balls into the tax and regulatory systems of countries around the globe, that image is gone. None of this was necessary, even for Ireland's sake. The ever-penetrating Fintan O'Toole summarises Ireland's predicament today. 'They blew it,' he said. 'The Irish elites amused themselves with monarchical lifestyles and frittered away the opportunity to break cycles of deprivation and child poverty. They practised the economics of utter idiocy, watching a controlled explosion of growth turn into a mad conflagration and aiming petrol-filled pressure hoses at the raging flames. They turned self-confidence into arrogance, optimism into swagger, aspiration into self-delusion.'

Irish self-delusion, unfortunately, went on to conquer the world.

The global financial crisis had terrible consequences in Ireland, and Ireland transmitted those effects around the globe, but at the end of the day it was a small player compared to the beast across the Irish Sea, 300 miles to the east, in London. And here lies one of the greatest untold stories of that crisis.

7

The London Loophole

In 2012 and 2013 Gary Gensler, a top US financial regulator, made a couple of speeches surveying the wreckage left by the global financial crisis. It was, he said, financial institutions operating complex 'business in offshore entities that nearly toppled the US economy'. He had a particular set of offshore jurisdictions in mind, he said, as he reeled off a list of well-known disaster stories from the crash. There was the US finance and insurance giant American International Group (AIG), which was felled by a freewheeling unit called AIG Financial Products, run out of an office in Mayfair in London. AIG's $180 billion bail-out in 2008 was the largest of any private company in US history. He cited Bear Stearns, which came to grief through two investment funds incorporated in the Cayman Islands. There was Lehman Brothers and its London-based derivatives operations (financial derivatives are contracts whose value is derived from the performance of something else, like the price of gold or a government bond), which were central to that firm's demise. Then there was Citigroup, which set up structured investment vehicles (SIVs) to shift assets and risks off its balance sheet, away from investors' and regulators' eyes, and whose collapse hit US taxpayers with two multi-billion-dollar bail-outs. 'And from where were the SIVs launched?' Gensler asked. 'London. And incorporated? The Cayman Islands.'

A decade earlier there had been the saga of Long-Term Capital Management (LTCM), the Connecticut-based hedge fund with $1.2 trillion in derivatives contracts which went sour and almost triggered a gigantic US bail-out. 'We had no idea what the ramifications would be in our financial system, and where, because these trades were booked in the Cayman Islands,' Gensler said. 'It was a terrible feeling.' Then there was JP Morgan Chase's multi-billion-dollar trading loss from credit default swaps executed in its UK branch by a trader known as the London Whale.[1] Gensler could have mentioned, but didn't, the case of Enron, the financialised US energy company whose collapse in 2001 was the largest bankruptcy in history at the time, and which turned out to have parked assets out of view in hundreds of financial vehicles in the Caymans and in the even murkier Turks and Caicos, both British overseas territories. He could have mentioned BCCI. He could have mentioned other scandals that posed financial stability risks, which used the British spider's web. In each case Britain and its satellite havens had taken the cream from the trading activity while the going was good, then when the risks eventually crystallised into disaster, 'it comes right back here, crashing to our shores,' Gensler continued. 'If the American taxpayer bails out JP Morgan, they'd be bailing out that London entity too.' Carolyn Maloney, a US Democrat, summarised it: there was 'a disturbing pattern,' she said, 'of London literally becoming the centre of financial trading disasters'.

To the extent that anyone in Britain paid attention, City analysts briefed furiously against the allegations. The head of one London-based fund management firm told me that the US financial system was just as full of bad actors as London. As he bluntly put it, 'The Americans are full of shit.'[2] Meanwhile the US commentariat, accustomed to the bats' cave of horrors that had been spewing out of Wall Street, simply could not swallow the idea that the country of the Beatles, Princess Diana and tea with the Queen could be so appalling. This did not compute. The accusations sank back out of sight.

But Gensler's point is important. Were Britain and the City of London somehow 'worse' than Wall Street in terms of financial regulation, so more to blame for the global financial meltdown? If the answer was yes, then this could be the most important silence that surrounds the crisis.

And the answer is, without a doubt, yes.

Any reader of this book should by now have a sense of the central role London and its offshore satellites have played in helping turn global markets into a hothouse for organised crime, corruption, tax evasion and the cross-border stashing of looted wealth. Following the collapse of the cooperative Bretton Woods system of managed finance in the 1970s, the Euromarkets that London created went fully global, and by the 1980s people had mostly stopped talking about them because once capital was allowed to flow more freely across borders there was no longer a meaningful separation between the Euromarkets and domestic economies, prompting London and the British web to find ways to redouble their offering as a rules-free offshore escape route for finance.

The growth of global finance not only fostered a step change in Britain's contribution to the rising global crime wave, but also put it at the centre of a series of changes that would lead to the global financial crisis. In both areas London and the spider's web affected other countries' financial systems in two main ways: first by providing an escape route, and second as a 'competitive' battering ram, offering Wall Street lobbyists an example and a threat to justify further deregulation at home along the lines of 'Do this, or we'll decamp to London.' The British web led New York into the global deregulatory race, while Zurich, Luxembourg and a handful of other offshore financial centres played supporting roles. It is almost inevitable that Britain is more deeply 'captured' by the City of London than the United States is captured by Wall Street: the two global financial centres are similar in size, but Wall Street is diluted in a much larger democracy, and it also doesn't have the centuries-old historical roots in the British establishment that are enjoyed by the City and its institutions.

Bill Black, a financial criminologist and former US bank regulator, talks of the 'three Ds' that incubated the crisis: deregulation, desupervision and the de facto criminalisation of financial firms, which led to fraudulent lending practices and much more. Onshore deregulation in the United States was bad enough on its own, but the regulatory race to the bottom had been far more destructive, led by London's 'anti-regulators', as he called them. 'By God, London won the competition in regulatory laxity with the United States,' he told me in 2012, 'which is why it became the financial cesspool of the world.'[3] Black was talking about mortgage frauds and other related crimes but I'd go further: the high-octane world of risky financial derivatives and shadow banking entities and activities which fed the crisis was incubated in tandem with rougher criminal activity: the offshore world of BCCI, Colombian drugs money and global organised crime. The crisis and the crime were the result of essentially the same decisions by the same British elites as a result of the same deregulatory 'competitive' see-no-evil offshore ideology, all aimed at bringing money to London. These apparently very different trends emerged together, and they must be understood together.

The story of the global financial crisis can be traced as far back as you like, but a good place to begin is with the waves of financial deregulation that hit the US and UK from the 1980s. Each wave fed the next. In neither country did change have anything to do with the needs of the real economy: the financial system didn't start servicing its customers noticeably better after deregulation. If anything, things deteriorated.

In Britain the biggest event after the collapse of Bretton Woods was Margaret Thatcher's Big Bang of sudden, massive financial deregulation in 1986. Thatcher's advisers had previously warned her that this would lead to 'unethical behaviour' and 'boom and bust' economics, but they were batted aside. 'The basic common sense of the British public,' assured John Redwood, the head of her policy unit, 'will not be tempted into Get-Rich-Quick Limited.'[4] Grown-up financial players and sophisticated customers could look after themselves.

But when the swaggering American investment banking giants burst into town from the late 1980s, laden with dollars, the flat-footed British players, who had grown complacent in their stitched-up old-boy networks were competitive roadkill. The Americans didn't just bring money, though; they also brought dangerous new ways of doing things. A lot of City business had until then been done by partnerships, whose members got rich when things went well but who risked collectively losing their shirts in a disaster. The real possibility of personal bankruptcy tended to focus minds and encourage prudence and vigilance, after a fashion. By contrast, the American banks were often listed on stock exchanges, so while their managers could get very rich indeed from success, they weren't personally liable for failure so could dump the costs onto bank shareholders or wider society. Under this 'Heads I win, tails they lose' formula, players were risking their own money less and less, and gambling more and more with what people in the markets call OPM – other people's money. OPM is arguably the biggest problem in financial markets today, and it can encourage spectacular recklessness.

The regulators demanded that banks had risk and compliance officers, whose job was to restrain financial traders from dangerous excesses, but company culture made it clear who dominated whom. The traders were the wolves, the tigers, the world's smartest people, the 'rock stars, rainmakers, the dark side, movers and shakers, the big swinging dicks', as one anthropological study of the City found. The compliance officers were the 'business blockers, deal killers, show stoppers, box tickers'. One compliance officer described himself as 'a dog that likes to be kicked', while another compared himself and his colleagues to football linesmen, the 'losers running back and forth across a line, stopping players from scoring or doing great things'.[5]

The Big Bang was attracting another American import to London too. Rowan Bosworth-Davies, a financial criminologist and former detective in the Fraud Squad, describes a variety of criminals arriving on his patch along with Wall Street culture: 'a tidal wave of fraudsters, con men, financial snake-oil salesmen, and assorted ne'er-do-wells, all masquerading under the title of "financial advisers"'. The City put no barriers in their way. 'Get off the plane at Heathrow at 10 a.m. and you could be in business at 3 p.m.,' he remembers. 'We started to see allegations of fraud coming through that we had never seen before … fraud in the derivatives markets, futures, options, that kind of thing. We started to see businesses set up in the City that were being run by mainstream US Mafiosi. Heavy American organised criminals,' he continues, reeling off names: Arnold Kimmes, Tommy Quinn. 'They were here to take advantage of the new relaxed atmosphere. We were talking to our friends in the US, particularly in the Manhattan District Attorney's office, and they'd say, "So is *that* where he turned up? We wondered what happened to him."'

Taking on this stuff, Bosworth-Davies says, made him feel like a salmon trying to swim upstream against a flash flood. His working-class accent and police background didn't help: in City circles, he says, he was treated with contempt, as a 'nasty little Mr Plod'. Law and order was simply beneath the City grandees. On a work trip to America he found US officials friendly enough, but scathing about Britain's approach to financial crime. A regulator took him aside. 'He said, "The problem with you Brits is that you assume that everyone who handles other people's money is a gentleman. You are then shocked when you find out the converse is true. Here in America we assume everyone who handles other people's money has the potential to be a criminal. And we legislate for the possibility.'"[6]

As Bosworth-Davies and his colleagues faced this influx of crime, the BCCI scandal exploded in Britain. As I described in Chapter 5, BCCI combined organised crime and murder with risky mechanisms threatening financial stability in a single Ponzi-scheme package run out of the bank's global headquarters in London. It was arguably the biggest single banking fraud of the twentieth century. As the scandal unfolded in the early 1990s, Britain and the Bank of England actively worked to frustrate US efforts to shut the rogue bank down. Robert Morganthau, the Manhattan district attorney who led the attempts to close BCCI down, remembers the Cayman attorney general, 'a crotchety British guy', refusing to help. The Americans turned to London, hoping to find a different attitude. 'We had no cooperation from the Bank of England,' Morgenthau remembers. 'We tried to get financial records out of London; they didn't provide us with anything.'

In fact, the Bank of England was working hard to protect the rogue bank. In April 1990 it helped BCCI shift its headquarters, officers and records away from Britain to Abu Dhabi. It also rebuffed a formal request from the US Senate Committee on Foreign Relations for a full copy of the British government's internal Sandstorm Report into the scandal, 'on the ostensible ground that to do so would violate British secrecy and confidentiality laws'.[7] After the Bank of England found out about BCCI's role in financing terrorism and laundering drug money, its response, according to a US Senate report, 'was not to close BCCI down, but to find ways to prop up BCCI and prevent its collapse. This meant, among other things, keeping secret the very serious nature of BCCI's problems from its creditors and one million depositors.' Robin Leigh-Pemberton, the Bank of England governor, revealed the British attitude: 'If we closed down a bank every time we found an instance of fraud, we would have rather fewer banks.'

After BCCI, Bosworth-Davies remembers giving a speech about money laundering in the City of London. He then sat down next to a director of a high street bank, who said, 'I listened with great interest to what you had to say but I can assure you if you think Her Majesty's

Government is ever going to prosecute people of my class, you are utterly mistaken. We are a protected species.'[8]

Compare this attitude in London in the early 1990s to what had happened in the United States after the savings and loan crisis of 1989, the fruit of Reagan-era deregulation, which felled more than 1,000 US 'thrift' financial institutions and was the biggest series of bank collapses in the US since 1929. Within six years of the crisis, more than 3,700 high-profile senior executives and owners of collapsed thrifts had gone to jail for fraud: the US Department of Justice secured convictions for over 95 per cent of chief executives or presidents of their institutions who were charged. Prison terms added up to many thousands of years.[9] The contrast with Britain could not be more jarring.

In the summer of 1994, around the time many of these American former bank bosses were emerging from jail, a group of JP Morgan traders from London, Tokyo and New York assembled at a luxurious hotel at Boca Raton, Florida. The usual drinking games went on; they hijacked golf carts and raced, giggling, around the lawns. Peter Voicke, a straight-laced German who was the most senior trader present, tried to calm them down; they pushed him into the pool. His deputy got pushed in too, and had his nose broken. Gillian Tett, a *Financial Times* journalist whose book *Fool's Gold* describes the episode in detail, said it wasn't possible to get a full account of the meeting because so many interviewees had 'only the haziest, alcohol-fuddled memories'. Yet it was on this weekend that the revellers came up with a new form of financial derivative. This would explode into the world's financial markets, and was one of the most important mechanisms driving the subsequent crisis.

A derivative is, in its simplest form, a contract between two players, whose value is *derived* from an underlying asset – a barrel of oil, a government bond or a bushel of wheat, for instance. Modern derivatives emerged around the 1850s in Chicago, at the time a major centre for storing and trading grain. Ahead of the harvest a wheat farmer might agree a contract with a speculator which effectively locked in a price for his wheat. For the farmer this was like insurance, while for the speculator it was like gambling. This idea proved popular, and the market expanded steadily. By the 1970s it had branched out beyond wheat, eggs and butter to include financial derivatives based on prices in foreign exchange, interest rates and other markets. By the 1990s a form of derivative called swaps was all the rage, in which you could swap one set of financial obligations for another. Let's say you've got a five-year fixed-rate mortgage, and your friend has a five-year floating-rate one. You think rates will fall, and she thinks they will rise. With a swap, you can agree to exchange your repayments: you will pay the floating rate for five years, and she will pay the fixed rate. This is a purely financial arrangement in which you don't actually exchange the mortgages, which is why these are called synthetic derivatives. And if you want to gamble you can exchange the swap payments without owning the underlying mortgages at all. The derivative the JP Morgan team came up with at Boca Raton was to become known as the credit default swap (CDS). This instrument enabled market players to bet (or insure themselves) not against movements in the *price* of something, but against the possibility that a bond or a loan would *default*.

The centre of experimentation for this stuff was London because the Glass-Steagall Act of 1933, which separated investment banking from commercial banking, prohibited some of the riskier, more lucrative aspects of this from happening in the United States.[10] And the rules of the European single market, which was launched in 1993, meant that banks could set up financial instruments in London and sell them across Europe without interference from national regulators in European countries. By the time the JP Morgan team met in Boca Raton in 1994, there were already an estimated $12 trillion in swaps outstanding, equivalent to the size of the US GDP. Serious concerns had emerged. Two years previously, a veteran banker had warned that derivatives were 'financial hydrogen bombs'.

To understand what happened next, it is important to grasp some principles about how banks make money. For centuries, banks had lent money out to companies or homeowners (who repaid these loans with interest), and they also borrowed money from depositors. Bankers used to speak of '3-6-3 banking', which meant paying 3 per cent on deposits, lending money out at 6 per cent – and being on the golf course by 3 p.m. If you can pay 3 and lend at 6, you can earn the difference – 3 per cent – for providing these useful services. But not quite; you have to pay staff salaries, the costs of bank buildings and other overheads – plus you must also take into account the fact that borrowers sometimes go bust and can't repay. Managing and understanding those latter risks traditionally involved quaint things like looking into the eyes of an applicant company's CEO while on the golf course, examining the company's balance sheet properly, and researching the competitive environment it operated in. With all these overheads, bankers borrowing at 3 per cent and lending at 6 per cent might find their eventual returns wouldn't be 3 per cent but 1 per cent. That may not sound like much, but 1 per cent of £10 billion in assets is good money.

Lending money is risky, so governments insist that banks have safety cushions. In theory, they ought to have more assets (things of value that they own) than liabilities (what they owe to others); the cushion is roughly the difference between the two – assets minus liabilities.[11] A bank's assets include things like cash, shares, property, computer equipment and perhaps your mortgage, which entitles the bank to receive a long-term stream of payments from you. Bonds are also assets; like mortgages, they promise interest payments to their owners over time, though with a bond the principal is repaid at the end of the term. Liabilities include deposits and other things the bank owes to those who have lent to it. If you pay a fifty-pound note into your bank account, the bank physically has it but it is still your money, so it owes you that fifty pounds and must give it back to you when you ask for it. Money deposited at a bank is therefore counted as part of the bank's liabilities. The balance sheet of a bank is simply a document laying out assets and liabilities. One side balances the other.

The safety cushion is called the bank's capital, and this – assets minus liabilities – should also be roughly what the bank's owners or shareholders think it is worth. If a company that has borrowed money from the bank collapses, and that loan is written off, then the value of the bank's assets falls by that amount, all other things being equal; the difference between assets and liabilities falls, and the bank's shareholders absorb that loss. The bank's share price falls, but nobody other than its shareholders is harmed – yet. The trouble begins when the bank's capital falls to zero or, worse, the bank owes more than it expects to be able to pay back. Such a bank might collapse, potentially wreaking havoc across the financial system. Nobody wants that, so regulators insist banks have a big enough capital cushion, expressed as a share of their total assets, to prevent such a catastrophe. The trouble is, many of these assets (like derivatives) are hard to value, and in a market panic, they can suddenly shrink dramatically, even to zero. That is why in any well-run economy, the safety cushions ought to be pretty large.

But modern bankers often hate such safety cushions, because they crimp the short-term profits which feed their bonuses. Imagine your bank has made £10 billion in loans (assets) and is earning a net 1 per cent on them, or £100 million, this year. If your bank is forced to hold a cushion (shareholders' equity) worth 10 per cent of its assets – £1 billion – then the shareholders are earning £100 million on their billion, a not-so-shabby 10 per cent annual return. But now imagine a different bank in a more lax jurisdiction which also has £10 billion in assets, also earning 1 per cent on them, but where now the capital requirement is only 5 per cent, so £500 million. A 1 per cent return on £10 billion still earns £100 million, but this is now worth a far sexier 20 per cent annual return on the shareholders' £500 million equity. Cut capital requirements to 2 per cent and your returns jump to 50 per cent. Just think: a 1 per cent return on assets gets transmogrified into a 50 per cent annual return for shareholders! This is a banking version of leverage, which the economist J. K. Galbraith in his classic book *The Crash of 1929* compared to 'a game of crack-the-whip [where], a modest movement near the point of origin is translated into a major jolt on the extreme periphery'. The danger, of course, is that if a bank has a cushion worth just 2 per cent of its assets, then a 3 per cent fall in the value of those assets could wipe out the bank. That's what happened, on a global scale, during the financial crisis.

The key point here is this: the lower the capital that regulators require you to have, the bigger your profits – and your bonus. Cutting capital requirements from 10 to 2 per cent could theoretically boost your profits fivefold. And this inevitably leads to great temptations. Banks desperately try to reduce capital requirements and lobby to water them down. Countries may try to lure greedy bankers with more 'competitive' (or lax) capital requirements; others may try to outdo them in laxity, and this can lead to a race to the bottom, driving down safety standards.[12]

Governments know about the dangers of this, so there have been efforts to agree common global standards. And here a merry-go-round of London-based shenanigans comes into view. UK regulators were in thrall to a group-think about financial risks that were similar to the libertarian attitudes in tax havens like Cayman. These attitudes relied on the Efficient Markets Hypothesis, which held that markets would sniff out trouble before it could happen – so clod-hopping regulators really should not try to second-guess what the clever, gentlemanly bankers were up to. Instead, regulators should simply promulgate 'principles' of good behaviour, then stand well back. The Americans, by contrast, relied much more heavily on rules and laws. The UK's principles-based regulation freed the UK to participate much more aggressively in the global race to the bottom.

The original global agreement on bank capital is the so-called Basel Accord, first agreed in 1988, under which international banks were required to hold a capital cushion equivalent to 8 per cent of assets, that headline number coming from the hard-nosed US regulator Paul Volcker. In theory, banks could not lend more than 12.5 times the value of their equity capital, but when Volcker went to Basel to discuss the accords with other central bankers, he discovered that European regulators had come up with a concept called risk-weighted capital.[13] The argument was that some bank assets, like cash or US Treasury bonds, were safer than others, so it should be possible to set risk weights below 8 per cent for them. At Basel it was agreed that corporate loans would get a 100 per cent risk weighting and residential mortgages a 50 per cent risk weight, so a $100 mortgage loan only required a $4 capital cushion, 50 per cent of the full $8. Loans to banks in other countries were considered even safer, under the gentlemanly assumption that counterpart regulators were doing a wonderful job, so these loans got a 25 per cent risk weighting, meaning just $2 in bank capital for every $100 lent out. The general principle was reasonable, but it increased complexity and with it the possibility of mischief. It also meant that banks reduced their lending to non-financial corporations – one of the most basic functions of any useful financial system – in favour of homeowners and other banks, since loans to them would gobble up less capital. (If you can't afford to buy your own home, this is one big reason why house prices are so high: Basel released enormous volumes of credit into housing markets.)

Banks' safety cushions were profitably smaller now, but they still wanted to pare the rules down further. And this is where those two great financialising innovations, derivatives and securitisation, came into the picture, and where things really began to go crazy. At each stage of this process the financial innovators found regulatory and other obstacles in their way, and at each stage they found ways around them with the help of the British spider's web.

Securitisation is an old craft, which emerged in its modern form in the US in the 1970s. This is where a bank takes income-generating assets like mortgages or government bonds and bundles them all together and sells them to a special purpose vehicle, which is typically a company set up for a particular function – in this case, to own these assets. SPVs are usually located in an offshore jurisdiction like the Cayman Islands. Imagine your SPV contains 1,000 residential mortgages, each worth an average £300,000 and each spitting out an average £1,500 in regular monthly mortgage payments, so £1.5 million a month, or £18 million a year. To fund its purchase of the mortgages, the SPV borrows money by issuing securities and selling them in chunks to outside investors at a profit, though the bank keeps a portion of the SPV for itself, let's say 10 per cent.[14]

Importantly, those mortgages don't belong to the bank any more; they belong to that Cayman SPV instead. They are no longer bank assets, so they are off the bank's balance sheet for capital purposes. Had the bank instead gone old school and held on to the full £300 million worth of mortgages, with a 4 per cent capital requirement it would have had to set aside £12 million in valuable capital against those home loans. But now the only thing it holds on its balance sheet is the 10 per cent it owns of the SPV, so must set aside only £1.2 million. The bank has still made its profits by parcelling up and selling off these mortgages to the SPV but now has used only a fraction of the capital that it would have needed if it held those mortgages itself. With the capital this frees up the bank can go out and repeat the trick. Then crank the handle and do it again. And again. And, hey presto, bigger bonuses for everyone, although (whisper it quietly) bigger risks in the financial system. So banks could use securitisation to slalom around the bank capital rules, and they did. It wasn't just mortgages either; they securitised bonds, credit card repayments, vehicle finance payments, student loans and all sorts of stuff.

It wasn't hard to find people to invest in these SPVs either. Financial deregulation had unleashed a flood of money and credit into world markets, and there were growing armies of cash-rich investors looking for places to put it all. Offshore SPVs had many attractions. For one thing, they gave investors financial exposure to residential mortgages without having to go through the grubby kerfuffle of dealing directly with actual homeowners – the banks had already done all the hard work. SPVs were made more enticing by giving investors access to different tranches of their output, slices of the annual £18 million in the above example. Those investing in the riskiest equity securities at the bottom would get the largest absolute returns in good times but would be the first to lose money if loans went bad. Above that there were progressively safer levels: junior debt, then mezzanine debt halfway up, then senior debt, and finally super-senior debt at the top – ultra-safe but paying tiny returns. Think of it like one of those cone-shaped towers of champagne glasses. Our SPV pours up to £18 million worth of champagne in at the top at regular intervals every year; if there's plenty to go around the champagne will sluice all the way down to the lowest levels, where there will be most glasses to catch it. But if a lot of mortgages go sour there's less champagne next time, so those at the bottom may go thirsty, while those at the higher levels should still be fine.

The SPV makes these payments automatically: it is a precisely tuned machine which determines precisely how the champagne flows – who gets how much, when and in what order of preference. In contrast to a normal company, with its board of directors, annual general meeting, corporate governance codes and managers' foibles and mistakes, the SPV is like a robot company, as the financial journalist Nicholas Dunbar explains:

In the brave new world of securitisation, that human element gets replaced with an engineered financial machine or structure, and for that reason it gets called *structured finance*. Unlike in a real company, where assets, revenues, and debt payments all involve real people and endless debate, the SPV doppelgänger is an android, programmed by a lawyer-crafted set of rules to mechanically transfer cash between various Cayman Islands mailboxes. In this world, the taxman is just another unpredictable creditor, best kept at bay by using a tax haven.[15]

In these androids lies a delectable, carefully calibrated smorgasbord of risk and reward for investors to pick and choose from, with each investor selecting their own preferred niche. But how to put a value on these things? To cut a very long story very short, the financial whizzes created some new water-into-wine mathematics and browbeat, bullied and corrupted the credit ratings agencies to give these complex securities top rating as low-risk vehicles, which allowed their creators to pay out less to the outside investors, thus boosting profits. The valuations invoked safety in numbers, the idea being that even if some loans defaulted, others wouldn't. The head of a Wall Street investment firm explained this idea to the finance writer John Cassidy: 'You take hundreds of drunks staggering down the street, and you make them put their arms around each other's shoulders and lock hands. Then you rely on the fact that they are all falling in different directions to keep the entire group upright. Oh, and you call it a Triple A Security.'[16] Of course a decent sized bump in the road would bring this happy group crashing down, just as such SPVs could never survive any proper market downturn.

Parking SPVs offshore in places like the Cayman Islands made them even more enticing to cash-rich investors. Tax was crucial, of course; a layer of tax at the level of the SPV could wipe out the whole margin of profit, so Cayman's zero-tax status was a huge plus. Also, if you had criminal money to invest, nobody in the Caymans was going to ask any questions. At a more fundamental level, there was another reason to go offshore: because these places are largely free of financial regulations. The Cayman Islands' entire model of financial legislation had always been to attract as much hot money as possible, while shaking off any associated risks. In the words of Anthony Travers, a stridently anti-government British libertarian who helped construct the Cayman Islands' modern financial centre, 'the responsibility of the Cayman government was managed by avoiding the concept of prudential regulation'.[17]

At the last count, the Cayman Islands' shadow banking sector held assets worth $5.8 trillion – equivalent to 170,000 per cent of Cayman's GDP, and over twice as big as the UK's own GDP.[18] And anyone in the Caymans who challenges the dirty-money machine – an important feeder for the securitisation business – comes up against terrifying mechanisms of administrative control in this financially captured state.

I heard about these control mechanisms when I interviewed a local personality at his house in Cayman in 2009.

During the interview there was a knock on the door and a stocky, dark-skinned man walked in, wearing a polo shirt and sunglasses. He introduced himself as 'the Devil' and declined to give me his real name; I still don't know it. He had a background in international law enforcement and said his pseudonym reflected how he was viewed locally, due to his having turned over financial stones that should never have been touched. He spoke of arms dealers, international terrorists and of Cayman-based hedge funds, mutual funds and SPVs. All of these sectors, he said, were riddled with crime and dirty money. He would not go into too much detail but instead gave me with a health warning: 'If we discuss this with you, you will end up like Salman Rushdie. There are things here not to be discussed. I mean it – this is a wicked, vicious place.' Transgressing the unwritten rules of the Caymans, he said, results in 'economic isolation. They destroy your credibility and your integrity. They will strip you of your dignity. We operate here under a code of silence – *omertà*.' He spoke of a local cabal of foreign financial interests, at which point our host interjected, saying this cabal was 'spoken of in terms you'd speak of a ghost'.[19]

Fuelled by shady money and various other sources of credit, and protected by the tax havens' anti-regulation regulations, the securitisation machine grew ever larger during the 1990s. But there were problems. One was that the banks had to provide a constant supply of new mortgages to feed the insatiable securitisation machine to churn out profits, and in the hunt for new mortgage customers they steadily dropped their lending standards. In the Hollywood film *The Big Short* the character played by Steve Carrell is shocked when he encounters a young stripper who owns five houses and a condo. This reflects what was actually going on: bankers were making loans to increasingly shaky lenders. In the real world a US bank whistle-blower, Michael Winston, recalls asking a colleague why his boss's car had a personalised licence plate that read FUND-EM.

'We fund all loans,' his colleague explained.

'What if the borrower has no job?' Winston asked.

'Fund 'em.'

'What if they have no assets?'

'Fund 'em.'

'No income?'

'If they can fog a mirror, we'll give them a loan.'[20]

There was another problem too: the banks' long-standing clients in the mainstream economy didn't much like being told that their loans had been sold off to an opaque SPV in a tax haven. As a result the banks wanted to find a way to keep these loans on their balance sheets, so they could say to their clients, 'We're still your bank. We've kept your loans in house, so can you please do your next M and A [mergers and acquisitions] transactions with us,' yet *still* be able to dance around the capital requirements. In other words, to have their cake and eat it.

And here we return to the wild world of derivatives, credit default swaps, Boca Raton – and London. The mechanism that the bankers invented during the wild weekend in Florida was based around the credit default swap, which enables players to bet (or insure themselves) against the possibility that a bond or a loan will actually go into default. A bank could keep loans on its balance sheet, use CDSs to insure those loans against default, then tell the regulators that these loans were insured and it had shed the risk, enabling it to obtain more lenient capital requirements. At the Boca Raton meeting in 1994 the JP Morgan whizzes hatched up a way to do this, using a scheme they called Bistro. They would still use securitisation – not to get the assets off their balance sheet this time, but to use those offshore androids to industrialise the process, converting CDSs into new and more appetising morsels precisely tweaked and tailored to the desires of global investors. And those investors, by buying into those income-generating morsels, would effectively be insuring those loans still on JP Morgan's balance sheet.

This was the moment when traditional securitisation techniques began to evolve into what would become known as synthetic securitisation. The investors in Bistro SPVs weren't buying exposure to underlying mortgages or corporate bonds, as with traditional securitisations; instead, these 'synthetic' vehicles were stuffed with bundles of credit default swaps – bets. So the banks had found a way to get investors to insure large amounts of their own corporate loans, in the process removing all that nasty default risk from their balance sheets and hopefully freeing up all-important capital for more profitable lending. Unlike traditional securitisations, which needed underlying mortgages to function, these synthetic bets could be replicated without limit. (If you bet on a horse in a race, that doesn't stop you placing a second bet on the same horse in the same race; you don't need to find another horse or another race.) And that is what began to happen. Bankers began to joke that 'Bistro' stood for 'BIS total rip-off' – referring to the Bank for International Settlements, which oversaw the Basel Accord. And the CDS concept at the heart of it all would turn out to be one of the most profitable – and dangerous – financial innovations of all time.

But before their full power could be unleashed, there were still a few hurdles to overcome. For one thing, regulators hadn't formally accepted the concept yet. Once again, the banks were able to find help in the usual place, light-touch London.

To understand what happened next, it is helpful to take a brief diversion to a blog written a few years ago by Jolyon Maugham, a UK tax lawyer.

I have on my desk an Opinion – a piece of formal tax advice – from a prominent QC [Queen's Counsel] at the Tax Bar. In it, he expresses a view on the law that is so far removed from legal reality that I do not believe he can genuinely hold the view he says he has. At best he is incompetent. But at worst, he is criminally fraudulent: he is obtaining his fee by deception. And this is not the first such Opinion I have seen. Such pass my desk all the time.

Maugham was referring to a lucrative industry in which law and accounting firms cook up tax schemes, usually involving tax havens, and flog them to banks and multinationals. When a multinational buys this kind of financial technology they need legal opinions as a kind of semi-formal seal of legitimacy and as reassurance that the scheme should defeat any tax authority's efforts to challenge it. A single planning idea could generate fees of £100 million pounds for the law and accounting firms that creates and sells it, Maugham continued, 'But without barrister sign-off, you have nothing to sell.'[21] And this creates predictable temptations. 'Assume that you are one of the Boys [who won't say no]. You write an Opinion of the type I have sitting on my desk. You collect your large fee – and you establish yourself in the mind of the House as an accommodative sort of professional. The sort of chap they might like to come see again in the future.'

In the absence of meaningful penalties, parts of the legal profession in London have become infected by this way of operating. So it will hardly come as a surprise, given the potential for profits, that this way of thinking also affected the world of credit default swaps.

Robin Potts, a British insolvency lawyer, was certainly an 'accommodative sort'. He was, as a colleague put it, 'the quintessential businessman's barrister', spending a lot of time in British tax havens. The chief justice of the Cayman Islands called him an 'outstanding advocate'.[22] David Marchant, a journalist who investigates tax haven scams and shenanigans with Offshore Alert, took a different view. He recalls Potts trying unsuccessfully to have him jailed for contempt of court in Bermuda in 1999, after Marchant refused to identify sources for an article he had written. As Marchant put it, '[Potts] wasn't likeable, coming across as a weasel – the sort of guy you wanted to punch in the face. Generally, the pomposity that Potts and the other English barristers brought to the Bermuda courtroom was insufferable. Not much in terms of collective ability but an abundance of sneering arrogance and a comical sense of superiority.'[23]

Potts took on some colourful cases on behalf of some colourful characters and made some colourful arguments. In one case he represented the interests of the British Conservative Party politician, donor and tax haven habitué Michael Ashcroft in an arcane appeal involving the valuation of millions of dollars in some shares. A judge in the case said in 2004 that Potts had effectively accepted that his clients were seeking to extract 'a ransom' from one of the companies involved, because it had them, in Potts' words, 'over a barrel'. Another judge called the Potts-Ashcroft petition 'an instrument of oppression' designed to unlock money that bore no relation to the true value of the shares:

This practice (which I understand is a not unheard of practice in the City) is described as 'green mail'. The proper word to my mind is blackmail. It is the kind of thing which brings the City into disrepute, to my mind. The purpose of the City is to raise finance to enable companies to develop businesses for their own and the country's well being. Where matters are dealt with in speculation and profits are made, which are then gathered off-shore, when there is no merit ... that to my mind is not legitimate.[24]

Long before this case, in 1997, the year that JP Morgan finally launched Bistro, the International Swaps and Derivatives Association (ISDA) commissioned the same Robin Potts to write a legal opinion about credit default swaps. This opinion hinged on a rather important question: were CDSs bets, or insurance? Should they be regulated and taxed under gambling or insurance laws? The answer that any reasonable person would give is that they are both insurance and gambling, depending on which side of the trade you are on. And some kinds of speculative CDSs are so dangerous that, as one commentator put it, 'the case for banning them is about as strong as the case for banning bank robberies'.[25]

Potts, however, managed to come up with the opposite answer – precisely the answer, as it happens, that ISDA and the hungry CDS traders at the big banks wanted. Credit default swaps weren't insurance or bets, the obliging Potts opined, in the process rubber-stamping the non-regulation of CDSs in London, and opening the gates to unlimited, unregulated betting on the credit defaults – the life and death – of companies. This overturned one of the most fundamental rules of banking: that a bank should have 'skin in the game', carrying some of the default risk of a loan on its own shoulders. The implications were immense. 'The business opportunities created by credit derivatives,' purred Blythe Masters, a top member of the JP Morgan team, 'is [sic] frankly staggering.' In 1996, the year before Potts wrote his opinion, there were an estimated $150–200 billion worth of CDSs already out there, already a very large number. Ten years later, as the financial crisis began to bite, that number had risen three hundredfold to over $60 *trillion* – roughly equivalent to the gross domestic product of planet Earth.[26]

So the banks believed they had obtained an exemption from regulation for these exciting new instruments – at least in London. Then, in 1998, the next big hurdle fell when the US Federal Reserve gave its blessing for JP Morgan to get capital relief via its Bistro deal. This would open the way for the Basel rules on bank capital to accept the deals too. But there were still obstacles to be overcome. Next was the Glass-Steagall Act of 1933, which had separated US commercial banking from investment banking to stop speculators gambling with depositors' money. Glass-Steagall didn't contain explicit provisions on derivatives – this was a grey area – so an army of lobbyists, armed with the example of London and the offshore centres, mounted a blitzkrieg in Washington to bring it all above board.

By then it was already getting generally easier for banks to find escape routes. It was not just about using derivatives and going offshore because there was another way, involving a different 'competitive' game. The US financial system is overseen by a patchwork of regulators, each the fruit of some past financial crisis, and 'regulator shopping' was all the rage, encouraging a 'competitive' race between US regulators to degrade standards in order to attract clients.

An ideological shift was well under way too. The hard man of American finance, Paul Volcker, had long ago stepped down as chair of the US Federal Reserve, the top regulator, and been replaced by Alan Greenspan, an extremist libertarian who had once called the welfare state 'nothing more than a mechanism by which governments confiscate the wealth of more productive members of society'. He had also said, channelling the wisdom of British tax havens, that he didn't believe there should be laws against fraud because it wasn't necessary: people would simply stop doing business with bad actors, he opined, and they'd be driven from the market.[27] Greenspan joined deregulatory forces with President Bill Clinton's treasury secretary, the former Goldman Sachs banker Robert Rubin, and Rubin's deputy Lawrence Summers, and this Third-Wayish trio cheer-led the frenzy of financial innovation now exploding across US trading rooms.

In November 1999 this new breed of American anti-regulators brought down their biggest trophy kill, the repeal of the Glass-Steagall Act, a singularly effective piece of antitrust legislation which had for six and a half decades prevented banks from gambling with their depositors' money. 'This historic legislation,' gushed Summers at the repeal ceremony in 1999, 'will better enable American companies to compete in the new economy.' Summers was by then US Treasury secretary and Rubin had moved onto the board of the newly merged Citigroup, which was to be the biggest beneficiary of the deregulation.[28]

Then, in 2000, came another giant deregulatory splurge: the Commodity Futures Modernisation Act (CFMA), which explicitly removed the US government's right to regulate over-the-counter derivatives such as CDSs and other exotic financial instruments. This had been spurred on by a 'president's working group' which asserted that deregulation was necessary to ensure that 'US firms and markets are not at a competitive disadvantage relative to their foreign counterparts' and warned that continued inaction 'could discourage innovation and growth of these important markets and damage US leadership in these arenas by driving transactions off-shore'. As ever, one 'competitor' in particular was on everyone's minds, the City of London. As financial criminologist Bill Black explained to me, in general terms 'London is vital to Wall Street's ability to argue that it needs weak regulation. The City is the bogey man.' Also in 2000, Britain's Financial Services Authority began approving aggressive risk models for Deutsche Bank and JP Morgan's London affiliates, which allowed them to build up dangerous levels of borrowing that US regulators would never have given. Other US banks soon noticed, and piled in. Not long afterwards, Goldman Sachs reached a deal with embattled US regulators for an arrangement that matched what London's was offering. The next American domino had fallen, courtesy of the City.[29]

By now, in the early 2000s, Greenspan's see-no-evil influence was all over Washington. But not all US regulators had fallen under his sway, and a group of them flew to London to join international discussions to set new Basel rules on banks' capital levels. By the time this was implemented in 2004, the rules looked like a Swiss cheese, not least because each country had its own banking system, and each wanted its own 'competitive' preferences reflected. The US officials arrived to discover that their top concerns weren't even on the agenda. They were told, especially by the British and Swiss, that the banks knew more about these issues than they did, so they shouldn't be telling them what to do about their capital ratios (and leverage ratios, a related measure of banks' indebtedness and riskiness). The regulators effectively capitulated and agreed to what was, in effect, a privatisation of bank regulation: the regulators would no longer calculate risk weightings but would let banks do their own calculations according to their own models. All the banks had to do was tell regulators what they were up to. Regulators moved from telling banks what to do, to merely asking banks what they were doing. A member of the Fed team recalled pleading fruitlessly at the London meeting, 'Look how little capital there is here. By any measure, you can't look at 800:1 leverage and say it's OK. I know it's not a true measure of risk. It just can't be true.' But it was no good. In that committee room the international regulators 'blew the last big chance to prevent a catastrophic financial disaster', explains derivatives expert Nick Dunbar. 'Assailed by arbitrage from all sides, the erosion of Basel began to resemble a time-lapse movie of an elephant being consumed by maggots.'[30]

The following year, 2005, was when Blair forcefully underlined the British anti-regulation approach, slamming Britain's Financial Services Authority for being 'hugely inhibiting of efficient business by perfectly respectable companies that have never defrauded anyone'. The FSA chairman responded cringingly 'that the FSA applied to the supervision of its largest banks only a fraction of the resource applied by US regulators'.[31] The UK continued to lead the way down the slope of laxity, as American regulators tried to 'compete' to stay abreast with London. Meanwhile, financial innovation proceeded apace across the Western world, spawning new vehicles and instruments, and the riskiest of these were mostly created in London.

The derivatives players were also overcoming a set of other obstacles, not with regulators this time, but in the market itself. The first problem was the ultra-safe super-senior tranches that the synthetic SPVs were issuing in large quantities. Nobody really wanted to insure them because they were only able to offer minute returns, but there was, it turned out, one player who would: the venerable insurance giant American International Group (AIG), specifically AIG Financial Products, based in Mayfair in London. This was led by Joe Cassano, a former employee of Drexel Burnham Lambert, the collapsed US junk bond firm at the centre of the fraudulent savings and loan crisis in the 1980s. AIGFP agreed to earn just 0.02 cents for every dollar it insured, each year, a model that has been compared to picking up pennies in front of a steamroller. (Cassano himself would take home 30 per cent of those pennies for himself, netting $280 million in 2000–8.) This deadly unit had been located in London, Dunbar explains, as part of a complex transatlantic corporate structure. 'So each country thought others were dealing with it, and thought, *What a relief we don't have to look at this thing.*' And of course that was what AIG wanted.'[32] When the global crisis struck, AIG weren't able to pay up on all the diseased financial instruments it had insured through its reckless London affiliate, and the ensuing financial vortex would suck down the parent company with 115,000 employees in 130 countries, and lead to the biggest government bail-out in US history.

AIG may have been the biggest bail-out, but Lehman Brothers remains the biggest bankruptcy. No bail-out this time. And once again London proved crucial in the story.

Underlying Lehman's bankruptcy was a mechanism called repo, which is now central to the plumbing of global finance. Essentially, this is a way for large corporations to deposit money. If you personally have £25,000 in a UK bank, your deposit is essentially safe; the government guarantees up to £85,000 and will repay you if the bank goes bust. But a corporation that wants to deposit £70 million doesn't have that protection. So it uses repo: it deposits cash with a counterparty – not necessarily a bank – and in exchange gets collateral, like a government bond or a securitised product from one of those Cayman androids, alongside a contract which says the bank will repurchase (repo) that collateral from the corporation very soon (often the next day or the next week) at a tiny premium equivalent to a day's or a week's interest. Typically this trick is repeated day after day. Corporations get slightly better interest rates in the repo market than with standard bank deposits, and if the bank goes bust, they've got the collateral to compensate them for the lost deposit. Banks can pay slightly better rates because repo gives them tax benefits and favourable accounting treatment.

Repo is everywhere now. It interconnects most financial markets in trillion-dollar webs of tightly coupled relationships, linking government and corporate bond markets with central banking, securitisation, taxes and spending, and more. It is so systemically important, in fact, that some people now call repo shadow money.[33] In times of crisis all this interconnection makes repo a transmission mechanism for shocks; the global financial crisis has been called, in part, 'a run on the repo market', and repo will be in the background of the next big crisis too.

Legally, repo hinges on a question: is the transfer of cash for collateral a true sale? If so, then the bond that a bank 'sells' in a repo operation is no longer the property of the bank, so the bank shouldn't have to set aside capital against it, and the cash injection it gets in exchange for that bond is also an asset that can be used to flatter the bank's balance sheet. In the real world, though, a repo obviously isn't a true sale, because the repurchase contract creates an umbilical link between the bank and that piece of collateral. In the years preceding the crisis Lehman wanted to hide assets from its balance sheet and approached a few American law firms to get a legal opinion that repo did constitute a true sale. Nobody would oblige.

By now it shouldn't be hard to guess where Lehman then went to find the opinion it wanted. The London law firm Linklaters helpfully wrote an opinion in 2001, which stated that the transactions in question – mostly called Repo 105 – were true sales after all. It also carefully mapped out a legal pathway for Lehman to make these trades through its affiliate in London in order to hide assets from investors, using the trades deceptively to flatter their balance sheet just before they issued a quarterly report, then unwinding them again just afterwards.[34] A senior Lehman official said that Repo 105 was just 'another drug we are on'. When the crisis hit, it emerged that Lehman had used repo to remove some $50 billion of bad assets from its balance sheet. Lehman's auditors in London, Ernst & Young, earned a reported $150 million in fees for signing off on Lehman accounts between 2001 and 2008, which didn't mention repo. Jon Moulton, a venture capitalist, sums up Lehman's subterfuge: 'They were jurisdiction shopping. They were trying to find the answer they wanted. They got it.'[35] In London.

As the financial system took on ever more risk, and found ever more ways to hide that risk, a crash was inevitable. It arrived in 2007 in a series of staggered explosions. Lehman was arguably the most dangerous of them all, prompting then President George W. Bush at one point to say, referring to the American economy, 'this sucker could go down'. And in this episode it turned out that Britain had played another, bigger role magnifying the repo risks.

When a corporation receives a government bond in exchange for cash in a repo transaction, it can pass that bond on to others in a second repo transaction. This is called rehypothecation. The receiver of that bond can then re-pledge it again, and so on.[36] US rules restricted this practice quite tightly, but Lehman and others were able to do it without limit in London, so a single sliver of collateral could get rehypothcated around the block until it ended up perched atop a daisy chain of interlinkages, with market players taking spreads and fees at each juncture. The longer the chain, the greater the risks. And any chain is only as strong as its weakest link. When Lehman Brothers fell it turned out that most of the assets had been transferred to its reckless London subsidiary, where many US funds found that a chunk of their assets, re-pledged across London markets, had gone up in financial smoke.

Making it all worse, rehypothecation meant nobody knew how much of this stuff was out there in the shadow banking system (that is, the hedge funds, repo traders and other arcane financial institutions and practices that lie outside traditional bank regulation). According to the IMF, this blind spot on rehypothecated assets meant that when the crisis hit, the shadow banking system was a full 50 per cent bigger – nearly US$ 5 trillion bigger, that is, than the regulators had thought. When things fell apart this worsened the chaos and deepened the crisis that followed. Once again, we have the City of London to thank.[37]

By this time, regulatory capture had been so deep and powerful in the United States that a casual observer might conclude that the US had finally caught up with Britain in the deregulatory race. Not so – not even close. My Exhibit A here is a remarkable lobbying document issued by New York City Mayor Michael Bloomberg and Senator Chuck Schumer in January 2007 entitled *Sustaining New York's and the US' Global Financial Services Leadership*. Its core argument rested on two words. One was 'London', which it mentioned 135 times in as many pages, and the second was 'competitive' (or variations), which got over 200 mentions.

New York, it maintained, was losing out in a great global race with London and other financial centres. The only way to keep up with London's 'more amenable and collaborative regulatory environment', it urged, was massive further financial deregulation. 'While our regulatory bodies are often competing to be the toughest cop on the street,' the authors urged in an article complementing the document, 'the British regulatory body seems to be more collaborative and solutions-oriented.' New York was still 'in the lead' in terms of size, the anxiety-inducing summary said, but London was ahead of the US in derivatives and some other areas. America risked being 'marginalised' in this 'ultra-competitive global marketplace'. The solution: relax regulations, stop policing the financial markets and copy London. It is hardly surprising that New York financiers had been calling London, where they could do things they weren't allowed to do at home, the Guantanamo Bay of global finance.[38]

Two months later the City of London issued its Global Financial Centres Index, announcing that, according to its own analysis, London had 'a narrow lead over New York'. It mentioned the United States 92 times and the same C-words over 200 times. The UK government had to ensure that a '"tipping point" is not reached'. The answer was even more deregulation in London too. In June Gordon Brown, Blair's chancellor, joined the financial love-fest, congratulating a group of City financial and political bigwigs on 'an era that history will record as the beginning of a new golden age for the City of London'. He crowed about having resisted pressure to tighten financial regulations in the wake of the Enron and Worldcom disasters, and added, 'Your success is critical to that of Britain's overall, and considering together the things that we must do – and, just as important, things we should not do – to maintain our competitiveness ... I believe it will be said of this age, the first decades of the twenty-first century, that out of the greatest restructuring of the global economy, perhaps even greater than the Industrial Revolution, a new world order was created.'

Two months later, in August, Britain's Conservative Party unveiled an even more spectacularly mistimed report. Entitled *Freeing Britain to Compete: Equipping the UK for Globalisation*, it wielded the C-words 226 times and spoke rapturously of the 'massively favourable trends' of easy credit, along with 'public/private partnerships, specialised credit-based funds and funds of funds, collateralised debt obligations, collateralised loan obligations, credit default swaps, special purpose vehicles' and many other mechanisms for taking on risk. Those were the very instruments that were about to bring the Western world to its knees. Within weeks Northern Rock customers would be queuing to empty their accounts. The global financial crisis had finally arrived.

Amid the rubble and the recriminations one thing became clear: the American judicial and regulatory system had been so degraded that US authorities no longer had the stomach or even the ability to jail the bankers who had been most responsible for blowing up the world. The term 'too big to jail' became common currency, and many noticed the contrast with the much smaller savings and loan crisis, which by 1989 had seen more than 3,000 bankers jailed. But in Britain it was worse, much worse. It's impossible to wrap your mind around the sheer extent of the difference between the two countries; I can only resort to a few statistics, quotes and anecdotes to give some indication.

At the time of writing, US authorities had levied over US$150 billion in fines just for activities related to the financial crisis out of a world total of over $320 billion for all activities. In comparison, the UK's financial regulatory authorities had imposed a total of $3.5 billion in fines on financial institutions between 2007 and 2018 – and that was *all* fines, including for run-of-the-mill misreporting or bad governance practices by small-fry brokers, payment protection frauds, insurance companies, the LIBOR scandal and the like. I have been unable to find *any* fines clearly related to the causes of the global financial crisis. Zero. It is true that British banks have been fined substantially, but it's been the American authorities taking action. In the United States nearly 250 people had been sentenced to prison by 2018 for misusing bail-out money, while in Britain, at last, four senior individuals at Barclays Bank now face charges relating to a deal with Qatar in 2008 to shore up the bank's position amid the crisis. They go on trial in 2019 and if convicted they will be the first significant exceptions to the long-standing apparent rule that, in Britain, bankers are a protected species. Still, their actions had nothing to do with helping cause the crisis in the first place.[39]

'Overall, the US government has become the world's most recent example of "bank capture", a dubious status usually associated with wealthy parasitic monocultures like Switzerland, Luxembourg, Singapore, Dubai or the City of London,' explains American offshore and financial crime expert James Henry. 'The United States has become a one-party state, presided over by the Bankster Party and its revolving doormen.' The Trump administration has aggressively deregulated US finance, while the UK, amid intense public fury after the crisis, has tightened up in some areas, in some cases more stringently than in the US. Yet for the main events that caused the crisis, there has been no accountability in London. According to the UK Financial Services Authority, AIGFP in London 'fell outside its jurisdiction'. As the *Telegraph* reported, 'to date, no British authorities have said anything about AIG. In the US, in contrast, there are multiple investigations.' Britain's Serious Fraud Office was prodded into launching a probe into AIG in 2009, but quietly dropped it in 2010 on the grounds of 'insufficient evidence' with hardly a ripple in the UK media, or anywhere else.

Few have understood how much more thoroughly Britain has been penetrated and captured by reckless global finance than the United

States has, and how this makes Britain's financial sector unusually dangerous for the world economy. 'There is a global geography of systemic risk, and London generates a disproportionate amount,' said one expert, 'for all the post crisis policy debate about containing and curbing it, [this] hasn't been touched upon.'[40]

And since the crisis, Britain's tolerance of financial innovations that pose financial stability risks has continued to be closely linked to its tolerance of money tainted with murder and illegal drugs. Take, for instance, the HSBC case, where the bank took money from Russian gangsters, organisations linked to al-Qaeda and Hezbollah, and sanctions-busting North Koreans, and helped launder at least $880 million for Mexico's Sinaloa drug cartel, people so evil, joked former New York Attorney General Eliot Spitzer, 'they make the guys on Wall Street look good'.[41] A Congressional inquiry into the US Department of Justice's decision in 2012 not to prosecute HSBC found that Britain's chancellor George Osborne and the Financial Services Authority had actively interfered at the highest levels of the US government and justice system, threatening 'global financial disaster' if 'their' bankers were prosecuted. London's intervention, the report said, 'hampered the US government's investigations and influenced DOJ's decision not to prosecute HSBC'.[42]

Americans are now waking up to the democracy-threatening perils of harbouring questionable foreign money, as revelations about links between Trump administration officials and Russian oligarchs continue to surface, but London had been in the game long before the US. 'America's experience [has been] but a faint echo of what hit London,' said Rick Wilson, a Republican political strategist. 'Russian mobsters in Brighton Beach, Brooklyn were buying taxi company medallions and running pump-and-dump stock scams. Some were picking up condos in Trump Tower. Russians in London were buying [...] Renaissance art and whole blocks of Knightsbridge.' A PwC report on Russian initial public offerings (IPOs) – companies being floated on the stock market – found that between 2005 and 2014 there were two listings on the New York Stock Exchange, two on the US technology exchange NASDAQ, 37 in Moscow and 67 on the London Stock Exchange. These weren't all criminal enterprises – far from it – but this huge preference for London reflected London's massively more permissive attitudes towards the rule of law.

Bernd Finger, a German former policeman specialising in organised crime, told me in 2017 that in his experience of trying to trace criminal assets, the German authorities usually got good cooperation from other countres, with two notable exceptions: Russia and Britain. Treaties require the Brits to provide information when asked, he said, 'but they simply do not answer'. When French authorities investigating money laundering and tax fraud at the phone company Lycamobile asked HMRC for assistance, they received an official letter stating that Lycamobile was 'a large multinational company' with 'vast assets at their disposal' and would be 'extremely unlikely to agree to having their premises searched ... It is of note that they are the biggest corporate donor to the Conservative Party.' Margaret Hodge, former head of the UK's Public Accounts Committee, called Britain 'the country of choice for every kleptocrat, crook and despot in the world'.[43]

'Our system for regulating markets and for prosecuting market crime is completely broken,' says Ken Macdonald, former director of public prosecutions in the UK. People and institutions operate 'as though they are beyond the reach of the criminal law. If you mug someone in the street and you are caught, the chances are that you will go to prison. In recent years mugging someone out of their savings or their pension would probably earn you a yacht.'[44] And so, it seems, would mugging a whole country – and indeed half the world.

8

Wealth and its Armour

On 17 September 2007 Richard Murphy, a British commentator and forensic accountant, published a short blog remarking on some odd items in the accounts of Northern Rock, the British mortgage bank. Long queues had formed outside the bank's branches after it had admitted a few days earlier that it had asked the Bank of England for emergency funding. This was the first proper run on a bank in Britain since 1866, and one of the first big shocks of the global financial crisis. Northern Rock had been playing the securitisation game hard, using whizzy special purpose vehicles. These vehicles got funding to buy mortgages by issuing short-term debt and selling it to global investors; when investors got the jitters and stopped rolling over their loans, the whole tightly interconnected financial machine ground to a violent halt.

On one level, this explained Northern Rock's sudden cardiac arrest. But the deeper Murphy probed, the odder it looked. It wasn't just that these vehicles were mostly based in the British tax haven of Jersey, or that they were *controlled* by Northern Rock but not *owned* by it – a distinction that allowed it to profit from them while claiming they were off its balance sheet, freeing up capital.[1] The really odd thing was the fact that the whole shebang, holding £40 billion or so worth of mortgages, was according to Northern Rock documents 'held on trust by a professional trust company under the terms of a discretionary trust for the benefit of one or more charities' and for 'other charitable purposes selected at the discretion of the professional trust company'. And the named beneficiary was Down's Syndrome North

East Association (UK) or DSNE, a charity run by volunteers to help children with Down's syndrome that operated out of a semi-detached house in a modest suburb of Newcastle. DSNE volunteers raised funds from sponsored swimathons, 'ladies' luncheons', theatre tickets and even a helpful fellow who had earned them £125 cycling across the United States. Nobody at the charity had a clue that there were £40 billion in offshore mortgage androids plugged into their semi-detached house, churning huge amounts of money through the financial ether. Apart from a whip-round from Northern Rock office staff in 2001, DSNE hadn't received a bean from the bank.

Anyone who read that blog would have had the same reaction I did: what the hell was this about? The whole thing, wrote Murphy, was 'a completely fabricated farce'. It was indeed. But nobody funnels £40 billion through such baroque financial and legal pipework without good reason. To understand why, we need to take a thousand-year dive into the history of one of the most useful, versatile, slippery, powerful and also dangerous mechanisms in the entire menagerie of modern global finance: the trust.

The basic idea of the trust emerged in the Middle Ages, when English knights and nobles went off to fight in the Crusades. They often left their lands and properties in the hands of stewards, who were supposed to manage them for the benefit of the knights' families until they returned. Sometimes, though, a knight would come back to find that his steward didn't want to hand his property back after all, maybe having also slept with the knight's wife or daughters while he was off risking his neck for the Pope.[2] So the departing fighters took to making their stewards swear oaths of loyalty to the stewardship arrangements under threat of fire and brimstone, sometimes in the presence of sacred relics. They got the Church involved. The prospect of spending eternity surrounded by demons with pitchforks tended to focus the stewards' minds, but it was still a messy business and over time a body of enforceable trust law grew up, which endures today.

A classic trust is a three-way relationship. First, there's the original grantor of the assets – in the old days a knight, but today maybe a billionaire grandfather – who bequeaths or gives assets into a trust before they die. Second, there's the person who manages those assets. Historically this would have been one of those stewards, usually a trusted family member, though today the trustee is likely a skilled lawyer. The third group comprises the beneficiaries – typically the knight's (or the grandfather's) family, who will benefit from the trust assets. This is all tied together with a trust deed, a detailed agreement which regulates who is to get what, when, how and under what conditions. This deed can be enforced in court. A trust isn't an entity like a company; it's a legal arrangement, more like a contract.

The assets in a trust can be anything: a couple of Swiss bank accounts, ten gold bars, a castle in Austria or luxury apartments in Chelsea, a portfolio of shares, a valuable patent, half a commercial porn empire, a bunch of special purpose vehicles registered in Jersey, the rights to a bad pop song, or several British Virgin Islands shell companies which in turn own all of these things or own other shell companies which own these things. Anything really. The alchemy begins when the grantor gives those assets away, and the very concept of ownership begins to separate out into different components: technical legal ownership versus the rights to consume or enjoy or control the assets, or the rights to receive income from them. Usually the trustee becomes the legal owner, which enables them to sign documents, make transfers and so on, according to the trust deed. But this is a narrow slice of ownership; the trustee cannot legally run off with the assets for themself or earn from them beyond carefully agreed management fees. (If they try, other parties to the trust can use the courts to get them back.) The beneficiaries have other rights over the assets. Maybe the trust gives the old man's grandson the legal right to live in that castle, and Grandpa's second daughter to get half the income from the royalties on that pop song when she is twenty-one, while an estranged wife gets the legal right to use the old man's yacht any time (except Thursdays) and is entitled to income from a portfolio of Facebook shares – but has no rights over the shares themselves. Maybe the trustees get discretion to dole things out as they see fit under a set of general guidelines. But in general terms Grandpa has given the assets away; other people get to manage them, and others get to use or benefit from them.

Now a lot of people who aren't familiar with trusts find this odd; it seems like serious overkill if Grandpa has to give away his assets just in order to, for example, escape paying tax on them. As an English wealth manager in Hong Kong put it, 'When you propose to an elderly Chinese gentleman, "Look, I'll tell you what, how about you give me control of your assets and I'll hold on to them for you and your kids until you need them, at which point I may or may not give the assets to you? And by the way, you'll be paying me a hefty fee all the while," the elderly Chinese gentleman laughs very hard for a long time.'[3]

To understand why trusts are so attractive you need to get a flavour of their power and flexibility. Grandpa, or the elderly Chinese gent, may be able to have their cake and eat it by only appearing to give away the assets, erecting that legal barrier between him and them, but then, with the help of a lawyer, creating discreet legal passageways, guards, permissions and code words to allow him back into the castle, to carry on with the feasting and the bacchanalia. Trusts, especially offshore trusts, can be used to shield assets and income from tax authorities, from the forces of law and order, from divorced spouses, from Grandpa's irate creditors – from all sorts of people who might otherwise have a claim on them. This legal separation is often more powerful than just the fact of having hidden the assets. Once Grandpa has given those assets to the trust, they are literally, legally, no longer his. If he sets the trust up properly he has created an impenetrable legal barrier. His tax authorities or creditors can huff and puff, but they can't get at those assets or the associated income. They're gone. And when Grandpa dies there won't be any inheritance tax on the assets, because they weren't his and there isn't anyone to inherit them; the assets just carry on, unmolested, safe inside the trust. You've seen that Patek Philippe watch advertisement in the glossy magazines, where a handsome father stands with his well-groomed young son in a vineyard or at the helm of an oak-panelled speedboat? The caption is 'You never actually own a Patek Philippe, you merely look after it for the next generation.' If that watch is held in a trust, then the caption is literally true.

That's not the end of the story though. Grandpa's tax authorities could try and tax the trust itself or the assets in the hands of the trustees. If they are located in the place where Grandpa is resident for tax purposes, it may be possible for the authorities to make some headway, though there are always loopholes, which helps explain why UK inheritance tax only yields around £5 billion a year, just 3 per cent of the £100–150 billion of British wealth passed down the generations annually. But if the trust or trustees are based offshore, where Grandpa's taxman doesn't have jurisdiction, then it becomes, to use HMRC's own words, 'very complicated'. They could try and tax the beneficiaries, but if *they* don't own the assets or are resident elsewhere, then HMRC will struggle to bring them into its tax net. Of course if the trust spits out income from those Facebook shares to the estranged wife, then that income may be within the reach of HMRC, Interpol or her creditors. But if the underlying shares stay inside the fortress walls of a well-constructed trust, they remain untouchable.[4]

Now there is one last tactic HMRC could try. They could say, 'Ah, now, the granddaughter may not have received any assets from the trust yet, but she is ultimately *entitled* to them, so we'll deem them to be hers and tax her accordingly.' Well, English trust lawyers found an answer to that one over four centuries ago, with an arrangement called the discretionary trust. In this case, there are no firm rules in the trust deed about who will get what, when, where, how and why; the trustee has discretion to decide. Maybe the granddaughter will only get her hands on the family stables if she passes all her exams or if the trustee decides on a whim to give them to her instead of her brother. Maybe a troubled son needs to satisfy the trustee that he has not used heroin in five years before he can get his hands on the family pile in Gloucestershire. But here's the crucial bit: until the trustee uses his discretion to decide who gets what, none of the beneficiaries is entitled to any of it, now or in future. So HMRC can't deem anyone to be entitled to anything. This defence has been so effective that trust lawyers have called it litigation-proof.[5]

This gives us a sense of how slippery and powerful trusts can be. Plain, crude ownership is for the little people. It also helps to explain that suspicious Northern Rock structure held 'under the terms of a discretionary trust for the benefit of one or more charities'. The structure was legally separated from Northern Rock by the legal walls of the trust, so those assets were considered off the bank's balance sheet. And yet the structure was economically connected to Northern Rock, with its financialised pipework of Jersey androids ultimately spitting profits out of the fortress and into the bank's bottom line. Northern Rock, too, got to have its cake and eat it.

And yet, you may still ask, what's with the *charitable* trust? Well, the truth is that there are many legitimate and excellent charitable trusts or foundations out there doing fine things, sitting on fortresses of endowed capital and paying out regular amounts to worthy causes. And because of this benificence, these trusts tend to get very favourable legal and tax treatment. However, many so-called charitable trusts have less benevolent purposes; their core goal is not to pay money out to beneficiaries but to create a legal fortress which enjoys super-favourable treatment, inside which all the misrule can take place, safe from scrutiny and from the laws of society. These structures must have nominated beneficiaries – otherwise the structure isn't legally a charitable trust – but in Northern Rock's case it was never intended that big bucks should be doled out to children with Down's syndrome. If Northern Rock hadn't collapsed, DSNE might have got a few thousand pounds after all the securitisation vehicles had been wound down and the loose ends tied up, but the donations would have been like scraps from the feast thrown over the castle walls to the peasants below.

For these reasons many of the world's greatest private fortunes and many of the world's biggest commercial financing arrangements sit inside charitable trusts – or foundations, which are similar to trusts. Trusts are vital mechanisms in the financialisation of our economies, separating the wealthy further from us and deepening the finance curse.

Nobody has ever calculated how much wealth is held in trusts worldwide – so many trusts are hidden in desk drawers in tax havens it's impossible to find out – but there are clues. One tax haven alone, the British Crown Dependency of Jersey, has published an official estimate that its trusts hold a trillion pounds' worth of assets, equivalent to the annual GDP of Spain. And private-sector sources there suggest that most Jersey trusts are discretionary. Compare that to the estimated £1.3 *billion* held in onshore UK discretionary trusts, and it's clear how important the offshore system is to this world. Jersey is just one of many players in trusts; the global total may be comparable to the amount of money in tax havens, estimates ranging between $9 and $36 trillion, the higher number likely the more accurate one.[6] And there are considerable similarities between trusts and tax havens: not just that they overlap so much, but also the fact that trusts are like personalised tax havens, mechanisms enabling wealthy people or institutions to shield their assets from the rules that bind the rest of us.

Trusts, especially offshore trusts, can create amazingly complex layers of secrecy which can be tougher than anything a plain-vanilla Swiss bank account offers, where bankers simply promise to take their clients' secrets to the grave. (Threats of jail can change their minds.) When the World Bank carried out a survey of how criminals use legal structures to hide stolen assets, it said trusts were so difficult to investigate or prosecute that they were rarely prioritised in corruption investigations, because they were so hard to crack open.[7]

Trusts can create secrecy in a couple of main ways. Most importantly, when billionaire Grandpa gives away his assets, he not only creates a legal barrier between himself and his assets; he also potentially creates a secrecy barrier. If he doesn't own the assets, how can they be linked to him? An ex-husband can use a trust to escape paying off a divorced wife; his assets aren't his any more to distribute. A politician could give a fat contract to a company held in a trust, then truthfully declare that she doesn't own it, even though she will benefit personally (this is just what Wilbur Ross, Donald Trump's secretary of commerce, did, helping him keep an estimated $2 billion worth of assets off financial disclosure forms).[8] A Muslim could profit from underlying assets which violate sharia laws, but truthfully say that they don't own those assets. Even if a Mafioso demands that Grandpa hands over the assets, he still can't because (in a properly constructed trust) they really are no longer his.

Then there is the trust deed, the agreement that outlines how the trust works, who benefits and so on. This may exist only as a piece of paper somewhere in a notary's office drawer, perhaps in one of the sleazier tax havens like Belize. It could even be a purely verbal agreement, made in front of witnesses. How could Interpol crack *that* open to find out what's inside? When Britain's government announced in 2018 that it planned to force its overseas territories to publish the real owners of companies registered there, it was rightly hailed as a step forward, but this measure will do little in itself to open up the real beneficiaries and controllers of assets held in trusts. And once Grandpa goes offshore, of course, the varieties of trust subterfuges get wilder and weirder.

While many trusts are above board, many exist in a grey area, where the legality of the arrangement depends on interpretations, questions about degrees of control, intentions, discretion, influence and the very meaning of ownership. Even writing about trusts requires extreme care, to avoid the many pitfalls and hidden traps. Perhaps the crudest trust subterfuge is the revocable trust, by which Grandpa gives the assets away while he's feeling the heat of a tax probe or criminal investigation, but once the smoke has cleared he just revokes the trust and gets the assets back. This is a sham, not really a trust at all, but to penetrate it you must prove it's a sham – and if the deed is locked away in a notary's desk drawer in Panama, that can be very hard indeed. Another strategy for Grandpa might be to put his nest egg in a trust with a pliable trustee, who can be persuaded or relied on to get one of the companies owned by the trust to lend money back to him along with a quiet understanding (nudge, wink) that the loan won't ever be repaid. There may even be trust 'protectors' and 'enforcers' with official powers to ensure the trustee does exactly what Grandpa wants.

Some trusts specialise in helping rich people, usually older men, provide for their ex-spouses not as a cast-iron entitlement but at the discretion of puppet trustees. Just think how much power that can give a rich old man over his unhappy ex-wife after a nasty divorce, even after his death. Or the trust could pay Grandpa consulting fees or invest trust money in his dodgy shell company, which sits outside the trust and can be milked at leisure. There are letters of wishes – invisible little side-deals that can guide the trustee in umpteen ways. There are dynasty trusts, which aim to keep family wealth cascading down through the bloodline for generation after generation. There are spendthrift trusts – particularly impregnable versions where trustees can cut off any potential beneficiary who gets into financial trouble, thus protecting the family's core assets. There are duress clauses, which are like steel portcullises that lock down the trust the moment there's an external threat, preventing any payments if a settlor or beneficiary comes under duress, such as from tax or crime authorities. There are flee clauses, where the trust flits to another jurisdiction the moment foreign forces of law and order come sniffing around. And tax havens create firewall laws to make it harder for foreign courts to get their legal crowbars into trusts. In the US you can get deliberately distorted things called beneficiary defective trusts, which give beneficiaries almost unlimited control over the assets, and beneficiary quiet trusts, which means beneficiaries can be kept completely in the dark about the fact that they are beneficiaries. There are also combinations of all of the above.

And then there are the Cook Islands, fifteen isolated microdots in the Pacific Ocean with a population of 20,000 which have made a tidy business out of some of the world's most outrageous asset-protection laws. Once someone has placed their assets into a Cook Islands trust, you can sue them all you like in American or British courts, but if the trust has been set up in the right way, you won't get them back. Well, you can try, but you'll have to fly out there, maybe changing planes in New Zealand for the five-hour flight to Rarotonga, then have the case tried in crooked Cook Islands courts under crooked Cook Islands laws, with Cook Islands lawyers, and then often have to prove beyond reasonable doubt – as in a murder trial – how rock-solid watertight your case is. The users of Cook Islands trusts include a monkey house of fraudsters, billionaire Ponzi schemers, hedge-fund swindlers, vicious patriarchs in vicious divorce battles, snake-oil salesmen peddling weight-loss nirvanas and many others. One of those others was Richard Edison, a Florida-based plastic surgeon nicknamed Dr Dread who was sued after five of his patients died and he left a sponge in a woman's breast. His assets, in a Cook Islands trust, were immune.

There's an image from one of the most influential wealth-protection bodies, the Society of Trust and Estate Practitioners (STEP), which shows an armed knight in chain mail standing before a couple of large bags of money, his hand raised defiantly. The caption reads, 'Armour for your Assets'. But I prefer a different, if related image. Terms commonly used by trust lawyers – 'firewall', 'protection from attack', 'impregnable', 'shelter', 'shield' and so on – suggest a slightly different medieval image, the castle. And each fortress has guards to extract tribute from the surrounding peasantry. This is where we enter the world of the super-rich, and the industry that has grown up to defend their wealth.

The medieval customs that accompanied the rise of trusts haven't died out; they have evolved to cope with a more complex world. The steward has become the wealth manager. Before the age of globalisation, these functions used to be carried out, as in the Middle Ages, by trusted, unpaid close confidants of the rich family, but as the world's financial markets opened up, ushering in an era of rapidly increasing complexity in financial affairs, the activity became more and more professionalised.

Wealth managers construct and manage large, complex international structures involving banks, tax havens, trusts and foundations, wills, law and accounting, corporations, share and bond portfolios, insurance products, hedge funds, and more – putting them right at the heart of the machinery of global finance. Often working in teams, often operating in 'family offices' catering to a single family, they are the elite general dogsbodies of the super-rich. To make their clients feel comfortable they ideally come from the same social class, having imbibed the same manners and customs from childhood: down-at-heel aristocrats for the old money and sophisticated smoothies for the new. Good wealth managers keep their clients' assets dancing freely between different legal systems, taking advantage of loopholes while avoiding getting snagged by rules and responsibilities, and staying permanently abreast of shifting legal and political tides in each country. If their clients are proper billionaires, they might help them set up art galleries, philanthropic foundations, vineyards and think tanks, or lobbying operations pushing to get estate taxes repealed, corporate taxes cut or anti-monopoly or anti-tax haven rules eviscerated. They provide savvy investment advice, navigate the fights and foibles of bickering families, organise personal security, pay gardeners and servants, serve as friends, as shoulders to cry on, psychologists, investment advisers, butlers, and guardians of mistresses, of misdemeanours and of family secrets. Really good wealth managers have enormous patience, diplomacy, humility, the ability to multi-task, and above all discretion.

One of the step-changes in the growth of wealth management as a wider industry came in 1990 when George Tasker, a middle-aged Liverpool accountant, wrote to *Trusts & Estates* magazine, a publication for professional wealth managers, offering to start a discussion forum. His letter was printed, and the result was, in terms of this, at the time, fusty old world, pandemonium. The editor rang him to say he had been inundated with correspondence from practitioners around the UK offering to start or join a local group. So, in 1991 they all got together in London to discuss setting up a body to cater for the pent-up demand Tasker had unexpectedly tapped into. When deciding on a name, the group toyed with possible combinations of T for trusts, E for estates, P for practitioners and S for society. 'PEST and PETS were quickly rejected,' he said, 'leaving the only other anagram, STEP.'

STEP was inaugurated in July 1991 and within a year had 1,000 members – and kept growing explosively, especially in the tax havens. Today STEP has over 20,000 members in 95 countries, and is now probably the most powerful and effective unified voice for trusts, tax havens and the 'wealth defence industry' on the planet.[9] When governments try to crack down on offshore tax haven secrecy, for instance, an army of STEP experts steps up, targeting policymakers, denigrating the reformers, persuading offshore centres like the Caymans to write new laws to spike the reforms, pushing sunny studies suggesting tax havens are wonderful – and of course shepherding their clients' assets around any incipient blockages before they emerge.

STEP is, depending on your perspective, a vast repository of top-class professional expertise or, as an offshore lawyer put it to me, 'a snake with many heads'. Its introductory training course is chock-full of tax havens and trusts, two of the world's most important inequality-boosting financial technologies. STEP's meteoric rise has accompanied a profound change in the wealth-management industry too, from an era when managers would stress solidity, reliability, trustworthiness, caution and loyalty, towards a more fast-paced Anglo-Saxon ethic, with an emphasis on speed and nimbleness and the chutzpah and derring-do to find pathways around the spirit of the law without actually crossing the line. Whereas bankers compete to grow their clients' assets and see legal compliance as a nuisance, wealth managers tend to focus on protecting wealth and their clients' reputations, which makes compliance more important.[10]

A fairly straightforward family wealth-management structure might involve a trust in one offshore jurisdiction with trustees somewhere else, a trust protector located in another, beneficiaries in other places again, and the original grantor of assets hopping around from one country to another. The trust might own a range of shell companies, maybe also scattered across several offshore and onshore jurisdictions; each company may have directors in more places; and the assets themselves may be in yet another collection of places, typically where the trust's grantors, beneficiaries and asset-enjoyers like to relax, go shopping or play. For citizens of the Commonwealth, the latter typically means London and New York; for Latin Americans it usually means Miami, Houston or New York; and for Francophone Africans it is more likely to be Paris and New York.

This is a fast-growing profession, expanding much faster than the global economy. By 2017, according to Credit Suisse, 36 million people could call themselves HNWIs, high net worth individuals, with assets each worth more than $1 million; these people make up the top 0.7 per cent of the world's population. HNWI numbers have been growing six times faster than the population as a whole, and in 2017 this group collectively held over $129 trillion in wealth, nearly half the world total. A good chunk of that is offshore, a good chunk is in trusts, and most is in both.

But wealth managers mostly don't work for these people, who are merely rich. Instead, they serve the 1.6 million worth over $10 million each, especially the ultra-HNWIs – those 150,000-odd people worth $50 million or more, a number that has been soaring by 10 per cent a year, helped along by financialisation, tax havens, mergers, technology and the rise of supranational criminal organisations. And these numbers are certainly underestimates, because national accounts can't usually penetrate trusts, tax havens and other mechanisms which disassociate assets from mainstream nation states, thus making it hard to pin down the true wealth of the super-wealthy.[11] And of course with trusts, if a grantor has given assets away, and beneficiaries haven't received them, they sit in a kind of ownerless limbo. So most statistics seriously understate the scale of the problem because of those missing trillions – which are linked to the world's super-wealthy but not actually owned by them.

At the heart of this world there's the same process of 'competition' going on, which I've returned to several times, in which jurisdictions constantly try to outdo each other with laws that are ever more helpful for billionaires and by implication ever more harmful to the other citizens of the countries they live in. Adam Hofri-Winogradow, a lecturer at the Hebrew University in Jerusalem, says this race to the bottom is leading to, among other things, 'stripping of the trust' – legal provisions supposed to protect society from the most egregious forms of trust and asset-protection mechanisms are steadily being whittled away.[12] This race is as fierce inside the United States as anywhere else. For example, US states are abandoning the long-standing rule against perpetuities – a bedrock of US trust legislation designed to prevent the creation of permanent wealth dynasties by making it unlawful to, say, leave your wealth to your great-great-great-grandchildren. Delaware, an especially roguish tax haven inside the United States, got the race going with aggressive new legislation in 1995, and within twenty years more than half US states had followed suit, abandoning or curbing the rule. (I say curbing advisedly – states like Alaska, Colorado, Utah and Wyoming now limit the life of a trust to 1,000 years.) It's a snowball effect: perpetual dynasty trusts can now pass wealth down family bloodlines for ever, free of taxes and effective scrutiny.

People without a lot of money might wonder why someone with £5 million, or £100 million, feels so strongly that they need more. It's a good question because the wealthy often don't seem to reap much benefit in terms of happiness and often pay a high price for their affluence. Nevertheless, it does seem that the more money people have, the further they will go to protect it. The private equity boss Guy Hands, for instance, said in 2010 that for tax reasons he had 'never visited' his school-age children in the UK, after he left Kent for tax exile in Guernsey (if you are in the UK for more than 183 days in a tax year, you fall into the tax net; presumably Hands reserved his days in the UK for work). 'I do not visit my parents in the United Kingdom,' he added, 'and would not do so except in an emergency.'

Studies suggest that wealth doesn't necessarily make people happier, and the reverse can be true, particularly when that wealth is inherited rather than earned. One 2010 study by the Israeli-American psychologist Daniel Hahneman and the British-American economist Angus Deaton found that happiness increases with income – but only up to around $75,000 per year, after which the rise stops. A study of 4,000 dollar millionaires from 2018 concluded that people with wealth above $8 million were happier than millionaires with less wealth – but only very marginally so, and only when that wealth wasn't inherited.[13] Over half of the respondents said that to become happy they would need to increase their wealth by 500–1,000 per cent. And even attaining that summit wouldn't necessarily help; when there's competition between family members to access a fixed pot of inherited money, it automatically pits them against each other. And money distances people from their friends too; because so many of those they meet are trying to wheedle or scam something out of them, they begin to get paranoid about everyone's motives.

Charles Davidson, a Washington DC-based publisher who inherited family wealth from a French oil and engineering fortune, has seen money destroy families. 'In my experience,' he says, 'wealth usually does hurt.' He has been told by wealth managers that most of the rich people they deal with are burdened by their money. The fact that they generally don't need to work to make ends meet is a big problem, and there is also often perceived illegitimacy to inherited wealth. 'Here in the US it's socially unacceptable to live from inherited wealth; everyone is supposed to be self-made,' he told me – although some are shameless about inheriting money, like Donald Trump's children, and it can be easier in places like Europe, where cultural codes and intermarriage between wealthy families has legitimised the passing down of capital from generation to generation. But even among wealthy European families, Davidson says, you only really hear about the success stories. 'You don't hear about the people whose lives have been trashed by this. This is not fuel for self-esteem.'

STEP has a whole Contentious Trusts and Estates division to deal with intra-family conflicts, and one STEP Journal article selling Bahamas-based offshore trust services to 'protect family wealth through the generations' explained that the 'enemy within needs to be considered. Putting it bluntly: how can you stop the family from pushing the self-destruct button?'[14]

Davidson points to a problem specific to trusts: that they allow patriarchs to control their families' finances from beyond the grave. The beneficiaries must sit around waiting for their wealth to be doled out by trustees, bit by bit, so they don't even have the psychological responsibility for that wealth; they are permanent supplicants. 'Given the choice, I would rather not have been born wealthy, but I never think of giving it up,' the late Duke of Westminster said. 'I can't sell. It doesn't belong to me.' When he died in 2016, the trusts and associated schemes that protected his wealth from tax reportedly cost the British public around £3 billion in inheritance taxes.

All these problems can be compounded when inherited fortunes were obtained or have been hidden using nefarious, criminal or objectionable means – which is all too common. When someone hacked the phone of a daughter of Donald Trump's adviser Paul Manafort, the leaked details revealed deep unease. Their father had 'no moral or legal compass', one sister wrote to another. 'That money we have is blood money.' (At the time of writing, Manafort is due to go on trial, facing charges including money laundering, bank fraud, obstruction of justice, and failing to register foreign lobbying work. He has pleaded not guilty to the charges.) And there seems to be a general spirit of heightened lawlessness suffusing the world of wealth. Quantifying this is tough, but a 2017 study of Scandinavia found that tax evasion rates, which stood at around 3 per cent for the general population, rose to 25–30 per cent for the richest 0.01 per cent. In less egalitarian countries it may well be higher: a study of Credit Suisse by the US Senate found that 85–95 per cent of accounts they looked at were not declared to their tax authorities.[15]

Extreme wealth also seems to generate unusual cruelty or vindictiveness. Traders in the City of London or Wall Street like to speak in violent terms: successful deals are 'rape and pillage' or 'slash and burn'. Greg Smith, a former Goldman Sachs partner who published an open letter to the *New York Times* outlining his company's culture, said 'it makes me ill how callously people talk about ripping their clients off'. Some of the strategies the super-rich adopt and the policies they advocate generate tiny rewards for them but astonishing pain for others. One of Donald Trump's proposed tax-cut packages in 2017 was projected to boost the average annual incomes of the wealthiest by just 2 per cent, while causing, among other human catastrophes, an estimated 200,000 preventable deaths.[16] Which brings us back to asking: where do these attitudes come from? And in the many cases where wealth brings unhappiness, what is it all for?

There are many answers. The journalist Alex Cuadros remembers getting an insight into one in 2012, a few days before of the publication of the Bloomberg Billionaires Index, to which he had contributed. He got a call from one of the press people working for Eike Batista, a Brazilian energy and logistics magnate. They'd already sent through a detailed list of Batista's assets, including photos of his Gulfstream and Embraer jets, his $42 million Pershing yacht, the *Spirit of Brazil VII*, and even a Mercedes-Benz McLaren sports car parked in the living room of his mansion. Batista's people had heard that Bloomberg was about to judge him the world's tenth-richest man, worth $30 billion.

This wasn't enough, the PR man said, then patched through Batista himself.

Bloomberg was underestimating the value of one of his gold mines, Batista fumed. His business empire was generating more and more cash, running 'like Usain Bolt', and when the next set of numbers came out, he promised, Bloomberg would look 'very foolish. I'm going to tweet it, actually.' Batista went on for a while, getting so excited that he started tripping over his words. Media reports had recently revealed that at a secretive meeting of Latin American billionaires and their heirs Batista had called out from the stage to the Mexican billionaire Carlos Slim, then the world's richest man, *'Te voy a pasar!'* (I am going to overtake you!) As people get richer, they increasingly define themselves by their wealth, and this intensifies their desperation to get their hands on ever more of it, to be seen by their peers to be doing so, and to be seen to be richer than them.[17]

Batista gave another reason, or self-justification, for his pursuit of extreme wealth, which connects to the competitiveness agenda and the finance curse. His money was productive capital helping Brazil move forward, he said. He liked to picture the lives of his workers: where they lived, what they ate, their children at school, happy faces around the dinner table – the self-image of the billionaire as wealth creator, job creator. 'Brazilians have always admired the American dream,' he said. 'What is happening in Brazil is the Brazilian dream, and I am the example.' He peppered his rant with the word 'honest' – a counter to the widespread suspicion in Brazil that the super-wealthy are all *malandros*, who get rich through unfair or dirty or criminal means.

The heroic, honest, wealth-creator meme that Veblen gave such short shrift to is indispensable for such people. It implies that whatever improves the fortunes of the business or the billionaire – including favourable tax treatment or smashing workers' rights – ultimately advances the fortunes of the nation as a whole in some sort of great global race. 'I want my country to compete openly with the international companies,' Batista said, confusing two very different forms of competition. 'It's Brazil's time to be number one.'

The finance curse analysis will be anathema to many billionaires because it transforms them from wealth creators to wealth extractors, no longer advancing the patriotic cause of their nations, but potentially dragging them backwards. If you look at the Bloomberg

Billionaires Index, nearly all of those at the top are wealth extractors and more specifically monopolists, whose corporate and sometimes personal financial affairs are typically spread across tax havens. At the top of the 2018 list sits Jeff Bezos, the head of Amazon, the everything-monopoly. Next comes Bill Gates, who created the Windows quasi-monopoly, followed by Warren Buffett, the port-folio monopolist who openly admits that he only tends to invest in businesses that have little competition. There's Mark Zuckerberg, the social network monopolist of Facebook, in fifth position, and Mexico's uber-monopolist Carlos Slim, now pushed down to seventh place by the new giants of technology. All these people have made their fortunes as a result of the evisceration or lack of anti-monopoly laws or enforcement, the rise of offshore finance, the financialisation of Western and other economies and the general retreat of government.

And here lies another reason, or justification, for the relentless and almost thoughtless pursuit of wealth: the heroic myth of the wealth creator is tied up intimately with a libertarian, anti-government, anti-society ideology which pervades tax havens, the world of global finance, upper income brackets and especially the super-rich.[18] Spend time talking to people offshore, in parts of the City of London or in the world of trusts and wealth management, and you'll crash into these attitudes again and again. Government is 'a self-seeking flea on the backs of the more productive people of this world', opined Matt Ridley, the wealthy old-Etonian son of the 4th Viscount Ridley. 'Governments do not run countries; they parasitise them.' Not long after he said this, the bank that he was chairman of, Northern Rock, collapsed and needed a huge government bailout.

I got a forceful verbal blast of these attitudes – typical of what I have encountered in tax haven after haven – from Adolfo Linares, a prominent Panamanian lawyer, who vented to me in a bar in Panama in 2016. High-tax countries like France or Germany were a 'tax hells', he said. The problem was not tax evasion by the rich, but overspending by government. I repeatedly asked Linares, who declared himself 'a proud member of STEP', about a number of near-empty residential skyscrapers in Panama, whose apartments are almost all dark at night, and which anyone you talk to in Panama City will tell you are substantially owned by big players in the Colombian drugs industry. Each time he angrily demanded why I wanted to know this, then finally relented, saying that 'our only tragedy is to be between the largest exporter and producer of drugs, and the largest consumer. That is our curse.' Which is a fair comment, but only up to a point: Panama deliberately courts dirty money. The OECD, a group of rich countries that oversees international systems to boost transparency in global finance and crack down on tax havens, was 'infested with socialists', he continued, and its initiatives represented 'tax imperialism, fiscal predation – in order to support welfare states that are collapsing under their own bureaucratic weight'. (The notion that welfare systems might be collapsing due to tax dodging or wealth extraction by the rich didn't seem to occur to him.) Offshore havens, by contrast, offered freedom. 'My funds are mine, only mine,' he continued. 'I believe in freedom as the most important thing in life.'

And it is remarkable how much freedom from the law money can buy. Brooke Harrington, a researcher who took a STEP management qualification in order to study private wealth, remembers a wealth manager telling her about when she flew out of Zurich airport with her boss to meet a client outside Europe. On the way she realised she'd left her passport at home but her boss told her not to worry, and sure enough they were waved through customs both in and out of Zurich and at the other end, where there was a limousine waiting to take them straight to the meeting. 'The CEO was right,' the wealth manager said. 'These people, our wealthiest clients, are above the law.' In 2005 Arkady Gaydamak, a billionaire Moscow-based financier and middleman, told me a similar story when I asked if he had visited France, Britain or the US, even though he was under an international arrest warrant. He would not confirm or deny reports that he had travelled to the UK, but added, 'Have you watched the movies? Don't you think I am able to go where I want to?'[19] Harrington remembers an instance of this mentality on her STEP training course, when learning how trusts can be used to shield assets from legitimate creditors. 'People can get sued and lose or incur debts they can't cover, but if their assets are in a Cook Islands trust, they can say, "Meh, I don't feel like paying. Come and get me,"' she explained.

Tax havens, trusts and the wealth management industry are about so much more than tax; they are all useful for managing the complexity of families' financial affairs. But if there is one theme that unites them, it is the pursuit of ways around the law or, in the case of criminal activity, straight through it.

Trusts and tax havens have created one set of rules for the rich and powerful, another set for the rest of us, and pose evident dangers for our democracies. Eva Joly, the Norwegian-born crusading French investigative magistrate who broke open the Elf Affair, Europe's biggest corruption investigation since the Second World War, explained how the real money is so often not created *in* countries, but extracted *between* them, in an elsewhere land, offshore, nowhere, where the rules fall away. 'Laws are made inside states. Money flows across borders,' she wrote. 'The magistrates are like sheriffs in the spaghetti westerns who watch the bandits celebrate on the other side of the Rio Grande. They taunt us, and there is nothing we can do.'

During Joly's investigations a friend introduced her to a man called Franz, who took her aside one evening. 'Madame, 98 per cent of felonies can be judged, but 2 per cent cannot. These are the state secrets. There are many powerful interests around you. Beware: the state secrets have their guardians, and they are not tender. Be reasonable.' Joly got armed police protection and a Kevlar jacket. 'I felt like I was penetrating into an unknown world, with its own laws.' A card was stuck to her office door, with a list of all the French magistrates killed since the Second World War. All the names were crossed out except hers. 'I have seen so many resemblances, in France and abroad, between the corruption of the state and all the mafias. The same networks, the same henchmen, the same banks, the same marble villas,' she wrote. 'We think crime lurks in the shadows of our societies. But we find it linked intimately to our great companies and to our most honourable politicians.'

Offshore, crime, money and politics aren't an aberration of the system; they are the system.

The law-escaping super-rich have their own reasons and justifications for the pursuit of ever more wealth, but how do wealth managers, in a world of rising inequality and oligarchy in many countries, justify helping billionaires to escape the rule of law, often hurting other parts of the societies where they themselves operate and the democracies they are part of? Though these people can often make a very good living out of it, unless they marry their clients they don't get super-rich themselves; their salaries, even those of very good ones, are usually some way below that of senior bankers.

Looking after the fortunes of very wealthy people is 'a very personal thing', said Pierre Delalande, a French wealth and advisory manager. 'The adminstrator is like a confidant, a family physician who is unaware of practically none of the fortunes and misfortunes of the family group.'[20] Wealth managers' motivations overlap with, but often differ from, those of their clients. Many have tricks for dealing with the ethical grey zone they operate in. Some love the technical challenges; an American wealth manager said he relished the 'intellectual challenge of playing cat and mouse with tax authorities around the world'.

However, since the profession also has a touchy-feely side, involving taking the best possible care of clients and their families, antisocial views aren't always as strong as they are among their charges. Harrington reckoned that only 20–25 per cent of the wealth managers she interviewed had 'really hardcore neoliberal attitudes' (like that of Panama's Adolfo Linares), in which 'socialists' lurk under every bed and where the world's ills stem from the grasping hands of high-tax nations. But they were plentiful enough – people who seemed 'completely unreflective about what they were saying. I don't think they realise how outrageous some of the statements are.' Those wealth managers who have some moral backbone simply cope, as a former Bahamas private banker once told me, by 'managing not to check in with your conscience' and clinging to the idea that you were at least helping *someone* – someone you know, and their damaged, vulnerable, families.

What about the tax havens themselves then? Is there much in it for them, helping the super-wealthy shake their own nations' laws and taxes from their shoulders? Not really. Where there are local benefits they are generally much smaller than might be supposed, and tiny when compared to the damage inflicted on other countries. The Cayman Islands, for instance, does manage to chip off tiny fractions of the trillions that wheel through the British semi-colony, but the lion's share is creamed off by transient white expatriates. South Dakota, an aggressive player in the US trusts game, earns 0.06 per cent of its state tax revenues and sees just 0.02 per cent of its workforce employed in this business, while helping some of the United States' richest families: the Pritzkers, heirs to the Wrigley chewing-gum fortune; the

Carlsons, owners of the Radisson hotel chain; and the hedge fund giant John Nash, shelter assets from the normal rules and laws that apply to ordinary Americans.[21] Around half this business is run out of a slightly down-at-heel two-storey building in Sioux Falls. All things considered, South Dakota, let alone the United States, may well be incurring a net financial loss.

'Nobody is winning in a lot of these situations,' says Charles Davidson, a wealthy US publisher. 'Lawyers want to lock this up so they can continue to feed off it, colluding against the interests of the client. Though I'd call them the victim.' It might be more accurate to describe wealth management as the unhappiness industry. Yet the super-rich, for all their sadness, have nothing to complain about when compared to the multitudes of victims who are at the receiving end of the many mechanisms of financial wealth extraction.

9

Private Equity

In a scrappy suburb in a town in middle England there's a low-rise building that houses the regional HQ of Careline Homecare Limited, a private firm owned by a private equity company. The local authority pays these companies to send carers out to the homes of elderly and vulnerable people to help feed or bathe them, shop for them, give them their medication, do their laundry or clean up after them and open windows to let the fresh air in. The council doesn't charge those who can't afford to pay, but patients who have enough assets incur fees. Most houses in the area sell for prices that wouldn't buy attic space in parts of London, so many patients here are council-funded.

The story of Careline, its patients and workers, is not an especially anguished tale by the standards of many that operate in this sector, and the firm that owns it also seems less aggressive than many other private equity players. Yet in my view it still illustrates clearly the dangers that the private equity model poses to our economies and societies.

Careline looks unremarkable from the outside, but if you burrow into the company's accounts, you don't have to have an awful lot of accounting expertise to see that what is happening here is pure financialisation: the injection of financial techniques, and especially the use of debt, to obtain wealth from a cash-strapped, government-funded system. At the time of writing Careline Homecare was owned by City & County Healthcare Group Limited. This, in turn, is owned by City & County Healthcare Holdings Limited, which is owned by C&C Bidco Ltd, which is owned by C&C Holdco Ltd, which is owned by C&C Midco Ltd, which is owned by C&C Topco Ltd. That's a seven-storey-high corporate tower already.

Up at the level of C&C Topco, things get murkier. In 2018 it listed twenty-four individuals as part-owners, alongside a bunch of funds with similar names, such as Graphite Capital Partners VIII A LP, Graphite Capital Partners VIII Top Up Fund A LP, and several others. Now who owns *these* creatures? Well, documents for Graphite Capital Partners VIII Top Up Fund A LP list a statement at the UK corporate registry signed 'for and on behalf of Graphite Capital General Partner VII LLP as General Partner of Graphite Capital Partners VIII (Guernsey) LP.'[1] Follow that 'VII LLP' upwards, and you come to an address on hyper-exclusive Berkeley Square in Mayfair, which is the headquarters of a private equity outfit called Graphite Capital. In its time Graphite Capital has owned or co-owned the Japanese-food chain Wagamama, the stationers Paperchase, the exclusive Groucho Club in London, the Golden Tulip chain of budget hotels, along with fashion and footwear firms, makers of diving gases, companies running dental payment plans, distributors of car tyres and City & County Healthcare, the owner of Careline.

One of the easiest ways to spot financialisation at work is to look at the kind of language investors like Graphite Capital use. The Graphite Capital website enthuses that the health and care 'market' enjoys 'favourable demographics' and that efficient firms 'can quickly gain market share'. Over 600,000 people work in home care in the UK, which is different from the similar-sounding care-home sector: with home care, patients stay at home, with care homes, they go into special residences staffed by carers. Around 900,000 people, mostly the over-sixty-fives, receive home care in the UK and around $5 billion is spent annually on this, mostly paid for out of the budgets of health trusts or local councils. Well over 80 per cent of this $5 billion is routed through private sector players including Careline.[2] The phrase 'favourable demographics' means that Britain's population is ageing, and ever more millions of people will need care, which is likely to mean more council money sloshing around.

Recent council budget cuts have hit services like this disproportionately, which means more suffering and need – which, for private equity firms, also means opportunity in the care sector. 'They can see the natural potential,' said Arnold Whitman, a private equity official who helped found a venture capital firm 'focused on the intersection of innovation and ageing'. Add in the role of technology in 'enhancing' home care, he said, 'and the sector only looks more attractive'. Private equity firms talk of 'smart bets' in this sector – buying care companies cheaply, 'unlocking value' by 'sweating the asset', followed by a successful 'exit strategy', where they sell up for a profit. They enthuse about 'dry powder' – a military term that once meant ready-to-use gunpowder but which today represents cash that investors have committed to their pool of investable capital but which hasn't yet been spent. Graphite Capital and its companies boast of seeking 'strong organic growth' and 'a move up the acuity curve in the provision of more complex care requirements'. If you find it unsettling to read this language describing a system to care for, well, perhaps your grandmother, you're not alone.

When I visited Careline in August 2017 there was nothing to indicate any connection with Graphite Capital, and a friendly woman taking a cigarette break by the front door told me nobody would have time to answer my questions that day. So instead I tracked down two long-standing employees. Jacqui[3] agreed to meet me in a coffee shop a few miles away. She struck me as the kind of carer I'd like when I grow old: a cheerful, unflappable, no-nonsense, hard-working tower of strength. She was officially earning £8.20 per hour, typically visiting twenty-five 'clients' a day on a shift which, with all the toing and froing, took her about twelve hours. 'So you might have someone with dementia,' she said. 'We medicate and make sure they eat. They'll tell you they've eaten, and they might think they have, but you have to be aware that they actually have. You get to know their fridge and cupboards.' She had been issued with two uniforms, so she washes one each day. It's a tough job, but she said she was driven to work hard by a love for her clients. 'You bond with certain people. A lot of times I take their problems home with me, I stay up all night worrying about them: that they will fall out of bed and there'll be nobody else there.' Her manager at Careline was tough but she got on with her 'because I do the job properly'.

Jacqui said her partner earns decent money and their kids have left home, so they aren't on the bread line. 'I'm not bothered about money,' she said, throwing her hands up. 'I haven't got time to think about stuff like that. I'm paid, and that's that. We don't drink, but I do smoke, which is extortionate. I couldn't survive on my own with the wage I get.' A committed Labour voter and a Remainer, Jacqui had no clue who owned Careline, though she had noticed a series of bumpy changes in ownership over the years. One, she said, was when an independent businessman 'had to sell us [her and her co-workers] as a package'.

It is hardly surprising that Jacqui did not know who owned Careline, given the complexity of its corporate structure and how very far her world is from its owners' in Mayfair. But the complexity and the separateness are integral parts of the private equity business model, which is itself an important element of the finance curse.

The basic idea of private equity is that the owners of a firm invite outside investors to contribute money to a pool of capital they've set up. The firm then invests this pooled money on buying up, or making large, concentrated bets on, another company – a chain of pizza restaurants, say. They borrow a lot more money, shake up the company and then hopefully sell it on for a profit. The big shots who run the private equity firm, the outsiders who invest alongside them and the financiers who lend to them then share out any gains from the pool, according to pre-arranged rules.

The heroic story that private equity officials like to tell is one where they take sickly, tottering firms, throw out the lazy bums in charge, make painful choices and re-engineer the companies into healthy, roaring new engines of capitalism, making everyone rich in the process. Investors call both private equity and hedge funds alternative investments, but the two differ from each other, mainly because of what they invest in. With hedge funds it's generally shorter-term stuff, flitting in and out of bonds, derivatives, commodities, shares or exotic debt instruments, betting on price differentials across markets and changes over time, sometimes selling only days or even microseconds after buying. Private equity, by contrast, tends to get involved in the heavy lifting of taking control of and restructuring companies wholesale, in processes that can take years. In both cases the titans running the show take annual fees, typically 2 per cent of the value invested, plus a cut, say 20 per cent, of any profits, before returning the rest of the pool to the outside investors (this basic formula is sometimes known as 2 and 20). A private equity firm isn't listed on a public stock exchange (which is why it is private), and this frees managers from short-term shareholder pressures to show high performance every quarter-year. That's the heroic story, at any rate, and as with most areas of finance there's a solid kernel of useful stuff in what private equity does. But behind this facade there's a much darker story.

There's certainly nothing wrong in principle with private-sector firms running care homes; a husband-and-wife team, for example, may be able to provide a better and more personalised service for forty patients than employees working directly for the council. The problem isn't the private *sector*; it's private *equity*, whose underlying business model is aggressive, financially engineered wealth extraction from as many stakeholders in a business as it can get its hands on. To borrow from the old Heineken commercials, private equity extracts from the parts that other companies can't reach. It represents perhaps the clearest example of financialisation at work in our economies.

The industry properly got going in the 1960s when Jerome Kohlberg Junior, a senior official at the US investment bank Bear Stearns, began urging his employers to stop merely advising companies and helping them raise money, and start buying them. And he proposed some interesting ways to juice up the profits. He persuaded the bank to set up a new division that would focus on buying up good, strong companies with healthy cash flows and then – here's the first trick – to get the companies it had acquired (called portfolio companies) to *themselves* borrow something like 90 per cent of the purchase price, then channel most if not all of this back to the new owner. Bear Stearns and its management could then take the profits from that portfolio company if things went well, and could also offset the interest payment costs on the new borrowing against the portfolio company's tax bill. But if the portfolio company went bankrupt Bear Stearns wasn't on the hook for its debts. That is because of the magic of 'limited liability' laws. If a limited liability company goes bust, the owners are only liable to lose as much money as they originally put in, but no more. So they make sure to put in as little of their own money as possible, and get others to put in the rest. It's a bit like if I set up a business with Joe Bloggs, give Joe little or no control and take the profits, but if the business goes bust I walk away and Joe shoulders the debts.

Why would the managers of a portfolio company accept such terms? The main reason is that the bank would sweeten the deal with appropriate 'incentive structures' for the bosses of the portfolio company, so they too can get rich. It's the other stakeholders of the portfolio company – like its employees and creditors – who are, like Joe Bloggs, on the hook for its debts. This 'Heads I win, tails you lose' formula – taking the profits while shifting losses onto other people – is another version of the age-old game of other people's money, or OPM, that I described in Chapter 7 in the context of the global financial crisis, and it is a generic recipe for reckless gambling. The more OPM Bear Stearns could get into the pool of capital, the more regular fees and profit shares they can then milk from the pool. And if they've a good story to tell and are plausible people with good references and backers, they will get their OPM.

This leveraged buyout (LBO) game, Kohlberg discovered, could be insanely profitable. So he left Bear Stearns in 1976 and with Henry Kravis, and Kravis's cousin George Roberts he set up a new company, Kolhberg Kravis Roberts, or KKR – the same company I mentioned in the Introduction, which now owns Trainline. This was the first proper private equity firm, though in those days they and the others that soon emerged were known as LBO firms. Yet these corporate raiders faced a problem: persuading bankers to lend them the funds they needed to make the game work. Fortunately for them, a new player had entered the scene, the investment bank Drexel Burnham Lambert, under the buccaneering junk bond king, Michael Milken. Drexel played a different OPM game: lending the money for LBO deals, it then sold the loans (which became known as junk bonds because of their riskiness) to other less clued-up players like insurance companies or dowdy savings and loan organisations, tempting them with high interest rates and persuading them that the reward was worth the risk. During the market upswing of the 'Roaring 1980s' there seemed to be a near-bottomless pit of optimistic investors willing to buy these junk bonds. LBO deals surged from $3 billion in 1981 to $74 billion by 1989. With fees often adding up to more than 6 per cent of a company's purchase price, Milken became the highest-paid financier in history.

However, in 1989 a US federal grand jury indicted Milken in the biggest ever criminal and racketeering action against a Wall Street figure. 'A serious criminal problem has infected Wall Street,' as the acting US attorney in Manhattan put it. LBOs came to a shuddering halt; debt markets dried up; market conditions changed, and swathes of heavily indebted companies acquired in leveraged buyout deals collapsed. But this was only a pause for breath. Though LBO had become almost a term of abuse, the titans were determined to try again, so they rebranded the sector with a fancy new name: private equity.[4]

At the same time a new intellectual saviour appeared, in the form of a Harvard Business School professor called Michael Jensen, who had trained at the University of Chicago and had some exciting new ideas about business strategy. Normal public companies – your BPs or your Tescos, say – are owned by a diverse group of shareholders, but run by a different group, their managers. These two groups' interests weren't necessarily aligned, Jensen argued in a couple of seminal papers in the *Harvard Business Review* in 1989 and 1990. Managers didn't have strong enough incentives to look after shareholders' money, and this led to what he called 'widespread waste and inefficiency'. He argued, first of all, that corporate America needed a new breed of superstar owner-managers in a financial 'market for corporate control' that would boost efficiency across the system. In pursuit of profits for themselves they would fight like tigers to buy bloated corporate has-beens and turn them into nimble, hyper-efficient profit machines. Second, he said, these firms should borrow heavily, because the 'discipline of debt' would make the owner-managers focus even more intensely on profits. Third, if you tied pay to performance, that would make those already laser-focused executives work even harder and focus even more fiercely on generating those profits. The general idea, explains Peter Morris, a veteran banker and commentator on private equity, was 'capitalism on steroids'.[5]

Jensen's ideas rest on the concept of shareholder value or, to be more accurate, shareholder primacy. This was a radical departure from previous eras, when corporations were run with many goals in mind. Peter Drucker's classic 1946 study, *The Concept of the Corporation*, argued that big business was 'America's representative social institution … its social function as a community is as important as its economic function as an efficient producer'. This was the corporate thinking that underpinned the high-growth Golden Age. Corporations didn't just create profits; they also produced good jobs, good products, taxes and healthy communities. Shareholders were just one among several key interest groups. This way of running companies was still the received wisdom at the end of the 1960s.

In 1970, however, Milton Friedman threw a firebomb into this consensus with a violent article in the *New York Times Magazine* entitled 'The Social Responsibility of Business Is to Increase its Profits'.[6] Business leaders had but one duty, he wrote: to their shareholders. Namby-pamby ideas like social responsibility, paying taxes, paying employees or setting safety standards higher than the minimum were, in his view, 'collectivist' and 'fundamentally subversive'. Business leaders who weren't nakedly pursuing profit alone were 'unwitting puppets of the intellectual forces that have been undermining the basis of a free society'. The money these wealth creators made, Friedman argued, would be reinvested somewhere else, and at the end of the day everyone would end up happy.

Friedman's freedom-laden arguments caught the zeitgeist and spread like wildfire. Chicago School ideas about efficient, beneficent markets were fanning out across America and the wider world. Soviet Union and Warsaw Pact forces had recently invaded Czechoslovakia to roll back moves towards liberalisation, injecting new urgency and legitimacy in the West towards the all-embracing word 'freedom'. When Jensen took up the baton, he elevated financiers to the apex of this new system for organising the economy, as 'rainmakers [who] draw from the people and institutions around them the dollars that are needed to build the nation's factories'. All this combined to spark profound changes that helped, as one account put it, 'Wall Street to replace the management-controlled firm with the finance-controlled firm'. A similar thing happened in Britain, but with a time lag: buyouts in the UK only really took off in the early 1990s.

When the Harvard Business School embraced Jensen, explains Duff McDonald, it transformed itself from an institution seeking to create a body of enlightened business people into a cheerleader for Wall Street. 'They basically threw in the towel and said, "Fuck it, let's go for the money."' Not coincidentally their fundraising improved spectacularly. Clayton Christensen, a dissenting professor at the school who specialises in business innovation, explains how destructive the new thinking has been. 'The professors of finance in the main business schools, the professors of economics have over the last forty years created a church. I call it the New Church of Finance. The doctrines are taught with the same force as the Catholic Church preaches their catechism.'[7] He describes a zealotry of financial ratios or fractions, generating an obsession with maximising financial returns to capital.

There are a number of these ratios: return on net assets (RONA), internal rate of return (IRR), return on invested capital (ROIC), earnings per share (EPS) and a few others. They are, in essence, profits or income divided by capital or assets employed, and they bind businesses into insanely powerful mathematics. Take any ratio or fraction. You can boost a fraction in two ways. You can either increase the numerator, which here represents profits or earnings or returns – what you get out. Or you can reduce the denominator, which is what you put in, usually something like investment. Often the easiest way to increase the ratio is to shrink the denominator. So a firm that earns £20 million for an investment of £200 million returns a ratio of 1:10 so is only half as successful by this financial yardstick as one that earns £2 million for an investment of £10 million for a ratio of 1:5. If you reduce your net assets to zero then RONA (Return On Net Assets) will give you infinite returns. Which is better for your economy: a firm that employs 5,000 people and invests a lot but makes small profits, or a private equity firm that borrows heavily and makes ten times the profits, while only employing a hundred people?

'As long as they can get more capital out than they put in, and the faster they can get it out, the higher the IRR,' Christensen said. 'So they invest in stripping things.' These ratios airbrush out and even work against the all-important world of employment, innovation, supply chains and livelihoods inside the company. Instead, these things are just data points in the financial market for corporate control. Such ratios help drive financialisation and the finance curse, as companies cut investment or outsource activities in order to get capital-intensive factories off their balance sheets. They also borrow more, reducing the capital they invest themselves. Any competent undergraduate economist could unpick Friedman's or Jensen's arguments, and many have. The biggest problem comes from the difference between operational engineering – fixing up badly run companies to create wealth – and financial engineering – good old wealth extraction. Private equity sometimes does both, often simultaneously, but it pretty much *always* does the second part. It is incentivised to do so, and it has a lavish smorgasbord of tricks to achieve this.[8]

The main event is borrowing, or debt, which provides a range of benefits – none of which focus managers' minds on building better and longer-lasting companies. The first joy of debt is that it magnifies returns. To take a simplified example, imagine you spend £100,000 of your own money to buy a house and its value rises by £20,000. You've increased your capital by 20 per cent. But if you instead borrow £900,000 to add to your £100,000 and buy ten such houses, which each rise in value by £20,000, you can sell the lot for £1.2 million, pay back the £900,000 loan and keep £300,000. You've tripled your money. This is the principle of leverage.

But there is a snag: if house prices fall, the debt magnifies your losses. Private equity titans engineer that risk away with the next trick, the one that Kohlberg learned. They don't take on the debts themselves, but instead load them onto the shoulders of the companies they buy. If the bet goes badly it's the company's other stakeholders – employees, suppliers and lenders – who take the hit. So imagine you put down £100,000 of your own money and take out a £900,000 loan from the bank to buy those same ten houses, then rent them out, having incorporated the whole shebang in a limited liability company. Now it is the business, not you, that is legally required to repay the loan, and your liability is limited to the amount of money you've invested yourself – in this case £100,000. If the business goes bankrupt then it's the bankers who are out of pocket, and you can walk away scot-free. With a profit, even.

But wait! You, the investor, have still lost your original £100,000.

Not necessarily. Let's say that after you set up the house business, you take short cuts on repairs and insurance costs. You do cheap paint jobs, mow the lawns and produce some glossy, doctored photos. You now raise the rents by 30 per cent, freeing up regular new cash flows. Investors will lend multiples of annual cash flows, so if you can produce an additional £30,000 a year in rental income, you might be able to borrow another £250,000, say, maybe even £350,000 if house prices and rental rates are generally rising. Next, you tell the house business to funnel all this back to you in a special dividend – you have no pesky shareholders to answer to so you can make it do what you damn well like. You have now got your full £100,000 back, and then some.

But now the economy tanks and a couple of tenants lose their jobs and fall behind on rent. The over-indebted house business goes bust. You've lost your original £100,000, but since the business is a limited liability company your liability is limited to what you've injected, that £100,000. Beyond that, the debts are on other people's shoulders: the bankers or investors, who will salvage what they can. You lost £100,000 but got that £350,000 special dividend, so you've still trousered £250,000 overall. And if you set up the company in the Caymans, you might be able to escape tax on that too.

So from this slash-and-burn operation, you've more than doubled your money! And if you can find more people crazy enough to lend to you, you can then take that £250,000 to repeat the trick, only on a larger scale, and those crazy people aren't hard to find. They aren't crazy either, because there is a logic to what they do.

There are oceans of global hot money out there, trillions of it, the product of immense changes in the global economy – capital looted out of poor countries, vast Chinese savings spilling over into world markets and new credit constantly created out of thin air by private banks and Western central banks. This money is looking for some- where, anywhere to invest – anywhere offering higher rates of return than low-interest German government bonds. And the lenders – maybe hedge funds or other specialist lenders – can get the debts off *their* backs via the great financial pass-the-parcel of securitisation, packaging these income-generating loans up into new income-generating collat- eralised loan obligations (CLOs) and flogging them to other cash-rich investors. CLOs are now a $500 billion industry globally and growing fast, another powerful vested interest demanding ever more private equity deals and mergers, and ever more debt.

And here is the next delight: whoever in the financial system is finally holding the baby when things fall apart usually isn't personally on the hook either. The investment manager or hedge fund opera- tive or banker has probably already earned their bonus, so it's other people's money as far as the eye can see. The ultimate victim is the sucker at the very end of the chain – very likely your private pension fund, if you have one, which has invested heavily in this stuff.

So this is one of private equity's great games: buy up a company, shake out new cash flows, use those to borrow more, then funnel the borrow- ings back to the company's owners, hopefully in large enough sums to pay them back for the original purchase of the portfolio company. There are myriad ways to free up cash flows. The most obvious is to cut costs: slash employee numbers, cut wages, reduce pension entitle- ments, skimp on investment. The private equity mogul Wilbur Ross, who would later become Donald Trump's commerce secretary, did this after winning control of a big chunk of the US steel industry. In 2005 he walked out with a $4.5 billion gain, pretty much the same amount as steelworkers and retirees lost in health and pension plans.[9]

If your mind is repelled by the brazenness and simplicity of this extraction device you're not alone, but it is common. In 2005, for example, the private equity giants Texas Pacific Group (TPG) and Apax Partners of London launched Project Troy, a €1.4 billion buyout of TIM Hellas, Greece's third-largest mobile operator, then a healthy company. Within a year its new owners had jacked up the company's debt nearly twenty-fold from €166 million to over €3 billion, funnelling payments from this new borrowing to themselves via some complex tax-minimising securities and a chain of Hellas companies. Had the Goldilocks era continued, Hellas might have survived. 'It was a free ride that took advantage of buoyant markets,' a private equity official said. 'In 2006 the world was beautiful and we thought we could walk on water.' They tried to flip the company to another investor for a profit, but when that failed they ramped up their withdrawals, milking the underlying company like a cash machine and eventually selling the creaking, debt-laden shell to an Egyptian investor in 2007, who in turn moved the company's domicile from Luxembourg to London, where the firm's debts could be wiped out through more lenient British bankruptcy laws. When it all went into administration in 2009, the liquidators said the company had been 'systematically pillaged'.[10]

Another common extraction technique is the Opco-Propco shuffle. In these cases a private equity firm buys up a company with lots of real estate and divides it into two parts: a property company (PropCo) and a separate operating company (OpCo) to run the business. The PE firm now sells Propco, but instead of investing the sale proceeds in productive activities like investing to build a responsible business, it funnels them straight up to itself. In rising real estate markets this might pay for the whole deal – again, effectively allowing the buyer to get the company for free, risk-free. But the sale can be made still more lucrative by including long-term guarantees that the Opco will lease back the properties it just sold at high rental rates. The friendlier the guarantees, the more cash the buyer of Propco will pay and the bigger the special dividend to the private equity owners. And the more likely the company will go bust.

This happened with Britain's Southern Cross Healthcare as it passed through the hands of three private equity operators including the US giant Blackstone, which eventually cashed out in July 2006 by floating the company on the stock market. When the financial crisis hit, cash-poor local authorities started cutting payments to care home operators and Southern Cross could not service its rental guarantees. These were costing £250 million a year, rising at 2.5 per cent per year no matter what. In 2011 the company fell apart, and its care homes, with almost 30,000 elderly residents, were taken over by their landlords or sold to other operators.

The direct human costs of this aren't hard to find. Undercover BBC filming in 2011 showed searing scenes at Winterbourne View, a property in Bristol owned by a Jersey-based company, itself owned by Lydian Capital Partnership, a private equity company operating out of Geneva. Vulnerable residents were taunted and slapped; one staff member stood on the wrist of a whimpering resident lying under a chair, a second was dragged screaming from her bed, another was teased about a suicide attempt, and yet another poked repeatedly in the eye. One resident was forced into a shower fully dressed, then pushed outside, where she was shown lying down, shivering with cold. A former nurse said a trainer had told him that if a patient gave him any problems he was to 'kick them in the bollocks'. Low wages and poor working conditions, of course, mean low-quality staff, and in this case, in the word of a clinical psychologist who saw the footage, 'torture'. Lydian was getting an average £3,500 a week per patient. A source close to Lydian described it to the *Telegraph* as 'a consortium of investors, they are very much hands off. They are very rich and remote people.' After the documentary, six former staffers went to jail.[11]

And back to Careline.

To be clear, Careline's patients and workers are treated far better than at Winterbourne View. Jacqui said her day-to-day job was usually 'fine'. But another Careline carer – I'll call her Sally – described much longer hours, with what she claimed were far tougher conditions. She said she was sickened by the conditions she worked under but, like Jacqui, stuck with the job out of love for her patients and a lack of time to even think about alternatives. She described the same pattern of worry-fuelled sleepless nights that Jacqui did. 'You're literally with these people till they take their last breath,' she said. 'That is my job: to be with them until right at the end. You don't let them down. It's sad. It's awful when you lose somebody, but at the end of the day you think, *I allowed them to do what they wanted to do, and stay in their own home.*'

Sally has worked in care for over twenty years and has seen the job change dramatically. 'It was more like a befriending service back then,' she said. 'You were going in, making cups of tea, washing up, having a chat and going on to the next one. You'd get half an hour on each call. You'd get travelling time between calls.' So carers got paid for the time they spent travelling between patients – not the case today. At the time of writing, most workers at Careline are paid only from when they set foot inside a client's home until they leave, often just a few minutes later. So travelling between clients is generally unpaid (or 'incorporated' into their hourly rate per assignment according to Graphite Capital, who may make additional mileage payments for greater distance). Careline doesn't provide cars. 'It is unbelievable the things we do,' Sally continued. 'There's no care as such because you literally go as fast as possible. It is horrendous. Horrendous. I'm not a machine. I can't carry on like that for ever.'

If this is bad enough for the carers, it is worse for the patients. 'They want to be in the community, but they are prisoners in the community,' Sally said. 'These elderly people are really vulnerable; their only contact with a human being is with that person. It shouldn't be five minutes, give medication, and "Bye bye,"' she said. 'People with dementia with night frights, they need people stroking their arms when they cry.' Careline used to issue mobile phones, but they were discontinued. 'They cost too much. We're back to paper rotas. The managers used to work with you, side by side. Now it is money, money, money, money. That's all they're interested in. The companies are so big now, you're literally a number, and they're not bothered.' (Graphite Capital reject Sally's characterisation, saying they invest significant sums in improving care quality, standards and career development, and that local authorities and the official Care Quality Commission had rated over three-quarters of its branches 'good' and none inadequate. It also said that it was the commissioning authority – usually the Local Authority or the Clinical Commissioning Groups – that determines how much time is allowed for the delivery of care to a particular individual, not Careline itself.[12])

The director of public health at a nearby council said the system of home care and residential care 'is close to collapse'. Councils impoverished by cutbacks and austerity, she said, think they can save money (and curb the reputational risks associated with poor service) by outsourcing home care to companies touting low-cost 'solutions', but it is a false economy. With carers no longer having time to perform preventive work like getting the patients to exercise or basic sanitary tasks, the patients often end up in residential care or hospital, which is 'the worst place for them' – vastly more expensive, unsanitary, disabling and alienating. Many of the companies also cherry-pick easy, profitable patients and dump difficult, expensive ones back onto the public health system. A further 'huge' problem, the director added, is that carers themselves regularly become ill from stress and overwork, then need care themselves.

I obtained a copy of the roster of another home carer who was currently employed by Careline and whose name was blacked out. This roster detailed the schedule to which she was previously subject when employed by a different home-care company. It showed their shift beginning at 7.30 a.m. and contained stuff like the following. Each entry represents a visit to a patient, and the numbers in brackets are parts of an hour.

10.21 – 10.31 *(0.17)*	Personal Care & Medication
10.35 – 10.40 *(0.08)*	Personal Care
10.47 – 10.53 *(0.10)*	Food preparation
10.53 – 11.02 *(0.15)*	Food preparation[13]

Those parts would have been totted up and multiplied per hour, then paid, net of tax. The roster showed over 140 visits between around 7 a.m. on a Friday and 11 p.m. on Sunday, and on the first night allowed the carer a bit over two and a half hours' sleep between midnight and her next shift at 2.40 a.m., with no allowance made for her (I was told she couldn't afford a car) getting home and back, going to the loo, eating or even speaking to her family. Look carefully at the timing of the last two entries, which allowed *zero* minutes to get from one client to the next, to say goodbye, to key in a security code, to greet the client, to deal with any of the emotional or other unexpected problems that may have developed since the last visit.

In fact, nearly all of the entries on this rota allowed zero minutes. Wonder Woman couldn't fulfil this schedule, nor would a vulnerable old lady even want the Amazing Wonder Woman barging in at 3 a.m.

They refer to it as call cramming or call clipping. The patients get horribly short-changed, the carers get horribly exploited. If you were to take travel time into account, carers would be getting far below the minimum wage, below £4 an hour in the case of some firms, a lot less than teenagers working at Aldi or Lidl get. These are zero-hour contracts too, which means the employers can cut hours on a whim. (Graphite Capital said that it would not allow such an intense roster, that its zero-hours contracts mean workers can also choose how much work to take on, that its businesses are routinely inspected by HMRC to ensure it is above national minimum wage or living wage standards, and that in its most recent careline worker survey, the majority of respondents – 31 in total – stated that they felt enabled to provide a caring service.) The care workers indeed aren't forced to accept these shifts, but the circumstances of their lives can mean they often have little option but to accept them.

The contrast between the language of 'smart bets' and Graphite Capital's plan to 'move up the acuity curve' and the real world of Jacqui and Sally can be summed up in a word: financialisation.

If you probe the complex corporate pipelines descending from Graphite Capital to Careline, you'll find different flavours of debt being injected, at various levels, for different reasons.

Harry, a private equity official, explained the general logic of corporate complexity to me. The aim, he said, is to split companies and their cash flows into a spectrum, as with Careline's seven-plus-high stack of Midcos, Topcos, Holdcos and Bidcos, in order to achieve a couple of things. The first is to create niches to attract all the different kinds of specialist lenders out there, each with different risk appetites and sectoral preferences, and each looking for particular niches to lend or buy into, either at the level of whole companies or just a particular subsidiary. Alongside straight bank lending and equity finance there is senior and junior debt, mezzanine finance, preference shares, warrants, varieties of hybrid debt, and more. Different companies in this stack may be located in different places, including tax havens. It's a bit like cutting a ten-pound pizza into ten slices worth a pound each, then rearranging the toppings to suit customers' tastes better – this piece has lots of salami, that has olives and capers, that has olives and artichokes – so you can now sell each piece for £1.50 each. And the more people you can get to lend to you, the more OPM you have to play with, and the bigger the pool of money from which to extract fees. These lenders are parts of a financial superstructure sitting on Jacqui and Sally's shoulders, a bit like invisible hansom cab drivers urging or even whipping their horses to work faster, adding to the pressure made inevitable by council budget cuts. But unlike shareholder equity, where financial problems in the underlying businesses hit the shareholders, the debt that the company owes to these lenders is more implacable: pay up in full, now.

A second big reason for corporate complexity, and also the use of debt, brings that other large stakeholder into view: the government, the shambling, unloved, grouchy giant that invests in the roads, the courts, educating workers, the sewage pipes under their homes and office buildings, and other essential things that underpin all private equity profits. After it has picked up the human flotsam from the lacerated pension pots, the lay-offs, the burnt-out workers and other damage to community life, government is at least supposed to get a payback in the form of tax levied on corporate profits. But the private equity titans want a free ride here too. 'The key to this is getting the cash out at the end,' said Harry. Everyone tries to avoid what he called 'trapped cash' – cash that is hard to get out of a subsidiary without triggering tax – and banks and the Big Four accounting firms are on hand to help find the right pathways through the tax laws – and the more complexity, the better.

The March 2016 accounts for C&C Topco, the top level in that seven-high stack of companies which owns Careline (but is still underneath the private equity firm), show the basic pattern. Topco recorded a total turnover of £124 million for the year ending March 2016, mostly from fees it received from patients for providing home care services. Out of this, it paid some £94 million in wages and benefits for its 7,700 full- and part-time workers and managers, an average annual £12,000; the top-paid director got £306,000. That leaves around £30 million outstanding.

A series of deductions then whittles that down further before it can be called taxable profit. One of those deductions relates to debt. When you borrow, you can deduct the loan repayments from your paper profits as business costs, and this cuts your tax bill. You can borrow either from outsiders, such as banks, or from insiders – from other parts of your corporate empire, through shareholder loans which Graphite Capital provides from the pool of invested capital from outside investors. And here we find an odd thing. The bank loans, repaid to lenders outside the corporate group, have an interest rate of around 5 per cent annually, but the £85 million in shareholder loans, theoretically repaid to lenders inside the corporate group, carry a fixed interest rate of exactly 10 per cent, and in some cases an amazing 15 per cent. (I say 'theoretically', because often those repayments aren't actually repaid; they just get added to the loan total.)

Why is one rate double, or even triple, the other? Well, there are a couple of reasons. Loan repayments to outsiders are genuine costs to the overall business, so it's best to keep them as low as the market will bear. But shareholder loan interest payable by C&C Topco turn up as revenues owed to the lenders in another part of the Graphite Capital empire with no net economic cost or benefit to the group. But in tax terms it's different. The taxman generously allows at least part of this interest payable to be offset against Topco's tax bill. And as long as the interest is to be received in a place or in such a way that it isn't taxed (perhaps in a tax haven or in a tax-exempt body like a pension fund) then there is no tax bill. The trick is to tweak the interest rate as high as you dare, before the tax authorities start to think you are taking the piss and disallow it.

So out of Topco's £30 million income after salaries, we find a £12.7 million deduction for interest, plus £12 million in 2015, mainly to service these shareholder loans at those stonking interest rates of 10 and 15 per cent.[14] Shareholder loans are, in the words of accounting expert Adam Leaver of Sheffield University, 'the straw into the carton of Ribena, to get the juice out' – a way for the owners to get their trapped cash out past the unhappy taxman. These very high-interest loans have another benefit: by adding 10 to 15 per cent to the loan total each year they also rapidly accumulate the amount that this corporate structure owes to Graphite Capital, which they can realise when they sell it on or if it goes bankrupt.[15]

At the end of all the deductions we find that Topco paid £727,000 in taxes in 2015, but then received a tax rebate of £639,000 in 2016, resulting in a net £88,000 payment for the two years. That's equivalent to less than 0.6 per cent of earnings or 0.04 per cent of turnover. Graphite Capital said that the corporation tax benefit from the shareholder loans was 'modest' and that the low tax payments reflect low underlying profits – though the latter part of this doesn't exactly sit comfortably with what it says on its website, which is that its portfolio assets in the health and care sectors have generated healthy returns of 2.5 times what they have invested.[16] They did not comment about returns from Careline, but if it does yield similar returns, this would be an example of a private equity firm obtaining large profits from a system that is woefully short of cash, through substantial use of financial techniques.

Graphite Capital hasn't done anything remotely illegal here. This is all standard practice. And once all those barely taxed corporate profits make their way up the pipelines to the private equity owners, tax cuts introduced in 2000 to make Britain's tax system more 'competitive' help ensure they pay very little tax too.[17]

It's not only private equity firms that use debt to cut their tax bills, of course; it's common across the business world. But private equity gets an especially large helping of this cream because it tends to use much more debt. One study estimates that up to 40 per cent of the value of companies bought by private equity firms is down to these tax deductions on interest payments alone.

This stuff is usually legal, but is it legitimate? One of my favourite answers comes from Scottish comedian Frankie Boyle. 'If you're rich, don't look at it as tax avoidance,' he said. 'Look at it as a children's hospital buying you a pool table.' This isn't a frivolous comparison: effective tax subsidies to a single private equity firm have in the past exceeded the costs of building a major new hospital.[18] Max Lawson of Oxfam has sarcastically proposed the creation of a new currency, the nurse, with the hospital as the larger denomination. Imagine the headline, he says: 'MILLIONAIRE RITCHIE RICH USED SWISS ACCOUNT TO AVOID 20,000 NURSES OF TAX IN ONE YEAR.'

Private equity firms, and others like them, create giant Bidcos which hunt and bid for healthy firms that haven't yet been sufficiently financialised, then put them through the financial wringer. It's like a financial harvest. This is so profitable that it has become a large part of our economy. A private equity official compared the remarkable growth of his sector with a cancer: 'a good idea gone bad, like a normal healthy process that has grown wildly in ways that were never envisaged'. One of the most careful in-depth independent studies of private equity is a quietly devastating 2014 book, *Private Equity at*

Work, by US academics Aileen Appelbaum and Rosemary Batt. 'What is striking,' they found, 'is how little of the earnings of the PE funds depended on business strategy or improvements in operations.' Firms bought out by private equity tend to have been more productive and faster-growing than their peers before the buyouts; afterwards, jobs and earnings tended to fall, and significantly so.[19] The authors of a 2018 study published in *American Affairs*, surveying 390 deals worth $700 billion, said that 'most private equity firms are cutting long-term investments, not increasing them, resulting in slower growth, not faster growth. If PE firms are not growing businesses faster, investing more in growth, or gaining much operational efficiency, just what are they doing?' The answer is, generally leveraging up returns by taking on more debt.[20] Collectively, private equity firms add little of value, extract a great deal and have persuaded everyone that because they're so rich they must be wealth-creating geniuses. They aren't; they are wealth-extracting geniuses.

German leftists use the term *Heuschrecken* – locusts – to describe private equity firms, which is often apt. Tamara Mellon, founder of the Jimmy Choo luxury shoe company, which worked with private equity for a decade, said that in her experience private equity attracted 'vultures and parasites ... none of these private equity firms have actually put capital in the business for growth. They have been more of a burden.' More interestingly, she also said she had never met a woman in a senior private equity role. And this brings up a depressing contrast: while 80 per cent of the health and social care workforce in the UK are women, only 6 per cent of senior private equity officials are women. If you exclude investor relations, legal work, operations and human resources – the softer side of private equity – this falls to 3 per cent. Theresa Whitmarsh, executive director of the Washington State Investment Board, remembers a private equity official telling her that women simply aren't cut out for their kind of deal making because private equity is 'a blood sport'.[21]

All this is troubling enough. But the most tragic part of this sorry tale is still to come.

Many people are dimly aware of the predatory nature of private equity and hedge funds, but reconcile themselves to it with the idea that if there are losers having wealth taken out of their pockets, this is balanced by winners elsewhere. This is the old Chicago School myth of shareholder value, the quasi-religious belief held by many in the financial markets that if you focus on profits and profits alone, it all washes out in the end and everyone is happy. There are other justifications too. With home care, the problem isn't just the presence of wealth extractors perched atop the system, but also the fact that there isn't enough money in the system in the first place as a result of savage cuts to council budgets. Council bosses may make the calculation that if they're going to have to give a raw deal to people being cared for, it's better to outsource it to private sector actors so they take the blame. The answer to this is that the private *sector* may or may not do a good job; the problem is private *equity* and its business model, which is spreading across the UK's corporate landscape.

Yet even if we were to take Friedman or Jensen's advice as gospel, it turns out that private equity and hedge funds are hopeless at the one thing they are supposed to be good at: generating good returns for investors.

In 2005 the billionaire investor Warren Buffett offered $500,000 to any investor who could select at least five hedge funds that outperformed a simple fund tracking the S&P 500 index over ten years. A brave asset manager called Ted Seides accepted the challenge. He chose a funds of funds, which instead of investing directly invested in more than a hundred hedge funds, which in turn invested in the markets. The results are now in: a million dollars invested with Seides would have gained $220,000 in ten years, a 2 per cent annual return. The passive, boring index fund in the meantime gained $854,000 – over 6 per cent annually. Buffett would have done better pinning a list of popular stocks to a board, getting a chimpanzee and then incentivising it with peanuts to throw darts at the board. The law of averages means the stocks selected by the chimp with the darts would almost certainly have been closer to the bigger number, and because its fees were peanuts, probably above it.

So, you may ask: how come so many private equity players have got so stupendously rich, if they are collectively so rubbish at generating profits for investors? The answer is simple. The PE titans who run the mother ship – the general partners in the parlance – set the ground rules for who gets what, when and how. The GPs simply write the rules so they get their hands on nearly all of the profits before the limited partners – those hapless, trusting outsiders like your pension fund manager who pour their money into the pool of investable capital – get their cut.

But how do they get this past those supposedly sophisticated outside investors? Let's say a private equity firm buys a successful pharma company and generates huge internal profits, whether from creating an even better pharma company or from debt-fuelled looting. The GPs' first trick is the famous 2 and 20 formula: they take 2 per cent of the value of invested funds annually as management fees, plus the so-called carried interest, which is typically 20 per cent of any internal profits generated, though often only after the fund has attained a 'hurdle rate' of profit. That formula may sound reasonable, but in the real world the mathematics rips surprisingly large chunks of the profits away from the outside investors and channels them into the moguls' pockets, especially when the portfolio company fares badly.[22]

Below that exists another world of chicanery of hidden fees, usually at the level of the portfolio companies the PE firms buy. Let's say PE Capital, a private equity firm, buys up ABC, which owns lots of office buildings. PE then sends in its affiliate PE Properties to run, maintain and service those buildings, charging ABC exorbitant, complex and often hidden fees. Or PE Capital buys a real consultancy business, then uses it to provide consulting services to ABC and all the other companies in its portfolio, charging outrageous prices. Government regulations prevent a listed company or a mutual fund from pulling this kind of stunt, but private equity is lightly regulated so the titans get a free pass here. And the GPs make sure they have near-total control over what happens to the companies they buy, which means the outside LPs don't get a look-in. So they get the scraps.[23]

This is like Hollywood accounting, which David Prowse, the actor who played Darth Vader in *Return of the Jedi*, now understands well. 'I get these occasional letters from Lucasfilm saying that we regret to inform you that as *Return of the Jedi* has never gone into profit, we've got nothing to send you,' says Prowse, even though it is one of the highest-grossing films of all time. 'I don't want to look like I'm bitching about it [but] if there's a pot of gold somewhere ... I would like to see it.'[24] The ageing actor now runs a rather low-grade website flogging signed photos of Darth Vader for thirty-five pounds each. Hollywood accounting – milking assets before they hit the balance sheet – turns profits into losses, which eliminates those pesky royalty cheques and tax bills. In private equity inflated fees are often buried deep in 100-plus-page documents sent to investors. And PE funds are also often invested via structures such as blocker corporations in secrecy havens like the Caymans or Luxembourg, making it harder for investors or tax authorities to see what's going on.

A standard index tracker fund that you or I might invest in typically charges its investors between 0.1 and 1 per cent of the value of the assets in management fees each year. By contrast, private equity fees, all told, add up to between 6 and 13 per cent of the value of the investment *annually*.[25] 'Investors continue to regard private equity fund managers as trusted business colleagues, even as they continue to pick investors' pockets,' says Yves Smith, an expert on private equity who runs the influential financial website *Naked Capitalism*.

What do investors get in return for all these fees? Well, there is a rich stew of studies out there claiming wonderful returns to investors; the problem is that the authors of these studies are usually beneficiaries of the industry in some way. They cherry-pick time periods and funds to make the firms look good, exclude the bad stuff or use the wrong benchmarks for comparison. Funds are labelled alpha when their returns are above market benchmarks, but much of what gets called alpha performance is really leveraged beta – average returns in rising markets, magnified by borrowing. Many tout a metric we have met before called internal rate of return (IRR), a financial ratio which cheerleaders can use to make pedestrian returns to investors seem stratospheric.[26]

Good independent studies of private equity returns do exist, though. The most positive suggest that the median PE fund outperforms normal stock indices by around 1 per cent per year, but that shrinks to zero when it's benchmarked against more appropriate indices of smaller companies, like the kinds of companies private equity firms buy out. Other independent studies are less rosy: 'The average private equity fund return is comparable or inferior to that of public equity,' stated Ludovic Phalippou of Oxford University, 'in sharp contrast to what industry associations report.' In a 2010 report entitled *Private Equity, Public Loss* investor Peter Morris contrasted private equity firms' high gross returns (before fees) and what arrives in LPs' accounts, showing many a tollbooth between. There's also an inbuilt positive bias in the research, as the less successful funds are less likely to share their data with researchers.[27]

And it's actually even worse than this. An iron rule of investing is that if you're taking risks, you should expect higher returns and good liquidity – which means you can sell when you want to. But private equity turns this around: outside investors not only have to lock their capital away, inaccessible, for years, with little influence on the underlying business, they also get plenty of risk with pedestrian returns. The GPs, by contrast, take very little risk – putting in typically 1–2 per cent of their own money into the business while potentially reaping enormous returns. Top PE titans are better paid – much better paid – than the CEOs of big banks. There's an old adage in finance: 'Where are the customers' yachts?'

Recently at a dinner party I sat next to a former private equity general partner, a smart, witty and engaging man. I ran these complaints past him and he replied by drawing for me on a napkin a simple picture of the typical capital structure of a private equity acquisition – those Bidcos, Holdcos and so on – to explain why the structure needed to be this way from the GPs' perspective. I pressed him to justify this baroque financialised apparatus from society's perspective instead. He then drew a graph of risk against return: investors need higher returns to justify higher risks. But, I pressed, how much of the money put at risk actually belongs to the private equity partners? One per cent, he replied sheepishly. And that's in line with the private equity norm: between 1 *and* 2 *per cent* of the investment pool tends to come from the titans' own funds.[28] He stopped drawing. Well, he continued, if you have three general partners and a $50 million fund, 1 per cent is £170,000 each, a lot of your own money to put at risk. Maybe so, if it's all you have, but most have plenty more, I commented, and a really good performance could multiply that stake by fifty. Within minutes he had gathered up his family and left without saying goodbye.

All this raises a big question. Why are sophisticated money managers throwing money at this sector? At the time of writing, money is pouring in to private equity in waterfalls. PE raised over $3 trillion from investors between 2013 and 2017, and a survey of institutional investors in 2017 found that on average they expected private equity to outperform markets by 4 per cent a year, even after underperforming in the S&P 500 index by 1.5 per cent a year for the past five years.[29] These hopes are fantasies: returns are only likely to get worse because so much money is now chasing the underlying assets in the productive economy that PE investors are having to pay a lot of money to buy companies these days. And in the next downturn private equity's borrowing binge will almost certainly make the value of their assets fall further than more conventional funds, and lead to more bankruptcies. So, once again, why do so many people invest in private equity?

Some of the reasons are so pitiful you may struggle to believe them.

There are two dull but important reasons: first, that ocean of money sloshing around the world has to go somewhere; and second, accounting and tax factors encourage this stuff. There is also the dodgy data stew, bamboozling investors and even sometimes private equity officials themselves into believing its claims of outsized performance.[30] Some funds also do genuinely and consistently outperform for investors, so everyone wants a piece of them, but the queues to invest in these are so long that only the Goldman Sachses and Harvard endowments of this world get in. As one researcher caustically put it, those funds 'will never manage *your* money'. If the sector has underwhelming returns overall, and if you're not Goldman Sachs, then mathematically you are more than likely to end up investing in a fee-eating donkey.

The reasons get sadder. When scarily underfunded pension pots can't be filled with normal market returns, many managers – with a duty of care over our private pensions, for goodness' sake – think the answer is to gamble by flinging money at these high-risk creatures, assuming that returns should correlate with risk. These investors may understand the predation in the care homes sector but fail to appreciate that they are unlikely to share in the fruits of that rapacity.

There are even less wholesome reasons. One is bribery. In 2009 the Carlyle Group, a private equity firm, agreed to pay a $20 million fine after a New York State official allegedly took a bribe in exchange for channelling a portion of the state's pension fund to Carlyle for it to manage – and cream fees from. And, as the *Guardian* reported, the episode 'did not prove to be isolated'. Less illegally, some big university endowment fundraisers chasing donations from wealthy PE alumni will offer to return the favour. Backscratching and favours for mates are rife.

But here's the most tragic part of this sorry mess: many fund managers invest our funds and pension pots into private equity and hedge funds because they want to be cool. I'm not kidding. Every single person I asked about this agreed it was a factor. Simon Lack, a former JP Morgan banker who advises on alternative investments, said he looked at 3,500 hedge fund proposals when he worked there, and remembered that 'there were no boring meetings. You meet some of the most talented people in investing, and that is pretty cool.' Lack also wrote a book, *The Hedge Fund Mirage*, which concluded that returns to investors in hedge funds are just as feeble as those from private equity.[31]

Another employee with a global bank with years of experience choosing how and where to invest clients' money revealed not just remarkable contempt for private equity and hedge funds, but also for those who invest in them. 'With some investors, there is nothing you can say to them that will ever persuade them they aren't going to make tons of money,' he told me. 'They want status. They open the *Financial Times* in the morning and read about KKR doing billion-dollar deals. They want to be at the table with the big boys.' He described a steady stream of chancers in hedge funds and private equity trooping through his office, pitching marvellous tales of why his bank should invest with them. Low fees were a no-no, he said; they smacked of desperation. They also simply *had to* operate out of swanky offices in exclusive areas like Mayfair. They would play mind games too. 'They put on this big show,' the banker continued. 'They will make you wait for six months just to get an "exclusive" meeting with their sales people.' They would shroud their proprietary trading strategies in mystery, a modern version of the lure to investors of the South Sea Bubble in the eighteenth century, where the company behind the scam offered a once-in-a-lifetime chance to invest in 'a company for carrying out an undertaking of great advantage, but nobody to know what it is'. The banker said he's had PE visitors who take themselves so seriously, and whose upper-class accents are so painful, that he has had to double-check that they aren't spoofing him. He always listened patiently to their pitches but almost never recommended that his bank invest with them.

But for all the savvy investors, there seem to be many more who fall for the hype and the glamour. Ludovic Phalippou says investors often tell him how dull it is to invest in standard stuff. 'They say, "I work in this bank. I am bored to death. I just have to invest in these equities and bonds. You can only invest passively; you don't trade, you don't turn over your portfolio; you try to minimise costs and taxes. How boring is that? If I don't invest in private equity and hedge funds then I am the biggest loser ever.'[32]

Peter Morris, the veteran banker and analyst, weaves all this together to explain why these people invest: 'The simple answer is: because it's not their money.' It's OPM. 'The private equity business is like sex,' says Howard Anderson, a professor at MIT, reflecting the industry's heads-I-win-tails-you-lose macho world view. 'When it's good, it's really good. And when it's bad, it's still pretty good.' That statement directly contradicts Jensen's claims about the 'discipline of debt' and the PE model sharpening managers' focus to build better companies. What we have instead is baroque internal financial flows, risk-shifting, tax games, debt darting in and out of corporate stacks and the OPM principle, which all blunt managers' focus on building good companies, while diminishing responsibility and accountability.

Private equity players sometimes get called locusts, vultures, parasites. These terms often fit, but I see a different creature: the octopus. When an especially aggressive PE firm buys a company it will reach its tentacles out to every stakeholder group it can think of: employees, pensioners, taxpayers, elderly and vulnerable recipients of home care, creditors, consumers, people living nearby breathing in the company's factory fumes, but also sophisticated co-investors and lenders – the GPs' supposed mates. It will grasp each group, turn it upside down and shake it to see what new cash flows will fall out, then reach out to lenders to multiply those cash flows with new borrowing, expanding the pool and expanding its fees.

Private equity firms advance several points in their defence. First, as one official put it to me, these firms channel 'oodles' of foreign investment into our countries. Which is true. But if much of that inward investment is in the form of crowbars to tear the wealth and soul out of our communities and businesses and siphon it offshore, is that a national benefit? And the profits thus extracted often flow to peculiar or dubious places. A trawl of Careline's connections, for example, reveals a menagerie of outside and offshore investors, which Graphite Capital says includes 'highly reputable' international investors. One investor is the Rising Tide Foundation, a libertarian Swiss group that has funded think tanks including the Reason Foundation ('choice, individual freedom and limited government'); and the UK's Centre for Policy Studies (co-founded by Margaret Thatcher, which pushes 'policies to limit the role of the state'). Rising Tide also donates to the Atlas Network, a discreet global network of more than 450 libertarian think tanks which frequently defend tax havens. Many of these organisations have defended the government austerity measures that are directly reducing council budgets and resources for home care.

A commonly used second defence is that the private equity sector contains some, and perhaps most, of the most experienced, brilliant corporate minds engaged in buying companies and fixing them up. This is also true, but in an important way it's a *bad* thing, because those people – who include a couple of friends of mine – have been lured away from true wealth creation and helping build great companies by a financial model that tends to reward them for engaging in predatory activities and financial engineering. This is a classic example of the finance-cursed brain drain out of useful sectors that I described in the Introduction.

A third defence of private equity argues that even if there is predation at one end, at least there are deserving beneficiaries at the other – private pension funds, for example, or the tax authorities. But this one doesn't hold water either; not just because the victims are generally poorer than the potential beneficiaries, but also because the pension funds and tax authorities are usually getting screwed over too.[33]

The sector's other big claim to social usefulness is in its role in building companies, using either so-called distressed investing, where they take failing firms, tune them up and make them hum again, or the buy-and-build model, where they create value by buying up lots of companies and joining them together, creating economies of scale, which can create real value. Careline is an example of buy-and-build: C&C Bidco is in fact a bidding machine which has bought over twenty companies offering care to vulnerable people.[34] Yet according to one in-depth study, distressed investing accounted for just 2 per cent of all private equity acquisitions.[35] The main action is elsewhere: in taking healthy companies, financially engineering their cash flows and often flipping them like hot burgers to the next investor. And as for buy and build, at the end of the day it is like the old corporate conglomerate model, but with two big differences. First, one of the other main reasons to bring companies together is to create monopolising market power in the niches where they operate, which was much harder to do in the old days before Robert Bork, when governments took monopolies seriously. As an example City & County, which owns Careline, is now the largest independent provider of home care services in the UK and is bidding to buy more 'assets' in this sector; its growing size undoubtedly boosts its bargaining power with workers, suppliers and local authorities. Second, PE firms are getting paid an order of magnitude more than their predecessors for doing the same thing. Neither development is healthy for countries that host them.

So, is there a legitimate role for private equity in an economy and society? It depends how you define it. If your definition includes 'financial engineering and extraction with enormous fees' then no, and this model should never in a million years be allowed near sectors like home care. If you prefer 'buying ailing companies and fixing them up in a private unlisted firm that does not have to answer to many impatient short-term shareholders', then certainly yes, but even then only if carefully regulated in the interests of society, and with the incentives to extreme predation stripped out. Better, perhaps, to parachute those brilliant fixer-uppers straight into afflicted firms and pay them decent money for doing what they do best. And this means a sector that looks nothing whatsoever like what private equity is today. Tony Blair once said, in a passionate defence of private equity, 'in today's global market, if you take the money off them, they will go and live somewhere else'. So how about rounding up the bin men, doctors, teachers, plumbers, engineers and home carers – and the richest and most aggressive private equity and hedge fund titans – and sending them all somewhere else for a long time. Then let's see who we miss the most.

Private equity is perhaps the clearest illustration of financialisation at work, but many of the techniques it pioneered have spread to other business sectors, egged on by law and accounting firms and the banks which set up so many of these schemes. The question now is: how do these techniques and financial flows play out across a whole country, and what other risks might they be storing up?

10

The March of the Takers

In 2012 Boris Johnson, then mayor of London, stood under an umbrella by a busy road, his blond hair whiffling in the wind. 'A pound spent in Croydon is *far* more of value to the country from a strict utilitarian calculus than a pound spent in Strathclyde,' he gushed.[1] 'Indeed you will generate jobs and growth in Strathclyde far more effectively if you invest in Hackney or Croydon or in other parts of London.' This was an urban geography variant of the competitiveness agenda: give London what it wants, and watch the wealth pour forth and spread bountifully across the land.

Many people share Johnson's image of London as the roaring engine of the British economy, to be treated with deference. 'London and the south of England have been subsidising the rest of the UK,' thundered Chris Giles in the *Financial Times* in 2017. His article, entitled 'Why London deserves a thank you note from the rest of Britain', cited official data showing that London generated nearly £16,000 in tax revenues per person, amounting to a surplus of £3,070 per head. 'The idea that London sucks the life out of other parts of Britain is absurd,' he said, and took up the theme on Twitter. 'HUGE subsidies from London and South East to rest of the country … Much of UK – worse deficit than Greece … London is the UK's cash cow. Endanger its economy and it damages UK public finances.' In the ensuing Twitter frenzy a senior official from a City financial advisory firm called for London 'to get itself expelled from England à la Singapore from Malaysia'.[2]

However, while some pundits call for more pampering for London, others urge Britain to rebalance its economy away from an excessive dependence on the capital and on financial services. As former chancellor George Osborne put it in 2011, Britain needed to be 'a country carried aloft by the March of the Makers'. He subsequently pledged that his government would build a 'Northern Powerhouse' to match London's strength.

This argument reminds me of what I used to hear on my radio almost every day when I lived in Angola in the early 1990s. Separatists in the northern province of Cabinda, historically the main oil-producing zone, have long battled for its independence so that they can keep for themselves the oil revenues that they see draining southwards to the rest of Angola. Meanwhile, other Angolan politicians constantly called (and still call) for a rebalancing of the economy away from oil and away from the country's dominant capital, Luanda, and for the oil wealth to be treated as seed money for other parts of the economy and the country. But this rebalancing never happened, even after the end of the civil war: according to the IMF, oil and diamonds make up 99.7 per cent of Angola's exports today, precisely the same proportion as when I lived there. One of the main reasons other sectors have not flourished is that the oil money undermines them, and also sets up political and economic strains that increase conflict and corruption and reduce overall growth and economic health. While oil flourishes, alternative sectors can't. This is common in mineral-rich countries and a central feature of the resource curse, which I introduced at the start of this book.

Likewise, many people argue that Britain is too dependent on London and its outsized financial sector, which has grown so large and powerful and extractive that other sectors of the economy struggle to survive, like seedlings starved of light and water under the canopy of a giant, deep-rooted and invasive tree. So does London subsidise the rest of the country? Is Boris Johnson right when he says that spending and wealth in Croydon, London and south-east England grow and spread out to places like Strathclyde? Or is London the centre of a financialising machine that sucks power and money away from the peripheries: a march of the takers, sabotaging the march of the makers? Can the City of London and the rest of Britain prosper alongside each other, or for the regions to prosper must the City of London be humbled?

To answer this, let's examine more closely the idea of wealth flowing in great rivers from Croydon in London up to places like Strathclyde.

Consider the Strathclyde Police Training and Recruitment Centre at East Kilbride near Glasgow, which was opened by Prince Charles in 2002. It was built and is operated under a private finance initiative (PFI), a now-notorious scheme set up under John Major's Conservative government then given an explosive boost under Tony Blair's New Labour after he came to power in 1997.[3] Traditionally, governments fund schools, roads and other infrastructure by raising taxes or borrowing, but under PFI private companies raise the finance for these projects from banks and specialist lenders on the basis of an agreement that the government will then lease that infrastructure from them, providing a steady stream of payments to the consortia that financed and built them, typically spread over twenty-five or thirty years. With PFI, immediate taxes and government borrowing are lower, since costs have been outsourced to the private sector. The catch is that future generations, or future governments, have to pick up the tab. This made PFI controversial from the outset.

If you examine the corporate structure of the PFI deal behind the police training centre in East Kilbride, it looks somewhat similar to the corporate tower that loomed over Careline in the previous chapter. The story begins with a special purpose vehicle called Strathclyde Limited Partnership, which commissioned the construction firm Balfour Beatty to build the police training centre. But the action above the Strathclyde SPV is more interesting.

Ten or so companies or partnerships above Strathclyde in the chain of ownership was, at the time of writing, a firm called International Public Partnerships Limited (INPP), a £2 billion Guernsey-based infrastructure fund listed on the London Stock Exchange. INPP's listed shares are owned by many diverse players, but include three large owners of its stock, all based in the City of London: the asset manager Schroder PLC; Investec Wealth & Investment Limited, a subsidiary of a South African investment company; and Newton Investment Management Limited, a subsidiary of the US banking giant BNY Mellon. Meanwhile, INPP's investments are managed by Amber Infrastructure Group Holdings Limited, which has a complex cross-shareholding relationship with INPP and whose glass-fronted offices sit just south of the Thames in central London, tucked between City Hall and London Bridge station. Public records show that at the last count around half Amber's shares belong to a firm called Hunt Companies, based in El Paso, Texas, while Amber's other major shareholdings include a company in Luxembourg, a Jersey trust company and a UK company owned by a top Amber official, whose address is listed as a large semi-detached house worth around £2 million in a leafy street near Wandsworth Common. INPP told its investors it earned £282 million in pre-tax profits in 2016 and 2017, and got a £2.5 million tax refund.[4]

Meanwhile, nearly all the companies above the Strathclyde SPV are registered to that same address near London Bridge, as are the company directors. At various points in this structure the public records show a series of charges – borrowing and debt. The lenders and arrangers include the British bank RBS, the BNY Trust Company based in Ontario, and the German Bayerische Hypo-und Vereinsbank, via its offices in the City of London. Most lenders aren't disclosed – most likely they are based in the City of London or offshore. The point here is that money flows from its source in the budget of the Scottish Police Authority and makes its way down to a series of addresses, people and institutions in wealthy parts of London or, via London, into tax havens and overseas countries.

Treasury data says that the police training centre cost £17 million to build, with Balfour Beatty as the main contractor. The government anticipates payments to the PFI consortium averaging well over £4 million a year over the contract's twenty-five-year life from 2001 to 2026, a total of £112 million. If the government had instead directly commissioned Balfour Beatty to build the centre and raised the £17 million construction cost by issuing a twenty-five-year bond paying 5 per cent, it would have paid out just £37 million.

Not all of that astonishing £75 million difference is wealth extraction. When the Treasury calculates PFI repayments, it not only incorporates interest costs but must also add running costs, insurance, bidding costs, dividends paid to company shareholders and a risk factor to reflect private-sector risk-taking when it invests.[5] It is impossible to unpick published numbers to get a precise sense of how large each of those factors are, but clues are available. One estimate suggests that nearly 60 per cent of total PFI repayments are down to the financially-enhanced costs of building the infrastructure: in Strathcylde's case, this percentage would work out at £66 million, nearly double the £37 million it would have cost if the government had done it directly. Part of the issue here is that governments can borrow much more cheaply than the private sector: official and independent studies estimate a difference of 2.5 to 4 percentage points annually, which if compounded over twenty-five years means, very roughly, doubling the financing costs.[6] Allyson Pollock, a leading authority on PFI, has called it a way of getting one hospital for the price of two, significantly because of these extremely high financing costs. What is more, amid claims and counter-claims, it seems that PFI providers may be, on aggregate, providing no better and perhaps a shoddier service.

Overall, it seems that the Scottish Police Authority (and, by extension, Scottish taxpayers) is paying a large and unnecessary surplus over and above what the project could have cost, money channelled down through financialised pipelines to a cluster of companies registered in London, then out to the many owners of, the bankers to and the fee-earners from companies in the City, Jersey, Guernsey, Luxembourg, El Paso, Germany, Canada and who knows where else.[7] All this appears to be fully legal, yet on this evidence, Boris's picture of money flowing from London to Strathclyde has it back to front.

The Strathclyde training centre was, at the last count, just one of over 700 PFI deals operating across the UK, every one via a special purpose vehicle and every one, as far as I can tell, with a similarly convoluted corporate structure. Every one that I have looked at also conforms to the same basic geographical pattern: a steady rain of payments from British regions outside of London and the south-east as well as poorer parts of the capital and into what I call the London nexus, by which I mean the City itself, the expensive residential areas of London and its surroundings where the main corporate actors live, and the mostly British tax havens and also other countries where the shareholders, creditors and other financial actors in these projects live and work.[8] Treasury data shows that while the capital value of assets under PFI schemes added up to £59.4 billion in 2016, the British taxpayer would end up paying out more than £306 billion over the lifetime of these projects, over five times that amount. And that's the official forecast; it is likely to be worse than that, because the private players can be adept at wriggling out of inconvenient or difficult contracts, while invoking ruthless penalty clauses at the first whiff of the government wanting to change anything.[9]

And these players have considerable market power, which gives them power over government. Most of the PFI structures have, at their top, a large conglomerate which specialises in bidding for PFI projects like Strathclyde. According to one report in 2017, just nine infrastructure funds, all based offshore, held controlling stakes in nearly half of all the 700-odd PFI projects in Britain – and this market concentration had been growing, as had the share of projects owned in tax havens. A study of the five largest PFI firms showed they paid no tax on their profits in 2011–15.[10]

The geographical picture is of course complex and varied. Not everything flows down the gurgling drains of the tax havens or into elite parts of Britain; some money reaches pension funds, for instance, which spread wealth rather more widely than to a handful of billionaires in Jersey or Monaco.[11] But even then, share ownership and pension fund ownership and benefits are heavily concentrated among the wealthy and in the London nexus, so the overall geographical pattern is clear.

This all might even be acceptable, if PFI was delivering an efficient low-cost service to places such as Strathclyde. The original idea of PFI was that by introducing competition into government activities, stodgy bureaucracies would be exposed to the fresh air of private-sector dynamism, flair, risk-taking and entrepreneurialism, squeezing out efficiencies and reducing pressure on public budgets. But the numbers I've just described suggest a very different picture: of large-scale extraction of wealth, far in excess of the value being added. Not only that, but horror stories associated with PFI and the wider picture of government outsourcing to the private sector are by now well rehearsed in the media. There are tales of police forces having to pay hundreds of pounds to repair a puncture, company employees taking bribes from criminals to fit loose electronic tags, firms charging government departments £1,000 to change a plug or invoicing them millions for services never performed, NHS health trusts crippled by repayment overloads, and PFI firms prioritising shareholder dividends over improving facilities at dangerous, overcrowded prisons. Taxpayers are still paying £12,000 a day for a PFI school in Liverpool that closed in 2014, because there weren't enough pupils. The City

Council will still be paying this in 2027: it can't change the contracts. And those who defend such practices as fair compensation for private-sector risk-taking do not appear to have a case. The National Audit Office, among others, has found that PFI firms were taking on hardly any risk because they had also become experts at using the corporate structures to shift it onto the shoulders of others.[12]

PFI is just part of a bigger picture of government spending via the private sector: around £240 billion, a third of the UK government's annual budget, now goes on privately run but taxpayer-funded public services. These arrangements also tend to involve similar geographical flows out from the British regions and down into the London nexus. But that's just money from the public sector. Arguably an even bigger issue is the financialisation of the private sector, which involves a wholly different kind of outsourcing and a very different set of flows of wealth – but with the same geographical pattern. And these rivers of money generate a host of different problems.

When the global financial crisis hit a decade ago, it soon emerged that big London banks had been for years generating outsized profits by taking considerable risks in financial markets, and when these risks crystallised into losses during the crisis, it was taxpayers across the country who bailed them out, paying the price in terms of austerity and cutbacks. The profits had gone to the London nexus, but the losses were spread across the country. Post-crisis austerity has hit the regions especially savagely. For instance, the UK's Local Government Association has said it expects council budgets to fall by an astonishing 77 per cent between 2015 and 2020 alone, as austerity continues. The impact of this is stark. Around two-thirds of local council spending in the UK comes from central government, and the rest from local taxes and fees, but in poorer regions there are fewer local sources of revenue, so councils rely more heavily on central government, while at the same time their more deprived populations have more need of public services. Yet the cutbacks have hit the poorest councils hardest: for instance, Knowsley and Liverpool, two of the most deprived parts of the country, saw council spending cut by around £400 per inhabitant between 2000 and 2016, while Wokingham and Elmbridge, two of the wealthiest, had theirs cut by £2.19 and £8.14 respectively.[13] Adam Leaver, professor of accounting and society at

Sheffield University, sums up the geographical impact of the boom years and the crisis: 'This quiet cross-subsidy from north and west to south-east has been running unnoticed for a long time,' resulting in 'a kind of regional moral hazard: the metropolitanisation of gains, and the nationalisation of losses.'

One major route for this flow is the stock market. Many people believe a stock market's main function is to channel investors' money to companies – to invest in productive things – but the shareholder value revolution that I described in the last chapter has turned this on its head, as companies increasingly prioritise channelling their profits not into investment but into buying back their own shares – thereby boosting the share price and with it shareholders' wealth and company executives' stock options – or buying other firms in monopolising mergers and acquisitions. (When oil companies spend their money this way instead of on oil rigs, American investors call it 'drilling on Wall Street'.)

These practices, which drain money from company investment budgets into shareholders' and bosses' pockets, are among the thirstiest of the financial sector's many syringes jammed into the veins of the real economy. Bill Lazonick, a leading US expert on business strategy, estimates that this kind of extraction via the stock market has been running at an average of over $400 billion per year in the United States, a gigantic hit to the productive economy which most commentators don't appreciate because it is disguised by its counterpart, soaring share prices. With the richest 5 per cent of the American population owning around two-thirds of shares listed on US stock markets, these wealth transfers are a key part of the inequality machine of financialisation.

Across the Atlantic, a study of 298 companies in the S&P Europe 350 share index found that they had spent a similar amount, a total of $3.28 trillion, on buying back their own stock and paying dividends to shareholders from 2000 to 2015. In 2015 they spent €350 billion – equivalent to 110 per cent of their net income – on shareholder dividends and stock buybacks. The comparable figure for the UK was 150 per cent. This is what Bank of England economist Andrew Haldane meant when he said firms were 'eating themselves'.[14] Given that much if not most corporate investment and employment happens in the UK's regions, where the customers are, whereas the large majority of profits are realised in the London nexus, this generates the same overall pattern.

Another manifestation of these flows is in the increasing tendency in most economies towards monopoly, which by its very nature is a centralising force. The effect, and often the whole point of, a merger is to increase the market power of the centre at the expense of peripheral players. These might be employees inside the corporation or, outside it, customers, suppliers and taxpayers. And as the monopolisers and centralisers gain more market power, high-street butchers, bookshops, small farmers, coffee shops and small and medium-sized businesses increasingly struggle to compete. We can see the effects on our high streets, as thriving communities and businesses give way to betting outlets, pound stores and charity shops: the businesses of poverty. London's dark star is exerting an increasingly powerful and damaging gravitational pull on British business, its profits and its employees.

More generally, increased financialisation means an ever-stronger focus on those financial ratios. These drive firms to get assets off their balance sheets, cut costs, cut jobs and cut taxes so as to boost returns to shareholders, or simply to focus on businesses that need little capital in the first place.[15] That's the big financial game in Silicon Valley, for instance, while the car-sharing platform Uber doesn't invest in cars, Airbnb doesn't generally own real estate, and Facebook or Google extract profit from content created by the sweat, hard investment and shoe leather of beleaguered newspaper employees and many others. These are variants of the downsize-and-distribute model, where you reduce costs and capital spending, and force firms to disgorge the resulting cash to shareholders rather than invest it in the underlying business. 'It is not short term versus long term; that is not the distinction,' says Lazonick. 'It is value creation versus value extraction.' Every corporate restructuring, every merger or private equity purchase that you read about in the *FT*, every corporate tax avoidance scheme and pretty much any other piece of financial engineering you can think of: nearly always has – is *designed* to have – the same profit-sucking effects, which nearly always conform to the same general geographical pattern.

A Manchester University study of outsourcing found another telling set of numbers to illustrate this. It compared the supermarkets with private train operating companies like Virgin, First Scotrail and so on. Whereas the supermarkets enjoyed a return on capital employed (ROCE, one of those shareholder-friendly financial ratios) of 8.5 per cent, the train companies got over 120 per cent. Why the huge difference? Simple: the train companies didn't own their trains but leased them. Their total capital investments had been just over £200 million, compared to supermarkets' £43 billion of mostly job-creating investment. The private train operators were piggybacking on the £36 billion that government-funded Network Rail ploughed into rail infrastructure: other people's money.[16] Which is why, as the Manchester study concluded, UK government contracts contain 'some of the richest margins to be had'. In such capital-light business models other people put in the investments, while the financialised interests sit at the economic choke points, extracting their tolls. And in Britain's case those choke points are typically located in the London nexus.

Ian Fraser, author of the book *Shredded* about the misbehaviour and the semi-destruction of RBS, illustrates how even finance itself has become financialised in pursuit of those shareholder ratios. 'When banks including RBS refocused on shareholder value in 1985–95, they changed their whole approach,' he wrote. Decision-makers were removed from the front line, branches were hollowed out, and authority was centralised. Local bankers taking deposits from local savers, who made a point of understanding and then lending to local businesses, were elbowed out and replaced by sales people. 'The holy grail became cross-selling, which often turned into misselling … sales, sales, sales became the goal and staff were incentivised accordingly.' Giving people financial inducements to sell complex financial products is generally a terrible idea. But shareholders loved it: a government inquiry into payment protection insurance found that returns on equity for this scam averaged 490 per cent in 2006. Some advisers, it found, were so strongly incentivised that they even sold fraudulent products to their families and to themselves. And they kept doing so, years after the crash.[17] Once again wealth was being extracted from the regions into the London nexus, in a symptom of what the late geographer Doreen Massey called the 'colonial relationship' between parts of London and the rest of the country.[18]

Now there is admittedly a big wrinkle in this overall picture. The City isn't just bringing in money from the British regions, it is also attracts foreign money. So, the argument goes, surely that balances things back out for the nation as a whole?

Not so fast. Leave aside for now the fact that much of this foreign inflow is what elites or global banks or multinationals have looted from other nations, often poor nations, to stash in London real estate or bank accounts. What is more pertinent for Britain is that over 55 per cent of the value of shares listed on the FTSE 100 is owned by foreigners, which means that much if not most of the inflow to the London nexus hardly touches the sides, even in central London; it flows straight back overseas again as dividends.[19] And these financialised flows aren't benefiting London either; they are enriching a wealthy subset of London, at the same time as they extract even more from poorer and even middle-class parts of the capital. Partly for this reason, in terms of wealth ownership London itself is one of the most unequal places in the Western world. At the last count, the richest tenth of its inhabitants owned 173 times the wealth of the poorest tenth.[20]

This great geographical sorting machine is also a racial sorting machine and a gender-based sorting machine. It is a disability-based and vulnerability-based sorting machine, taking value from clients and employees in the home care sector, who are disproportionately women, disproportionately non-white and all vulnerable, and handing it to people operating out of Berkeley Square in Mayfair and far beyond. It is a generational sorting machine too, handing money to parts of the baby-boomer generation from everyone else, as PFI, shadow banking profits and other aspects of financialisation allow jam for the winners today, with the bills sent out to all our kids.[21]

This hidden tide of money flows constantly from the tired, the weak, the vulnerable, the huddled masses and victims of discrimination and abuse, from across London and Britain, through an immense filigree of financial pipelines to a relatively small number of mostly white European or North American men in Mayfair, Chelsea, Luxembourg, Jersey, Geneva, the Caymans and New York. This is the finance curse in action. And it's nice work if you can get it.

*

Alongside the siphoning of cash from government and from productive parts of the private sector, there's another great one-way flow going on: a great draining of knowledge, skills and people.

'I never blog on cases, but today I must break my rule,' wrote the barrister and former Conservative MP Jerry Hayes in 2017. The case involved a private forensic science laboratory that had through shoddy work created a bogus match between a defendant and a sample, the sample being a Glock handgun and ammunition, and the defendant being an innocent man who could have gone to jail for years. Thanks to a government lawyer repeatedly pushing for more information, the private laboratory finally admitted to 'confusion' which had wrongly placed the defendant in the frame. In his blog Hayes traced the problem back to the privatisation of the UK's national forensic service a few years earlier, an announcement that had prompted horror from professionals. 'The National Audit Office warned that this privatisation "could spark a crisis within the justice system". They were right,' Hayes said. When he explained to the judge how the forensic lab had made its error, 'I will never forget the look of horror on his face. In forty years of practice at the bar this shook my faith in what was once the finest and fairest justice system in the world. Read this and weep. And mourn for British justice.'

As the government outsources more and more functions to the private sector, lines of accountability are cut and it understands less and less of how the economy works, leading to a steady loss of control. With a third of government now run through outsourced providers, operating in pseudo-markets in health, prison services, social care, police training and more, a river of talent and knowledge has flowed out of government, making it ever more reliant on the outsourcers. The result, says Abby Innes of the London School of Economics, has been 'the enforced stupidification of the civil service and a profound loss of institutional memory, strategic oversight and coherence'.[22]

Outsourcing state functions to the private sector has ironically created a system of bad incentives uncannily like Soviet central planning, says Innes, who is also an expert in former communist states. The top-down state sets long-term performance targets, which can never cover all the possible eventualities; the highly complex contracts are impossible to monitor effectively and inflexible in a changing world; the players constantly try to shirk and wriggle out of commitments; and whenever there is a clash, the government, which has outsourced a lot of its expertise to private actors, gets 'dragged into bargaining games it cannot win'.

Tom Gash, an independent consultant who worked in the Prime Minister's Strategy Unit, has seen how government can lose the capacity to be an intelligent customer and loses power in the relationship. When the government contracted big technology firms to provide information technology services, he said, 'it was sort of "We will take this problem off your hands, government; give us a seven-year contract."' But when the government wanted to change what it was doing, it was stuck in an expensive trap, in which the companies could charge large sums for the change. 'It really lost its ability to understand what was going on: "How does this stuff work, or how many people does this really need?"'

And this in turn led to sets of nested relationships and back-scratching in the private sector, where the different players work mutually towards extracting more from government. So a professional services firm might be advising the government on an IT project, say, while other bidders on that same project will be working closely with that firm on other projects. 'There is a nexus of relationships and power structures,' Gash said, 'lots of routes to influence knocking around in the bid: wheels within wheels, where everyone knows everyone.' He gave the example of Universal Credit. In 2010 consultancies played a big role in encouraging the government to launch a wholesale reworking of Britain's system for paying income support and other benefits to low-income people, even though civil servants thought it was a disastrous idea. 'Sometimes the consultancies want a big, disruptive project to happen, so they often say, "We can do these things much better and more efficiently, let's do this transformational mega-project, rather than making small tweaks to make things work 20 per cent better."' In the case of Universal Credit the civil servants have been proved right: it is years behind schedule and has cost billions more than expected.[23] Those costs mean it has been highly profitable for the private-sector firms involved.

Those claiming that 'the market' will make such processes more efficient often argue that when things go wrong you can always hire more private-sector consultants to fix things. But if fixing things is profitable, is it in their collective interest to provide lasting solutions in the first place? Outsourcing was originally supposed to drive down costs by introducing competition into areas dominated by a stodgy state. But the result has been to create a few large monopolistic providers like Serco, Atos, Capita and the now-collapsed Carillion, which specialise not in providing the most competitive services but in winning government contracts and maximising their own revenues. In the five years leading up to 2018, the five biggest companies won 80 per cent of all government outsourcing contracts.

Yet it's not just the state being 'stupidified' by losing talent and knowledge to the private sector; it is the private sector too, as those in thrall to financial ratios turn their talents away from wealth creation towards more profitable, capital-light, wealth-extraction activities. This is the private equity model, rolled out across the economy.

Take Railtrack, for instance, the ill-fated fruit of an ill-conceived privatisation. The company slashed costs by ridding itself of operations managers and engineers, instead favouring leaders 'great at privat-ising, great with the City', as one official put it. They began chasing fantasy technology which generated splendid profits forecasts for the City but was never going to work. Unfortunately the engineers who could easily have pointed this out had been sacked. As Chris Green, a private rail boss, put it, Railtrack took 'a really high-calibre engineering team and destroy[ed] it'. The fragmented, clueless firm then stumbled into a suicidal contract with Virgin Trains that it clearly didn't under-stand. Several months and several actual train crashes later, Railtrack collapsed among recriminations and a huge taxpayer bill.[24]

The financially driven push towards private-sector outsourcing, breaking up large, vertically integrated corporations and reassembling them into entities that look more like trading companies, linked to extensive supply chains that provide the functions previously carried out in house, has yielded tremendous profits and in some cases has even delivered lower costs for consumers. But it has also hollowed out a once-thriving industrial ecosystem. Expensive functions like research or training, which used to create beneficial economy-wide spillovers and nourish diverse businesses, have leached away. Government could step in to fill in the holes, but it has steadily stripped itself of resources and knowledge about how its own economy works. The holes have

been filled instead with cheap and easy credit and laissez-faire plati-
tudes. Somewhere here must lie a large part of the explanation
for the fact that British productivity is an astonishing 15–25 per
cent lower than that of its European peers France, Germany, the
Netherlands, Belgium and Sweden.[25] For decades the British establishment has demonised trade unions for damaging British productivity
with demands for higher wages, but the more recent financial re-engineering of 'organised money pursuing high returns', as the Manchester
study of outsourcing put it, is a 'much more disruptive force'.[26]

These two great neoliberalising pipelines – government outsourcing
and the financialisation of the private sector – are emptying wealth,
people and talent out of both. And this raises a new question: where
do all these people end up?

The answer is that they are feeding into the pool of consultants
and advisers, an amorphous group that is steadily growing in size and
power. According to one recent count, in the UK there were 477,000
management consultants, 382,000 accountants, 311,000 employed in
legal services and 421,000 bankers. There are the consulting firms
like Boston Consulting Group, McKinsey & Co, Accenture, and Bain
Consulting – the latter a group whose global revenues hit an estimated
£140 billion in 2017. There are also London-based law firms, the top
hundred of which generated £22 billion in revenue in 2017.

'Everywhere one looks, there are more and more consultants,' wrote
John Gapper in the *Financial Times*, 'on strategy, investment, operations, compensation, digital transformation, technology, marketing.
Some businesses seem to have been entirely occupied by consultants.'
We all need lawyers, and we sometimes need consulting advice – just
as we all need finance – the question is how much is socially useful.
Once they get in the door, they can be hard to eject. I am reminded
of the 1958 film *The Blob* starring Steve McQueen, in which an alien
red jelly falls to earth and is found by an unsuspecting old man. It
gloops onto his hand and eats him, then moves on, consuming every
life form it encounters, growing bigger and sowing panic.

Many exotic private-sector actors of different sizes inhabit this Blob.
Some are rougher than the average management consultant. One of
these people, who called himself an 'arranger', told me how he and
his colleagues would scour the world for overtaxed companies then

approach them and offer to plug them into aggressive tax-efficiency machines. The way he described it was a bit like plucking ripe fruit. Before the global financial crisis, he said, 'We were seeing the tax market growing very strongly: bigger and bigger deals, and more and more jurisdictions coming in – Poland, Spain, and so on. The tax professionals turned to countries where pockets of tax were still being paid by banks and others, and they were saying, "Let's go in, and do them a deal."'[27]

Also in the Blob are the business schools, which relentlessly push the shareholder-value ideology and don't seem to have changed their position since the global financial crisis, which surely should have shattered that illusion. The financial ratios they teach constantly urge us to do more for less, faster. The business world's obsession with these financial ratios helps to explain why you feel there's never enough time to do anything, why Amazon inflicted a 'continual performance improvement algorithm' on its employees and why banks take such risks with *your* money while flogging you fraudulent services. These ideas are everywhere now. Arnaldo Lago de Carvalho, a veteran Angolan economist and businessman, outlined to me in 2017 how damaging this world view can be. Gesturing sadly towards a seafront skyline filled with decaying half-built office blocks and hotels, the fruit of get-rich-quick schemes which collapsed in an oil price crash in 2014, he sighed as he described how a generation of young Angolans who had left the country returned when the civil war ended in 2002 after having studied in Western business schools. 'Everyone who goes outside to study comes back to this country with the idea that they have to get rich quickly,' he said. 'You don't think about really producing something, creating wealth. People finishing MBAs, they want to be consultants or be in financial institutions. Nobody wants to go and manage an agricultural industry or anything like that. When you have a very undeveloped country, people with this mentality do not help.'

'Blob' is an unkind term for a large and diverse group containing many fine individuals, some of whom are friends or relatives of mine. But the members of this group, particularly at the most senior levels, tend to share views, characteristics and linkages reflecting the financialising needs of the clients they serve. They are paid to help these clients – large banks and multinationals, hedge funds, private equity firms and so on – to avoid tax, disclosure, laws and rules, so it is all but inevitable that they have developed an anti-state, anti-tax, anti-regulation corporate culture and the obsession with shareholder value that I described in the last chapter. As a result, they comprise an interest group which incubates and accelerates a financialising London-centric shared world view. The Blob is not centrally organised, but given its members' common affinities, standard duties to increase shareholder value to clients, and deep penetration of government offices, it is almost a political actor in its own right.

The advisory, consulting and accounting firms that populate the Blob have become what Professor Adam Leaver of Sheffield University calls 'super-spreaders' of finance fever across the private sector, as public listed companies increasingly learn the extractive techniques pioneered by private equity, with towering stacks of companies plugged into tax havens using clever mixes of debt and equity to suck income out of subsidiaries while keeping the risks inside those same subsidiaries, so resting on other people's shoulders. 'The advisory firms, the consultancy firms come in and say, "You are not managing your income flows efficiently enough,"' he said. 'It used to be almost unheard of to see the parent company as a speculative investor in its own subsidiaries, sucking the income out. Tentacles descending into pots and streams of cash – this was seen as kind of profane. Now it seems like the way it is done.'[28]

The Blob is not just financialising the private sector, but also the government too, through the revolving doors of influence. The more outsourcing, the greater its penetration. As I explained in Chapter 5, HMRC itself has been transformed into something of an anti-tax tax-raising authority, at least for certain kinds of taxpayers. Its staff have been cut by over 45 per cent in ten years, with the promise of still more cuts, which means yet more outsourcing. One of the UK's government advisers on tax, David Heaton, was caught on film at a conference advising people how to keep 'the money out of the chancellor's grubby mitts' and offering a 'bump plan' – manipulating maternity pay rules to 'get the government to pay your bonuses for you'. Another more senior government tax official, Edward Troup, who now chairs the board of HMRC, has previously said that tax is 'legalised extortion'.[29] Before he became Britain's chancellor, George Osborne was filmed advising a caller to Britain's Daily Politics TV show how to dodge inheritance tax 'and then get personal care paid for by the state. I probably shouldn't be advocating this on television.' A smirk plays around the edges of his mouth as he speaks, then breaks fully into a guilty smile.[30]

Of all the different players who inhabit the Blob there is one group that may be the most influential, insidious and dangerous of them all: the Big Four audit, accounting and consultancy firms, KPMG, PwC, EY, formerly Ernst & Young, and Deloitte.

In the true-to-life Hollywood blockbuster *The Big Short* a small band of scruffy oddballs, played by Brad Pitt, Steve Carrell, Ryan Gosling and Christian Bale, probes the numbers behind America's soaring housing market in the mid-2000s and sees a crash coming. Nobody believes them, but they are of course proved right in the end. If any group should have raised the alarm ahead of time it was the Big Four, with vastly better resources and access to companies than the *Big Short*'s misfits ever had. But the audit firms gave clean bills of health to all the Western banking giants shortly before they descended into financial chaos. *Every single bank.* And they signed up on all sorts of aggresive, dangerous and risky trades too. PwC, for instance, accepted one valuation for a bunch of toxic collateralised debt obligations (CDO) contracts held by Goldman Sachs, while happily accepting a wildly different valuation for the very same CDOs held by the counterparty, AIG. Those CDOs helped bankrupt AIG. Charlie Munger, one of America's best-known investors, looked at the deals and reached a simple conclusion. The accounting profession, he concluded, was a 'sewer'. And this was a problem older than the financial crisis: Big Four auditors were signing off the accounts of Enron, BCCI, the many savings and loan frauds, the WorldCom and Tyco scandals and various others right up to the moment the companies collapsed.

Auditors are supposed to do the job of a watchdog: checking companies' accounts to protect their investors, employees and wider society. The financial crisis shone a light on the field the watchdogs were supposed to be guarding, and revealed them to be feasting on the sheep alongside the wolves in what looked like some sort of tacit deal – the wolves being the big banks and other players who made billions in the go-go years before the crisis, and you and me being the sheep.

How has the auditing industry joined the predators against the rest of society? Tax writer and former corporate tax inspector Richard Brooks answers the question in his book *Beancounters*, a devastating exploration of the corruption of a once-proud profession. 'At this point,' he wrote in a section about Enron, 'it might be asked where the auditors were. The answer was that they were in the building. That was the problem.' The auditors had become so closely intertwined with Enron that the company's chief accounting officer went on holidays and golf junkets with auditor Arthur Andersen's lead accounting partner.

The Big Four have become so entangled with the companies they audit because they aren't just auditors. They reach into multiple areas: cooking up tax-dodge schemes for those same companies (and for wealthy individuals), helping governments design tax systems, and providing advisory and consultancy services on IT systems, on whether to set up SPVs in tax havens, on how to oversee nuclear power plants, on how to manage healthcare systems, on how to wind down bankrupt firms, and more. They pop up in the most unexpected places. At the Oscars ceremony in 2017 Warren Beatty mistakenly announced that the film *La La Land* had won best film, even though the judges thought *Moonlight* was better (it was.) PwC had given Beatty the wrong envelope. The question many people asked was: why on earth was PwC involved in the Oscars?

Essentially, the Big Four fill holes in public- and private-sector knowledge that exist because functions have been been outsourced. These roles have become so lucrative that auditing now makes up less than 40 per cent of their roughly $130 billion in global revenues, and less than 25 per cent in the UK. At the last count the Big Four earned nearly $30 billion a year from tax advice alone, helping private clients both to comply with tax laws and to escape tax, usually both at the same time. To get a sense of how those apparently opposite functions work together, ponder the word 'loophole'.

These firms are now, in Brooks's words, 'consultancy firms with auditing sidelines'. And this generates enormous conflicts of interest. If a Big Four firm makes tens of millions selling consulting advice to a big bank or multinational (Arthur Andersen, for instance, was at one point anticipating $100 million in annual fees from Enron), then how likely is it they will ask that company difficult questions when they check its books? And if these conflicts of interest helped increase the risks ahead of the last crisis, the same thing is probably happening again now, but this time with apparently solvent mainstream firms at risk. The more financialised they are, the greater the risk may be.

Solvent firms have more assets than liabilities. When the construction company Carillion collapsed it turned out that well over a third of its assets were under an accounting item called 'goodwill' – a rather nebulous term which basically reflected the accountants' assessment of Carillion's future income streams. In good times the more goodwill assets on Carillion's books, the stronger it looked, and the more it could borrow. This mechanism was used to bring forward value from the future, in order to make jam and bonuses today. But when the firm fell apart this nebulous notion evaporated, leaving a super-sized hole in its balance sheet and severely burned creditors. Bonus-generating goodwill games are increasingly common across the corporate sector, cheered on by the Big Four firms signing off on accounts. In the next major downturn, if interest rates rise or if investors lose faith in will-o'-the-wisp goodwill, there could be system-wide losses for the economy all over again.[31]

Why are the Big Four signing off on these phantom assets? When the official receiver came in to salvage what it could from Carillion's carcass, they found a big part of the reason: the firms had between them earned over £70 million in fees from Carillion in the decade before its collapse. KPMG and Deloitte had been its auditors, signing off on the accounts; EY had been doing large-scale consulting work for the company, and PwC had provided advisory services. And there was more. When the receiver sought a firm to handle the insolvency it concluded that PwC, which had earned 'only' £17 million from Carillion, was the least conflicted of the four, so it got the job – but with a twist. PwC 'was unable or unwilling to provide an estimate of how long its work would take, or what the eventual bill would be', a parliamentary commission concluded. 'PwC could name its price. The oligopoly had become a monopoly.' And the Big Four are expected to earn £50 million or so from the clean-up.[32]

The essence of the problem is one that any pre-Robert Bork anti-monopolist would recognise: firms with immense market power derived from profitable conflicts of interests embedded in their business models, incentivised to exploit and profit from those conflicts. Their audit role makes the Big Four, as accounting professor Prem Sikka puts it, the 'private police force of capitalism'. Companies are required by law to have their accounts audited, and the biggest firms are now so insanely complex that nobody but the Big Four is able or willing to take on the job. Yet unlike the real police, whose salaries are paid by government, these accountants of fortune are paid by their clients. The Big Four have for decades audited between 99 and 100 per cent of the FTSE 100 firms. Barclays had the same auditor for 120 years, until an EU wrist-slap forced it to change. The watchdogs aren't only in league with the wolves; they have, like couples that have been living together for decades, increasingly grown to resemble them.[33]

The scale and number of conflicts of interest that the Big Four firms are now able to milk are enough to make the head spin. They simultaneously provide financialising services for large corporations, secure lucrative contracts to help onshore governments around the world design their tax laws, assist tax havens with *their* laws to help multinationals and billionaires escape onshore tax, and help multinationals and banks to use these tax havens to their advantage.

Paying these firms to help design Britain's tax laws is like paying burglars for advice on the best locks for your house. Burglars are certainly experts in home security, but they are also the people most capable of breaking in. (The difference with burglars is that the Big Four try to help their clients navigate carefully around the law, and not brazenly break it.) And the Big Four aren't just passive providers of advice; they work diligently to punch holes in national tax laws. Ernst & Young, for instance, had a 'tax policy and controversy network' for multinationals, which boasted that in sensitive areas where the media might sniff out a story about tax cheating 'policy development offers a low risk alternative' where tax changes could be 'implemented with the minimum of delay'. 'Policy development' is of course a euphemism for lobbying and influencing tax laws.[34] As all this happens, Big Four officials rotate in and out of government in a game of 'poacher, turned gamekeeper, turned poacher again', as a parliamentary committee was told.

The Big Four have become 'a solvent dissolving the boundary between public and private interests', says Brooks. 'Running the economy and working in banking or the Big Four are really all part of the same career now. The revolving door means they and the politicians see the world in the same way, and the politicians –

Osborne, Obama and the rest – make a mint once they leave office. All the bright forty-somethings who were running the Treasury have gone to work for Blackrock, places like that. People who've done stints restructuring the health service then go to work for KPMG in this new, competitive, fragmented health service.'[35] And so the Blob steadily spreads its influence.

The newspapers tend to call the Big Four's corporate tax-minimising activities tax avoidance, which by definition is not illegal. But this is often false: truly independent and well-resourced tax courts would likely knock down many of their strategies if the schemes were challenged. In 2013 a senior PwC employee told the UK's Public Accounts Committee (PAC) that the firm would flog a tax avoidance scheme to a multinational even if it reckoned there was only a one in four chance of it surviving in court. In other words, as PAC chair Margaret Hodge put it, 'you are offering services to your clients – knowingly marketing these schemes – where you have judged there is a 75 per cent risk of it then being deemed unlawful'.[36] (Another PwC official denied that, responding 'I don't know where that came from; I don't recognise that statement.' Another official, from Ernst & Young, said that standards had improved since the early 2000s.)[37] With Big Four partners' earnings tied to revenues, it's hardly surprising to see a steady downward trend in ethics and a tendency to push against – and often beyond – the limits of the law. Hodge put this in clear finance-curse terms: 'What really depresses me,' she said in one of her trademark public roastings of hapless tax officials from multinationals, 'is that you could contribute so much to society and the public good, and you all choose to focus on working in an area which reduces the available resources for us to build schools, hospitals, infrastructure.' What was so shocking was its industrial scale, she said, across a vast array of businesses. The Big Four stand firmly on the multinationals' side against wider society, showing a 'barefaced lack of respect for Parliament and the British public'.

For developing nations, which tend to rely much more heavily on corporate tax revenues than rich countries, the problem is worse. A government attempting to enforce its tax laws against a large multinational may only be able to send a couple of inexperienced, under-paid tax officials to fight the case, sometimes in a foreign court. The officials will be faced with a large team of top-notch lawyers and their

Big Four advisers. It's like trying to fight off lions with a stick. The British charity ActionAid published a report with a front-page image of a Ghanaian stallholder, Marta Luttgrodt, who sells SABMiller beers for a tiny profit. Although she pays less than fifty pounds in annual income taxes, that sum, the report notes, exceeded SABMiller's entire tax payments in Ghana that year. When told this, Luttgrodt said simply, 'I don't believe it.' What else *could* she say?

As government outsources its brain to the Blob, it falls more and more under its sway.[38] But this influence goes deeper: the Blob's values have captured our culture and society. Journalists, bemused by the complexity of the latest business or tax story, tap into the anti-tax, deregulatory Blob for the expertise they need, nodding along as they're educated in its views. Outsource homecare! Financialise the universities! Sell the tax inspectors' own offices out from under their feet to a tax haven company! Privatise prisons and forensic laboratories! Sell this healthy company to that private equity firm! Merge these two supermarket giants! And each move tends to extract more wealth from the regions, to pump it into the London nexus.

One government after another has failed to prosecute the Big Four or even enact the most obvious of all reforms: break the firms up, most especially split the audit functions away from their other business. They have swallowed noisy public inquiries, probes by the National Audit Office and whatever UK or US regulators throw at them with little more than a burp. A 2011 probe by the UK competition authorities into their awesome market power was batted aside effortlessly. Fines rarely exceed half a million here, a few million there: flea bites when set against their elephantine global revenues. Big Four bosses, including partners at the helm ahead of the financial crisis, now sit on the boards of regulators, are given peerages and knighthoods.[39] And the same old geographical pattern emerges: in the London nexus riches for Big Four partners and for the owners of firms that benefit from their lax audits, and in the rest of the country much larger eventual losses for everybody else.

This cannot be a formula for national prosperity.

11

The Evidence Machine

In July 2015 a senior official at a Big Four accounting firm was telling me about the wonders of Britain's latest cuts to the corporate income tax rate. The cuts, she gushed, would make Britain's economy grow, and there was even a table in the latest summer budget to prove it. I looked it up and there it was, on page 55, a pretty blue and grey graph under the heading 'Competitive Taxes' alongside a twenty-year forecast apparently showing that the series of programmed corporate tax cuts (from 28 per cent in 2010 to an expected 18 per cent in 2020) would save British businesses nearly £17 billion and attract so much inward investment and new economic activity that GDP would be boosted by £18 billion in the long run. Happy days!

Under the graph, though, I noticed in small print, 'Source: HMRC Computable General Equilibrium model output and HMT analysis'. What could that be? A tedious official document online explains it: you plug lots of inputs about taxes and the state of the economy into one end of the box and turn the handle; the model churns these inputs through some equations and spits out answers at the other end. But, I still wondered, what was in this model? How did it work? No clue was given, so I sent HMRC a Freedom of Information (FoI) request to find out more and waited patiently for their reply.

Everyone knows big money skews evidence in its favour and seeks to hide the traces of its meddling. Few will be surprised, for example, to learn that left-wing think tanks are more transparent about their sources of funding – *much* more transparent – than tax-cutting right-wing free marketeers and financial deregulators. The interests of finance constantly filter into our economic news and analysis in ways that are usually invisible. If you watched the historian Niall Ferguson's acclaimed series *The Ascent of Money*, for instance, were you aware that it was sponsored by the Cayman Islands for an undisclosed six-figure sum? Economists also sometimes get pilloried for creating mathematically elegant models that don't make sense in the messy real world.[1]

What this chapter will make clear is that, no matter how skilled, honest and independent researchers are, the very act of measurement tends to skew the evidence systematically in favour of big banks and multinationals. That's for many reasons, but especially because the stuff that benefits large corporations is easier to measure than the stuff that benefits wider society, so as the numbers pass through the evidence machine from research and measurement to newspaper headline and evidence-based new policy, the benefits to corporations win out.

Before telling you about HMRC's curious response to my FoI request, it is worth exploring the battleground of 'evidence' and how it gets weaponised against progressive policymaking.

People who call for corporate tax cuts make three main arguments. First, they claim such tax cuts put more money in the hands of local businesses, which then invest and create jobs and economic growth. Second, they argue that lower taxes attract investment from overseas. And third, they say cuts reduce corporations' incentives to cheat on their taxes. These claims are frequently accompanied with old dog-whistle phrases like 'competitive tax system' and 'losing out in the global race' to get everyone's blood pumping. The three core propositions, though, seem reasonable. A diligent government policymaker will nevertheless be expected to present evidence that this is what actually happens, so he or she goes off and does some measurement or, more likely, finds an expert.

If the policymaker is predisposed towards a tax-cutting conclusion, they might turn to a business-friendly organisation like the Oxford University Centre for Business Taxation. Now 'Oxford University' has a wonderful ring to it, but our policymaker will probably know that this body was set up in 2005 with a £5 million grant from the Hundred Group of big multinationals under the guiding hand of Chris Wales, a former top Goldman Sachs official. At the outset it was tasked with using its academic weight to 'achieve a more competitive tax system for British businesses', as a profile of Wales in *Accountancy Age* magazine put it, and if you look at its output you will discern the competitiveness agenda everywhere. The centre's director, Professor Mike Devereux, once wrote an opinion piece in the *Financial Times* entitled 'The best reform of corporation tax would be its abolition'. Chatting to him, it's clear that his views are more nuanced than the *FT* headline suggests, and the centre does produce plenty of complex, technically skilled and varied work. However, it won't say how much of its funding comes from big banks and multinationals, but it's a lot. And its output tends to veer towards the same broad conclusion: corporate tax cuts are not a bad idea.[2]

But let's now assume that our policymaker is an idealistic sort bound by quaint old traditions of public service and wants the work done by a fully independent academic without conflicts of interest. There are plenty of these about, and an independent academic is appointed and gets to work. She might start by studying lots of countries over different time periods, then look at what happens when those countries cut or raise corporate taxes and try to find patterns. Are corporate tax cuts followed by increases in corporate investment or foreign inward investment or more jobs? She may use regression analysis, a mathematical technique to get a better sense of whether one thing causes another or if the measured changes and correlations are caused by other things. She may produce numbers, expressed in 'elasticities' or 'semi-elasticities', which indicate how strongly economic sectors respond to tax changes. If she has the time and resources, she will look at different kinds of taxes, and at different kinds of corporations and investors. Are they greenfield foreign investors, who literally dig up green fields to build new factories from scratch, or are they simply shifting money around, buying up shares in existing local companies, contributing little to the local economy? She may also try to make allowances for the fact that a corporate tax cut is unlikely to have the same effect in Germany as in tiny Luxembourg or poverty-stricken Tanzania. There's endless stuff to grapple with, and oceans of research out there. Measurement probably won't be easy – our boffin must sweat to tease out the numbers – but she can get some numbers.[3]

Often the evidence leads straight to a story along the lines of 'Corporate tax cuts increase investment,' which of course is a good thing. You will get this line from quite a lot of mainstream published research. But now imagine that our researcher and policymaker are especially diligent. They dig more deeply and ask more searching questions, and when they do, the story starts to fall apart. And the more they dig, the more it disintegrates.

To get to the heart of this matter let's make a brief detour to middle America, to examine a particularly influential part of the corporate tax-cutting ideology. In 2011 Kansas elected as governor a man called Sam Brownback, a self-styled farm boy from one of the state's wealthiest families. Obstreperously anti-government and reflexively in favour of big business, he had earned a name for himself with stunts such as scrawling regular updates on the size of the national debt on a whiteboard in his office and washing the feet of a retiring aide in a biblical show of humility. He has called evolution 'a theory, not a fact' and once signed an executive order allowing state employees to be fired for being gay. After thundering about the role of lobbyists and big money in politics, he got re-elected with extensive help from a shadowy lobbying firm which, according to a US Senate deposition, bypassed campaign finance rules to help him.[4]

After being elected, Brownback signed into law the biggest tax cut in Kansas history, slashing personal and business taxes.[5] 'We'll have a real live experiment, and we're right next to some other states that haven't lowered taxes,' Brownback said. The tax cuts, he promised, would be 'a shot of adrenaline' in the heart of the Kansas economy.

He flew in Arthur Laffer, a gravel-voiced economist famous for the Laffer curve, an economics graph that the academic drew on a cocktail napkin for Dick Cheney in a hotel lobby in 1974. The curve resembles the blunt nose cone of a rocket pointing up. The idea is that at a zero per cent tax rate you get no revenue – but you also get nothing at 100 per cent because nobody will do any work. So the graph rises then falls, and somewhere in the middle there's a sweet spot of maximum tax revenue. Laffer was interested in the downward part of the slope on the right-hand side of the curve, where if you cut taxes, revenue increases! It is not hard to see why Dick Cheney and so many after him were enthralled by this apparent free lunch: people get taxed less, and the government gets more taxes. Everyone wins! 'More employment, more output, more production, more sales taxes,' Laffer said of Brownback's 'shot of adrenaline'. Standing side by side, the two men predicted people and businesses moving from Missouri to Kansas in great waves.[6]

More than seven years later the results of the experiment are in. The cuts proved an instant deficit bomb and have left piles of economic wreckage: school closures, potholes, educated Kansans fleeing the state, higher taxes for the poor and private-sector job culls. 'Email after email after email I get from constituents say "Please, let's stop this experiment,"' a Republican senator explained. Headlines appeared in local and national papers: SAM BROWNBACK GUTTED KANSAS: HOW AMERICA'S WORST GOVERNOR AND AN ULTRA-CONSERVATIVE IDEOLOGY WRECKED AN ENTIRE STATE.[7] In 2014 more than a hundred prominent Republicans publicly endorsed Brownback's Democrat rival for governor. Things got so bad that the Kansas supreme court ruled that educational spending was unconstitutionally low, and in June 2017 the Republican-controlled state legislature reversed many of the cuts. Brownback then quietly discontinued quarterly reporting on state GDP growth rates while publicly urging newly elected president Donald Trump to replicate his tax cuts nationwide – which Trump did.

There's a long and dishonourable history to the Laffer curve: suffice to say that the theory falls apart in practice, and Kansas is just the latest piece of evidence in an immense file that has proved it useless as a general guide to policy. You might think, for instance, that cutting corporate tax rates would indeed curb corporations' appetite for schemes to escape taxation, but if anything the opposite has happened: huge worldwide cuts in corporation tax rates since the 1980s have been accompanied by a rising tide of corporate tax planning (cheating) – a fivefold surge in tax-related profit-shifting in the last fifteen years alone, now costing governments $300–650 billion per year, with developing countries particularly hard hit. Why, after all, would a tax cut from 25 to 20 per cent stop companies lobbying for a further cut to 15 per cent? And why would a corporation accept 20 or even 15 when it can pay zero in a tax haven?[8]

The big point is: tax cuts really do reduce tax revenues, despite many lobbyists claiming the opposite and despite HMRC's endorsement of Laffer's fantasy curve in some of its models, skewing and distorting the evidence in favour of tax cuts.[9] And this brings us to the next really big point.

Let's assume, for the sake of argument, that our genuinely independent researcher found or created a study showing clearly that corporate tax cuts did increase local investment or attract foreign investors. This still wouldn't say anything useful about whether the tax cut was a good idea because the researcher only looked at the benefits of the tax cut; she didn't look at the costs. She knows there are winners and losers: the winners are interest groups such as multinational corporations, whose gains can usually be measured by looking at increased profits, investment and so on. But the costs are usually inflicted on a much more diffuse range of stakeholders, often through impacts that can't ever be measured.

But the politicians want numbers! Since 1981, for instance, US federal agencies have been required to use cost-benefit analyses as a basis for rule-making. So our researcher produces what numbers she can but only warns about unmeasurable costs. The thirst for hard numbers means the benefits get prominence and the warnings get ignored.

Take the UK's corporate tax cuts from 28 to 20 per cent, which the Big Four official was rejoicing about at the beginning of the chapter. The government has estimated that this will reduce UK tax revenues by £16.5 billion per year. With this much money you could run twelve Oxford Universities at full tilt. Or you could run nine Oxfords, and with the spare change double the resources of Britain's Financial Conduct Authority, multiply government cybersecurity resources three times over and double staff numbers at HMRC. Or you could build the Barts mega-hospital in London fifteen times over, every year. Or you could send nearly half a million kids to Eton each year, if you could fit them all in.[10]

Are these tax cuts a good trade-off? Do they make Britain more 'competitive'? Will they improve productivity?

The truth is that there is no way of answering these questions using numbers. Even though the research has produced a precise number for the cost – £16.5 million a year – you still aren't close to a real answer on the benefits. If budget cuts cull our schools or our crime-fighting sentinels, or just offend voters' sense of fairness and undercut popular support for the tax system, do these costs outweigh any possible investment increases? The costs are not only unmeasurable, there is no scientific or economic basis for deciding whether these trade-offs are worth it.

Our independent academic researcher may by now be feeling dizzy, but if she is a good researcher she will explain that only politics and democracy can answer these questions; the numbers don't help. Yet the myopic desire for numbers permeates some of Britain's most respected institutions and ultimately undermines their reliability. Take the Institute for Fiscal Studies (IFS), for instance. It is 'explicitly a *micro*economics research institute', its director Paul Johnson told me, and the impact of corporate tax 'is a firmly microeconomics issue'. They do not, he continued, do *macro*economics. This matters because microeconomics looks at the behaviour of individuals and institutions, one part of an economy, while macro looks at the level of a *whole* economy.

Policymakers ultimately need macro not micro answers to see the costs and benefits of tax slashing for a whole country. Micro thinking, if not very carefully handled, generates what economists call 'the fallacy of composition'. A benefit to one section of an economy – in this case big corporations – doesn't mean it's good for the whole economy. When the Labour Party in 2017 proposed hiking corporate income tax, the IFS produced a study saying this would increase revenue but warned that Britain would 'move down the competitiveness ranking relative to some other EU countries'.[11]

This same IFS study also pushed another tax-cutters' favourite, the old story that a significant share of the burden of corporation tax tends to get shifted to labour, suggesting that if you tax corporations more, they will hire fewer workers or pay them less. This claim is generally nonsense. Corporate taxes fall largely on the owners of corporations, who are overwhelmingly the mostly wealthy people. Donald Trump's giant tax cuts in 2017 are a case in point: he promised that the cuts would translate into a $4,000 pay rise for working families, whereas at the last count an estimated 83 per cent of the windfall went to the richest 1 per cent of Americans. Wall Street banks, big technology firms and big pharmaceutical firms earned massive windfalls from the tax cuts, while only 4 per cent of workers were expected to get an increase in pay or benefits. In fact, essentially the opposite proposition is true: corporate tax *cuts* shift the tax burden onto workers, who pay an increased proportion of the revenues raised by governments.[12]

It turns out that there is a long list of other hidden costs associated with cutting corporate taxes. Here's one example. If you slash corporate tax rates far enough, high earners may ask their employers to pay their salaries or fees to personal shell corporations rather than directly to them. This way they may pay tax at the corporate rate instead of the higher income tax rate, and they can often then use accounting devices to get money out of their shell corporation without triggering more tax. So a corporate tax cut also risks eating into income tax and National Insurance revenues.[13] In fact, in many countries a key reason for establishing corporate income tax in the first place was as a backstop to protect the take from personal income tax. This is another reason why cutting the corporate tax rate can actually increase overall tax avoidance, the opposite of what you might expect.

Imagine what might happen if, as some lobbyists want, corporate taxes were abolished entirely. You could perhaps make a heroic effort to estimate the damage this might cause to income tax revenues, and add that to the £16.5 billion. Given that in the UK personal income tax and National Insurance deliver over six times the revenue of corporate income tax, these losses could be large. But I am not aware of any academic effort to estimate this: there are so many imponderables and moving parts it may be impossible to produce serious numbers.

Worse, there's a feedback loop here. Cut corporate taxes too far, and people will say, 'Look, it's undercutting income tax! Let's cut the top rate of income tax to stop this!' It's a race to the bottom inside the tax system – not between two countries this time, but between two taxes.[14] As ever, this race shifts yet more wealth and power upwards.

Here's another problem. Corporate tax cuts tend to reward predatory rent-seeking behaviour over genuine wealth creation. Compare a business that has invested £100 million in a factory and its 500 workers and generates £5 million in taxable profits, with a debt-fuelled, financialised share-flipper with five employees, which invests £2 million in IT systems, also for a £5 million annual profit. If you cut the corporate tax rate from 40 to 20 per cent, the after-tax profit for both of them jumps by a million, from £3 million to £4 million. The factory owners find their returns on capital rise by 1 per cent – £1 million divided by £100 million. Nice free money if you can get it, but certainly not a game-changer. The share-flipper, by contrast, gets a 50 per cent boost – £1 million divided by £2 million for an after-tax return on capital fifty times bigger. That's serious money worth lobbying for.

This simple calculation illustrates how corporate tax cuts tend to incentivise and reward exactly the wrong sort of investor, adding fuel to the shareholder-value disaster that I described in the last chapter.[15] Corporate tax cuts for our economy are like refined sugar in the human body – empty financial calories with adverse long-term health effects.

How would you even start to try and measure the long-term costs of any of these things, and against what yardstick? You can't, even if you want to. Even UK government officials have recognised the problem – then dismissed it with a rhetorical smirk. 'It is not the government's intention to assess all businesses and divide them into producers and predators and then apply different tax rates to them, perhaps with a "predator surcharge",' said David Gauke, exchequer secretary to the Treasury. 'Such an approach would place considerable extra demands on HMRC.'

Mr Gauke should not joke about this, and he's also wrong. Remember, countries need investment that's embedded in the local economy, bringing jobs, skills and long-term engagement, where managers send their kids to local schools and the business supports an ecosystem of local supply chains. This is the golden stuff, and if it's nicely embedded, then a whiff of tax won't scare it away. If an investor is more sensitive to tax, then almost by definition it has shallower roots; tax will tend to frighten the less useful, more predatory stuff, which bring fewer jobs and local linkages.[16] So a corporate tax increase, Mr Gauke may be interested to learn, is in itself a predator surcharge, a fine way to sift out the socially useless chaff and retain the nourishing wheat.

Gauke should also have known what happened when Britain introduced its so-called controlled foreign company (CFC) reforms – essentially a watering-down of its defences against corporate tax haven activity, in the hope that it would entice foreign multinationals to set up tax-light operations in the UK. In 2014 the *Telegraph* ran an article suggesting these reforms were already proving a massive success, citing Big Four officials who predicted they would create over 5,000 jobs. 'Hundreds of multinational companies are lining up to establish oper-ations in the UK,' the article gushed, 'paving the way for thousands of new jobs and billions of pounds in extra tax revenues.'[17] The reforms 'would add £1bn to corporation tax revenues' apparently.

Yet what actually happened? First, that £1 billion appeared to refer to government estimates that the reforms would *cost* £1 billion a year in lost revenues. In a small investigation in 2015, I found only sixteen companies that said they were relocating their headquarters to the UK. Of these, I could only identify two – Lancashire, a Bermuda-based insurance company, and the advertising and PR company WPP – which said tax was the decisive reason. WPP didn't announce any new jobs in the UK; Lancashire said the move had created 'probably five or six' jobs in the UK. Aon, the world's largest insurance broker, said its relocation to the UK would bring twenty senior jobs, but added that tax wasn't decisive. The Italian car maker Fiat, which also announced that it was moving its tax domicile to the UK, said tax was *a* factor but not *the* factor, and said the move would have 'no impact on headcount in Italy or elsewhere'. An earlier Reuters poll of US firms that had relocated to Britain for these reasons could only positively identify around fifty jobs created in total, but then added that one partly tax-motivated transaction, in which Liberty Global took over Virgin Media, had involved 600 job *losses*. The benefits flowed overwhelmingly to large companies and their owners.[18] So, using the government's own estimates, this 'competitive' move would cost £1 billion in tax revenues per year and might well end up killing jobs.

And this particular pro-tax haven reform affects other countries: NGO ActionAid estimated it would cost developing countries around £4 billion in lost taxes per year, equivalent to over a third of Britain's foreign aid budget. Overall the research is clear: 'competitive' corporate tax cuts tend to attract profit-shuffling activities, don't usually create jobs or improve welfare, and generate a wide array of costs.[19] An estimated 40 per cent of measured global FDI is, as the IMF put it in 2018, 'completely artificial' – that is, investment in empty corporate shells in tax havens carrying out no real economic activity; conduits for financial flows en route to somewhere else. This inconvenience drives a coach and horses through of a lot of the research that policy makers have been relying on that claim that corporate tax cuts are a good idea.

If a researcher could somehow overcome this enormous obstacle, they would then be confronted with several others.[20]

One of these others is the alarming fact that the world is now a very different place, awash with capital. And this changes the calculations in a deeper way. Large corporations are sitting on fast-growing piles of uninvested money, nearly $3 trillion of it in the United States and Europe by mid-2017, according to Moody's. These are from large profits and are being squirrelled away in cash, treasury bills and more exotic financial instruments, instead of being invested in the businesses. This is an outcome and a reflection of inequality, as large firms and their owners bust unions, escape taxes and use mergers and monopoly powers to wrest a rising share of the economic pie away from workers, consumers, taxpayers and others. Since the rich spend a lower share of their income than the poor, this upward transfer of wealth saps overall spending power in our economies, so there's reduced demand for the goods and services produced by corporations, meaning they invest less. This is one of the main reasons why, as the IMF and others have found, inequality tends to reduce economic growth. This is an old economic problem. As John Maynard Keynes once put it, discussing financial globalisation and inequality in the oligarchical Gilded Age before the First World War (no relation of the Golden Age after the Second), 'society was so framed as to throw a great part of the increased income into the control of the class least likely to consume it'.

This three-trillion-dollar fact poses a large question for the tax cutters to answer. Why would a corporate tax reduction – adding to already vast uninvested cash piles – spur corporations to invest? Corporate tax cutting is like pushing on a string. And, given how quickly cash piles have been growing – a hefty 6 per cent a year, at the last count – any research based on past evidence can't take this factor into account.[21]

How can our diligent researcher incorporate all this stuff into a serious cost-benefit analysis? She can't. No one can.

The real experts in academia, government departments and think tanks – including those at the IFS – know all this. Government departments are beset by tensions between those who insist on using and framing evidence properly and those who want to please their bosses or the *Daily Mail*. 'It's not credulous little toadies with greasy forelocks just doing what some mad politician with glaring eyes tells them to do about corporate tax,' said an expert in evidence-based policymaking who has worked in government departments in the UK and many other countries. 'It's a real internal battle, and it's political.'[22]

Honest civil servants and academics will try to frame their evidence using a proper narrative, but somewhere in the evidence machine the nuances are wiped away. In the particular case I looked at, HMRC's model fed directly into a pretty graph 'showing' that corporate tax cuts would boost the economy even though no honest model could ever generate such a conclusion.[23]

The US anti-monopoly expert Kenneth M. Davidson has carried a small piece of paper in his wallet for years, containing a footnote from a 1977 article. 'The first step is to measure whatever can be easily measured,' it reads. 'This is OK as far as it goes. The second step is to disregard that which can't be measured or give it an arbitrary quantitative value. This is artificial or misleading. The third step is to presume that what can't be measured easily really isn't very important. This is blindness. The fourth step is to say that what can't be easily measured really does not exist. This is suicide.'

Like the giant fish in Ernest Hemingway's classic novel *The Old Man and the Sea*, the evidence has been progressively stripped of its meat until there's nothing left but a skeleton, whose bones are sold to an unsuspecting public as if they were nourishing tuna steaks. The sharks come in waves: the 'competitive' consensus nudging certain academics towards certain conclusions; the wall of corporate money selecting the 'right' academics in the research institutions; partisan players in the media cherry-picking numbers from a nuanced picture; and policymakers and politicians desperate to reach conclusions that will find favour with, say, the *Daily Mail* or the City establishment. Honest civil servants and researchers have to fight their way through all that. This is how corporate taxes get cut, through what is called evidence-based policy.

It didn't take HMRC long to respond to my Freedom of Information request about their evidence-based policy machine. The email was a terse official refusal to explain their 'Computable General Equilibrium' model; neither how its inner machinery worked nor what they had plugged into it. They told me that being transparent about this might 'prejudice commercial interests [which] could weaken our contractors in a competitive environment'. 'Commercial interests'? I queried. They told me to get lost again but did assure me that the model had been peer-reviewed by a private-sector outfit called Loch Alpine Economics.

Who were they? I wondered. Loch Alpine turned out to be an outfit run out of a large, pretty house in a leafy suburb of Madison, Wisconsin staffed by Christoph Böhringer and Thomas F. Rutherford, two fairly mainstream experts on modelling climate change who have clearly expanded their scope beyond climate issues.

Their review, which is available online, said HMRC's use of the model, which it called 'a multi-sector dynamic Ramsey model of intertemporal saving and investment', was 'poorly documented' but OK overall. Still none the wiser, I called Rutherford. He was defensive, suggesting that my criticisms were 'incredibly naive, on a par with Fox News's reporting on climate change'. But he agreed heartily that the model's credibility depended on what assumptions are plugged in. Loch Alpine's review does give a couple of clues about HMRC's black-box evidence machine; it relies on 'the neoclassical efficiency paradigm of competitive markets', adding that 'an optimal tax system under pure efficiency considerations boils down to equalising the MCPF of different taxes at the lowest level possible'. Whatever that may mean, anyone familiar with Chicago School economics and the concepts I've mentioned in this book will recognise the language.

This black box is an example of a recent fashion in tax policymaking circles for what is called dynamic scoring or dynamic modelling. The underlying idea is sensible: when government changes a tax, economic agents will respond by building or consuming more or less stuff or trying to dodge the tax. So you anticipate their responses and build them into your model. Which is fine. In theory. But the trillion-dollar question is: how do these models work, and what evidence gets put into them? Anyone can tweak the inputs and inner workings of these models to create whatever output suits them, which is why US tax expert Edward Kleinbard calls dynamic scoring 'a Republican ruse to make tax cuts look good'. Indeed, Loch Alpine's Christoph Böhringer has authored a paper which says that the models HMRC uses are 'doomed to remain a "black box" for non-experts'.[24] Here is a fabulous Panglossian machine that HMRC *may be* using to produce a predetermined output, then slapping an 'evidence-based policy' sticker on it. Why are they keeping it secret? At the time of writing, the Trump administration was using the dynamic scoring technique to justify a claim that $2 trillion of tax cuts would pay for themselves, Laffer style.

'Taxation, in reality, is life,' says Sheldon Cohen, a former top US tax official. 'If you know the position a person takes on taxes, you can tell their whole philosophy. The tax code, once you get to know it, embodies all the essence of life: greed, politics, power, goodness.'

And greed, politics, power, goodness, democracy and any number of other things – you can't put numbers on them. HMRC's black box can't handle those unmeasurables; it can only cope with the benefit side of the equation. This reminds me of the banker played by David Walliams in *Little Britain*, who if he had been presented with a proposal to hike corporate taxes would have tapped languidly at a keyboard before announcing in a bored voice, 'Computer says no.'

After all this, our honest academic researcher may be feeling that the task is hopeless, but in fact she still has a last card to play. Instead of trying to weigh iffy benefits against unmeasurable costs, she might take a short cut and try to figure out how corporate tax cuts affect the *whole* economy, measuring macro things like economic growth or total job creation. Many have tried to do this, often in ways that are more honest than plugging secret numbers into secret black boxes, but now a new set of obstacles heaves into view.

The main problem is that corporate tax cuts normally only represent a tiny share of economic activity, usually much less than 1 per cent of GDP, so it would be astonishing if this factor stood out clearly among all the myriad other ingredients of growth. And in any case, GDP growth is a narrow prism through which to judge success. A fast-growing country in which most of the benefits of growth flow to a few oligarchs isn't necessarily one you or I would want to live in. Nor is one where growth comes with poisoned rivers and choking pollution. Economists' myopia about GDP growth, explains Harvard economist Dani Rodrik, is a key reason why they have misunderstood trade globalisation so badly, failing to take seriously the question of how economic benefits are distributed across societies. This myopia has made it a lot easier for extremists and demagogues to win public support.

And beyond even this, the tax cutters need to overcome some awkward historical facts. The Golden Age, lasting for a quarter century after the Second World War, was an era of higher corporate and income taxes amid a much broader environment of progressive economic policies, and the era of fast-falling tax rates since then has accompanied long-term declines in growth and rising inequality. It's also inconvenient for the tax cutters that highly taxed Scandinavian and other European countries have grown just as fast as the lower-taxed Anglo-Saxon economies but with lower inequality and significantly better human development outcomes. It's more complex than simple cause and effect, but these indisputable facts give the tax cutters an Alp-sized mountain to climb before making their arguments.[25]

The best Petri dish for studying corporate taxes is again the United States. Juxtaposing US states provides useful insights, partly because there's so much data, and partly because it's much more reasonable to compare Michigan with Missouri than it is to compare Belgium with Bermuda or Bangladesh. In an exhaustive review of the evidence on state tax systems, Michael Mazerov of the Center on Budget and Policy Priorities concluded that 'Numerous academic studies find no correlation between state tax levels and various measures of state economic performance ... other studies find that higher taxes are actually associated with better economic performance.'[26]

Let's go back to Kansas again, this time to Marquette, a fading, slightly rusty agricultural hamlet of 600 souls deep in the countryside. In 2014 Marquette's last school closed as a direct result of Brownback's 'shot of adrenaline' experiment in tax cuts. At the final school meeting, angry parents held up pieces of paper with numbers on them to indicate how many children in their home were losing their school, but local businesspeople weren't cheering the tax cut either. 'For a business owner, you're better off having those teachers in those jobs here in Marquette; they shop in town and help you out that way,' said Steve Piper, who owned the grocery store. 'If your sales are down, if you are not making any money to start with, taxes mean nothing. It's a percentage of a smaller amount of money. When I sell my stores, is anyone going to want to buy a store in Marquette without a school in town?'[27]

And here Piper puts his finger on a crucial and often ignored point about corporate taxes. Income taxes on businesses are levied on profits, which are essentially the difference between two large numbers: revenues minus costs. Even relatively small changes to one or other side of that balance can have massive effects on your profits. Let's say, for example, your costs are 96 and your revenues are 100, for a profit of four. A tiny 3 per cent fall in revenues down to 97 slashes your gross profit from four to one, a full 75 per cent. A 5 per cent fall, down to 95, could bankrupt you. By contrast, a massive corporate income tax rate cut from 40 to 30 per cent will hardly move the needle: your profit goes up 10 per cent from 4 to 4.4.[28] So tax cuts that result in poorer public services can be especially damaging to small businesses because they can mess heavily with revenues and the ingredients of success while hardly reducing total costs. Not only that, but lower-margin businesses with big cost components, which tend to be hit hardest by tax cuts, are often the best kind of business to have in your state because large costs will tend to reflect a large and well-paid labour force or perhaps deep local supply chains – the stuff with which thriving local communities are built.

And business survey after survey reflects this. Corner store or globe-trotting multinational, tax cuts just don't matter that much. Corporate CEOs constantly bellyache that they need more tax cuts. Of course they do, but in the same way that my children say they *need* more ice cream. But asked to order what they're looking for when deciding where to locate real business units, company officials consistently rank factors other than tax as more important: the rule of law, a healthy and educated workforce, good infrastructure, access to prosperous, thirsty markets, good inputs and supply chains, and economic stability – and most of these require tax revenues. Low taxes usually come a distant fifth, sixth or seventh.[29] As Warren Buffett put it, 'I have worked with investors for 60 years and I have yet to see anyone [. . .] shy away from a sensible investment because of the tax rate on the potential gain. People invest to make money, and potential taxes have never scared them off.'[30]

You can slice this a different way. Among rich nations, high-tax countries have performed just as well as low-tax countries in overall GDP and growth terms, but with better health and social outcomes and less inequality. Or, as Martin Wolf, the *Financial Times'* chief economic commentator, put it, 'High-tax countries have been more successful in achieving their social objectives than low-tax countries. They have done so with no economic penalty.'[31]

The case against corporate tax cuts is so strong and the reasons why the research is wrong are so numerous that it is tedious to lay them all out. The ones I have described here are only a few of many.[32] But there is a more important point. It turns out that nearly all the arguments I have made or could make in this area can be modified and applied in other economic arenas – in fact almost any arena that involves big banks or multinational corporations.[33] And that's for a simple reason: the benefits to corporations of any particular policy are usually much easier to measure than many of the costs to other actors. It's child's play, for instance, to generate numbers showing how cutting workers' wages and benefits will boost company profits. But those cuts inflict costs such as more family breakdowns, higher inequality, less spending power, increased drug use, weakened faith in our shared economy and society. Most of these things are unmeasurable and long-term but no less important, so cost-benefit analyses based on numbers will systematically favour corporations against people. The result is, as the former IMF economist Simon Johnson put it, that 'the attitude took hold that what was good for Wall Street was good for the country ... A whole generation of policymakers has been mesmerised.'[34]

Perhaps the most important arena where the evidence machine works this way involves finance. How Britain treats and regulates its financial sector is immensely more important than what its corporate tax rates are. The biggest question here for Britain is: what are the costs and benefits of hosting a large financial centre like the City of London? This brings us back to the heart of this book: the finance curse. Here we find the same problem with the evidence machine and another peculiar, spectacular dimension to the story.

In 2009, in the teeth of public fury about the bankers' role in the financial crisis, New Labour Chancellor Alistair Darling and the UK Treasury set up an initiative to deliberately deepen and formalise the financial capture of the British government, or, as they put it, 'to strengthen further the quality of the promotional work for the UK-based international financial services industry'. The aim was not so much to clean up and reform the City after the crisis, as to head off the outrage threatening its privileges. The result was TheCityUK, a one-stop shop for financial lobbying run by the City of London Corporation, the local authority for the square mile of financial real estate that sits around the Bank of England at the geographical heart of London.

The City Corporation, as it is known, is not just a local authority; it is also *officially* a lobbyist for the UK financial sector and for financial liberalisation around the world. Its history stretches back a thousand years. It pre-dates the British parliament and is so special and different from other UK local authorities that when the Queen crosses into the square mile she is met by the lord mayor of the City of London (not to be confused with the mayor of London) and asks the lord mayor's permission to enter; he then offers her his sword as a symbol of his loyalty to her. The City Corporation also has an official called the remembrancer permanently installed in parliament, facing the speaker, whose job is to report back to the City what is going on – and of course to spread City influence in parliament.

Banks, law and accounting firms, and other private corporations get to appoint voters in local elections, meaning that the Chinese Communist Party, for instance, is effectively able to vote in British elections via the Chinese banks in the City. The City Corporation is also a giant old boys' network steeped in endless arcane traditions, and this network is constantly being renewed. Alongside the worshipful companies – of Skinners, Tallow Chandlers, Pewterers and many more, all City livery companies descended from old trade associations – there is the more modern Worshipful Company of Tax Advisers, founded in 1995, whose members have included many well-known names on the British tax scene. The City Corporation is in, the words of Baron Glasman, a long-standing critic, 'a medieval commune representing capital'.[35] It is certainly unlike any other institution in the world.

TheCityUK was set up as 'a coherent, strategic and focused City–Treasury nexus, which would sit at the heart of British development strategy and economic policymaking'.[36] Its official core mandates are to support 'the competitiveness of the financial services sector' and 'to demonstrate the importance of the UK financial services industry to a broader British audience' and further afield. Its board of directors and its advisory council are filled with representatives of British, American and Swiss banks, of tax havens like Jersey, of the Big Four accounting firms and other players. The president of its advisory council is the lord mayor of the City of London.

TheCityUK showers newsrooms with reports listing the benefits of financial services to the UK economy. At the last count, in late 2017, it was boasting of Britain's net $77 billion trade surplus in financial services, more than the United States and Switzerland, the two next largest, combined. Financial services, it continued, contributed $72 billion in annual tax revenues and employed a million people, with a further 1.2 million employed in related professional services such as management consultancy and law and accounting. These are big numbers – *huge* numbers – and their impact on public opinion is immense. But to anyone who has read this far, it should be obvious that this is just one side of the story. TheCityUK scrupulously does not mention the costs that oversized finance imposes on other parts of the British economy – and its data is dodgy too: even the benefits are much smaller than it claims.[37]

The costs include the so-called Dutch disease: inflows of money into Britain push up prices and the exchange rate, harming exporters by making their goods more expensive. There is the brain drain: the most talented people leave other economic sectors, civil society and government for high-paying jobs in the City. There is financialisation. There are regional economic distortions and rising inequality, which among many other things damage democracy and social cohesion. There is the widespread loss of faith in the British government and establishment following the public bailouts and the apparent immunity of bankers. Many of these costs are unmeasurable. What is the price of democracy? Society?[38]

The real price is what Gerald Epstein and Juan Montecino sought to estimate in the introduction to this book: a cumulative net £4.5 trillion hit to the UK economy. This number is, as the authors admit, subject to all kinds of provisos and uncertainties, just like everything else I've described in this chapter. But the point is that, unlike TheCityUK figures, which measure only benefits, this one includes both sides of the equation. It is a better, more honest estimate. And it is conservative, not least because it too cannot give a numerical value to many costs.

Yet despite all this, not only do we have TheCityUK promoting an entirely false, even meaningless, one-sided story about the financial sector's contribution to the British economy, it has also been official government policy to support this statistical conjuring act as a matter of strategic national importance. How's that for financial capture?

All this provokes two big questions.

First, if the evidence being wielded in support of corporate tax cuts or financial deregulation or any other pro-corporate neoliberal policies isn't there – and I'm saying here that it is *impossible* to create honest numbers, no matter how clever or honest your models are – then what is the poor policymaker to do?

Well, it's not as desperately difficult as it might seem. Evidence matters, and there is a place for numbers. But bad evidence is worse than no evidence. And there are other forms of evidence, which don't come from spreadsheets. One is called analysis: you make sensible arguments and judgements, and discuss and debate those openly with colleagues or the public. You beef this up with what the pioneering US economist James Henry called investigative economics. Get out of your armchairs, recognise those uncertainties, judge where your spreadsheets might help and, crucially, where they won't. Go out and *talk* to people. Discover the blood and guts of what's going on: who's doing what with whom, how and why. For many economists that's difficult. It can be scary to pick up the phone to busy and important people making economic decisions, but it is a great way to find out how the world actually works.

And there are two more words to guide policymakers forsaken by data. One is 'politics'; the other is 'democracy'. In these two infuriating concepts lies the wisdom of centuries. And these, for me, are the most legitimate of all guides to policy.

The second question is this. If the numerical estimates for costs and benefits of certain policies affecting multinationals are all bunk, then why believe our estimate? To answer this, turn back to the part where our honest academic, instead of measuring benefits to one part of the economy and then trying to subtract unmeasurable, incomparable costs from other parts, decided to use measures that encompass the whole economy, such as the effects these policies might have on long-term economic growth. For corporate taxes this wasn't feasible, mainly because corporate tax cuts are such a small part of the economic pie that it is impossible to disentangle their effects from all the other crazy stuff happening. But finance is a much bigger beast: with financial assets equivalent to more than ten times Britain's GDP it is the largest sector of our economy by far, certainly big enough for its impact to be teased out and measured.

For all the uncertainties, our numbers are a better starting point for understanding what is going on. They show that the UK's oversized financial sector is inflicting a staggering net cost on the people of Britain. This book has shown some of the many ways in which this happens. Indisputably, Britain has a bad case of the finance curse.

Conclusion

In October 2013 Britain's Chancellor George Osborne said on a visit to Beijing that it would be his 'personal mission' to make London the world's top global centre for trading, investing and making payments in China's renminbi currency, whose international use had been heavily restricted by official Chinese controls. On Osborne's visit the two sides signed a deal granting London an initial £8 billion quota for foreign institutions to invest in China using renminbi, and also agreed that Britain would bend its own banking rules to let Chinese banks operate in London with reduced oversight. On the same visit, Osborne announced that Chinese companies would be allowed to own stakes of up to 100 per cent in British nuclear power stations. At the heart of the many agreements reached on that visit was a simple quid pro quo: mouth-watering financial appetisers for the City of London, which is determined to be the top global centre for trading renminbi as China slowly relaxes official controls – in exchange for Chinese access into Britain's nuclear industry.[1]

When China's president Xi Jinping visited London two years later, the same quid pro quo was evident. China's central bank completed a 30 billion renminbi ($4.7 billion) sale of Chinese Treasury Bonds on markets in the City of London, its first ever debt offering in any currency outside China – and this happened within hours of the state-run China General Nuclear Power Corporation (CGN) signing a deal to take a large stake in the Hinkley C nuclear power plant in Somerset, the most expensive power plant in world history. CGN also signed preliminary agreements to get involved in two more nuclear power projects, Sizewell C in Suffolk and Bradwell B in Essex, the latter of which would involve a fully Chinese design. Xi received a 41-gun salute fired from Green Park, plus another 62 from the Tower of London, and a ride with the Queen in the royal carriage along The Mall to Buckingham Palace. Chinese and British officials described it as a 'golden time' in Britain's relationship with China. Only three months earlier, US authorities had indicted CGN for a two-decade-long conspiracy to steal nuclear secrets.

When Theresa May became prime minister in July 2016, she briefly paused the nuclear deals on security grounds but gave the final go-ahead two months later under pressure from the City of London, and after the Chinese gave 'a series of warnings' that rejection would damage the 'golden era of relations'.

In economic terms, the Hinkley C project is 'a dreadful deal, laughable', as one expert put it: not just financially and technically risky, but also likely to be obsolete once it comes on stream in 2025 or later, as renewable energies and 'smart grid' technologies provide ever cheaper and safer alternatives. British consumers are expected to pay tens of billions, over and above the normal price of electricity, to subsidise this project if it goes ahead as planned.[2] Britain is pursuing an economically unviable nuclear industry for many complex and varied reasons, including lobbying by big-money interests and genuine disagreements about the future price of electricity. But one other reason is to support Britain's military nuclear forces: without a civilian nuclear programme behind these forces it is hard to keep the ecosystem of relevant knowledge alive to support a nuclear weapons programme. And this last reason touches on an aspect of the finance-for-nuclear deals that could ultimately be more important than the financial side: national security.

British nuclear and security experts have greeted news of this Chinese entry into such a sensitive industry with horror. 'If you build a plant yourself, you can get into the guts of our energy infrastructure through the back door, with cyber keys and so on,' said Paul Dorfman, a nuclear expert at University College London who also advises the Ministry of Defence, among others. 'Everyone knows that China hacks in an unbelievable way: it is almost a joke. No other OECD country would let China anywhere near its critical energy or communications infrastructure.' While we are right to fret about Russian cyber attacks on Britain, and the penetration of corrupt and criminal Russian elements into the City of London and the British establishment, China – and specifically, the Chinese Communist Party

(CCP) under Xi Jinping – potentially poses a deeper, richer, more multifaceted long-term threat to Britain's and the West's security.

The CCP's policies on building up Chinese industry and economic strength have had the wonderful effect of lifting hundreds of millions of Chinese people out of poverty, and China's industrial miracle has spread many positive economic effects across the world, not least the low-cost imports from China that we all enjoy. But this, of course, is not the full story. The Chinese opening to world trade since the 1970s has done little to make the CCP less repressive. This is often couched as a human rights issue – the CCP is well known for its attacks on the Dalai Lama as a 'wolf in monk's robes', for instance – but for Western countries the dangers are much broader. The CCP has global ambitions, under a plan that Xi once said aimed to 'make the foreign serve China' – a vast, single-minded and all-encompassing three-dimensional game of global chess to achieve world dominance. Its 'United Front Work Department', which gets an estimated $10 billion a year in state funding, seeks to 'charm, co-opt or attack well-defined groups or individuals' in order to strengthen CCP's political control at home and gain influence overseas, and gather intelligence. United Front training manuals describe it as 'a big magic weapon which can rid us of 10,000 problems in order to seize victory'.

China's new global assertiveness is hardly a surprise for such a fast-rising power, and it may seem a bit rich for British people in particular to criticise its sharp-pointed tactics: after all, Britain in centuries past was the ruthless, expansionist, predatory power bent on world domination. And the United States, the superpower that took over after the collapse of the British empire, has not – to put it mildly – always served as a shining example of benevolent leadership to the world, particularly in its increasingly oligarchical and financialised form of economic expansion of recent decades, for instance, or its 'global war on terror'. Yet our hypocrisy and often appalling history in exerting our global power does not alter the fact that the rise of China will not just be a story of one ugly hegemon replacing another. This shift potentially threatens many of our most cherished and valuable ideals and beliefs. Liberal values such as freedom of expression or religion, academic independence and individual rights are anathema to the CCP, and it is seeking to undermine these ideals where it can – including in Britain and the West.[3] Western democracies once hoped to export liberal values to China: now we are already finding ourselves having to defend these values on our home ground.

Meanwhile the CCP, and other foreign powers, would like to shatter the Western alliance that has underpinned Western security and prosperity since the Second World War. To this end it is exploiting rifts and weaknesses in foreign societies: it has already made considerable headway in Australia and New Zealand, where it has channelled funding to certain political players as one component of a broader strategy to 'gradually wean the two countries off their alliance with the United States while boxing in their public debate about China'.[4]

The finance curse, in all its divisive, weakening, oligarchical effects, means that, among major Western economies, Britain is the most vulnerable to Chinese influence. The nuclear deals of 2013–16 are a clear sign of this, as was Britain's City-influenced decision in 2015 to become a founding member of the Chinese-led Asian Infrastructure Bank, a decision that led to US officials taking the rare step of publicly rebuking Britain for its 'constant accommodation with China'. Britain is especially vulnerable because of the City, which contains the CCP's strongest levers of influence over the British government *by far*. That is the fruit of a simple formula: the CCP has wide influence over financial players in the City, and the City has long ago overrun and captured large parts of British policymaking, regulatory and crime-fighting apparatus.

Other, less visible, hostile interests can use the City to spread malign influence. A US counter terrorism expert who has worked with large banks told me that the City's willingness to do deals with the world's worst scoundrels threatened the UK's traditional role as a solid US ally. 'I always say to colleagues: don't assume the British are our friends in everything – especially for anything finance related,' he said. 'That is where I think in general Britain is really playing with fire. The US especially will start asking – very reasonably – to what extent exactly is Britain with us or against us in this area.' Some in the US are now waking up to the City's dangerous game, he said, and Britain will pay a 'big price' internationally for this, which won't be mitigated by any 'special relationship' the UK thinks it has with Washington. 'If it's ever necessary to throw Britain under the bus, the US will not hesitate.'[5] As we have seen time and again in this book, the City's 'capture' of the British establishment is anchored in the Competitiveness Agenda: the constant threat by the owners of rootless or foreign capital that they will relocate to more welcoming places if they don't get what they want.

The City has always looked after its own interests, at the expense of other parts of the nation if necessary, and when it comes to national security, things are no different. City financial institutions answer to shareholders, often foreign shareholders, ahead of the interests of the people of Britain. Hostile powers know this: they can deliberately manipulate City institutions to be secretive transmission belts for influence. Take, for instance, the biggest of the City's banking beasts, HSBC – originally the Hong Kong and Shanghai Banking Corporation, a multinational giant with its headquarters in London. Its international balance sheet is around $2.5 trillion, which is the same size as Britain's GDP. In 2015 HSBC announced a strategic 'pivot to Asia', transferring resources away from Europe and other markets to this rising centre of world growth. By 2017 it said that over half its employees and nearly 90 per cent of its $17 billion in global profits came from Asia: most from Hong Kong and China.[6] For this reason alone, HSBC is more likely to do what the CCP tells it to do than what the British government tells it to do. But it is more significant than that: HSBC has shown that it can, and does, tell the British government what to do. One of the bank's favourite levers is drawn straight from the Competitiveness Agenda: its periodic, widely flagged 'reviews' of whether it will keep its headquarters in London or move it to Hong Kong. HSBC officials brief selected journalists and pundits with the message that it is 'considering' moving its headquarters out of the UK, maximising British national anxiety. Its last such review, in 2016, was widely credited with persuading the government to weaken its approach to taxing and regulating the City of London.[7]

If Britain keeps pursuing the City's agenda, especially its desire to keep London at the forefront of the internationalisation of China's renminbi currency and in the global expansion plans of Chinese financial institutions, this route to influence will grow – meaning that we will keep bleeding concessions to the CCP in potentially all sorts of other areas, not just finance. Brexit will worsen our anxiety, as the potential loss of some European markets sparks more calls for the UK to show that it is 'open for business'.

Oversized finance and its agenda is an open doorway that has already let in some of our worst nightmares: poverty, soaring inequality, rising social conflict, economic crisis and stagnation, cross-border organised crime, and lawless elites lording it over the rest of us with impunity. If that door isn't closed, and soon, even bigger global threats will creep in – some armed with nuclear weapons.

This is a new competition being played out on multiple fronts; economic, strategic, diplomatic and military. What is now unrolling across the world, with Russia seeking to sow divisions and undermine the West, and China's CCP playing a longer game to dominate it and everyone else, is a genuine competition between nations: very different from the fake economic 'competition' between nations under the Competitiveness Agenda that I've described in this book. Britain is trying to stay strong in the real competition by trying to get ahead in the fake one, by racing faster than the rest to attract ever more dubious money to the City.

It should be obvious by now that this is not a winning strategy. In fact, the finance curse points us in exactly the opposite direction for Western countries. The *Financial Times* columnist Rana Foroohar puts this in terms of a leading question: in the great global game of strategic rivalry in the twenty-first century, 'which country will be better able to control its moneyed elites?'[8]

Those elites, in the era of financialisation and the finance curse, are increasingly the wealth extractors instead of the wealth creators, and they are weakening our countries. I am reminded here of an advertising jingle for the Weebles: small egg-shaped children's toys that you could push around but which always stayed upright: 'Weebles wobble but they don't fall down.' They stayed standing because the weight was concentrated at the base. And so it is for our unequal, beleaguered democracies. The more economic weight that is retained by our hard-working poorer and middle classes, the stronger and more unified our nations will be. And the more wealth is concentrated at the top, the more of a pushover our countries will be.

Inequality caused by wealth extraction is especially dangerous and divisive. That's not just because the poor and middle classes feel increasingly left out, and have less and less to lose, but also because the billionaire classes need to distract us away from focusing on how they got rich. So they revert to the old political formula: using their control over the media to deflect popular fury in other directions, towards people with the wrong skin colour or the wrong sexual orientation, or from the wrong religious groups. The world has seen this hate-filled formula before.

*

I hope that some readers will respond to this book by asking themselves a question: what can I do to change things?

Reform is difficult, the City's power is immense, and recent events aren't encouraging. Fortunately there is a clear path forwards, and enormous space is now starting to open up for those who wish to push for the necessary change.

To understand how to move forwards, we can start by learning something from a relatively recent reform movement: the global fightback against tax havens. Before my last book, *Treasure Islands*, was first published in 2011, most people thought of tax havens as exotic, colourful sideshows to the world economy, mostly restricted to a few palm-fringed islands and Switzerland. Since then, however, the Panama Papers and a string of other revelations about tax havens have helped to show the problem in much more detail, confirming its immense global scale. Few people now dispute the central role that the global tax haven racket has played in the world economy, or Britain's and the US's role at the heart of it. It's not uncommon now to hear people angrily discussing tax havens in pubs and in cinema queues. The movement's success in raising awareness in Britain and several other countries has been stunning.

Yet despite this groundswell of public awareness, actual progress in Britain's fight against tax havens has proved underwhelming so far. This is for a couple of big reasons, beyond the obvious fact that influential offshore interests are resisting change. For one thing, people in Britain are often ambivalent about Britain's role in the offshore game: we wring our hands about the damage tax havens wreak on other countries, but we struggle to mobilise large domestic coalitions to fight on behalf of foreigners – and (whisper it quietly) we like the money that the City brings in to Britain. Many people think that this money must be benefiting them somehow: even if they know it's a harmful race to the bottom, they sigh and lament that Britain is trapped in this global race and that despite all the ugliness we must keep racing, even if only for Britain's sake. The only way to stop or curb the race, many believe, is to agree some sort of multilateral armistice with other countries, through international cooperation and collaboration. And this belief creates new hurdles: not least that getting countries to collaborate on complex problems such as taxing multinationals across borders is like herding squirrels on a trampoline. In each country, powerful elites getting rich off the race have an incentive to ensure that their countries cheat. And most voters aren't that interested in this complex, distant global stuff. Good luck trying to get 150,000 people on the streets with placards to support the OECD's Common Reporting Standard (an international scheme to increase transparency in global finance by getting countries to share financial information with each other).

The really good news here is that there is a much more powerful way forwards.

In the 1983 movie *War Games*, the actor Matthew Broderick plays a computer geek who hacks into the US Department of Defense's supercomputer and gets dragged into a game of strategy called Global Thermonuclear War. As the game merges with reality, the machine races through thousands of scenarios before concluding: 'A strange game. The only winning move is not to play.'[9] We are in the same position now. If the finance curse analysis that too much finance hurts your economy is correct, then it makes sense to shrink the role of finance in your economy – so, logically, you can and should step out of the race, unilaterally.

That last word 'unilaterally' is key. With this understanding we open up tremendous democratic space to tax, regulate and police our economies and our societies. Our nation will feel less need to accede to the demands of potentially hostile foreign powers, monopolists, tax haven operators, private equity titans, and a host of other wealth extractors. Global coordination and cooperation can help and are worth trying where possible, but they aren't the prerequisites for the change that we need. And this much more straightforward approach to strengthening our nation in the face of the coming storms carries another enormous benefit: by tackling the finance curse through appealing to national self-interest, we can mobilise far larger and more powerful constituencies for reform than in the fight against tax havens.

If we decide to tackle the finance curse, there are some easy targets we can begin with.

The global fightback against tax havens was originally led by the Tax Justice Network, with which I have worked. One crucial part of its stunning success in raising awareness was to combine deep, cross-disciplinary professional expertise – including accountants, bankers, lawyers, journalists and economists – with a truly radical voice and a willingness to take robust, uncompromising, even violent positions against the prevailing establishment consensus. We engaged the media, but we also deliberately targeted different constituencies, one after another, seeking to wake each up and explain how tax havens mattered to them. We began with non-governmental organisations (NGOs) focused on helping developing countries, explaining to them how tax havens helped elites in poorer countries steal their nations' wealth, in quantities much larger than were being delivered to those countries in foreign aid. We moved on to groups worried about inequality, organisations worried about the overweening powers of big banks and multinationals, and to groups focused on the impact of local austerity policies – asking why citizens were facing cutbacks when multinationals or billionaires weren't paying their taxes. We engaged with labour unions, human rights organisations, and even some receptive governments whose tax revenues were being undermined by tax havens. Each time, our aim was to act merely as the kindling or spark to get these bigger players burning. Soon, we could count on powerful allies.

With this approach, we can now generate awakenings in related areas. Take anti-monopoly, for instance, which is at least as big an issue as tax havens. In Britain and in Europe there is no comparable organised platform to challenge the establishment consensus on monopolies: to put it harshly, most civil society groups and their funders are all but asleep on this issue. As with the fight against tax havens, this is a battle against the corruption of markets with the potential to build alliances and support all across the political spectrum, from people on the traditional left concerned with inequality and oversized corporate power, to those on the traditional right who fret about the corruption of markets and the disappearance of effective competition. What is needed now is an expert, radical, new civil society movement to create a complete and revolutionary reappraisal of how our democracies deal with monopolies. Such a counterforce is now emerging in the United States, focused around a poorly resourced but highly influential expert group called the Open Markets Institute.[10] We urgently need something like this in Britain and in Europe.

We need a new movement to overturn this corrupt status quo. How have our competition authorities allowed our too-big-to-fail banks which crashed the economy to become even bigger now than they were before the crisis? Why are the Big Four accounting firms not broken up, along the fault lines of their conflicts of interest? Why are they not regulating tech monopolies like Amazon, Google, Facebook effectively in the public interest, sitting back while they drain most of the advertising profits away from the media groups and others who do the hard work of creating all that content, and shovel the profits into tax havens? Why do they tolerate all those 'middleman monopolies' where powerful interests park themselves on the crucial choke points in global supply chains, extracting wealth from all the players in the network, like Veblen's smug toads snapping up passing flies? Change here will be immensely hard, of course – but without any organised counterforce, it will be impossible.

Here's another way we can think about tackling the finance curse. This is, in essence, the exact opposite of the Competitiveness Agenda, and you might call it 'smart capital controls'. The aim here is not so much to try and control flows of capital *out* of our economy, but to be selective and careful about what flows *in*. These controls would usually not come in the form of barriers to flows of capital at the border, but instead in the form of policies designed to make the economy work better by protecting us from the more dangerous forms of global money.

For example, billions of dollars of money flooding into our property market from former Soviet republics is not helping Britain as a whole: while it may make wealthier homeowners feel richer and deliver windfalls to estate agents and City bankers, it squeezes others out of the property market – and also poses many other dangers, such as feeding boom-and-bust economics, or serving as a vector for wealthy foreign owners to corrupt our politics.[11] Policies to control these inflows could range from outright bans on certain kinds of investment in the property market; to radical transparency, forcing the names of the beneficial owners of all real estate in Britain into the public domain; to a land value tax, levied on the value of each square metre of underlying land, which could jimmy a stream of tax revenues out of wealthy foreigners who own land in the UK, and channel this towards compelling social priorities, such as a basic income. A land value tax would be, if set up right, unavoidable: even if the land were held under an impenetrable Cook Islands trust, if whoever owns or controls or benefits from it does not cough up the right amount of tax each year, the land (or a portion of it) would be forfeit and you can send the bailiffs in. These kinds of 'smart capital controls' would rebalance our housing markets, reduce housing booms and crashes and the number of empty homes, curb inequality, and keep potentially criminal elements out of our markets. Separately, we can find smart ways to discourage flows of money into Britain from the abusive private equity firms. If this inward investment serves as a crowbar for looting and hollowing out our productive economic base, then we are much better off without it. Smart capital controls would remove the tax breaks and incentives for looting, while leaving Britain open to genuine productive job-creating investment.

A policy of smart capital controls may also discourage London from serving as an offshore hub for renminbi trading, not just because of its potential as a vector for CCP influence over British policymaking, but also because such trading tends to increase the size and influence of finance in the British economy, which the finance curse shows us is to our detriment. Smart capital controls would favour dramatically increased capital safety buffers at big banks, reducing City profits but making the banking sector more stable and less prone to gambling at the taxpayers' expense, delivering overall benefits to our country. Smart capital controls would give the police the authority and resources to properly police criminal activity in the City, for the first time in many decades. Britain's people would similarly benefit if we were to impose radical transparency on the British-controlled tax havens, and force them to stop creating regulatory and tax loopholes for global banks and multinationals.

In essence, we need to engage in a huge clean-up, to drive out the bad and preserve the good. The finance curse shows that the British economy would grow more strongly as a result, and gain in many other ways.

None of this would be *easy* – there would be short-term dislocation and political fallout – and European principles of free movement of capital may stymie some of these progressive measures. But it is within reach. Until now, the Competitiveness Agenda has proved to be the great intellectual blockage preventing people from seeing the possibility for change, and protecting the City of London. People wrongly believe that there is a trade-off between democracy and economic prosperity, thinking that more democracy damages the City, which reduces our prosperity. But the finance curse reveals this agenda to be a billionaire-friendly hoax: a house of cards, ready to fall. Most competent economists already know that this version of the competitiveness story is foolish. Millions of struggling people across the country also know it isn't working for them. But judging by the punditry and the mainstream media, most of the influential people in the country don't get it yet. But this blockage is quite easily dislodged, and the finance curse analysis gives us the tools to do it. There is no trade-off. More democracy means more prosperity and higher economic growth. And a smaller, better City. Once this blockage is cleared, sweeping new vistas of political possibility open up. If the City of London has imposed a £4.5 trillion hit on the British economy, as the research in the Introduction suggests, then reversing the finance curse would deliver transformational gains. This is a vast opportunity for any political party in Britain. Such a brazen approach would upset many in the establishment – but if put together in the right way it could prove immensely, election-winningly popular. People who often feel hopeless about prospects for change often forget that democracy is a mighty weapon, and it remains very much alive.

If Brexit goes ahead, as seems likely, Britain could go in two different directions. It could try to pursue the Singapore-on-Thames model, as a 'competitive' island racing ever faster and abasing itself ever more submissively in pursuit of the wealth of the world's oligarchs, criminals and tax-escaping multinationals. Or it could go the other way, and pursue the interests of its own people instead. So we are at a crossroads: a particularly crucial moment for setting Britain's future direction. The changes that are now needed are revolutionary ones. But we are already in revolutionary times, whether we like it or not. Trump and Brexit are probably the harbingers of bigger changes to come. The new threats that are now rapidly materialising, including those posed by growing financial stability risks, climate change, Russia, China, the monopolising technology giants and artificial intelligence, and the growing divisions in our societies fed by growing inequality, are on a fall-of-the-West scale.

If you want to help push change in the right direction, there is much you can do: political action, donating to an influential reform group, or going on a demonstration (and you'll find that 'Break the Finance Curse' fits neatly on a placard). The time for timidity has passed. It is no longer good enough to be a Facebook warrior, sending out messages to communities of people who already agree with you. If you can persuade just one other person to genuinely change their mind about the dangers posed by the oversized financial centre in our midst, you will already have made a strong contribution.

The old political divisions between left and right are dead. In today's Britain, one of the greatest political divisions is between those who support financialisation and the finance curse, and those who want to return finance to its proper place, serving society. Which side are you on?

Acknowledgements

Many people helped me write this book. After my family, John Christensen takes top credit. We developed the finance curse concept together over several years, but his influence on my thinking is older. As Director of the Tax Justice Network he introduced me properly to the world of tax havens, which in my view is the best possible entry point for understanding modern global finance. Others who have been more than generous with their time and/ or contacts include Andrew Baker, Richard Brooks, the group at Manchester University formerly known as CRESC, the Enlighten project, Andy Green, James Henry, Abby Innes, Adam Leaver, Peter Morris, John Singleton, Jim Stewart, Matthew Watson, Duncan Wigan and others who wish to remain unrecognised. Beyond these people, I offer great thanks to the many others who generously offered their time and insights over the past few years.

Notes

1. Trainline.com Limited is owned by Trainline Holdings Limited, which is owned by Trainline Group Investments Limited, which is owned by Trainline Junior Mezz Limited, which is owned by Trainline Investments Holdings Limited, which is owned by Victoria Investments Newco Limited (Jersey), which is owned by Victoria Investments Bidco Limited, which is owned by Victoria Investments Midco Limited, which is owned by Victoria Investments Pikco Limited, which is owned by Victoria Investments Intermediate Holdco Limited, which is mostly owned (around 300 million out of 311 million shares) by Victoria Investments Finco Limited – the remaining 11 million or so shares are owned by named French people linked to Trainline's operations in France. However, the Finco company is owned by Victoria Intermediate Topco Limited (Jersey), which is owned by Victoria Investments S.C.A. (Luxembourg). The general partner (GP) of this Luxembourg entity is Victoria Manager SARL (Luxembourg). All the companies so far are UK companies unless otherwise stated. The Trainline.com accounts for 2017 list Victoria Investments Finco Limited as the ultimate parent company, and list KKR & Co. LP as 'the ultimate controlling party, on behalf of the funds under its management'. It is possible that some details have changed, since some of the annual returns outlining the shareholdings date to as early as January 2016. A prospectus for KKR Acceleration Aggregator LP, a company owned by KKR but otherwise unrelated to Trainline, published in December 2016 by the German financial regulator BaFin, lists KKR Management LLC as the General Partner of KKR & Co.

LP. It also lists several other companies which appear to be linked to Trainline: KKR Victoria GP Limited (Cayman), KKR Victoria Co-Invest LP (Cayman), Trainline International Limited, Trainline.com limited branch (Luxembourg) and KKR Victoria Aggregator LP, a Cayman exempted limited partnership, which is represented by its general partner KKR Victoria Aggregator GP Limited (Cayman). This adds up to twenty-two companies in the Trainline cluster. As of 25 June 2018 KKR listed 183 active (i.e. 'real') portfolio companies on its website. • **2.** By the 'Trainline Group' I am referring to Victoria Investments Finco Limited, which Trainline.com describes as the ultimate parent company. Its accounts show total revenues of almost £153 million, of which around £148 million was from the UK. Staff costs were just £33 million or so, and 'finance costs' were £45 million. It is hard to know what those are, since these payments flow upwards to a company in Jersey, where the information is not available. See 2017 accounts, p.25, for the £148 million, and p.26 for staff costs. Trainline also makes money selling digital services to rail companies. • **3.** The resource curse thesis was first properly aired in Jeffrey D. Sachs and Andrew M. Warner, 'Natural Resource Abundance and Economic Growth', NBER Working Paper 5398, National Bureau of Economic Research, December 1995. Another early classic was Terry Lynn Karl, *The Paradox of Plenty: Oil Booms and Petro-States*, University of California Press, 1997. • **4.** The 500 per cent/100 per cent UK/ US statistics for 2006 are from Andrew Haldane, 'The Contribution of the Financial Sector Miracle or Mirage?', Future of Finance Conference, London, 14 July 2010. More recently the IMF, taking a wider view beyond banking to include insurance and other financial sector assets, found that the equivalent figure for the UK was around 1,000 per cent of UK national income in 2015. See 'Spain, Financial System Stability Assessment', IMF, October 2017, Figure 1: 'Aggregate Assets of Financial Institutions', 2015, p.11. See also 'UK national balance sheet: 2017 estimates', Office for National Statistics, Table 2: 'Value of UK financial assets and liabilities', showing total financial assets of £31.5 trillion. By comparison, UK GDP was $2.6 trillion (£1.9 trillion) at market prices and US$2.8 trillion (£2.1 trillion) at purchasing power parity, meaning that on this (different) measure, financial assets were equivalent to 12–15 times GDP. • **5.** As *The Economist* put it, 'Britain's various elites once directed their most gifted offspring towards Parliament. Today it is as if they have all decided to stop sending their best.' For a much deeper exploration of all this, see Aeron Davies, *Reckless Opportunists: Elites at the End of the Establishment*, Manchester University Press, 2018. • **6.** This phenomenon is widely recognised and known as the Dutch disease, named after a long slough of economic despond that the Netherlands fell into after making giant gas discoveries in the 1950s. Large net financial inflows to the UK due to the activities of the City of London can have similar 'Dutch Disease' effects, potentially damaging other sectors, though this has not been extensively researched. However, recent patterns suggest there is an effect. For instance, when sterling fell by 20 per cent after being ejected from the European Exchange Rate Mechanism in 1992, this was followed by four years of manufacturing growth – within a long-term pattern of decline. Then in 1996 and 1997, amid a great City financial boom, sterling rose by 25 per cent and stayed there for over a decade, and suddenly the manufacturing sector started shedding jobs again. Sterling fell after the global financial crisis, which may help explain why manufacturing employment did not fall at a faster pace in the ensuing recession. On this, see Tony Dolphin, 'Don't bank on it: the financialisation of the UK economy', Institute for Public Policy Research, 2012, especially p.36. • **7.** See, for instance, 'Time for Change: a New Vision for the British Economy', Institute for Public Policy Research, August 2017. It notes on p.47 that manufacturing as a share of the European economy has fallen from 19 to 17 per cent since the mid-1990s, but has fallen from 17 to just over 10 per cent in Britain. While Japan and Germany display a wide range of competitive industries, Britain's revealed comparative advantage is concentrated massively in just two sectors: financial services and insurance. On inequality, this is widely documented. See, for instance, 'Understanding the Socio-Economic Divide in Europe', Organisation for Economic Co-operation and Development, 26 January 2017, Figure 2.1. Gini coefficients (a measure of inequality) for 22 European countries range between 0.25 for Denmark, the least unequal, and just below 0.36 for the UK, whose Gini is a shade lower than that of the most unequal country, Estonia, whose Gini is just above 0.36. What is more, Gini is an imperfect measure of inequality because it does not adequately reflect extreme wealth concentration among the top 1 or 0.1 per cent, which is an especially British phenomenon. • **8.** See *Are firms underinvesting – and if so why?* speech given by Sir Jon Cunliffe, Deputy Governor Financial Stability, Bank of England, 8 February 2017. Also see, for a visual breakdown, Fig. 7 p.21 in *Our friends in the City: Why banking's return to business as usual threatens our economy*, New Economics Foundation, 2016. • **9.** On investment rates, see 'An international comparison of gross fixed capital formation', Office for National Statistics, 2 November 2017. It states that between 1997 and 2017 'the UK had the lowest average value of GFCF [gross fixed capital formation] as a percentage of GDP of any Organisation for Economic Co-operation and Development (OECD) nation'. On a GDP per capita basis at market prices, World Bank data showed for 2016: France $41,400, UK $42,400, Finland $43,400, Belgium $46,600, Sweden $48,900, Germany $48,900, Denmark $49,000, Netherlands $50,600 and Norway $58,800. (France is a shade lower than the UK, but that is because French people work fewer hours each year.) On productivity (GDP per hour worked), OECD data showed France at $59.90 against the UK's $48.30; the other countries in the previous list lay between $60 and $65, except for Finland at $52.70. • **10.** For a discussion of the 'let them eat credit' era, see in particular Greta R. Krippner, *Capitalizing on Crisis: The Political Origins of the Rise of Finance*, Harvard University Press, 2012. The phrase comes from Raghuram Rajan, *Fault Lines*, Princeton University Press, 2011. • **11.** John Kay, *Other People's Money: Masters of the Universe or Servants of the People?*, Profile Books, 2015, pp.2–3. See also Mick McAteer, *An Economic and Social Audit of the City*, Financial Inclusion Centre, July 2017. • **12.** Baker, A., Epstein, J., Leaver, A., Montecino, J., Fields, D. and Atkinson, R., 'The UK's Finance Curse? Costs, Processes and Future Research Agendas', Sheffield Political Economy Research Institute Working Paper, 2018. The £4.5 trillion figure has three components. First is 'misallocation growth costs', which measures the economic impact of the financial sector reallocating production away from its most beneficial uses, through draining the cleverest and best-educated people out of more socially productive sectors via Dutch disease effects or by redirecting investment away from where it is most useful and into wasteful wealth-extracting activities. The two main research documents on which this calculation is based are Enrico G. Berkes, Ugo Panizza and Jean-Louis Arcand, 'Too Much Finance?', IMF, 1 June 2012; and S. Cecchetti and E. Kharroubi, 'Reassessing the Impact of Finance on Growth', Bank for International Settlements, 2012. Also see N. Gupta and I. Hacamo, 'Superstar (and Entrepreneurial) Engineers in Finance Jobs', Kelley School of Business research paper No. 18, 8 March 2018, which shows significant flows of highly qualified people out of engineering into better-paid finance. More recently, see Nico Valckx, 'Rising Household Debt: What It Means for Growth and Stability', IMF, 3 October 2017. This concluded: 'a 5 percentage-point increase in the ratio of household debt to GDP over a three-year period forecasts a 1.25 percentage-point decline in inflation-adjusted growth three years in the future. Higher debt is associated with significantly higher unemployment up to four years ahead. And a 1 percentage point increase in debt raises the odds of a future banking crisis by about 1 percentage point.' This research shows credit (or lending) to the private sector boosts growth for an economy but only up to a point; after that, more credit starts to reduce growth. On a graph it's an inverted U-shaped relationship. The turning point seems to be where credit is equivalent to about 90–100 per cent of GDP, and in the UK credit to the private sector has averaged around 160 per cent of GDP. Epstein and Montecino estimate these misallocation costs to Britain at £2.7 trillion accumulated over 1995–2015, equivalent to around 1.5 times average annual economic output.

The second component is the cost of the financial crisis. The standard way of calculating this is to look at how the economy has grown since the crisis, and compare this against the long-term trend of economic growth. Epstein and Montecino calculate the cumulative cost from the crisis to 2015 at £1.8 trillion and counting for the UK. Simon Sturn and Gerald Epstein discuss possible double counting in 'Finance and Growth: The Neglected Role of the Business Cycle', Sheffield Political Economy Research Institute Working Paper 339, 2014. As they note, further research is needed to investigate all this more deeply. The way Epstein and Montecino calculated the £1.8 trillion means it can be added to the £2.7 trillion to create a total cost of oversized finance, so far, of £4.5 trillion. The third component of damage is called 'excess financial profits and compensation'. This measures the excess pay and profits financial players receive over and above the value of the services they would provide to customers in an efficient, competitive capitalist economy. This is a bit more complex than the other two components, because at first glance these profits are not outright losses to the economy but transfers within it – from ordinary people and businesses to highly paid financiers. But think of it this way. Imagine a country with a million poor people and one multi-billionaire who owns all the big businesses and banks and uses his power to extract an unwarranted $1,500 from each citizen each year. The billionaire's income doesn't meaningfully offset the losses to everyone else; any reasonable person would agree that the population, and therefore the economy, is losing $1.5 billion each year (and the billionaire is probably stashing these winnings offshore anyway). Britain doesn't have such stark inequality, but there are perhaps fewer than half a million real winners in the City's game of wealth extraction among a total population of 65 million or so, so it is still reasonable to call these transfers outright losses to the UK. Epstein and Montecino put these costs to the UK at £680 billion for 1995–2015. It doesn't make sense to add this to the £4.5 billion total, however: the City is an international financial centre, so a lot of this premium is extracted from foreigners, not from people in Britain. What is more, some tax would at least have been paid on this excess income, redressing the balance somewhat. There *is* an number to be added to the £4.5 trillion, but it's less than £680 billion, which explains my reference to an estimate of '£4.5 trillion, plus some'. • **13.** For a more general discussion of this, see John Christensen, Nick Shaxson and Duncan Wigan, 'The Finance Curse: Britain and the World Economy', *British Journal of Politics and International Relations*, 5 January 2016. This was based on an earlier document, John Christensen and Nicholas Shaxson, 'The Finance Curse: how oversized financial centres attack democracy and corrupt economies', Tax Justice Network, May 2013.

1 *Sabotage*

1. Nils Gilman, 'Thorstein Veblen's neglected feminism', *Journal of Economic Issues*, September 1999. • **2.** Cited in Sidney Plotkin and Rick Tilman, *The Political ideas of Thorstein Veblen*, p.16. The friend was a professor called Jacob Warshaw. • **3.** As Matthew Watson of Warwick University put it, *Leisure Class* was in a sense merely a scene-setter for *Business Enterprise*: 'It might very well be described as one of the subject field's most important forgotten books; it raises barely a stir in the collective consciousness of contemporary economists.' Watson sent me these comments via email, 2016. See also Matthew Watson, 'Thorstein Veblen, The Thinker Who Saw Through the Competitiveness Agenda', foolsgold.international, 29 February 2016, to be posted on financecurse. org. • **4.** William Heath Robinson was a cartoonist famous for drawing ridiculously complicated machines for achieving simple goals. • **5.** As Watson put it, 'A repeated theme throughout pretty much every chapter of the 900-page *Wealth of Nations* is that productive labour is good and should be encouraged, whereas unproductive labour is bad and should be discouraged. We wouldn't have a finance curse if we really did live in Adam Smith's world.' • **6.** From Steve Weinberg, *Taking on the Trust: how Ida Tarbell brought down John D. Rockefeller and Standard Oil*, W.W. Norton & Co., 2008, pp.219–20. Rockefeller defended himself by arguing that he had found a solution to the tragedy of the commons, where too many oilmen were drilling on the same bounteous oilfield, leading to overproduction and mayhem in oil prices. • **7.** The Hancock episode is from Henry Demarest Lloyd, *Wealth Against Commonwealth*, Harper, New York, 1899, p.162–3 • **8.** The quote is from Weinberg, *Taking on the Trust*, p.83. The death of Franklin Tarbell's business partner is recorded in several accounts, but none gives his name or date of death. • **9.** Steve Weinberg, *Taking on the Trust*, p.149. • **10.** The Standard Oil Trust was created in 1882, and its assets transferred to a new company in 1899, after state laws on corporations were relaxed somewhat. See Eliot Jones, *The Trust Problem in the United States*, Macmillan, 1921, pp.58, 60. Jones adds that beyond Standard Oil's control of 90 per cent of the market (p.58), 'Not all of the remainder could properly be considered as independent.' • **11.** Pujo Report, see especially US Senate Subcommittee on Banking and Currency, 'Money Trust Investigations', 18 December 1912, especially Exhibit 134-B: 'Table Showing Affiliations of J.P. Morgan & Company, Guaranty Trust Company, Bankers Trust Company, First National Bank and National City Bank with Other Corporations Through Interlocking Directorates'. • **12.** I discovered this second family connection to the Vesteys after a relative of mine read *Treasure Islands*, which has a chapter on the Vesteys, and emailed me a summary of their history. The Vesteys' descendants still own interests in South America: I also worked for six weeks as an assistant cowboy on a Vestey-owned farm in São Paulo state in Brazil in 1988. • **13.** See for instance the Tomlinson Report, originally released in 2014 but eventually published by the UK Treasury Select Committee on 22 Februry 2018. The Financial Conduct Authority appointed the City of London firm Promontory Group to lead an investigation into the scandal. Promontory has been called a 'safe pair of hands' but has been accused by US regulators of helping banks cover up scandals it was supposed to unearth. See for example 'Promontory Financial Settles with New York Regulator', *New York Times*, 18 August 2015. The ensuing report cleared RBS of the worst accusations, but even then the bank had to pay out hundreds of millions of pounds. Also see 'Watchdog "forced" to keep RBS scandal report secret over fears bank would sue', *The Times*, 5 December 2017, and 'The Dash For Cash: Leaked Files Reveal RBS Systematically Crushed British Businesses For Profit', Buzzfeed, 10 October 2016. • **14.** I use 'know-nothing' provocatively, to make the point about people in the financial sector who are often highly educated and intelligent yet who view the relevant issues through the prism of finance, which is often directly at odds with the wider needs of the population. In any case, financial market players' knowledge is exceedingly restricted, even in their own fields. John Kay, one of the astutest observers of the financial system, describes this phenomenon: 'Many senior executives talk with contempt of the analysts who follow their company . . . most of what is called "research" in the financial sector would not be recognised as research by anyone who has completed an undergraduate thesis, far less a PhD . . . anyone who comes from outside the financial sector to the world of trading is likely to be shocked by the superficiality of the traders' general knowledge.' Kay, *Other People's Money*, p.86. • **15.** These sections are from Weinberg, *Taking on the Trust*, pp.225–6, 227–30 and 258.

2 *Neoliberalism Across Borders*

1. Telephone interview with Lee Hansen, 21 November 2016. The 'communist' quote is from Charles Leven, 'Discovering "voting with your feet": Remembering Charlie Tiebout on the occasion of awarding the Tiebout Prize to Tracy Gordon', *Annals of Regional Science*, 2003. • **2.** McCarthy drank himself to death in 1957, which may have amused Tiebout, whose father, a psychiatrist, was a pioneer in the Alcoholics Anonymous movement. • **3.** Another Chicago suburb, next to Evanston. • **4.** This section is largely based on Leven, 'Discovering "voting with your feet"', and from John Singleton, 'Sorting Charles Tiebout', *Working Paper Series 2013–20*, Center for the History of Political Economy, 8 January 2014. Leven was at the lunch, and his seems to be the only first-hand account of this episode. Singleton expressed some scepticism over the precision of Leven's recollections. Tiebout seems to have had the germ of the idea some time before this conversation, however. On citations Singleton said, 'Forty-five years on from Tiebout's passing, Tiebout (1956) boasts nearly 11,500 citations, ranking it among the most cited articles in economics. By comparison, Samuelson (1954) claims under 6,000, while Musgrave (1959) and Buchanan and Tullock (1962) own approximately 5,400 and 8,000 citations respectively.' • **5.** Tiebout himself designed it as an explicit riposte to Samuelson. The name of his 1956 paper, 'A Pure Theory of Local Expenditures', was almost identical to Samuelson's 1954 paper about the free-rider problem, 'A Pure Theory of Public Expenditures'. • **6.** According to William Fischel, an expert on Tiebout and public sector economics at Dartmouth College, Tiebout was making an argument to 'stop dissing your local government – because this is the one you chose.' From my telephone interview with Fischel, 22 November 2016. As Tiebout (1956, p.422) put it: 'Spatial mobility provides the local public-goods counterpart to the private market's shopping trip.' For a good summary see Matthew Watson, 'Paul Samuelson and the Provision of Collective Consumption Goods: A Rejection of Competitiveness Logic', foolsgold.international, 23 July 2015, to be posted on financecurse.org. • **7.** Telephone interview with Singleton, 3 November 2016. • **8.** See for instance Walter Scheidel, 'The Only Thing, Historically, That's Curbed Inequality: Catastrophe', *Atlantic*, 21 February 2017. • **9.** John Maynard Keynes, 'National Self-Sufficiency', *Yale Review*, Vol. 22, no. 4 (June 1933), pp. 755–69. • **10.** For example, the iPhone and iPad were less the result of Steve Jobs's 'foolish genius' than of massive state investment in the revolutionary technologies behind these objects of consumer desire: the Internet, GPS, touch-screen displays and communications technologies. See Mariana Mazzucato, *The Entrepreneurial State*, Anthem, 2014, particularly Chapter 5, 'The State behind the iPhone'. For example, Figure 12 on page 92 shows that Apple spent the equivalent of just 2.8 per cent of its sales on research and development between 2006 and 2011, compared to 13.8 per cent for Microsoft. Jobs's genius was mainly in making these technologies consumer-friendly (p.93). Financiers talk of 'Death Valleys' – stages in the design, investment, development and marketing of technologies where private bankers rarely dare to venture and the entrepreneurial state has to step in. • **11.** For growth rates, see for instance 'The Rise and Fall of the Golden Age: An Historical Analysis of Post-war Capitalism in the Developed Market Economies', with Glyn, A., Hughes, A., Singh, A., seminar Money, Finance and Trade Reform of WIDER/UNU, Helsinki, published in Marglin, S. and Schor, J. (eds), *The Golden Age of Capitalism*, Clarendon-Oxford UP, Oxford, 1990, cited in S. Marglin and J. Schor (eds), *The Golden Age of Capitalism*, Clarendon-Oxford University Press, 1990. Table 2.1 shows annual average GDP growth per capita for sixteen major advanced countries of 1 per cent 1920–70, 1.4 per cent 1870–1913, 1.2 per cent 1913–50, 3.8 per cent 1950–73 and 2 per cent 1973–9. For developing countries, the growth rate was an unprecedented 3 per cent in 1950–1975. Golden Age growth was, moreover, much more equitable than in other eras, benefiting the poor and middle classes disproportionately. Older growth rates are much, much lower. According to Ha-Joon Chang, *Economics: a User's Guide*, Penguin, 2014, pp.54–68, per capita growth in western Europe averaged 0.12 per cent between 1000 and 1500, and a mere 0.04 per cent in Asia and eastern Europe, and between 1500 and 1820 in Western Europe just 0.14 per cent. Growth rates rose sharply to 1 per cent in the Industrial Revolution (1820–70) and 1.3 per cent 1870–1913. The 4.1 per cent statistic for western Europe comes from Ha-Joon, *Economics*, p.79. • **12.** For data and analysis comparing wage rates, see Thomas Philippon and Ariell Reshef, 'Wages and Human Capital in the U.S. Financial Industry, 1909–2006', NBER Working Paper 14644, National Bureau of Economic Research, December 2008. • **13.** For the Harlech letter, see David Kynaston, *The City Of London, Volume IV: A Club No More, 1945–2000*, Pimlico, 2002, p.19. • **14.** The Metcalf quote is from Stephen Metcalf, 'Neoliberalism: the idea that swallowed the world', *Guardian*, 18 August 2017. The Davies quote is from Will Davies, *Limits of Neoliberalism: Authority, Sovereignty and the Logic of Competition*, Sage, 2014, pp.3 and 8; and from Will Davies, 'How "competitiveness" became one of the great virtues of contemporary culture', LSE blogs, 19 May 2014. • **15.** The history of the Mont Pelerin Society is well known. For the financing of the Mont Pelerin meeting, see Nicholas Shaxson, *Treasure Islands: Tax Havens and the Men Who Stole the World*, Vintage, 2012, pp.83–4 and 301. • **16.** Wallace E. Oates, 'The Effects of Property Taxes and Local Public Spending on Property Values: An Empirical Study of Tax Capitalization and the Tiebout Hypothesis', *Journal of Political Economy* 77:6, November – December 1969, pp. 957–71. • **17.** For example the economist Joseph Stiglitz said, 'The so-called Tiebout hypothesis is one of the predominant rationales for decentralisation.' See Joseph Stiglitz, 'Redefining the Role of the State: What should it do? How Should it Do it? And How should these decisions be made?', World Bank, 17 March 1998, Tokyo, fn.19.

The Fischel quote is from William A. Fischel (ed.), *The Tiebout Model at 50: Essays in Public Economics in Honor of Wallace Oates*, Lincoln Institute of Land Policy, 2006. • **18.** Most of the Davies quote comes from Will Davies, 'There is no such thing as UK Plc', foolsgold.international, 2 April 2015, republished as '"National Competitiveness": a crowbar for corporate and financial interests', Tax Justice Network, 2 April 2015. I commissioned the blog from Davies. • **19.** Cecil Andrus, *Politics Western Style*, Sasquatch Books, 1998, pp.22–3, quoted in Greg LeRoy, *The Great American Jobs Scam*, Berret-Koehler, 2005, p.59. • **20.** The LeRoy quote is from Greg LeRoy, *The Great American Jobs Scam*, pp.2–3, 69, 70 and 90. Good Jobs First has identified a total of 500,000 deals costing $250 billion in subsidies from more than 740 federal, state and local incentive programmes in all fifty states and the District of Columbia. • **21.** *Kansas County Profiles: Johnson County*, Kansas University Institute for Policy & Social Research, 2017, pp.41 and 43. • **22.** On exploitation see, for instance, Jon Swaine, 'New Jersey grants $1.25bn in public funds to firms that back Republicans', *Guardian*, 26 June 2014: 'Corporations that contributed millions of dollars to the Chris Christie-led Republican Governors Association and other GOP campaigns have received public funding deals worth almost $1.25bn from his New Jersey administration in less than two years.' Such donations are not necessarily illegal. • **23.** See *Financial Statements and Supplementary Information* for the years ended 31 December 2015 and 2014, Jackson County Community Mental Health Fund. • **24.** See Thomas Cafcas and Greg LeRoy, 'Smart Skills versus Mindless Megadeals; Cost-Effective Workforce Development versus Costly "Buffalo Hunting," with Proven Policy Solutions', Good Jobs First, September 2016. As the report notes, it is nearly always legal to take the money and run – promise jobs, take the subsidies and then either not create the jobs or enact layoffs. For the tech jobs, see 'Study: State and Local Governments Pay $2 Million per Job to Tech Giants for Data Centers', Good Jobs First, PR Newswire, 11 October 2016. A 2012 *New York Times* investigation of 150,000 deals estimated that Kansas spent 17 per cent of its state budget on incentive programmes; West Virginia and Oklahoma each spent 37 per cent, and oil-rich Texas 51 per cent. The subsidies figure comes from the *New York Times* series and database 'United States of Subsidies' authored by Louise Story, 1 December 2012. The richest states of Maryland, California, New Jersey and Connecticut spent between 2 and 5 per cent. The $600 job training figure is from Steve Duscha and Wanda Lee Graves, 'The Employer as the Client: State-Financed Customized Training 2006', US Department of Labor, 2007. • **25.** See also Albert Hirschmann's 1970 book *Exit, Voice and Loyalty*, which argues that citizens dissatisifed with their lot can opt for either exit (relocate elsewhere), voice (get angry and lobby for change) or loyalty (give up and accept your lot). He thought voice was particularly important, as it bred accountability, energised civil society and provided useful information about what was going on. Tiebout had already developed the exit option into a formal theoretical framework. As Fischel puts it, 'Everyone knew that Americans were mobile, but no economist had previously connected mobility with demand for the services of local government.' George Stigler had pointed out that taxpayer mobility undermined local government's ability to redistribute wealth, but neither he nor his students developed this insight further. • **26.** The academic literature talks about the 'California effect' – a race to the top on standards, and the 'Delaware effect' – a race to the bottom. • **27.** According to Fischel and Singleton, Tiebout first offered this idea during a Richard Musgrave seminar at the University of Michigan. Singleton states, 'In a characterisation fitting Tiebout's personality, Musgrave described the suggestion as offered jokingly.' The 'fuckers' quote is from Leven, 'Voting with your Feet'. • **28.** Even Oates's measurements were a special case: in the places he looked at, around half of state spending went into education, a far higher proportion than in most countries. See also Wallace E. Oates, 'The Many Faces of the Tiebout Model' in William A. Fischel (ed.), *The Tiebout Model at 50*, Lincoln Institute of Land Policy, Cambridge, MA, 2006, pp. 21–45. This looks at the substantial academic literature which followed Tiebout, is somewhat sympathetic to the idea of 'Tiebout sorting' but also outlines several other weaknesses in the original model.

3 Britain's Second Empire

1. See for instance Ha-Joon Chang, *Economics*, especially the sections 'Britain: the pioneer of protectionism' and 'The United States: Champion of protectionism', pp.61–4. See also Dani Rodrik's *Straight Talk on Trade: Ideas for a Sane World Economy*, Princeton Press, 2017, especially p.210, which draws the distinction between the two main arguments for trade: first, David Ricardo's that trade encourages specialisation and efficiency and delivers benefits through imports; second, the mercantilist position – that the benefits come from exports creating jobs. • **2.** For a country with such a large financial centre relative to its population, Britain has nearly the lowest rate of investment among large industrial economies. See for instance 'Time for Change: A New Vision for the British Economy, Interim Report of the IPPR Commission on Economic Justice', Institute for Public Policy Research, 2017, pp.37–9. As the report put it, 'The juxtaposition of a highly successful financial sector and weak investment might appear paradoxical, but it is not difficult to explain. Many of the UK's financial services serve the global market, not the domestic one: their purpose is not financing investment in the UK economy.' Also see 'Peter Cain: unused interview', published on Vimeo at Spiderswebfilm.com. Cain explained that most industrialists in Lancashire, Yorkshire and the West Midlands financed their investments out of their own profits and through informal regional networks. Physical distance reinforced a cultural and economic separation. 'People didn't know each other, and all kinds of rumours could float around,' Cain said. 'Also, if you're a gentleman, industry isn't something you want anything to do with, because it means work and labour, and that's not culturally very nice.' As agriculture declined in the nineteenth century, the City grew rapidly, and Britain's landed aristocracy began to intermarry with its emerging elite, creating a unified lobby, while industry, split between Manchester, Sheffield, Liverpool and other parts of the industrial north, was fragmented and thus sidelined. By the start of the First World War dividends and income from overseas investments alone amounted to almost 10 per cent of all national income, making fabulous fortunes in the City, and the Treasury saw the City as the motor of the economy, with industry dependent on it. • **3.** David Kynaston, *The City of London, Volume IV: A Club No More*, Pimlico, 2002, p.22. • **4.** See Note 10 in Chapter 2. There were already leaks in the system. For instance a Bolton memo from 1952 summarises a meeting with American bankers, citing an official from the Guaranty Trust complaining that 'only yesterday one of our oldest and most respectable customers – tea importers – rang me up to know how he could buy tea with cheap sterling. He said his competitors were doing it ... we told him we could not help him and pointed out that it involved breaking UK exchange restrictions, but he was unconvinced and we had to pass him on to one of the firms which do the business ... Lincoln Johnson of the Manufacturers Trust said ... branches of British Banks in the Far East were engaging in the business.' From George Bolton's diary, a file marked 25 Febrary 1952 in the National Archives. • **5.** The first Bolton quote in the paragraph is from Gary Burn, *The Re-emergence of Global Finance*, Palgrave, 2006, p.80. 'The 'slushy socialism' quote is from the last handwritten line of a letter from Macmillan to Bolton of 23 June 1952, obtained from the UK National Archives. • **6.** Nyasaland, a small British protectorate in Africa, where my father had served as a colonial officer, became Malawi, whose first president Kamuzu Banda appointed my mother head gardener at his presidential palace. I was born there in 1966, two years after independence. • **7.** The New Deal regulations involved a set of strong curbs on banking which included, among other things, splitting speculative investment banking activities from deposit-taking banking in order to stop bankers accepting customers' deposits and effectively taking them to the casino. • **8.** I got the cloud computing analogy from Harold Crooks' excellent film *The Price We Pay*. • **9.** The Roosa quote is from Burn, *Re-Emergence*, p.164. The Cohen report is mentioned ibid. pp.158–64. The earlier Cohen quote is from a telephone interview with him on 28 February 2017. 'Transnational reservoir' is from *Records of the Undersecretary for International Monetary Affairs (RUSIMA)*, Burn, *Re-Emergence*, p.161. Roosa added (ibid. pp.161–3) that Eurodollars 'involved dubious pyramiding of interrelated credits … the classical case of the sort of pyramiding which preceded the 1929 collapse … the same pack of cards structure'. • **10.** See Bank of England quarterly bulletin, First Quarter 1970, 1 March 1970, Table D, p.48. Total non-sterling liabilities of all UK banks rose tenfold in nominal terms in 1963–1969 from £1.8bn to £16.9bn. Of that, US banks' liabilities rose 20-fold, from £440m to £9.1bn. See also Bank of England, *The International Banking Markets in 1980–81*, Table A, which shows the 'gross size of the Eurocurrency markets' as $1.6 trillion. The figures in this paragraph aren't directly comparable with this, since they aren't inflation-adjusted and they measure different things. • **11.** James S. Henry, 'The Debt Hoax: an economic detective story', *New Republic*, 14 April 1986 is thought to be the first major article linking the cycle of Euromarket lending, debt and offshore wealth. Years later, Henry would create the first credible in-depth estimates for the quantity of wealth stashed offshore: see James S. Henry, *The Price of Offshore Revisited: New Estimates for Missing Global Private Wealth, Income, Inequality and Lost Taxes*, Tax Justice Network, July 2012. For a more recent and excellent account of the recycling of debts into flight capital, see Léonce Ndikumana and James K. Boyce, *Africa's Odious Debts: How Foreign Loans and Capital Flight Bled a Continent*, Zed Books, 2011. Tim Congdon, a City of London financier, said, 'Fly-by-night rascals effectively stole the proceeds of syndicated loans and did not have to carry the burden of debt service … It fell on the general body of taxpayers, not the jet-setting fraudsters, to meet the demands of the international bankers', in Susan Strange, *States and Markets*, Bloomsbury, 1998, p.124. With thanks to John Christensen. The Thatcher quote comes from 'Speech at Lunch for President of Mexico (Miguel de la Madrid Hurtado)', 12 June 1985, at margaretthatcher.org. • **12.** Burn, *Re-Emergence*, pp.90–1, and Niall Ferguson, *High Financier: The Lives and Time of Siegmund Warburg*, Penguin, 2011, p.216. The justification given for building up London was so that 'the balance of payments be no longer denied earnings that the services of the City can provide'. • **13.** As Lord Cromer put it, the Bank did not believe 'the existence of risks provided any reasons for our seeking to restrict the development of this market' (Burn, *Re-Emergence*, pp.161–6). Evidence of ongoing muddle is provided by a 1976 report by the US Congressional House Committee on Banking, which expressed amazement that the growth of the Eurodollar market had passed almost unnoticed. 'Its growth has been encouraged by the absence of regulatory restraints and perpetuated by bank regulators who know too little to be able to determine whether and what form of regulation will be beneficial', *ibid.* p.168. • **14.** Even the Bank of England has now admitted, 'The evidence is that today's system has performed poorly against each of its three objectives [efficiency, stability and internal balance], at least compared with the Bretton Woods System, with the key failure being the system's inability to maintain financial stability and minimise the incidence of disruptive sudden changes in global capital flows.' See Oliver Bush, Katie Farrant and Michelle Wright, 'Reform of the International Monetary and Financial System', Bank of England Financial Stability Paper 13, 12 December 2011. The Bank could have added other criteria, such as fairness and equity or the rule of law, in which case its conclusions might have been even starker. • **15.** Other countries had offshore territories, and there was the Tangier International Zone, which served as an offshore Gomorrah for years before it became part of independent Morocco in 1956, when Swiss central bankers noticed a sudden influx of money, bankers and banks. 'Planes are rushing out the last few tonnes of the free zone's gold,' a Swiss news report at the time put it. In 1962 *Le Monde* described 'waves of capital' fleeing to Monaco, not just from Tangier: 'the Indochina wave, the wave of old African colonies, the wave of the Congo, and others perhaps to follow'. See Vanessa Ogle, 'Archipelago Capitalism: Tax Havens, Offshore Money, and the State, 1950s–1970s', *American Historical Review* 122:5, December 2017, pp.1431–58. • **16.** A Bank of England memo dated 11 April 1969, obtained from the National Archives by Paul Sagar for *Treasure Islands*, funded by the Tax Justice Network. The memo was written by Payton to someone identified as A. D. Neale and to 'O'Brien' at the Foreign and Commonwealth Office. • **17.** A Bank of England official, declining an invitation to dine with the popular Labour chancellor 'Big Jim' Callaghan at Downing Street in 1967, denounced the event as a 'mad hatter's tea party' and fumed that he refused 'for reasons of conscience an invitation to sup at No. 11 with the Devil'. See Kynaston, *The City of London*, Chapter 1. • **18.** For the quotes in this paragraph: See Ogle, 'Archipelago Capitalism', pp.1443–5 in particular. Ogle wrote, 'The Cayman law was particularly perfidious, as it was based on a close reading of Britain's tax laws, with its own language carefully chosen so as to fall outside those laws.' The Cayman Council is called the Private Sector Consultative Committee and you can find the official list of its members easily on the web. • **19.** See confidential letter from J. G. Littler to an official identified only as 'Packman', 3

September 1971, National Archives, 26.8.01. • **20.** As one international banker, A. E. Moore, remarked in 1979, 'The development of the concept of the Eurocurrency market ... can be seen as leading directly to the phenomenon of offshore banking centres, based away from any country in which regulatory, monetary or fiscal controls might apply.' See A. E. Moore, 'The phenomenon of the offshore centre', speech delivered to the International Conference of Banking Supervisors, 5/6 July 1979, National Archives. *Treasure Islands* popularised the idea of a British 'spider's web' of tax havens, though I first saw the term in an email from James S. Henry, a senior adviser to the Tax Justice Network. There is now a film, *The Spider's Web: Britain's Second Empire*, about this episode, co-produced by my close collaborator on *Treasure Islands*, John Christensen. As it happens, the Scythian philosopher Anacharsis offered us a very different, though similarly appropriate, analogy using the humble spider's web. 'Laws are like spider webs,' he said. 'They catch the little flies, but cannot hold the big ones.' • **21.** The question of what powers Britain has and doesn't have over its Overseas Territories is complex and contested. But behind the complexity its powers to change tax haven legislation are almost unreserved. See, for instance, 'Britain can force its tax havens to curb secrecy. But will it?', Tax Justice Network, 13 November 2015, and associated links. A well-known BVI lawyer who wanted to remain anonymous told me by telephone on 29 January 2013 that the UK has 'complete power of disallowance' over all its legislation. Britain's extensive powers in this respect go back to the early post-independence era. For instance, a confidential letter of 18 May 1973, signed by N. B. J. Huijsman of the West Indian and Caribbean Department, to someone called Mr Larmour, states clearly Britain's extensive powers over these territories. It begins by noting that the Caymans' abusive 1967 trusts law was 'reserved' by the governor for approval in London, but a desk officer 'signified non-disallowance of the Bill without previously submitting it ... the effect of this was to drive a coach and horses through the Treasury's carefully constructed defences against abuse of tax havenry'. The letter goes on to state, 'As far as our control over Cayman Islands legislation goes ... the Governor has a reserved legislative power which would where necessary be applied in cases if the Governor considers that it is expedient in the interests of public order, public faith or good government (which expression shall, without prejudice to their generality, include the responsibility of the Islands as a territory within the Commonwealth etc)' to exercise this power. The practical effect of this is that he can introduce appropriate legislation, and if the legislative assembly fails to pass it, to declare it passed under his reserve powers, whether in original or in amended form. Furthermore, his instructions require him to reserve for royal approval 'any bill establishing any banking association or altering the constitution, rights or duties of any banking association'. He must also reserve any bill 'of an extraordinary nature and importance whereby … *the rights or property of Our subjects not residing in the islands … may be adversely affected.* … Finally, even in respect of bills to which the governor has given his assent, the secretary of state has a back-stop power to disallow the legislation.' (My emphasis. This explicitly covers harms transmitted elsewhere.) • **22.** From 'British Development Division in the Caribbean: Report on a team Visit to the Cayman Islands 14–17 April 1969', National Archives, marked FIN/CMS/1407/15. • **23.** See 'Panamanian Law Firm Is Gatekeeper to Vast Flow of Murky Offshore Secrets', International Consortium of Investigative Journalists, 3 April 2016. • **24.** Jeremy Green, 'Anglo-American development, the Euromarkets, and the deeper origins of neoliberal deregulation', *Review of International Studies*, 42(3), 2016, pp.425–49. • **25.** The best-known exposition of financialisation comes from Gerald Epstein, who defined it as 'the increasing role of financial motives, financial markets, financial actors and financial institutions in the operation of the domestic and international economies'. See Epstein, G. A., *Financialization and the World Economy*, Edward Elgar Publishing, 2005.

4 The Invisible Fist

1. Director, Stigler and Friedman had also been at the all-important Mont Pelerin meeting in Switzerland in 1947. • **2.** See Edmund W. Kitch, 'The Fire of Truth: a remembrance of law and economics at Chicago, 1932–1970', *Journal of Law & Economics* 26:1, April 1983, pp.163–234. Further testimony about Director's influence is on pp.185–6. Coase said (p.192), 'When I came to the University of Chicago I regarded my role as that of Saint Paul to Aaron Director's Christ. He got the doctrine going, and what I had to do was to bring it to the Gentiles.' • **3.** Ibid. The drama itself is mostly on p.221. The list of attendees at Director's dinner is not available but the group recalled George Stigler, Milton Friedman, Aaron Director, John McGee, Gregg Louis, Reuben Kessel, Lloyd Mintz, Al Harberger and Martin Bailey as being present. • **4.** Ibid. The Holy Grail quote is from Lynn Parramore, 'Meet the Economist Behind the One Percent's Stealth Takeover of America', *INET*, 30 May 2018, referencing Nancy MacLean's book *Democracy in Chains*, Viking, 2017. • **5.** Alan Greenspan, *Antitrust*, Nathaniel Branden Institute, New York, 1962. This was based on a paper given at the Antitrust Seminar of the National Association of Business

Economists, Cleveland, 25 September 1961. The ideas began moving out of academia and into policy when Stigler led a government task force in 1969 whose final report was a flimsy document slamming antitrust regulators and citing 'nebulous fears' about corporate size and power, a report which one expert said, 'felt no need to cite either data or scholarly literature'. See Kenneth Davidson, *Reality Ignored: How Milton Friedman and Chicago Economics Undermined American Institutions and Endangered the Global Economy*, CreateSpace, 2011, pp.35–6. • **6.** Alexis De Tocqueville, *Democracy in America*, Vol. II, 1840. 'Caesarism' is from Charles Francis Adams Junior, 'The Government and the Railroad Corporations', *North American Review* 112:230, January 1871, pp.31–61. • **7.** David Gerber, a law professor at Chicago-Kent College of Law, said the rise of antitrust law was spurred by 'resentment towards the new super rich and their lavish and ostentatious lifestyles ... located primarily in New York and other cities on the East Coast'. Another catalyst, he said, was 'rising anger among Midwestern farming communities at what they saw as rapacious and monopolistic conduct ... manipulating prices paid to farmers for their grain and livestock'. See David J. Gerber, 'US Antitrust: from shot in the dark to global leadership', Chicago-Kent College of Law, spring 2013. • **8.** The 1931 analysis is from 'Summary Competition Policy under Shadow of "National Champions"', Fifteenth Biennial Report 2002/2003, Monopolkommission, p.581, Section 24. The Roosevelt quote is from Franklin D. Roosevelt, 'Message to Congress on Curbing Monopolies', 29 April 1938, available at the American Presidency Project, http://www.presidency.ucsb.edu/ws/?pid=15637. The Stoller quote is from Matthew Stoller, 'How Democrats Killed Their Populist Soul', *Atlantic*, 24 October 2016. As the US monopolies expert Barry Lynn puts it (p.52), monopoly powers give the corporation 'the ability to kill at will, which means that its power to govern the political economic systems under its control is entirely despotic in nature'. The Celler quote is in Kenneth Davidson, *Megamergers: Corporate America's Billion-Dollar Takeovers*, Beard Books, 1985. The US Supreme Court summarised the 1890 Sherman antitrust act as 'a comprehensive charter of economic liberty ... providing an environment conducive to the preservation of our democratic political and social institutions'. Cited ibid. p.31. • **9.** See for instance Brett Christophers, *The Great Leveler: Capitalism and Competition in the Court of Law*, Harvard University Press, 2016, p.171. • **10.** The Treaty of Rome, particularly Articles 85–88, enshrined classic antitrust, though it was rather vaguely worded. By 1960, the year of Director's dinner, four of the six founder members of the European Economic Community – France, Germany, Netherlands and Belgium – had enacted antitrust laws to put the treaty into effect. Its terms focused heavily on pre-emptive market regulation: 'concerted practices that *are likely* to affect trade between member states and that *intend* or *effect* the prevention, restriction, or distortion of competition within the Common Market' as opposed to the Chicago School's later approach – regulating only after the event. Japan found the concepts more alien, but by the 1960s the benefits were increasingly obvious, and though Japan's world-beating industries were giant, sprawling conglomerates, they still competed with each other across many activities. In the words of Angela Wigger of Radboud University, a European academic antitrust expert, 'competition regulation [was] centre-stage for European integration from the outset', but a coalition of government and representatives of industrial capital successfully blocked the introduction of merger control rules into the emerging EEC treaty structure. See, for instance, Angela Wigger, *The Political Interface of Financialisation and the Regulation of Mergers and Acquisitions in the EU*, Institute for Management Research, Radboud University, 3 August 2012. • **11.** Telephone interview with Blum, 5 May 2017. Wigger, *Political Interface*, says the British government changed tack on monopolies in the late 1960s under Labour prime minister Harold Wilson, who decided 'to fundamentally rethink British hostility to monopolies and to restructure British industries "on a scale and at a speed such as we have not seen in this century"'. The spur to the change was the desire to allow large British corporations to compete with the then-dominant US multinationals. • **12.** This section on Robert H. Bork brings together different time periods. For the Kennedy quote, See Congressional Record – Senate, 1 July 1987, p.18519. Bork's allies took a different view of him. Edwin Meese III, the attorney general, who shared some of Bork's constitutional views, asserted that there had been a witch-hunt by a 'small band of special-interest lobbyists and left-wing groups' who engaged in 'gutter politics' and a 'highly organised, well financed political campaign'. The section on 'homosexuals, American Indians, etc.' is drawn from Bork's 1996 book *Slouching towards Gomorrah: Modern Liberalism and American Decline*, Regan Books. Bork didn't have it all his own way: his nomination to the US Supreme Court was rejected after a ruthless grilling at the same hearings where Ted Kennedy spoke in 1987. The grilling was so intense that the *Oxford Dictionary of English* even created a verb – 'to bork' means to defame or vilify systematically, often in the media, usually to stop someone getting into public office. • **13.** Bork's idea that predatory pricing didn't exist was based on mathematical modelling which suggested that predators would have to spend too much on loss-making strategies to make those losses worthwhile. He credited Director with some of these insights (see for instance Robert H. Bork and Ward S. Bowman Junior, 'The Crisis in Antitrust', *Fortune*, December 1963), which laid out some of the arguments that would emerge in Bork's *Antitrust Paradox*, Basic Books, 1978. Both the *Fortune* article and the 1978 book include extraordinary displays of magical reasoning. The *Fortune* article, for instance, includes the sentence: 'Professor John McGee, an economist now at Duke University, reviewed the entire case record of the Standard Oil litigation and reported that there is not one clear episode of the successful use by Standard Oil of local price cutting or other predatory practices.' (One of many counter-examples to McGee would be Rockefeller's use of dynamite and cannon against the independents trying to lay pipe in Hancock, which I outlined in Chapter 2.) On buying up rivals, Bork said, 'the modern law of horizontal mergers makes it all but impossible for the predator to bring the war to an end by purchasing his victim. To accomplish the predator's purpose, the merger must create a monopoly', and law 'would preclude the attainment of the monopoly necessary to make predation profitable'. Also, 'those who continue to buy after a monopoly is formed pay more for the same output, and that shifts income from them to the monopoly and its owners, who are also consumers. This is not dead-weight loss due to restriction of output but merely a shift in income between two classes of consumers.' • **14.** Telephone interview with Berk, 28 July 2017. • **15.** See, for instance, Spencer Weber Waller, 'Review – Market Talk: Competition Policy in America', *Law & Social Inquiry* 22:2, spring 1997, pp.447–8. Intellectual property rights were given new teeth too, on the similarly shaky justification that this would, by promoting big American high-technology champions, promote exports. See Christophers, *Capitalism and Competition*, pp.237–8: Reagan-era lobbying to weaken anti-trust was specifically 'in order to promote better international "competi-tiveness" for the United States'. • **16.** See Kenneth Davidson, *Reality Ignored: How Milton Friedman and Chicago Economics Undermined American Institutions and Endangered the Global Economy*, 2011, p.39. Other indirect quotes are from my interview with Davidson in March 2016. For the histories of these consultancies, see Jesse Eisinger and Justin Elliott, 'These Professors Make More Than a Thousand Bucks an Hour Peddling Mega-Mergers', ProPublica, 16 November 2016. One such professor was Joshua Wright, a vocal defender of economics as the touchstone of antitrust law, whom Donald Trump has appointed (at the time of writing) head of antitrust. Brett Christophers, a monopolies expert at Sweden's Uppsala University, said, 'The upshot today [of all this merger activity since the Bork era] is a sector as concen-trated as any other in the US economy.' This goes a long way towards explaining the massive rise in US financial-sector profits, from a little over a sixth of US corporate profits in 1960, to over 45 per cent ahead of the crisis. See Brett Christophers, 'Financialisation as Monopoly Profit: The

Case of US Banking', *Antipode*, January 2018. • **17.** The day I am writing this, 16 March 2017, the *Financial Times* is carrying a story entitled 'Unilever investors favoured talks with KraftHeinz'. Even entertaining the idea of this proposed $143 billion merger would have been inconceivable under classic antitrust. The 'false cornucopia' phrase is from Barry Lynn, *Cornered: The New Monoply Capitalism and the Economics of Destruction*, John Wiley & Sons, 2010. • **18.** The Luxottica information is largely drawn from its 2017 annual report. See also Sam Knight, 'The spectacular power of big lens: how one giant company will dominate the way the whole world sees', *Guardian* Long Read, 10 May 2018. The Open Markets Institute in the US has written repeatedly about Luxottica. On Oakley, this was widely reported, including on *Corporate Consolidation: Last Week Tonight with John Oliver*, HBO, 24 September 2017, which carried a clip of Luxottica CEO Andrea Guerra saying, in response to a reporter's challenge that the Oakley episode represented an exertion of market power, 'I understand your theory, but they understood that life was better together' – a comment that is reminiscent of Rockefeller's offers to buy up the ownership shares of weakened rivals with Standard Oil stock and saying, 'I have ways of making money you know nothing of.' • **19.** See 2017 list of global system-ically important banks (G-SIBs), Financial Stability Board, 21 November 2017, and 2016 list of global systemically important insurers (G-SIIs,) 21 November 2016 list not updated in 2017). • **20.** See 'The British Experiment', *The Economist*, 4 March 2017. For the Blackrock statistic, see 'Too Much of a Good Thing?', *The Economist*, 26 March 2016. • **21.** This episode is from a telephone interview with Barry Lynn, 21 March 2017, and 'Boosting Resilience through Risk Governance', OECD paper, 2014, p.37. See also Yossi Sheffi and Barry C. Lynn, 'Systemic Supply Chain Risk', *The Bridge* magazine, National Academy of Engineering (US), Vol. 44 Issue 3, 22 September 2014, and Barry Lynn, 'Built to Break: the International System of Bottlenecks in the New Era of Monopoly', *Challenge*, March–April 2012. • **22.** Gazprom has frequently cut off or threatened to cut off gas supplies to countries to further Russia's political and geostrategic ambitions. See for example Alan Riley, 'European Commission v. Gazprom: the antitrust clash of the decade?', Centre for European Policy Studies 285, 31 October 2012. • **23.** The trader/manager spoke to me on condition of anonymity in an interview in London in March 2017. On LIBOR US attorney general Loretta Lynch called the small group setting LIBOR rates 'a cartel ... a brazen display of collusion'. See 'Attorney General Lynch Delivers Remarks at a Press Conference on Foreign Exchange Spot Market Manipulation' 20 May 2015, available at www.justice.gov. • **24.** The thesis that current patent systems tend to stifle innovation is hardly controversial. For example, see

Lynn, *Cornered*, particularly the chapter 'Lightning Escapes the Bottle' and a series of articles linked on 'Do Patents Stifle Cumulative Innovation', Economist's View, 17 July 2014. • **25.** On Gilead, see 'Gilead Sciences: Price Gouger, Tax Dodger', Americans for Tax Fairness, July 2016. On South Africa, see 'HIV drugs boost South African life expectancy', BBC News, 1 August 2004; Linda Nordling, 'South Africa ushers in new era for HIV', *Nature*, 13 July 2016; Sarah Boseley, 'Big Pharma's Worst Nightmare', *Guardian*, 26 January 2016; and 'SA drops price of ARVs, saves R11bn in six years', timeslive.co.za, 22 September 2017. • **26.** The changes included the Airline Deregulation Act of 1978, the Depository Institutions Deregulation and Monetary Control Act of 1980, the Staggers Railroad Act of 1980 and especially the 1982 Merger Guidelines under the Reagan administration, which explicitly cited 'efficiency' and 'consumer welfare' as the only legitimate goals of antitrust. • **27.** For a shocking exposé of monopolisation in American agriculture, see Christopher Leonard, *The Meat Racket: The Secret Takeover of America's Business*, Simon & Schuster, 2014. Leonard describes a 'vast, hidden territory of finance, economics and power' that includes farms, processors, transporters and consumers, which he claimed was helping Tyson to gain astonishing influence over significant parts of America's meat supply, reshaping US rural economies wholesale. In Arkansas Leonard's investigations revealed a company he thought was behaving 'like an economic dark star that has drawn into itself all the independent businesses that used to define a small town like Waldron, the kinds of businesses that were once the economic pillars of rural America'. Tyson responded with a statement, saying 'We provide opportunities for farmers to prosper ... We depend on them and want them to succeed. No one company is big enough to control the market.' See 'Tyson Foods, American Meat Institute respond to "The Meat Racket"', MSNBC, 20 February 2014. Four companies – Tyson, JBS, Cargill and National Beef – now control around 85 per cent of US beef processing. On Bloodworth, see Shona Ghosh, 'The undercover author who discovered Amazon warehouse workers were peeing in bottles tells us the culture was like a "prison"', *Business Insider*, 18 April 2018. The Harvie quote is from Deena Shanker, 'Farmers' Beef with Trump over Big Meat', Bloomberg, 21 April 2017. • **28.** Amazon said, in response, that it provides a 'safe and positive' workplace for employees with 'competitive pay and benefits', and that it is 'committed to treating every one of our associates with dignity and respect'. It did not recognise Bloodworth's portrayal as accurate. See Amazon's full response published in Shona Ghosh, 'The undercover author who discovered Amazon warehouse workers were peeing in bottles tells us the culture was like a "prison"', *Business Insider*, 18 April 2018. • **29.** The Bartlett quote comes from 'How Fox News Changed American Media and Political Dynamics', *The Big Picture*, 21 May 2015. On the Trump rollback of local news broadcasting restrictions, see Tom Wheeler, 'On local broadcasting, Trump Federal Communications Commission "can't be serious!"', Brookings.edu, 12 April 2018 • **30.** On Amazon, see Lina Khan, 'Amazon's Antitrust Paradox', *Yale Law Journal*, Vol. 126, January 2017. On the Gazelle Project, the *New York Times* speculated that Amazon's owner Jeff Bezos had described it thus as 'a joke, perhaps, but such an aggressive one that Amazon's lawyers demanded the Gazelle Project be renamed the Small Publishers Negotiation Program'. On Amazon admitting its strategy, Jeff Bezos's first letter to shareholders stated, 'We believe that a fundamental measure of our success will be the shareholder value we create over the long term. This value will be a direct result of our ability to extend and solidify our current market leadership position ... At this stage, we choose to prioritise growth because we believe that scale is central to achieving the potential of our business model.' • **31.** The US net corporate profits number comes from Gavyn Davies, 'The Real Underpinning for Equities', *Financial Times*, 10 June 2013. For an overview of labour and profit shares, see 'The Labour Share in G20 Economies', International Labour Organisation and Organisation for Economic Co-operation and Development, 26–27 February 2015, Annex B, Panel B, on p.15, where, since the mid-1970s, the share of GDP going to workers' compensation declined by roughly 15 percentage points peak–trough (though the long-term moving average declined by around 10 percentage points). See also 'Time for Change: A New Vision for the British Economy', Interim Report of the Institute for Public Policy (IPPR) Research Commission on Economic Justice, September 2017 (Figure 2.6 shows a roughly 10 per cent decline in the labour share of national income). Also see 'Closer to equality? Assessing New Labour's record on equality after 10 years in government', Compass, 2007, p.21, which showed the share of GDP going to workers in the form of wages fell from around 65 per cent in 1975 to 56 per cent by 2005. More recent data from the ONS (which may not be exactly comparable) said that the worker share in 2015 was £930 billion out of £1.89 trillion GDP, for a share of 49.2 per cent (see 'UK Quarterly National Accounts April–June 2017', Office for National Statistics, Table D, 'GDP by category of Income, compensation of employees'). The difference in GDP between the 1975 figure and the current figure for these reports ranges between 10 and 15 per cent of GDP, which on the ONS figure of GDP is £189–285 billion. Dividing this by the size of the British workforce (32 million, see ONS: Table 1: summary of UK labour market statistics for May to July 2017, seasonally adjusted) gives roughly £6,000–9,000 per employee. For the US, see also Matt Stoller, 'Bigger corporations are making you poorer', *Vice*, 5 April 2017, summarizing research which found that wages would be $14,000 higher per year in the US if the economy had the level of competition it had in 1985. See Simcha Barkai, 'Declining Labor and Capital Shares', Stigler Center for the Study of the Economy and the State, November 2016, New Working Paper Series No. 2. • **32.** See for instance David Autor, David Dorn, Lawrence F. Katz, Christina Patterson and John Van Reenen, 'Concentrating on the Fall of the Labor Share', NBER Working Paper 23108, National Bureau of Economic Research, January 2017. Also presentation by Peter Orszag at Stigler Center Conference, 'Is there a Concentration Problem in America?', 27–29 March 2017 and Jae Song, David J. Price, Fatih Guvenen, Nicholas Bloom and Till von Wachter, 'Firming Up Inequality', NBER Working Paper 21199, National Bureau of Economic Research, May 2015. This latter paper summarises: 'Virtually all of the rise in earnings dispersion between workers is accounted for by increasing dispersion in average wages paid by the employers of these individuals. In contrast, pay differences within employers have remained virtually unchanged, a finding that is robust across industries, geographical regions, and firm size groups.' Going further back in history, Christophers, *The Great Leveler*, pp.165–6 and 212 summarises the research findings of Michal Kalecki, Josep Steindl and others, suggesting that degrees of monopoly go a long way to explaining relative changes in the share of income going to labour versus capital.

5 *The Third Way*

1. The BCCI Ponzi scheme is outlined on page 51 of Senator John Kerry and Senator Hank Brown, 'The BCCI Affair: A Report to the Committee on Foreign Relations', United States Government Publishing Office, Washington DC, December 1992. Also see Austin Mitchell, Prem Sikka, Patricia Arnold, Christine Cooper and Hugh Willmott, *The BCCI Cover-up*, Association for Accountancy and Business Affairs, 2001. Even the summary of this detailed investigation is horrifying. Sikka subsequently forced the British government to reveal key details of the Sandstorm Report, a suppressed British official report into BCCI. My own parents banked with BCCI during part of my childhood in Brazil in the 1980s, but withdrew their money when the first scandals emerged so didn't lose their savings when Blum and a handful of other US crime fighters took BCCI down in the early 1990s. For the 'tissue paper' quote, see Maurice Punch, *Dirty Business: Exploring Corporate Misconduct: Analysis and Cases*, Sage Publications, 1996, p.12. Luxembourg didn't regulate BCCI, it said, because the local holding company wasn't technically a bank. • **2.** The trip was in October 2011. The writer of the email, whom I met later, declined to be identified by name. For the *FT* quote, see Paul Murphy, 'More Evidence in the Case Against Luxembourg', FT Alphaville, 9 March 2017. • **3.** The controversial Juncker quotes are from 'Jean-Claude Juncker's most outrageous quotations', *Daily Telegraph*, 15 July 2014. Also see 'Who is Luxembourg's most popular politician?', *Luxembourger Wort*, 9 October 2012; 'Farewell to Juncker, Eurogroup president', Jeroen Dijsselbloem at a farewell dinner for Juncker, 11 February 2013. • **4.** On Luxembourg sabotaging European efforts to counter financial secrecy, this mainly concerned the EU Savings Tax Directive, a scheme for the sharing of financial information across borders. See 'Austria's and Luxembourg's Anglo-German fig leaf', Tax Justice Network, 22 February 2011. On Luxembourg's history as a tax haven, see 'Narrative Report on Luxembourg, Financial Secrecy Index 2018', Tax Justice Network, January 2018, and for Juncker's role see especially pp.10–11. Luxembourg as a financial centre was already well established when Juncker took office. Its original architect was probably Pierre Werner, Luxembourg's prime minister 1959–74 and 1979–84, who was more of a financial specialist and oversaw Luxembourg's growth as a centre for Eurobonds from the early to mid-1960s, and then its development into an increasingly diverse financial centre. • **5.** Brooks said in his email that his suspicion of 'mass tax crimes' was based on the fact that these schemes relied on the Luxembourg affiliates (Luxcos) being tax resident in Luxembourg (the companies are incorporated in Luxembourg, but that does not automatically mean they are tax resident there). In general, the test for tax residence is whether management decisions are actually taken in Luxembourg. If the Luxcos' management decisions were usually taken in these groups' home countries, where they have their headquarters, the schemes ought to fail on this basis. An extra ingredient needed for crime to have taken place is that the companies' management would have to have known that they were providing false returns, which they likely would have, if they were really taking the decisions in London. Yet it can be very hard to prove in court where management decisions are taken. This is different from other kinds of tax avoidance schemes which fail on technical legal details of the complex avoidance structure set up. Unfortunately, the media has routinely and inaccurately labelled these schemes 'tax avoidance', so not illegal, yet the legality of many such schemes is in fact indeterminate until there has been a court challenge and a resolution. For a general discussion of the problems involved in distinguishing between tax evasion and avoidance, see 'Risk Mining: what tax avoidance is, and exactly why it's anti-social', Tax Justice Network, 26 August 2014. • **6.** Juncker's role was more to provide political protection to the financial centre as it grew fast under its own steam. See Simon Bowers, 'Jean-Claude Juncker can't shake off Luxembourg's tax controversy', *Observer*, 14 December 2014 and 'Jean-Claude Juncker blocked EU curbs on tax avoidance, cables show', *Guardian*, 1 January 2017; also 'Junckergate: when it becomes serious, you have to lie?', European United Left/Nordic Green Left European Parliamentary Group, 28 September 2015. Bob Comfort, Amazon's top tax negotiator, said of Juncker in 2003, 'His message was simple: "If you encounter problems which you don't seem to be able to resolve, please come back and tell me. I'll try to help."' To see how dramatically Luxembourg grew as a corporate tax haven under Juncker, see 'Jean-Claude Juncker and tax haven Luxembourg, in a picture', Tax Justice Network, 30 January 2015. This is a graph showing US corporate profit-shifting into the world's tax havens. Until the late 1980s, most of it was destined for the 'big five' – Switzerland, the Netherlands, Ireland, Bermuda and Singapore. Juncker became finance minister in 1989, and at this point Luxembourg's share started to grow sharply, accelerating when he became prime minister, and today Luxembourg is one of the 'big six'. The graph is from Gabriel Zucman, transl. Teresa Lavender Fagan, *Hidden Wealth of Nations: The Scourge of Tax Havens*, University of Chicago Press, 2015, with Juncker timings added by David Walch of Attac Austria. By 1992, soon after Juncker became finance minister, the offshore mutual fund industry, which in Luxembourg was a classic tax evasion ploy, was growing at an annual rate of 60 per cent. See Rupert Bruce, 'Luxembourg thrives as an Eden for Funds', *New York Times*, 13 November 1993. • **7.** 'In Luxembourg there's even a little competitiveness observatory to keep everyone's eyes on the ball. Nothing of substance is disputed in the consensus,' said Benoît Majerus, associate professor at the University of Luxembourg. For a deeper exploration of the consensus in tax havens, see the 'Life Offshore' chapter in Shaxson, *Treasure Islands*, or look up 'Stuart Syvret' on my blog treasureislands.org for a series of more recent articles on the culture of secrecy in Jersey. An example of the bubble-like thinking in Luxembourg comes from Nicolas Henckes, secretary general of Luxembourg's business round table, who accused the recently launched Tax Justice Network Luxembourg of being a *'faux-nez'* – a puppet – of the City of London (see 'Tax Justice Lëtzebuerg: à peine créé, déjà critiqué', *Luxembourger Wort*, 13 January 2016). Majerus said that the Tax Justice collective, which he had helped found, was part of a 'tiny minority' of critics of the financial centre. After its launch, he said, Henckes came into his office and lectured him for an hour. • **8.** In a rare outburst in October 2011, Luxembourg's state prosecutor general Robert Biever said that of 50,000 criminal cases in the previous year, two-thirds had involved traffic offences and only seven the financial sector because the Police Judiciaire were unable to handle the latter. Is it really true, he wondered aloud, that 'criminal energies in Luxembourg are really concentrated on traffic offences'? He blamed the government for not giving prosecutors enough resources or backing. See 'Justice: Robert Biever dénonce', *Le Quotidien (Luxembourg)*, 14 October 2011 and 'Robert Biever dénonce', Paperjam.lu, 14 October 2011. • **9.** The Bomans comments come from my telephone interview with him on 10 March 2017 and subsequent emails. On conflicts of interest, in 2016 Belgian and German newspapers revealed that Claude Marx, head of the Commission de Surveillance du Secteur Financier (CSSF), the main Luxembourg financial regulator, had been involved in setting up offshore companies with Mossack Fonseca, at the heart of the Panama Papers scandal. See 'Claude Marx, directeur de la CSSF, très impliqué dans les Panama Papers', *Luxembourger Wort*, 15 March 2017. Luc Frieden, Luxembourg's finance minister, said of the Madoff cases in June 2009, 'The principle is very clear: the custodian bank has to indemnify investors,' and, 'Regarding the law, the situation is not that difficult: the custodian bank has a responsibility to make restitution for these assets.' Yet Luxembourg's courts did not hold the banks responsible. See Stephanie Bodoni, 'Madoff's European Victims waiting to recover loss', *Bloomberg Businessweek*, 7 February 2014. • **10.** In the words of Peter Mandelson, Tony Blair's top aide, and his co-author Roger Liddle in their book *The Blair Revolution*, the main aim of the Third Way project was 'to overcome Britain's continued slide in international competitiveness ... based on partnership between the private and public sectors, and to create a more equal and cohesive society'. See Peter Mandelson and Roger Liddle, *The Blair Revolution: Can New Labour Deliver?*, Faber and Faber, 1996. • **11.** The Patman history is mostly from Alexander Cockburn and James Ridgeway, 'Why they sacked the Bane of the Banks', *Village Voice*, 3 February 1975, and Matt Stoller, 'How Democrats Killed their Populist Soul', *Atlantic*, 24 October 2016. Patman's Federal Reserve quote is from an obituary in the *Beaver County Times*, 8 March 1976. The Coelho history is drawn from multiple sources, including the US House of Representatives biography of him at history.house.gov, as well as Gregg Easterbrook, 'The Business of Politics', *Atlantic*, October 1986, 'The Tony Coelho Factor', *Washington Times*, 17 January 2006, and several stories in the *New York Times* about Don Dixon. Coelho resigned in 1989 amid the savings and loans scandal but reappeared ten years later as general chairman of Al Gore's presidential campaign committee – brought in, as one senior Gore official put it, because they needed 'an adult' to run it. • **12.** Wall Street players also rode this cultural wave, on occasion portraying shareholder democracy as an issue of inclusion and civil rights. In 1999, for instance, US brokerage company E*Trade advertisements featured a photograph of black passengers sitting at the back of a bus – recalling racial segregation – and a caption reading 'They Said Equality Was Only For Some Of Us'. The civil rights leader Jesse Jackson in a speech in 1999 asked, 'Why are African Americans continuing to invest in the bear lotto when they need to be included as participants in the bull market? Why are our youths buying hundred-dollar Nike shoes instead of Nike stock?' See Karen Ho, *Liquidated: An Ethnography of Wall Street*, Duke University Press, 2009, pp.22–3. • **13.** Paul Krugman also dissects Thurow's ideas in his 1994 paper 'Competitiveness: a dangerous obsession', *Foreign Affairs*, March/April 1994. The Democratic National Committee in 1982 sanctioned seven groups as official party caucuses: women, blacks, Hispanics, Asians, gays, liberals and business/professionals. See Ronald Elving, 'Debating Length, Language, Democrats Ponder Platform', *CQ Weekly Report*, 11 June 1988, p.1583, cited in Jon F. Hale, 'The Making of the New Democrats', *Political Science Quarterly* 110:2, summer 1995, pp.207–32. See also Michael Lind, 'Trumpism and Clintonism Are the Future', *New York Times*, 16 April 2016. • **14.** The ERT has argued that 'every economic and social system in the world is competing with all the others to attract the footloose businesses', and its 160-page official history (as of 2017) mentioned 'competitiveness' or 'competitive' 153 times. However, when Bastiaan van Appeldoorn asked a former ERT secretary general, Keith Richardson, what was meant by 'competitiveness' he was told that it was 'just a word, a container, a paper bag – and you can put different things into it', van Appeldoorn remembers. 'Richardson saw the task of the ERT as not just to promote the concept of competitiveness, but to make sure that the right things are put into this paper bag' (phone interview with van Appeldoorn, 31 March 2017). When I asked the ERT in May 2017 for an interview to explore how it thinks nations 'compete', Bert D'Hooghe sent me several ERT documents, including 'benchmarking reports', which he said would explain the concept. These reports *seemed* to equate European competitiveness with the competitiveness of European companies, especially large companies, but didn't make this explicit. The ERT's own competitiveness ranking spelled out its ideas more explicitly than most: the most 'competitive' country is the one that is best at attracting mobile capital. See also Neil Brenner, Bob Jessop, Martin Jones and Gordon Macleod (eds), *State/Space: A Reader*, Wiley, December 2002. • **15.** On the price-obsessed nature of European antitrust law, see 'Antitrust: Overview' and 'Competition Overview: making markets work better', both at ec.europa.eu. The top summarising line of 'Competition Overview' states (April 2018) that the aim of competition policy 'is to provide everyone in Europe with better quality goods and services at lower prices'. Lower down, it adds 'more choice', 'innovation' and 'better competitors in

global markets'. 'Antitrust: Overview' cites two main articles from the Treaty on the Functioning of the European Union. Article 101 prohibits vertical and horizontal agreements between two or more independent market operators which restrict competition. Article 102 'prohibits firms that hold a dominant position on a given market to abuse that position, for example by charging unfair prices, by limiting production, or by refusing to innovate to the prejudice of consumers'. This is significantly, though not wholly, the Chicago School approach. On anti-cartel fines being relatively small, see 'Cartel Statistics: Table 1.1. Fines imposed (not adjusted for Court judgments) – period 2013–2017', Eurostat, updated 27 September 2017. Compare this to European gross business income of €3.4 trillion in 2016 ('Annual Accounts by Institutional Sector, Entrepreneurial Income Account', Eurostat, 2016, item B.2g, financial + nonfinancial gross operating surplus).
• 16. Michael Porter, 'How Competitive Forces Shape Strategy, *Harvard Business Review*, March 1979. Porter built a lucrative consulting business out of these ideas. See Steve Denning, 'What Killed Michael Porter's Monitor Group? The One Force that Really Matters', *Forbes*, 20 November 2012. The Watson quotes come from my Skype interview with Watson, March 2015.
• 17. Michael Porter, *The Competitive Advantage of Nations*, Harvard Business Review, March/April 1990. He says 'Government has critical responsibilities for fundamentals like the primary and secondary education systems, basic national infrastructure, and research in areas of broad national concern such as health care. Yet these kinds of generalised efforts at factor creation rarely produce competitive advantage. Rather, the factors that translate into competitive advantage are advanced, specialised, and tied to specific indus-tries or industry groups ... investments in focused educational institutions or other specialised factors.' As regards British government funding, see for example Tom Hale, 'University Challenge: the race for money, students and status', *Financial Times*, 23 June 2016. The article says: 'What money the state does commit is heavily weighted towards the highest-achieving universities, particularly those with state of the art science and research facilities.' David Harvey also described this process, especially as regards cities, in a famous 1989 article in which he described a shift from 'manage-rial' governance of cities and localities, which focused on providing services and benefits to urban populations, towards 'entrepreneurial' governance systems, focused on attracting and building local businesses. See David Harvey, 'From Managerialism to Entrepreneurialism: The Transformation in Urban Governance in Late Capitalism', *Geografiska Annaler*, Series B, Human Geography Vol. 71, No. 1, *The Roots of Geographical Change: 1973 to the Present*, 1989, pp. 3–17. • 18. William Davies, *The Limits of Neoliberalism: Authority, Sovereignty and the Logic of Competition*, Sage, 2014, p.110. • 19. For

an example of John Major's use of 'competitiveness' see 'Mr Major's Press Conference on the Competitiveness White Paper', May 1994, www.john-major.co.uk. He doesn't mention corporate taxes directly, but puts great emphasis on skills and innovation, and while he does mention 'a competitive Britain', most references to competition refer to business competition in markets. • **20.** Conor Burns, a Conservative MP, remembers Margaret Thatcher being asked by a dinner guest what her greatest achievement was. 'Tony Blair and New Labour,' she replied. 'We forced our opponents to change their minds.' See 'Margaret Thatcher's greatest achievement: New Labour', Conor Burns, Conservative Home blogs, 11 April 2008. Mandelson added, 'It is still arguable today whether Lady Thatcher went too far – including in her hostility to manufacturing that accompanied her favouring of finance. But undoubtedly the process of 'opening up' the UK economy to the global economy drove a lot of our growth.' See Andy McSmith, 'Margaret Thatcher's legacy: Spilt milk, New Labour, and the Big Bang – she changed everything', *Independent*, 8 April 2013. • **21.** The letter comes from Richard Brooks, *The Great Tax Robbery: How Britain Became A Tax Haven For Fat Cats And Big Business*, Oneworld, 2014, p171. • **22.** For a good dissection of Blair's 2005 speech, see Bill Black, 'New Labour leaders want to go back to policies that blew up the UK', *New Economic Perspectives*, 13 May 2015. Also see Atul K. Shah, *The Politics of Financial Risk, Audit and Regulation: A Case Study of HBOS*, Routledge, 2018, and Neil Hume, 'PM attack angers City watchdog', *Guardian*, 6 June 2005. • **23.** Paul Krugman, 'Competitiveness: A Dangerous Obsession', Foreign Affairs, March/April 1994. The 'teach our undergraduates to wince' quote comes from Krugman's 1996 book *Pop Internationalism*, MIT Press, 1997, p.125. • **24.** On the 'national competitiveness' rankings, comparisons are generally inappropriate because you are comparing apples with monkeys. Hong Kong's overwhelming national advantage is that it is the pre-eminent economic gateway to China, while Bermuda's is its ability to market its sovereignty to global tax haven players then divide up the meagre proceeds among a tiny population. What can it possibly mean to rank these places against industrialised France or impoverished Chad or oil-rich Kuwait? The Portes comments are from my telephone interview with him on 18 June 2015. Portes clarified: 'It doesn't necessarily mean that what they're proposing is wrong; to say "We need to do this to make Britain more competitive" begs the question "What actually is this proposal supposed to achieve?"' As an example, he raised the question of whether investment in education would make Britain more 'competitive'. 'Well, possibly, on some definition of competitiveness, but that is not really why. Yes, we do need to improve education, but the reason is that we will become more productive, possibly more equal, richer, and other good things. Competitiveness is a distraction from what the point of improving education is.' On 'competitive' taxes he said, 'That is less obvious and more dangerous, in the sense that it is equally meaningless and imprecise, and possibly more dubious. What exactly are we going to achieve? If we want to reduce taxes to encourage MNCs [multinational companies] to locate here as opposed to somewhere else, that may or may not be a legitimate policy objective, but it is not really about competitiveness. You have to work out the costs and benefits of that.' It is sometimes possible to make comparisons between governments and companies. As Professor Simon Wren-Lewis of Oxford University points out, companies that channel all their profits into paying dividends to investors instead of investing in upgrading their business will tend to wither, just as austerity-obsessed countries that prioritise paying down debt instead of upgrading public infrastructure or investing in education or research and development will find that things steadily get trickier. • **25.** See, for instance, the work of Professor Bob Jessop of Lancaster University on bobjessop.org/tag/competitiveness/. During my interview with Jessop on 24 June 2015, he spoke of a 'high road to competitiveness' – which might be summarised as 'upgrading' – and a 'low road' via deregulation. He opposes critiques by Krugman and others because, he says, their starting point is neoclassical economics, which airbrushes out a lot of messy institutional and other real-world factors. He added, 'My critique of competition is: be brutally clear about how competition works, and how competitiveness works, and don't just dismiss it as so much rhetoric because it is misused by politicians and ideologues.' See also Erik Reinert, 'Competitiveness and its predecessors – a 500-year cross-national perspective', paper for the Business History Conference, Williamsburg, Virginia, 11–13 March 1994. Martin Hellwig, director of the Max Planck Institute for Research on Collective Goods and former head of Germany's Monopolies Commission, was fiercer still. 'The notion of competitiveness of an economy doesn't make sense. It is a semantically nonsensical use of the term,' he said. See 'An interview with Martin Hellwig: competitiveness as doublespeak,' foolsgold.international, 2015, based on my telephone interview with Hellwig, 29 June 2015. • **26.** The Martin Wolf quote comes from 'Optimistic about the State: Martin Wolf's searing attack on the competitiveness agenda', foolsgold.international, 7 May 2015. The Simon Wren-Lewis quote comes from his article 'Bemoaning the cost of national debt is missing the point – we must invest in the economy', *New Statesman*, 28 November 2017. • **27.** For a deeper discussion of this, see Thomas Fazi and Bill Mitchell, *Reclaiming the State: A Progressive Vision of Sovereignty for a Post-neoliberal World*, Pluto, 2017, or Dani Rodrik, *Straight Talk on Trade*, Princeton, 2018. • **28.** For instance, the Corporate Europe

Observatory showed that of the 517 available seats across all of the European Central Bank's advisory groups, 508 were assigned to representatives of financial institutions – 'corporate capture at its most extreme'. See '"Open doors for forces of finance": 500 financial lobbyists at large at the ECB – by invitation', Corporate Europe Observatory, 3 October 2017. • **29.** The Kroes speech was 'European competition policy in a changing world and globalised economy: fundamentals, new objectives and challenges ahead', 5 June 2007. In the speech she also said, 'competition is the key means to increase consumer welfare, to ensure an efficient allocation of resources, to keep market players on their toes', reflecting two Chicago School attitudes: the obsession with price rather than market structure and the belief that market processes are the route to efficiency. The quote on Kroes comes from 'EU Antitrust Nominee Didn't Disclose All Ties', *Wall Street Journal*, 21 October 2004. Kroes was later exposed by a leak from the Bahamas corporate registry, showing she had failed to declare her directorship of an offshore firm set up by a polo-playing private equity boss from the United Arab Emirates, which had tried (but failed) to buy billions of dollars' worth of Enron assets. See 'Writing the Script: The European Roundtable of Industrialists', Chapter 3 in *Europe Inc.: Regional & Global Restructuring and the Rise of Corporate Power*, Corporate Europe Observatory, 2003. The merger figures come from Figure 1.5 on page 16 of 'Value of cross-border M & As in relation to the value of FDI flows' in 'UNCTAD World Investment Report 2000: Cross-border Mergers and Acquisitions and Development'. An acquisition is a kind of merger. On page 14 it is explained that the ratio can rise above 100 per cent because of time lags, and also that the data suffer from measurement problems making these figures imprecise. The report defines M & As as 'the acquisition of more than 10 per cent equity share', clearly a broad definition. The Mahatir quote is from the same UNCTAD report. • **30.** In a piece on UK policy on competitiveness *The Economist* in 1994 noted, 'Mr Heseltine has already expressed more interest in nurturing national industrial champions than in championing the interests of the nation's consumers' (Christophers, *The Great Leveler*, p.242). It was also argued that competition in banking generated reckless behaviour, so banks should be excepted from antitrust laws. The financial crisis revealed this as nonsense: the biggest banks had caused most of the havoc. On Germany see 'Summary Competition Policy under Shadow of "National Champions"', Fifteenth Biennial Report 2002/2003, Monopolkommission, especially Sections 23 and 24. The whole document contains an excellent critique of the competitiveness agenda, although from a rather market-focused perspective. • **31.** Even European leaders declared the Lisbon Agenda a failure. In 2009, a month before his country assumed the rotating presidency of the European Union,

Swedish prime minister Fredrik Reinfeldt and his finance minister Anders Borg declared, 'the Lisbon Agenda, with only a year remaining before it is to be evaluated, has been a failure'. See 'Sweden admits Lisbon Agenda "failure"', Euractiv.com, 3 June 2009. • **32.** The European Parliament, a bolshier but weaker European institution which often tries to push back against the Commission's neoliberal agenda, declared in December 2015 that it 'regrets that the Commission chose not to use the ordinary legislative procedure for the decisions regarding National Competitiveness Boards'. • **33.** Singapore enjoys a package that is as unrepeatable as Luxembourg's. Its economic model is heavily statist, with 90 per cent of housing stock government-owned, rents tightly controlled and strong social democratic policies. Singapore's Ministry of Manpower estimated its workforce at 3.67 million in 2016, of which 1.39 million – 38 per cent – is foreign. • **34.** On employees and cross-border workers, see 'Population and multiculturality' on www.luxembourg.public.lu (the official Luxembourg government portal), accessed 6 April 2017. For the composition of the workforce, see also OECD Luxembourg Survey, 2008, Figure 1.4. Nearly 45 per cent of the workforce were French, German or Belgian by origin. Figures 1.5 and 1.6 show that around 82 per cent of employees in financial and business services were foreign, as opposed to less than 30 per cent in public and social services. Box 1.1 outlines labour market policies. According to official data, 45 per cent of Luxembourg employees were 'cross-border employees' commuting in every day, while another 25 per cent were people with foreign passports who lived in Luxembourg. See also '2015 Sozialamanach', Caritas annual report on Luxembourg, Graphique 2, p.204, Graphiques 3 and 4, pp.207 and 208. On European comparisons, see Paul Zahlen, 'Regards 01', Statec/Institut national de la statistique et des études économiques, January 2012, and 'Statistics Explained: National Accounts', Eurostat, accessed 6 April 2017. Luxembourg also has plenty of non-financial businesses, from steelmaking, once its biggest industry, to smaller stuff like diamond trading, luxury clocks, high-end restaurants and information technology. On banknotes, see Paul Murphy, 'More Evidence in the Case Against Luxembourg', FT Alphaville, 9 March 2017, and 'Big bills: let's recall them all', Tax Justice Network, 23 February 2016. As this last notes, Luxembourg printed the equivalent of more than 200 per cent of its GDP in banknotes in 2014, compared to a European average of 10 per cent. • **35.** For a detailed exploration of this episode, see Brooks, *Great Tax Robbery*, pp.104–13. Brooks authored the *Private Eye* piece too. After an HMRC inquiry into the leak to *Private Eye*, all five expert tax inspectors with the relevant experience were moved sideways into other jobs, and most of that potential tax bill evaporated into the Luxembourg mists. • **36.** A separate study by Actionaid reckoned the tax haven move alone would reduce the tax revenues of developing countries by £4 billion annually. See 'Collateral damage: How government plans to water down UK anti-tax haven rules could cost developing countries – and the UK – billions', Actionaid, March 2012. The special partnerships include a 'Business Forum on Tax Competitiveness' and a 'CFC Liaison Committee' involving UK Treasury officials and mostly the tax directors of large global multinationals. In terms of legalising tax haven loopholes, I am talking especially about 'controlled foreign company' (CFC) reforms. See 'Closed Consultation: controlled foreign companies (CFC) reform', HM Treasury, 29 November 2010, along with 'The Principles of Tax Policy, written evidence submitted by Richard Brooks', www.parliament.uk, 31 January 2011, criticising the proposed reforms. A few of the details but none of the substance had changed by the time the reforms were enacted in 2012. For the $1 billion estimate, see Helen Miller and Thomas Pope, 'Corporation Tax Changes and Challenges', Institute for Fiscal Studies Briefing Note BN 163, February 2015, Table 2.1, p.9. The estimate was for the 2015/16 year. See also 'Corporate Tax Reform: Delivering a more Competitive System', HM Treasury, 11 January 2011. • **37.** From OECD data: GDP per hour worked.

6 The Celtic Tiger

1. Fintan O'Toole, *Ship of Fools: How Stupidity and Corruption Sank the Celtic Tiger*, Faber and Faber, 2009, p.12. The sentence has been abridged to remove a comment about Uruguay, but the sense is intact. • **2.** When premier Wen Jiabao visited Shannon in 2005 the Chinese ambassador insisted that his Irish hosts allow him to pause for reflection on 'the plateau' – a spot on Tullygrass Hill overlooking the industrial estate – to ponder where it all began. The main sources for this are Matt Kennard and Claire Provost, 'Story of cities #25: Shannon – a tiny Irish town inspires China's economic boom', *Guardian*, 19 April 2016; Paul Quigley, 'Why do Chinese leaders love visiting Shannon?', *Journal*, 23 February 2012; and '70 years a-glowing as Shannon Airport celebrates milestone with launch of photographic exhibition', *Shannon Airport News*, 2 December 2015. With thanks to Mic Moroney for the Shannon tip-off. For O'Regan, also see Patrick Neveling, 'Export Processing Zones and Class Formation', in James Carrier and Don Kalb, eds, *Anthropologies of Class: Power, Practice & Inequality*, Cambridge University Press, March 2015. • **3.** Initially, Export Profits Tax Relief gave a 50 per cent reduction on taxes on income from export sales, but this rose to 100 per cent in 1960. See John Bradley, 'Foreign Direct

Investment and Institutional Co-Evolution in Ireland', *Proceedings of the British Academy*, 1999, especially p.48, which shows employment in manufacturing rising from 175,000 in 1960 to 232,000 in 1990, a rate which averages out at around 1 per cent annually. See also Frank Barry, *Foreign Investment and the Politics of Export Profits Tax Relief 1956*, Trinity College Dublin, February 2011, especially p.10, and *Foreign Direct Investment and Institutional Co-Evolution in Ireland*, University College Dublin, February 2006. See also Kenneth Thomas, 'Ireland's Recent Success Not Built on Low Taxes', Middle Class Political Economist, 1 August 2011, and associated links, for a broad summary. • **4.** For the foreign direct investment data, see Clare O'Mahony and Frank Barry, *Making Sense of the Data in Ireland's Inward FDI*, Dublin Institute of Technology, 2005, Table A1: FDI inflows. • **5.** In 1973 59 per cent of Irish exports went to Britain; by 1987 this had fallen to 34 per cent. See Ray MacSharry and Padraic White, *The Making of the Celtic Tiger: The Inside Story of Ireland's Boom Economy*, Mercier Press, 2001. • **6.** See for instance '10 things a woman couldn't do in Ireland in 1970', Irish Central, 10 May 2017. The McCarthy quote comes from my interview with her in Dublin on 22 September 2016. • **7.** For a graph showing this trend, see Nicholas Shaxson, 'Did Ireland's 12.5 per cent corporate tax rate create the Celtic Tiger?', Naked Capitalism, 12 March 2015, originally at foolsgold.international. The background data came from 'Statistical Annex of the European Economy', Autumn 2014, ec.europa.eu, p.24. This records gross domestic product per capita as a share of the European average. However, Ireland's GDP data is skewed by artificial profit flows from multinationals, which don't meaningfully connect with the Irish economy, so GDP data has to be converted into gross national product (GNP) to strip out much of this profit-shuffling. Irish gross national income is around a third lower than Irish GDP. For further details on why even GNI or GNP overstates Irish performance, see, for instance, 'Tax Avoidance and the Irish Balance of Payments', Council on Foreign Relations blog, 25 April 2018, which states, 'At this point, profit shifting by multinational corporations doesn't distort Ireland's balance of payments; it constitutes Ireland's balance of payments.' Ireland's performance until the 1990s was probably a little worse than the graph suggests because of the accession to the European Union of Greece in 1981 and Spain and Portugal in 1986. These relatively poor countries depressed the European average, thus flattering Ireland's relative position. The underlying tables show significant or even dramatic growth in the other low-income countries in Europe, much of which was generic 'catch-up', a factor for Ireland too. For instance, the Czech Republic's GDP per capita relative to the EU average trebled from 16 per cent in 1990 to 43 per cent by 2007, with an average corporate tax rate of around 30 per cent; Estonia's, with an average 23 per cent corporate tax rate, grew sevenfold in 1993–2007; and Portugal's nearly doubled, with an average 33 per cent corporate tax rate and little foreign direct investment. Among the poorer countries, only Spain was lacklustre, its GDP per capita rising from 70 to 79 per cent of the European average in 1991–2007. • **8.** Joe Joyce and Peter Murtaugh, *The Boss*, Poolbeg Press, 1983, pp.48, 62 and 100–2. • **9.** The Deutschmark punt is described in Elaine Byrne, *Political Corruption in Ireland, 1922–2010: A Crooked Harp*, Manchester University Press, 2012, pp.96–7. • **10.** From my interview with McCabe at the Dáil Éireann in Dublin, 22 September 2016. • **11.** For an analysis of Haughey's many different corrupt methods, see Byrne, *Crooked Harp*, especially p.148. • **12.** This Third-Way attitude of giving wealthy people wide leeway to operate with minimal interference, then using the tax system to get society to share in the proceeds, was summarised by Bertie Ahern in 2004, when he told the *Irish Times*: 'If there are not the guys at the Galway races in the tent who are earning wealth, who are creating wealth, then I can't redistribute that.' • **13.** See 'Bono rejects criticism of U2 tax status', *Irish Times*, 27 February 2009. • **14.** Fintan O'Toole, *Ship of Fools*, p.36. • **15.** 'World Bank, Foreign direct investment, net inflows (percentage of GDP) for Ireland,' available at data.worldbank.org. For a brief summary of the two booms, see Jack Copley, 'The Celtic Tiger: the Irish banking inquiry and a tale of two booms', foolsgold.international blog, 5 May 2016. He in turn cites D. O'Hearn 'Globalization, "New Tigers", and the End of the Developmental State? The Case of the Celtic Tiger', *Politics and Society* 28:1, 2000, pp.67–92; and P. Kirby, *Celtic Tiger in Distress: Explaining the Weaknesses of the Irish Model*, second edition, Palgrave Macmillan, 2010. • **16.** The Apple subsidiary was Apple Sales International. See 'Offshore profit shifting and the U.S. tax code – Part 2 (Apple Inc.)', US Senate Permanent Subcommittee on Investigations, 21 May 2013. The loopholes ensure that only a tiny portion of a company's profits get taxed at that 12.5 per cent rate; the rest is kept outside the tax system completely. The tax loopholes were to a large degree a question of historical omission: Ireland did not adopt significant transfer pricing legislation to combat such abuses until 2010, long after other Western countries had enacted them. • **17.** As Peter Sutherland put it, 'The Italians, the French – a lot of the European countries – used every conceivable barrier to stop goods being exported into their dometic markets, even from other EU countries. It was the 1992 project that really changed this.' See Peter Sutherland interview in Paul Sweeney, *Ireland's Economic Success: Reasons and Lessons*, New Island, 2008, pp.17 and 19. • **18.** 'World investment report 2016', Annex Tables, Annex Table 2, FDI Outflows by Region and Economy, UNCTAD, June 2016.

• **19.** For the economic data, see Helen Russell and Philip J. O'Connell, 'Women Returning to Employment, Education and Training in Ireland: An Analysis of Transitions', *Economic and Social Review* 35:1, spring 2004, pp.1–25. • **20.** As Sutherland put it in Sweeney, *Ireland's Economic Success*, pp.14–15, 'Our GDP per capita was distorted in the period up to the 1990s, because we had a much higher dependency ratio and a much lower labour participation rate – by women in particular. When our dependency ratio dropped (because there were fewer young children, because of birth control and everything that happened in the 1990s), this increased the GDP per capita … this was a significant issue.' The Ballmer quote is from ibid. p.112. The worker-to-dependent ratio is from O'Toole, *Ship of Fools*, p.17. • **21.** There is a good collection of these images at 'What's the Big IDA then?', broadsheet.ie, 9 December 2015. On education, as MacSharry and White put it (*The Making of the Celtic Tiger*, p.47), 'The rate of economic recovery was … underpinned by another important and visionary political development from the sixties – the introduction of free second-level education. Its ecomomic impact … ensured Ireland in the late eighties was well placed to exploit the employment opportunities created by the new knowledge-based industries.' On the Industrial Development Authority survey and marketing strategy, see ibid. pp.244–5 in particular. • **22.** Part of the traditional story is one of virtuous Irish 'fiscal consolidation' but the true picture is mixed: government spending rose steadily in absolute terms from 1980 until 2007, though it fell from around 40 per cent to around 30 per cent of GDP at the same time, as GDP boomed. See, for instance, 'Expenditure Strategy' from the 2014 budget document, available at budget.gov.ie, p.10, accessed 16 November 2016. • **23.** See MacSharry and White, *The Making of the Celtic Tiger*, pp.29 and 153–5. They report that Ireland's Economic and Social Research Institute later estimated that the structural funds from the period 1989–99 had increased Irish GNP by 3–4 per cent. Also see ibid. pp.179, 193 and the chapters 'The Evolution of the IDA' and 'The IDA Philosophy through the Decades'. European funds also financed carefully targeted IDA training grants, helping the latter to further fine-tune the offering to the world's investors. For information on telecoms, see James Burnham, 'Why Ireland Boomed', *Independent Review* VII:4, spring 2003, pp.542–4. • **24.** The O'Neill quote is quite widely reported. The Big Four accounting firms are especially enamoured of Ireland's tax breaks, partly because they are expected to lobby for them on behalf of their multinational clients, and partly because the tax side of foreign investments generates such enormous fees for them: easily the majority of the total $1.3 billion in fee income for PwC, Deloitte, KPMG and EY in Ireland in 2016. See 'Brexit boost for Ireland's "big four" as fee income jumps', *Irish Times*, 2

May 2017. • **25.** A history of the famine for the BBC described three components to the ideology that would prove so deadly for Ireland: 'the economic
doctrines of laissez-faire, the Protestant evangelical belief in divine
Providence, and the deep-dyed ethnic prejudice against the Catholic Irish
to which historians have recently given the name of "moralism"'.
Encyclopaedia Britannica said, 'The emphasis shifted to reliance on Irish
resources and the free market, which made disaster inevitable.' Jim
Donnelly, 'The Irish Famine', BBC, 17 February 2011. • **26.** It's not exactly
seven storeys: different parts of the building are different heights. • **27.**
'Poorest of the rich. Ireland Survey', *The Economist*, 16 January 1988. See
also 'Patriots who knew how to play the power game', *Irish Independent*,
5 September 1999. • **28.** For this history of how the International Financial
Services Centre emerged, the two main sources are MacSharry and White,
The Making of the Celtic Tiger, particularly pp.317–55; and Fiona Reddan,
Ireland's IFSC: A Story of Global Financial Success, Mercier Press, 2008. Also
see 'An Irish player on the global stage, Profile, Dermot Desmond', *Herald
Scotland*, 17 December 2005. • **29.** Desmond seems so proud of the IFSC
that he would later sue a newspaper which reported a claim that the
financial centre wasn't his idea. See 'Desmond extracts an apology from
the Sunday Times', villagemagazine.ie, 5 November 2014. For background,
see also Desmond v. Doyle and Others, Supreme Court, 17/12/2013. In
1984 the coalition led by the conservative Fine Gael party had also put
forward a white paper recommending a new focus on promoting financial
services and offshore banking, but this had got nowhere. • **30.** See 'Dermot
Desmond on the IFSC past and future', Finance-magazine.com, undated.
See also Reddan, *Ireland's IFSC*, pp.26–9 and pp.38–40. On London, see ibid.
p.54. A careful marketing process examined which aspects done in London
could be done in Dublin instead, and an industrial policy for the IFSC was
partly crafted around that. The Childers quote comes from Jamie Smyth,
'Great tax race: Ireland's policies aid business more than public', *Financial
Times*, 1 May 2013. Irish democracy finally caught up with the Clearing
House Group in 2015, long after the financial crisis erupted, and it was
replaced by a purely industry body without government involvement. 'The
appropriateness of the group, given the apparent ability of private interests
to influence government policies, had been brought into question in recent
years' (*Irish Times*, 22 June 2015). • **31.** Finance Act, 1987, Section 30. Also
see Jim Stewart, 'How the IFSC "HQ" became a shadow of its intended
self', *Irish Times*, 6 September 2010. In this Stewart states, 'By law, the
financial regulator was required to promote the development of the financial services industry. Considerable resources were devoted by the regulator
to "meeting and greeting" prospective regulated entities – instead of to

the overriding need for adequate regulation. Aspects of this policy have now changed, particularly in regard to regulation. But the broad thrust of economic policy remains the same.' • **32.** One German official said that the IFSC and Shannon were little more than 'tax havens for many big foreign investment companies', in particular for special purpose investment companies handling huge funds but with 'no real trading function'. See Reddan, *Ireland's IFSC*, pp.29–31. Statistics from Conor McCabe, *Sins of the Father: Tracing the Decisions that Shaped the Irish Economy*, The History Press, 2011, especially pp.56 and 166–8. The German quotes are from the *Irish Times*, 14 November 1992, cited in McCabe, *Sins*, p.168. • **33.** Report of the European Commission's High-Level Expert Group on Bank Structural Reform, Chaired by Erkki Liikanen ('The Liikanen Report'), ec.europa.eu, October 2012, p.12, Table 2.3.2. • **34.** As the US economist Barry Eichengreen noted, 'borrowing by property developers and aspiring homeowners was fueled by the decline in interest-rate spreads that flowed from the advent of the euro ... Claims on the Irish banking system peaked at some 400 per cent of GDP ... this was an exceptionally large, highly leveraged banking system atop a small island. It grew out of the high mobility of financial capital within the single market. It reflected [among other things] the freedom with which Irish banks were permitted to establish and acquire subsidiaries in other EU countries' (*The Irish Crisis and the EU from a Distance*, University of California, Berkeley, 2015). O'Toole (*Ship of Fools*, p.21) noted that the number of manufacturing jobs in Ireland fell by 20,000 between 2000 and 2006, and prices in 2004 were 28 per cent above 1997 levels, compared to an EU-wide increase of 14 per cent. • **35.** See Stewart, 'How the IFSC "HQ" became a shadow', pp.13–16 for Depfa, and pp.3–4 for 'competitive' regulation and for a brief exploration of the Ormond Quay debacle. Also see Derek Scally, 'Near-collapse of German bank and its Irish subsidiary shrouded in mystery', *Irish Times*, 30 August 2013. • **36.** See Stewart, 'How the IFSC "HQ" became a shadow'. • **37.** See 'Offshore profit shifting and the U.S. tax code – Part 2 (Apple Inc.)', US Senate Permanent Subcommittee on Investigations, 21 May 2013, especially the opening statement by Senator Carl Levin, which explains the issues clearly. • **38.** See 'AIB to pay no corporate tax for 20 years: CEO', *Irish Examiner*, 27 September 2017. • **39.** For instance, an Oxfam / Tax Justice Network study in November 2015 estimated that in 2012 US multinationals alone shifted $500–700 billion to low-tax countries, almost all of which went to Ireland, Luxembourg, the Netherlands, Bermuda and Switzerland. Had the US reached out and taxed those profits well over $100 billion would have been collected. Separately, Citizens for Tax Justice in the United States estimated that multinationals cached $2.5 trillion offshore in 2015, avoiding up to $717.8

billion in US taxes. Ireland plays a central but unquantifiable role in this. See News Release 367: 'Fortune 500 Companies Collectively Maintain 10,366 Tax Haven Subsidiaries', Citzens for Tax Justice, 4 October 2015; and 'Still Broken: Governments must do more to fix the international corporate tax system', Oxfam, Tax Justice Network, PSI, Global Alliance for Tax Justice, November 2015. • **40.** 'Report of the Tribunal of Inquiry into Payments to Politicians and Related Matters', by Justice Michael Moriarty ('The Moriarty Report'), Part 1, March 2011, available at moriarty-tribunal.ie. The Isle of Man mentions came mostly in Part 2. • **41.** See 'In the event, DIRT was a brave event,' *Irish Times*, 21 July 1999. Also see O'Toole, *Ship of Fools*, pp.48–55. The Moriarty Report, Part 1, pp.513, 515 and 520. See also O'Toole, *Ship of Fools*, pp.55–60, and Elaine Byrne, *Political Corruption in Ireland 1922–2010: A Crooked Harp?*, Manchester University Press, 2012, particularly p.156. O'Toole adds (*Ship of Fools*, p.72), 'This ... was entirely unspoken. There is absolutely no evidence of direct political interference in the workings of the Central Bank. There are no threatening phone calls and no Fianna Fáil moles on the bank's staff. Things are much subtler, and much more insidious, than that ... people knew who Des Traynor was and for whom he worked. They knew that there was a system of networks and connections, with the ruler of the country at its centre ... it was reinforced by the utter impunity from legal consequences of those who had engaged in flagrant fraud.' • **42.** For the ceramic flowerpot example and others, see Jim Stewart, 'PwC / World Bank Report "Paying Taxes 2014": An Assessment', International Institute for International Integration Studies, Trinity College Dublin, Discussion Paper 442, February 2014, and 'Now Brazil puts Ireland on its tax haven blacklist', Tax Justice Network blog, 15 September 2016. Even Jim Stewart, one of the bravest and most outspoken critics of the financial and tax vortex that Ireland has become, chooses his words carefully. He tends to avoid calling Ireland a tax haven outright, and instead says that Ireland's tax system has aspects of tax havens. • **43.** At the time of writing, the most vocal lobby was the Northern Ireland Economic Reform Group, run by the head of KPMG in Belfast but whose funding is not clear. NIERG states on its website that it is 'an independent group consisting of economists, accountants and businessmen based in Northern Ireland who wish to see a more successful and competitive NI economy ... the group take the view that reduced corporation tax is the best way to ensure a rapid acceleration in investment and productivity'. I submitted a question about its funding to NIERG on 17 November 2016, via its website, but received no reply. • **44.** David Begg, a former general secretary of the Irish congress of Trade Unions (quoted in Sweeney, *Ireland's Economic Success*, p.119), put this in context. 'Ireland's great *economic* success could have generated a great *social* success if we had done things differently,' he said. 'If the government had not cut taxes so sharply on incomes and on companies, we would have had much more to spend on health, on education and on earlier investment.' • **45.** Hong Kong's big selling point is its role as the world's gateway to China, while for the eastern European countries it was the transition away from communism rather than the much less important issue of corporate tax cuts that sparked their growth lift-off. As for China's economic zones, what the government learned from Ireland was how to enact reforms in controlled, geographically restricted ways, which allowed the Communist Party to remain firmly in control. The reforms in the zones initially allowed farmers to sell excess production – after state quotas were fulfilled – at uncontrolled prices. For more on this, see Rodrik, *Straight Talk*, especially p.57.

7 *The London Loophole*

1. See 'Chairman Gary Gensler's Keynote Address on the Cross-border Application of Swaps Market Reform', Sandler O'Neill Conference, 6 June 2013, available at cftc.gov; 'Statement of Support, Chairman Gary Gensler', 29 June 2012, cftc.gov; and Rana Foroohar, 'The Myth of Financial Reform', *Time*, 23 September 2012, reprinted in Rana Foroohar, *Makers and Takers: The Rise of Finance and the Fall of American Business*, Crown Business, 2016, p.189. Maloney's statement and part of the quote from Gensler came from a year earlier: see Tom Braithwaite, Sahien Nisiripour and Brooke Masters, 'US Watchdog hits at "risky" London', *Financial Times*, 20 June 2012. • **2.** My interview was on 1 October 2012. The fund manager, who subsequently moved offshore, declined to be identified as the source of this quote. • **3.** From my telephone interview with Black, 30 September 2012 and Bill Black, 'New Labour Leaders Want to Go Back to Blair's Policies That Blew Up the UK', *Naked Capitalism*, 15 May 2015. The banking data is from the five banks that hold more than 44 per cent of US industry's assets, SNL Financial, 2 December 2014; derivatives data from Office of the Comptroller of the Currency's 'Quarterly Report on Bank Derivatives Activities, Second Quarter 2007', www.occ.gov, Table 1. The Riegle-Neal Interstate Banking and Branching Efficiency Act of 1994, which removed obstacles to banks opening branches in other states, contains the competitiveness justification: 'Equalising competitive opportunities for United States and foreign banks.' The 'staggering' quote comes from Christian A. Johnson and Tara Rice, 'Assessing a Decade of Interstate Bank Branching', *Federal Reserve Bank of Chicago Working Papers 2007*; 3 April 2007. The Bill Black quotes come from my telephone interview with him on 15 September 2012, and from 'Bill Black: Thomas Friedman – Deregulation Makes Banking Safe', Naked Capitalism, 11 August 2016. • **4.** Archives 1985 & 1986: Jim Pickard and Barney Thompson, 'Thatcher policy fight over "Big Bang" laid bare', *Financial Times*, 30 December 2014. • **5.** These quotes are from the superb *Swimming with Sharks* by Joris Luyendijk, Guardian Faber, 2015, about the City of London. Similar accounts are provided in Karen Ho, *Liquidated: An Ethnography of Wall Street*, Duke University Press, 2009. • **6.** Bosworth-Davies's most detailed comments on the arrival of criminal elements in London after the Big Bang are recorded in 'Financial Crime – Staring failure in the face', Rowan's Blog, 13 December 2006 and subsequent blogs. Some of these quotes come from my telephone conversation with Bosworth-Davies on 17 September 2012, and subsequent email correspondence. • **7.** Senator John Kerry and Senator Hank Brown, 'The BCCI Affair: A Report to the Committee on Foreign Relations', United States Government Publishing Office, Washington DC, December 1992. The Morgenthau quotes are from my interview with him on 4 May 2009 in his office in New York shortly before his retirement and the committee report. The committee obtained a heavily redacted copy of the Sandstorm Report. Prem Sikka obtained a less redacted version in 2011, after a five-year Freedom of Information fight. The confidentiality quote is from p.54; the shift to Abu Dhabi is on p.13. The report said US investigators 'were hampered by examples of lack of cooperation by foreign governments, including most significantly the Serious Fraud Office in the United Kingdom'. • **8.** Ian Fraser first related the 'protected species' quote to me by email; I emailed this to Bosworth-Davies and he replied that it was '100% accurate'. Also see Rowan Bosworth-Davies, 'Has the UK rediscovered its appetite for prosecuting "white collar" crime?', Ianfraser.org, 16 March 2012. Bosworth-Davies said a watershed was the collapse of the Blue Arrow case against rogue bankers in 1992, then Britain's costliest criminal trial. Afterwards he said a friend in the Serious Fraud Office told him that 'the message had come down from on high that there would never again be any similar kind of prosecution of any City institution or its senior executives'. The BBC had reported on Blue Arrow: 'the Appeal Court ruled that due to the length of the trial and the complexity of the subject matter the jury could not have reached a fair verdict'. (See 'Did Blue Arrow make bank fraud untriable?', Sam Francis, BBC News, 14 April 2014.) But Bosworth-Davies took a different view, saying the reason that Blue Arrow was so terrifying for senior financiers 'was that it demonstrated that ordinary juries *could* understand the ramifications of complex fraud cases, and that they *could* convict'. • **9.** See Michelle Singletary, 'Justice Dept. hails prosecutions at banks, S & Ls', *Washington Post*, 14 November 1995; 'Hundreds of Wall Street Execs Went to Prison During the Last Fraud-Fueled Bank Crisis', Billmoyers.com, 7 September 2013; and 'S&L Fraud Sentences Average 3.2 Years: Thrifts: The Justice Department says federal cases in general typically draw 2.5-year terms', Associated Press, 4 September 1990. • **10.** See Gillian Tett, *Fool's Gold*, Little Brown and Company, 1 September 2009, p.18. London's role as a regulation-escaping platform had also been massively enhanced with unfettered access to the single European market from the early 1990s, boosting its attractions in the same way that Ireland was now serving as a beachhead for US tax-escaping corporations wanting to operate across Europe. Hedge funds were fast getting into this exotic game, and again it was London, not New York, where most of the innovations debuted. As Tett puts it (p.107), 'while funds were springing up in New York and Connecticut, it was London where the evolution – and mutation – appeared to be most densely concentrated'. On p.116 she also fingers London as the key locale for SIVs, another related vehicle which had been especially problematic. • **11.** In fact, the value of bank assets and liabilities is highly uncertain. As one analysis put it, 'Bank of America had $27.7 billion of "assets and liabilities where values are based on valuation techniques that require inputs that are both unobservable and are significant to the overall fair value measurement", a technical term meaning that Bank of America takes its best guess about how much those assets are worth.' See Matt Levine, 'Bank of America Made $168 Million Last Quarter, More or Less', Bloomberg View, 15 October 2014. • **12.** For instance, see the testimony of Richard Berliand, managing director, global head of futures and options, J.P. Morgan Securities Limited in 'Transcript of meeting of the CFTC's Global Markets Advisory Committee', 12 January 2005, available at CFTC.gov. He says, 'We have a lot of non-domestic customers who very much can choose whether they sign up with a US FCM [futures commission merchant] or whether they sign up with an FCM in some other jurisdiction. Therefore, what we do today has significant tax dollar, economic implications on what happens to our US businesses and, therefore, it's very important … that we do not produce a structure that makes a Cayman Island-based customer, for example … in a position that they would not have if they were signing up under English law or some other environment. So just a caution that everything we do is so connected internationally and such a high proportion of our clients truly can arbitrage the legal environments in which they work that we must keep that in mind. I don't think we want to see a wholesale exit of business to other jurisdictions.' • **13.** See Nicholas Dunbar, *The Devil's Derivatives: The Untold Story of the Slick Traders and Hapless Regulators Who Almost Blew up Wall*

Street . . . and Are Ready to Do It Again,' Harvard Business Review Press, 2011, especially pp.116–17 for a discussion of this episode. In the book Dunbar talks of 'European regulators' but in an interview on 16 May 2018 said that he was referring to British and Swiss regulators in particular. • **14.** This paragraph describes 'mortgage securitisation'. The 'outside investors' that buy these securities are generally represented by a second SPV, which issues its own debt, in tranches, and sells it to a wide variety of other investors. This second SPV is the Collateralised Debt Obligation (CDO). • **15.** Ibid. p.59. • **16.** John Cassidy, *How Markets Fail: The Logic of Economic Calamities*, Allen Lane, 2009, p.270. • **17.** Travers is quoted in Alan Markoff, 'The Cayman Islands: From obscurity to offshore giant', *Cayman Financial Review*, 5 October 2009. Travers was in this instance talking in the context of a regime for attracting funds to Cayman, not specifically with respect to special purpose vehicles. As John Kay put it (*Other People's Money*, pp.122–3), 'These offshore locations ("treasure islands") are often described as "tax havens" but they are every bit as much regulatory havens.' Travers has publicly called me an 'imbecile' for criticising the Cayman Islands. • **18.** See 'Global Shadow Banking Monitoring Report', Financial Stability Board, 2016, pp.18 and 92. See also Thomas Rixen, 'Why reregulation after the crisis is feeble: Shadow banking, offshore financial centers, and jurisdictional competition', *Regulation & Governance* 7:4, December 2013, pp.435–59: and Markoff, 'The Cayman Islands'. Responsibility lies with both onshore and offshore regulation: regulators in the US, for example, could prohibit financial players from operating offshore like this. • **19.** I described 'the Devil' in slightly more detail in *Treasure Islands*. It is true that Cayman is now, under international pressure, somewhat less tolerant of dirty money than it was back then, but that's not saying much. • **20.** See David Dayen, 'Wall Street's greatest enemy: the man who knows too much', Salon.com, 28 August 2013. • **21.** Jolyon Maugham, 'Weak Transmission Mechanisms – and the Boys Who Won't Say No', Waiting for Tax blog, 8 July 2014. • **22.** An obituary of Potts, who died in 2009, said he was in great demand, particularly in Britain, Hong Kong and Bermuda. See 'Robin Potts, QC: Lawyer', obituary in *The Times*, 9 September 2009. • **23.** David Marchant, via email, 8 March 2018. • **24.** Between: Rock Nominees Ltd Petitioner – and – (1) RCO (Holdings) Plc (in members' voluntary liquidation) (2) ISS Brentwood Plc (3) ISS (UK) Ltd. (4) Jahanger Ahmed, Simon Cox, David Openshaw, UK High Court of Justice, Chancery Division, Companies Court, Hearing dates: 7, 8, 9, 10 and 14 April 2003, Case No: 3249 of 2002; and Rock (Nominees) Ltd Appellant – and – RCO Holdings Ltd (in members voluntary winding up) and Ors Respondents, Court of Appeal (Civil Division) on appeal from High Court Chancery Division (Mr Justice Peter Smith),

Case No: A3 2003 1086. • **25.** A fundamental concept in insurance is 'insurable interest', by which you are only allowed take out an insurance policy if you have an identifiable interest in the thing you are insuring. You'd be deeply uneasy if you discovered that a stranger had taken out an insurance policy that would pay them a million pounds if you died or if your house burned down. So by law you are allowed to insure your own life, but not a stranger's. Credit default swaps involved the same problem: you could use them to insure a loan against default (against the death of a company, as it were). Using CDSs, for instance, you could easily and secretly build up huge incentives to destroy a perfectly healthy company or destabilise a government – at the time financial institutions were being investigated for their role in destabilising Greece. See Wolfgang Munchau, 'Time to outlaw naked credit default swaps', *Financial Times*, 28 February 2010. Naked CDSs are where you can take out insurance on the bonds without actually owning them. On Robin Potts and insurable interest, see John Kay, 'Of cows, communities and credit default swaps: Why gambling with CDS should be banned', *Financial Times*, 6 April 2010; and Kay, *Other People's Money*, pp.61–3 and 72. • **26.** The $60 trillion number comes from 'OTC derivatives market activity in the second half of 2007', Bank for International Settlements, May 2008, p.1. The market value of these swaps was about $2 trillion. See also Oskari Juurikkala, 'Credit Default Swaps and Insurance: Against the Potts Opinion', *Journal of International Banking Law and Regulation* 3, 2011, pp.132–9; and John Cassidy, *How Markets Fail*, p.282. • **27.** For Greenspan, see 'Brooksley Born, the Cassandra of the Derivatives Crisis', *Washington Post*, 25 May 2009. • **28.** The repeal of the Glass-Steagall Act was essentially forced onto Congress by the merger of Citicorp with Travelers to make Citigroup, which under the act was illegal. Either the merger or the act would have to go, and in this battle of finance versus society, finance won the day. As banking analyst Kenneth H. Thomas said, 'Citigroup is not the result of that act but the cause of it.' See 'Sandy Weill: How Citigroup's CEO rewrote the rules so he could live richly', Chris Suellentrop, Slate.com, 20 November 2002. • **29.** From 'Over-the-Counter Derivatives Markets and the Commodity Exchange Act: Report of The President's Working Group on Financial Markets', US Treasury, November 1999; and from my telephone interview with Black, 15 September 2012. As Dunbar described (in a telephone interview on 16 May 2018) the general dynamics of the regulatory processes to me in the decade or more leading up to the global financial crisis, the UK Financial Services Authority was seen as a light-touch regulator, so 'US banks were then able to go back to the SEC or whoever it was in Washington, and say, "We are doing all our business over in London, because you are not being flexible enough." I think they used that as a stick to beat US regulators with, and that created this race to the bottom.' • **30.** The US regulator's quote and the 'maggots' quote are from Dunbar, *The Devil's Derivatives*, pp.131 and 141. The number of risk weight categories has grown from five in the original Basel accords to several thousand today: see Thomas M. Hoenig, director, Federal Deposit Insurance Corporation, 'Back to Basics: A Better Alternative to Basel Capital Rules', delivered to the American Banker Regulatory Symposium, Washington DC, 14 September 2012. In the end, the US never implemented Basel II: in 2007 it issued binding regulations covering the largest US banks, but delayed individually approving these banks' risk model systems; in the meantime, the banks remained subject to Basel I. It was only after the Dodd-Frank Act of 2012 that the Basel II framework of using banks' internal models became part of US bank supervision. A new Basel agreement, Basel III, was announced in 2010; at the time of writing, its implementation was ongoing. • **31.** Britain made a very similar boast when it came to corporate tax. For instance, Ian Barlow, a top UK tax adviser, boasted that US corporations found the UK taxman's approach 'refreshing' and that HMRC was 'much easier to deal with than their own tax authorities'. See Tom Bergin, 'Special Report – How the UK tax authority got cosy with big business', Reuters, 27 December 2012. The story emerged in the Cameron years but dates the cultural sea-change to the period 1999–2001. Also see Atul K. Shah, *The Politics of Financial Risk, Audit and Regulation: A Case Study of HBOS*, Routledge, 2018. The contempt of the London banking community for American law enforcement was as strong as ever. The year after Blair's speech, the New York branch of the UK-headquartered Standard Chartered Bank expressed concern about possible reputational damage from the London office helping cloak at least $250 billion in transactions violating sanctions against Iran. The reply from London was blunt. 'You fucking Americans. Who are you to tell us, the rest of the world, that we're not going to deal with Iranians?' See NY State financial services on Standard Chartered, http://www.dfs.ny.gov/banking/ea120806.pdf. • **32.** Technically AIG Financial Products (AIGFP) was registered in Delaware and theoretically overseen by the Office of Thrift Supervision in the US, while the London-based entity was the UK branch of an AIG subsidiary in France called Banque AIG. This was all about playing international hopscotch with regulation. As Dunbar explained in my interview with him on 16 May 2018, 'It was better to do that in London because in the US there was always the possibility that the Fed would find out and might ask more questions than the FSA would. It was a perception that they were going to get a better regulatory environment in London … It was quite complicated, with AIGFP in London, the parent company in US, and between all three of them could then get the lightest possible touch regime. They optimised it for the lowest possible regulation they could find.' In *The Devil's Derivatives* (p.159) Dunbar explained: 'Banque AIG was really just a front for AIGFP ... the bank was a shell where Cassano booked his default swap trades. But because it was a European bank it fell under the Basel umbrella and ensured the capital benefits from the super-senior default swap trades [with AIGFP]' (see later in this chapter for an explanation of this). See also Richard Northedge, 'AIG London unit not regulated by FSA', *Independent*, 15 March 2009; 'The causes and effects of the AIG bailout', Committee on Oversight and Government, US Congress, 7 October 2008. • **33.** See for instance Daniela Gabor, 'The (impossible) repo trinity: the political economy of repo markets', *Review of International Political Economy*, 2016, particularly pp.10–11. • **34.** Linklaters said it had reviewed the opinion and was 'not aware of any facts or circumstances which would justify any criticism', adding that the US Examiner 'does not criticise those opinions or say or suggest that they were wrong or improper.' See 'Linklaters cleared Lehman Brothers deals after US firms said "No"', *Evening Standard*, 12 March 2010. • **35.** The Valukas report quoted Lehman's global financial controller Martin Kelly, who said he believed 'the only purpose or motive for the transactions was reduction in balance sheet' and that 'there was no substance to the transaction'. See Report of Anton R. Valukas, Lehman Brothers Holdings Inc. Chapter 11 Proceedings Examiner's Report, US bankruptcy court, Southern District of New York, 11 March 2010. Nathan Powell, an independent research analyst, said Lehman conducted toxic transactions in Britain 'to take advantage of the lack of limits on re-hypothecation'. See 'MF Global trustee reviewing firm's practice of repledging collateral', Reuters Financial Regulatory Forum, 21 December 2011. On Ernst & Young earning $150 million, see Richard Brooks, *Bean Counters: The Triumph of the Accountants and How They Broke Capitalism*, Atlantic Books, 2018, pp.131–3. • **36.** As with money creation by the banking system, which is kept in check by reserve requirements, so rehypothecation is theoretically kept in check by the 'haircuts' involved in repo. Therefore, for Lehman's Repo 105, the bank would have to pledge $105 in collateral in exchange for $100 in cash. An IMF paper in 2010 estimated that just before the crisis hit US banks were getting over $4 trillion in funding via rehypothecation and said the shadow banking system – the parts that fall outside bank regulation – was 50 per cent bigger than people had previously thought because they had ignored rehypothecation. See Manmohan Singh and James Aitken, 'The (sizable) Role of Rehypothecation in the Shadow Banking System', IMF Working Paper 10/172, July 2010. • **37.** A similar thing happened on a smaller scale when the derivatives broker MF Global went bankrupt in a financial crisis aftershock in 2011. Again, it was MF Global's loosely regulated London unit that was the epicentre of the disaster. • **38.** The report was 'Sustaining New York's and the US' Global Financial Services Leadership', the Office of the Mayor of New York and the US Senate, 22 January 2007. The quotes are drawn from an op-ed in the *Wall Street Journal*: Charles E. Schumer and Michael R. Bloomberg, 'To Save New York, Learn From London', 1 November 2006. See also Lehman examiner's report: 'London was the "Guantanamo Bay" of finance', Ianfraser.org, 12 March 2010. • **39.** The figures for US and global bank fines are from Kara Scannell, 'US haul from credit crisis bank fines hits $150bn', *Financial Times*, 6 August 2017; and 'Banks paid $321 billion in fines since financial crisis', Boston Consulting Group, Reuters, 2 March 2017. Also see 'Sigtarp: quarterly report to Congress', Office of the Special Inspector General for the Troubled Asset Relief Program, US Treasury, 26 April 2018, and 'How many bankers were jailed for their part in the financial crisis?', *Channel 4 Fact Check*, 20 November 2017. The Financial Conduct Authority data is based on a table I constructed from the FCA's published data on fines levied, and on that published by its predecessor, the Financial Services Authority, on the UK National Archives web archive. This data includes fines levied by the FCA, the Prudential Regulation Authority (PRA) and the FSA. I excluded fines below £250,000, all fines levied on individuals and fines on non-financial institutions such as mining companies. My finding of zero fines related to crisis-related activities is a subjective assessment based on activity type. I sent separate Freedom of Information requests on this specific point to the FCA, the PRA and the Serious Fraud Office (SFO) on 4 May 2018. The SFO replied on 12 June 2018, outlining seven fines imposed and deferred prosecution agreements reached as a result of SFO prosecutions since 2012: only one was on a bank (Standard Chartered) but it was for bribery not for the financial crisis. In 2018 Labour's John McDonnell asked a parliamentary question about how many bank employees and directors had been prosecuted for their role in the financial crisis. The Attorney-General Jeremy Wright responded in June 2018, citing the Barclays case, in which Barclays PLC and four individuals were charged (on 20 June 2017) with conspiracy to commit fraud and for providing unlawful financial assistance, contrary to the Companies Act of 1985. The criminal investigation was ongoing (the High Court dismissed the charges against Barclays in May 2018, but two months later the Serious Fraud Office applied to have the charges reinstated). In addition, Wright cited five convictions and eight acquittals for bankers for rigging the Libor markets 'in the run up to and during the crisis', plus the charging of 11 individuals for rigging Euribor markets. However, none of these activities caused or even helped cause the financial crisis, except (perhaps) in highly tangential ways. See *Financial Services: Prosecutions: Written question – 155658, parliament.uk*, 20 June 2018. In summary: ten years after the crisis the number of prosecutions for activities that helped cause it was zero. • **40.** Professor Andrew Baker of the University of Sheffield, via email, 20 June 2018. • **41.** That $880 million was just what they knew about; overall, HSBC excluded $60 *trillion* in wire transactions from money-laundering monitoring each year. • **42.** 'Too Big to Jail: Inside the Obama Justice Department's Decision not to Hold Wall Street Accountable', report prepared by the Republican Staff of the Committee on Financial Services, US House of Representatives, 11 July 2016. The $60 trillion figure is on p.180. • **43.** The Rick Wilson quote is from 'America is in the middle of a Russian influence campaign – not at the end', *Spectator USA*, 10 May 2018. The Bernd Finger quote is from my interview with him and follow-up emails, January 2017. The PwC report is 'An overview of Russian IPOs: 2005 to 2014 Listing centres, investment banks, legal counsels, auditors and issuers' jurisdictions', PwC, 2014. For a more comprehensive look at these questions, see a collection of essays edited by David Whyte: *How Corrupt is Britain?*, Pluto, 2015. • **44.** For a profile of Green and the forces arrayed against him, see Suzi Ring and Franz Wild, 'Britain's White Collar Cops are Getting Too Good at their Job', *Bloomberg Businessweek*, 1 March 2018. See also 'Serious Fraud Office needs funding boost, warns OECD', *Financial Times*, 23 March 2017.

8 *Wealth and its Armour*

1. See 'Northern Rock – the questions needing answers', taxresearch.org. uk, 17 September 2007. The distinction between ownership and control is outlined on p.28 of 'Granite Master Issuer plc: annual report and accounts for the year ended 31 December 2006', where it states, 'The Company's ultimate controlling party is Northern Rock plc ... the Company's ultimate parent is the Law Debenture Intermediary Corporation plc, a company registered in England and Wales, the shares being held under a trust arrangement.' Also see Ian Cobain and Ian Griffiths, 'A twisty trail: from Northern Rock to Jersey to a tiny charity', *Guardian*, 28 November 2007; 'Memorandum from the Financial Services Authority', Parliament.uk., 9 October 2007; Paul Murphy, 'The (un)charitable core of Northern Rock', FT Alphaville, 8 October 2007. I emailed Down's Syndrome North East Association for comment on 9 May 2017 but received no response. • **2.** In fact, the basic idea was probably imported from the Middle East. The prophet Muhammad is said to have endorsed a legal structure called a *waqf*, which is much like today's charitable trust. • **3.** Brooke Harrington, *Capital Without Borders: Wealth Managers and the One Percent*, Harvard University Press, 2016, p.107. • **4.** 'Very complicated' comes from HMRC's own guidance on taxing non-resident trusts. Two of the biggest loopholes in the taxation of onshore UK trusts are domicile rules, and business reliefs and agricultural property. UK trusts currently carry a 6 per cent (value of assets) tax every ten years, so trustees will often move trust portfolios into assets that benefit from these tax reliefs as the ten-year charge date approaches, then move them back to other assets afterwards. For a discussion of this, and the 75p out of £100, and the £5 billion, see 'Passing On: Options for reforming inheritance taxation', Resolution Foundation, May 2018. On the £200 billion passed down annually, this is my own calculation based on Figure G 'Transmitted Wealth as a % of national income' in A. B. Atkinson, *Wealth and Inheritance in Britain from 1896 to the Present*, Centre for Analysis of Social Exclusion, London School of Economics, November 2013. He estimated an average ratio of around 5–8 per cent from 1950 to 2010, which, applied to the UK's £2 trillion annual income in 2016, gives a very rough £100–150 billion (Source: ONS, GDP at Market Prices, annual, adjusted seasonally). Facundo Alvaredo, Bertrand Garbinti, and Thomas Piketty gave a 9 per cent figure for the UK in 2010: see Figure 4, 'The inheritance flow in Europe 1900–2010', in 'On the share of inheritance in aggregate wealth Europe and the United States, 1900–2010' Post-Print halshs-01511115, HAL, 2017. Another reason for the low tax haul is not a loophole but the fact that a substantial amount of inherited wealth is in small enough individual sums to not incur top tax rates. • **5.** See 'Review of the operation of the Council Directive 2003/48/EC on taxation of income from savings. Response to questions posed in the working document of the expert group on taxation of savings', Society of Trust and Estate Practitioners, undated, available on Wayback machine, 9 March 2016. It said, 'It would appear difficult to draft practicable trust-related amendments to the Savings Directive of the kind referred to in the Working Document which would be "litigation-proof". Beneficiaries of discretionary trusts do not own trust property until it is distributed to them, nor do they control anything.' • **6.** Jersey Finance, the official arm of the offshore centre, has stated: 'Over £1 trillion of assets are held in Jersey trusts and other asset-holding vehicles, of which £400 billion are held in private trusts and roughly £600 billion in corporate asset vehicles.' From 'Evaluating the economic, financial and fiscal linkages between Jersey and the United Kingdom', a report by Capital Economics for Jersey Finance, October 2016. Giles Corbin, a partner at Jersey-based Mourant, said 'something like 90 per cent of Jersey trusts we draft are fully discretionary ones.' (A practitioner in the British Virgin Islands stated that 'most British Virgin Islands Trusts tend to be discretionary trusts.') Both comments are quoted in Jersey: '90 per cent of our business is discretionary trusts,' Tax Justice Network Blog, 12 June 2013. For a comparison of jurisdictions by amount of trust activity, see 'Cayman Islands Monetary Authority Annual Report 2016', p.21, Table 4: Number of Licensed Trust Companies – Selected Jurisdictions, 2012–2015 Calendar Year-end. This shows Jersey, Guernsey, the Isle of Man, the BVI, and the Caymans each having 150–190 trust companies (each trust company servicing many clients) suggesting a similar-sized trust industry. For the UK total, see Inheritance Tax Statistics, www.gov.uk, Table 12.7: Assets held in taxpaying discretionary trusts at 10-yearly charge date. The $9–36 trillion estimates for the size of assets in tax havens are from James Henry, 'The Price of Offshore Revisited', Tax Justice Network, July 2012, updated in James S. Henry, 'Taxing Tax Havens: How to Respond to the Panama Papers', Foreign Affairs, 12 April 2016. Henry partly pioneered this method of estimation, triangulating using three separate statistical methods, combined with 'investigative economics' which involves talking to players in the industry. The widely publicised estimates by Gabriel Zucman, at the lower end, were published in his book The Hidden Wealth of Nations, Chicago, 2015. Zucman uses a novel method to estimate assets in tax havens by using data on cross-border holdings of assets and liabilities, and establishing mismatches between them. This number in my opinion misses out a large section of the data for several reasons: first, large amounts of assets are held in vehicles (like trusts) where the beneficial owner is not unrecorded but misrecorded (such as in the name of the trustee) – so no mismatch shows up in the cross-border data, even though the asset is offshore. Second, banks will usually be quite happy handing over aggregate data on client assets to balance-of-payments data collection authorities like the BIS – which is the main international source used by Zucman – but they will be far less happy handing over client-level data to tax authorities. So his method misses a large amount of assets hidden from tax authorities. For further discussion of 'missing' data see Nicholas Shaxson, 'How to Crack Down on Tax Havens: Start With the Banks', Foreign Affairs, March/April 2018 issue, as well as John Christensen and James Henry, 'The Offshore Trillions', New York Review of Books, 10 March 2016, letter in reply to Cass R. Sunstein, 'Parking the Big Money', 14 January 2016. • 7. E. Van der Does de Willebois, E. M. Halter, R. A. Harrison, J. W. Park and J. C. Sharman, 'The Puppet Masters – How the Corrupt Use Legal Structures to Hide Stolen Assets and What to Do About It', Stolen Asset Recovery Initiative, World Bank, UNDOC, 2011, pp.45–6: 'Investigators and prosecutors tend not to bring charges against trusts, because of the difficulty in proving their role in the crime ... Even if trusts holding illicit assets may well have been used in a given case, they may not actually be mentioned in formal charges and court documents, and consequently their misuse goes unreported.' • **8.** See Dan Alexander, 'The Mystery Of Wilbur Ross' Missing Billions', *Forbes*, 16 October 2017. • **9.** For a lobbying document in favour of tax havens, see 'Memorandum from the Society of Trust and Estate Practitioners (STEP), Treasury – written evidence: Offshore Financial Centres', parliament.uk, 17 March 2009. This contains statements such as, 'The overwhelming consensus among economists who have examined this area is that low-tax finance centres provide significant economic benefits to higher-tax economies,' when in fact no such consensus exists except perhaps among economists who have been commissioned by tax havens to provide such analyses. For an example of these, see 'The (-ve) Value of Jersey to the UK Economy', Tax Justice Network, 14 October 2014, responding to a report commissioned by Jersey portraying tax havens as beneficial. • **10.** Tax havens are often about wealth protection rather than wealth appreciation. As a Citibanker in Mexico told the financial investigator James Henry, 'The money my clients put offshore is for safekeeping: when they want 200 per cent returns, they keep the money here.' James Henry, 'The Price of Offshore Revisited', Tax Justice Network, July 2012. • **11.** The inequality data comes from Thomas Piketty, *Capital in the 21st Century*, Belknap Press, 2014. The high net worth individuals data comes from the Credit Suisse 'Global Wealth Report 2016', principally Figure 4, p.26. But this data raises the question: what constitutes 'ownership'? Does it include 'ownerless' wealth held in, say, discretionary trusts? The Credit Suisse report does not mention trusts, foundations and the like, but says (also p.26) that it uses survey data – which it notes is unreliable – supplemented with 'rich lists' such as the *Forbes* billionaires' list, collated by journalists. *Forbes* says (in Kerry A. Dolan, 'Methodology: How we crunch the numbers', 7 March 2012) that it simply measures 'holdings' and 'wealth' and 'stakes', but does not mention trusts or foundations and the like. (I haven't checked all the methodologies of all the billionaire lists.) *Forbes*'s methodology may capture some 'ownerless' wealth, particularly if the billionaires listed are prone to boasting, but it surely misses plenty too, so, given the popularity of offshore trusts, the true numbers are probably significantly bigger. The 'six times' figure comes from the Cap Gemini World Wealth Report, 'Build your view', showing the world HNWI population growing from 10 million in 2009 to 15.4 million in 2015, a 7.5 per cent annual growth, while World Bank annual population growth figures show an average 1.2 per cent for that time period. • **12.** Adam S. Hofri-Winogradow, 'The Stripping of the Trust: From Evolutionary Scripts to Distributive Results', *Ohio State Law Journal* 75:3, 2014, pp.529–70. • **13.** See Daniel Kahneman and Angus Deaton, 'High income improves evaluation of life but not emotional well-being', *PNAS*, 1 September 2010; and Grant Edward Donnelly, Tianyi Zheng, Emily Haisley, and Michael I. Norton, 'The Amount and Source of Millionaires' Wealth (Moderately) Predicts Their Happiness', *Personality and Social Psychology Bulletin* 44:5, May 2018, pp.684–99. Also see Andrew T. Jebb, Louis Tay, Ed Diener and Shigehiro Oishi, 'Happiness, income satiation and turning points around the world', *Nature Human Behaviour*, 2018, which noted, 'Globally, we find that satiation occurs at $95,000 for life evaluation and $60,000 to $75,000 for emotional well-being.' • **14.** Timothy Colclough, 'To PTC or not to PTC', *STEP Journal*, November/December 2009, pp.51–3, quoted in Brooke Harrington, *Capital Without Borders: Wealth Managers and the One Percent*, Harvard University Press, 2016. • **15.** Annette Alstadsæter, Niels Johannesen and Gabriel Zucman, 'Tax Evasion and Inequality', National Bureau of Economic Research, Working Paper No. 23772, 28 May 2017. The 85–95 per cent undeclared figure comes from ibid. for HSBC; and 'Offshore Tax Evasion: The Effort to Collect Unpaid Taxes on Billions in Hidden Offshore Accounts', US Senate Permanent Subcommittee on Investigations, 26 February 2014, p.64. • **16.** See Paul Krugman, 'Understanding Republican Cruelty', *New York Times*, 29 June 2017 • **17.** Alex Cuadros, *Brazillionaires: The Godfathers of Modern Brazil*, Profile, 2016. • **18.** See Benjamin I. Page, Larry M. Bartels and Jason Seawright, 'Democracy and the Policy Preferences of Wealthy Americans', Northwestern University, March 2013. Based on interview material, they found that wealthy people 'are extremely active politically and that they are much more conservative than the American public as a whole with respect to important policies concerning taxation, economic regulation, and especially social welfare programs. Variation within this wealthy group suggests that the top one-tenth of 1 per cent of wealthholders (people with $40 million or more in net worth) may tend to hold still more conservative views that are even more distinct from those of the general public.' • **19.** From my interview with Gaydamak in Moscow in 2005. In addition, the London-based NGO Global Witness reported in 2002 that Gaydamak 'may have even visited the UK, possibly even as recently as late November 2001' despite the international arrest warrant being issued by France on 6 December 2000. Gaydamak held an open press interview at the Dorchester Hotel in London two days afterwards – with no action from British authorities. See Global Witness, All the President's Men, 1 March 2002. • **20.** Michel Pinçon and Monique Pinçon-Charlot, *Grandes Fortunes: dynasties familiales et formes de richesses en France*, Payot, October 2006, pp.14–16 • **21.** See Zachary Mider, 'South Dakota, little tax haven on the Prairie', Bloomberg, 1 September 2014; and 'US tax havens: the new Switzerland', *Financial Times*, 8 May 2016. Bret Afdahl, director of the South Dakota Division of Banking, sent me data via email on 19 May 2017 showing total trust company assets of $234 billion, roughly double the figure for 2012, and 89 trust companies employing '136.5 full time equivalents'. The trust companies paid a total of $840,000 in annual supervision fees in 2016 plus $309,000 to finance 26 examinations, plus $1.4 million in Bank Franchise Tax.

9 *Private Equity*

All responses on behalf of Careline in this chapter come from a representative of Graphite Capital and its portfolio company City & County who I refer to as Graphite Capital throughout this chapter.

1. There seems to be some confusion in Graphite Capital's published accounts and statements about which funds are which. Note 23 in C&C Topco's accounts for 2016 say that most of the equity shareholding is held by Graphite General Partners VII, but Graphite Capital said via email that this was incorrect: it should be Graphite General Partners VIII. (The 2017 accounts do say 'VIII' instead of 'VII' in the relevant section.) Separately, a document dated 14 January 2014 for Graphite Capital Partners VIII Top Up Fund A LP say it was signed 'For and on behalf of Graphite Capital General Partner VII LLP as General Partner of Graphite Capital General Partner VIII (Guernsey) LP', but Graphite Capital said via email that the VII should also be VIII. When asked, Graphite Capital did not explain whether this was due to a change or an error in its accounts. All the company's comments in this section have been provided by City & County and/or its controlling party, Graphite Capital. • **2.** These figures come from 'An Overview of the Domiciliary Care Market in the United Kingdom', UK Home Care Association, May 2016; 'The Size and Structure of the adult social care and workforce in the UK', 2017, Skillsforcare.org.uk; and 'The Home Care Business', Corporate Watch, 3 December 2016. Graphite Capital said via email in July 2017 that 95 per cent of home care in the UK was already outsourced. • **3.** Not her real name. • **4.** This was, as the Chicago-based private equity investor John Canning explained, 'really a marketing concept'. See Josh Kosman, *The Buyout of America: How Private Equity is Destroying Jobs and Killing the American Dream*, Penguin Random House, 2010. • **5.** Jensen delivered the goods in two short pieces in the *Harvard Business Review*. One was 'Eclipse of the Public Corporation' in 1989, the other, in 1990, 'CEO Incentives: It's not How Much You Pay, but How', a rousing defence of performance-based executive pay. Don't worry about workers, suppliers, taxpayers or lenders, he said, as long as the company's financial performance delivered returns to shareholders, all was good. He didn't mention Milken or Drexel. Morris is quoted from my interview with him on 2 June 2016 and subsequent emails. He added that Jensen's ideas resonated far beyond private equity. They allowed quoted company CEOs to use what their peers were earning at PE-owned companies as an argument for ratcheting up their own pay. In the early 2000s Jensen began admitting he was wrong about pay. Jensen did not respond to an emailed request for an interview for this book. • **6.** There are endless take-downs of Friedman's and Jensen's ideas. See, for instance, Steve Denning, 'The Origins of "The World's Dumbest Idea:" Milton Friedman', *Forbes*, 26 June 2013. For a deeper investigation, see Lynn Stout, *The Shareholder Value Myth: How Putting Shareholders First Harms Investors, Corporations, and the Public*, Berret-Koehler, 2012; and Karen Ho, *Liquidated*, 2009, Chapter 3 and particularly p.124 onwards. • **7.** From 'The New Church of Finance: Deeply held belief systems and complex codes must be changed', *Deseret News*, 9 December 2012, and from my phone interview with Clayton Christensen, 24 May 2012. • **8.** As Eileen Appelbaum and Rosemary Batt put it in *Private Equity at Work: When Wall Street Manages Main Street*, Russel Sage Foundation, 2014, pp.7–8, 'with the portfolio companies of most private equity firms located in many different industries, private equity's expertise is typically financial, not operational'. • **9.** For the Wilbur Ross episode, see ibid. pp.206–9 and 233. For Delphi, see ibid. pp.211–13; Lynn, *Cornered*, pp.69–70; John D. Stoll, 'Delphi gets $6.2 billion bailout of pensions', *Wall Street Journal*, 23 July 2009; and Greg Palast, 'Mitt Romney Bailout Bonanza', *Nation*, 17 October 2012. • **10.** Various sources including Helia Ebrahimi, 'How private equity plundered profitable Greek telecoms company Hellas', *Daily Telegraph*, 7 January 2012; 'Another Greek Tragedy', *The Economist*, 20 June 2015; 'Private Equity's Trojan Horse of Debt', *New York Times*, 13 March 2010; and court documents. • **11.** This was widely reported, including in Steven Swinford, 'Rich investors with a stake in care home abuse hospital', *Daily Telegraph*, 2 June 2011. Morris argued that Lydian wasn't necessarily mainstream PE, and may have been more a case of 'a few wealthy individuals taking advantage of PE techniques (and high debt levels) – while also cloaking themselves in the mystique that came with the term PE'. • **12.** Specifically, on hourly payments, Graphite Capital said: 'In most areas, where distances between calls are minimal, care workers are paid an hourly rate per assignment. This rate incorporates payment for the relatively short travel time between calls. This is standard practice within the industry ... in areas where travel distances between calls are greater (for example in rural regions), separate mileage payments may be made to staff in addition to their hourly rate, unless it is already incorporated in their base rate ... we do not determine how much time is allowed for the delivery of care to a particular individual. That is the responsibility of the commissioning authority, being usually Local Authorities or the Clinical Commissioning Groups. We, like many others in the industry, feel more time should be given to caring for those we look after and we regularly seek from our commissioners increases to the length of the visits that make up care packages.' • **13.** The actual times have been changed slightly to ensure that this rota cannot be identified – which is why I describe the rota as containing 'stuff like this' – but the timings shown do not distort the overall picture. • **14.** Graphite Capital's position is that it has received no interest or loan notes repayments from C&C since the investment was made in December 2013. • **15.** Shareholder loans are an injection of capital that is actually like shareholder equity – but they are potentially another extraction technique, not just because at least part of the interest payments can be deducted for tax purposes. If the firm goes bankrupt, liquidators will tend to prioritise repaying shareholder loans over the interests of equity holders and other unsecured creditors such as workers, suppliers and HMRC, which may receive very little. For a general discussion of this, see Prem Sikka, 'To end bad management, we need to look at who bears the risk in Britain's broken economy', *Left Foot Forward*, 24 May 2018. It cites PwC, the liquidators of the Private Equity-owned Maplin electronics firm, as estimating that unsecured creditors would receive less than 1p in the pound after its collapse, substantially for these reasons. Sikka, a professor of accounting at Essex University, also documented shareholder loans with annual interest rates of 25 per cent in 'Here's how Caffè Nero made £2bn in sales but didn't pay a penny in corporation tax', *Left Foot Forward*, 12 March 2018. (Maplin was once owned by Graphite Capital, though not in the period investigated by Sikka.) Graphite Capital said its shareholder loans in the case of City & County were unsecured and that they 'would not be ranked ahead of other creditors'. However I'm not convinced about this – in my experience, in the event of bankruptcy, shareholder loans tend to take priority over equity holders but not necessarily over all other unsecured creditors. • **16.** At the time of writing Graphite Capital said on its website 'Our realised investments have generated a return of 2.5x times cost, with no investment returning less than 1.6x cost.' It said via email in July 2018 that only a 'minor' portion of the interest payments on shareholder loans were deductible against tax, following international initiatives to curb such practices. When Graphite Capital said its low tax payments were due to 'modest underlying profits' I then pointed out that this was unclear because there is a difference between *accounting* profits and genuine *economic* profits, and that their comment did not sit comfortably with its website's claim about its returns in this sector. In response, it provided no further detail on this point. • **17.** Brown cut the long-term rate of capital gains tax for business assets in 2000 from 40 to 10 per cent, as part of his drive for a more supposedly 'competitive' tax system and to 'recognise risk, reward effort and encourage innovation'. Worse still, these rewards to owners are income, so ought to attract income tax but instead are classified as capital gains, which by any reasonable definition they are not. • **18.** Normal companies typically use something like three times as much debt as equity (the owners' own money), while with private equity it's roughly the other way around. See Appelbaum and Batt, *Private Equity at Work*, p.77, which also has the 40 per cent figure for enterprise value. On the tax changes in the UK, see 'Private equity execs face bigger tax on "carried interest"', *Financial Times*, 31 March 2016. Research shows that private equity firms are significantly more aggressive in using tax havens and other schemes to escape paying tax, and this is particularly true of the larger firms, which can afford the armies of lawyers and accountants necessary to design the complex schemes that really shake the taxman off. See Brad Badertscher, Sharon P. Katz and Sonja Olhoft Rego, 'The Impact of Private Equity Ownership on Portfolio Firms' Corporate Tax Planning', Harvard Business School Working Paper 10–004, 4 March 2010. Not only that, but when private equity owners earn income, they generally get taxed at lower rates than the rest of us, though the UK government in 2016 did announce changes that would help redress this balance. • **19.** The 2 per cent figure, which relates to the years preceding the global financial crisis, is from Appelbaum and Batt, *Private Equity at Work*, pp.194 and 196. On employment growth, see ibid. p.233. Chapter 7: 'Private Equity's Effects on Jobs and Labor' goes into these questions in more detail. The exception to this trend, they found, was in finance, insurance and real estate, where earnings rose – yet the finance curse shows that those are precisely the sectors where high earnings can be a curse, not a blessing, for the economies that host these sectors. Also see Daniel Rasmussen, 'Private Equity: Overvalued and Overrated?', *American Affairs*, Spring 2018. • **20.** The Appelbaum and Batt quote is from *Private Equity at Work*, p.65. The AA quote is from Daniel Rasmussen, 'Private Equity'. • **21.** See 'Tamara Mellon puts the boot into buyouts', *Financial Times*, 6 April 2012. On gender, see Theresa Whitmarsh, 'My locker room rally cry for women in private equity', World Economic Forum, 2 November 2015; and 'Overview of the health and social care workforce', kingsfund.org.uk, undated. The comparable figure for investment bankers is 16 per cent women. • **22.** The 2 and 20 is especially lucrative for bigger funds, principally because the overheads are relatively smaller: it doesn't take fifty times as many people to run a £5 billion fund as it does a £100 million fund. The 20 per cent profit share is usually taken only after an agreed 'hurdle' rate of internal profit, typically 8 per cent, is reached. Appelbaum and Batt (*Private Equity at Work*, p.52) estimate that two-thirds of general partners' total revenue derives from the 2 rather than the (performance-based) 20. The 2 in this formula, which is not based on financial performance, is the big one, especially for large funds; it accounts for around two-thirds of the titans' income. • **23.** For an explanation of this, see 'Interview: Dissecting the truth about the private equity market', Thomson Reuters, 18 April 2018. The 'near total control' quote is from William J. Magnuson, 'The Public Cost of Private Equity', *Minnesota Law Review*, Vol. 102, 2018. • **24.** 'How Hollywood Accounting can make a $450 million Movie "Unprofitable"', *Atlantic*, 14 September 2011. On 22 June 2017 I asked Prowse for an update via his website at message@darthvader-starwars.com but he did not reply. • **25.** See Ludovic Phalippou, 'Synopsis of Private Equity Laid Bare', LinkedIn, 5 December 2017. O. Gottschalg, L. Phalippou and F. Lopez-de-Silanes, 'Giants at the gate: Diseconomies of scale in private equity', Social Science Research Network, 25 December 2009; and Peter Morris, 'Private equity, public loss?', Centre for the Study of Financial Innovation, 2010, p.27. Phalippou said in a summary of his 2017 book *Private Equity Laid Bare* (Wiley), 'Headline fees are remotely related to the actual fee bill. Fees depend on how every single clause is written and how each element is defined. Contracts are incredibly difficult to read and understand … recording (and discussing) headline numbers is pointless.' • **26.** Firms also like to use a metric called x – so they can say 'I got 3x' or '5x', meaning they sell companies for three or five times what they paid for them. (Graphite Capital boasts historical returns averaging 2.5x costs.) Two company officials with long experience with private equity told me how the new players chase high numbers especially hard. You start aiming for 3x or more, to make a name. Once you are known and trusted to deliver high returns, you can sit back and watch investors' money roll in, chasing your track record, and rake in those easy 2 per cent annual management fees. Appelbaum and Batt discuss the various studies of private equity performance in *Private Equity at Work*, Chapter 6. • **27.** Ibid. pp.51 and 52: 'GPs invest just $1 or $2 in the fund for every $100 invested by the fund's LPs, yet they claim 20 per cent of the profit.' See also Ben Protess and Michael Corkery, 'Just How Much Do the Top Private Equity Earners Make?', *New York Times*, 16 November 2016. • **28.** See Applebaum and Batt, *Private Equity at Work*, p.53. • **29.** The $3 trillion figure is from Bain & Company, 'Bain & Company's Global Private Equity Report', *Bain.com*, 26 February 2018; and Prequin, 'Private Equity & Venture Capital Spotlight', Vol. 14, Issue, *preqin.com*, June 2018. It is widely accepted that returns are getting worse, largely because when investment funds were small, there was a rich menu of highly promising companies to choose from. The low-hanging fruit are now gone, and the more money there is, the harder it is to find good deals. The 'outperform' quote is from Daniel Rasmussen, 'Private Equity'. • **30.** For example, a standard metric is the value bridge, which systematically overstates performance. The value bridge seeks to split out success into its component parts: general market increases, stock picking, market timing, financial engineering and genuine operational skill. Even if the mathematics are usually correctly calculated, they only capture one dimension of debt. See Peter Morris, 'Evaluating Private Equity Performance: Approach the "value bridge" with caution', KPMG, 2016. Phalippou said the value bridge 'is biased to exaggerate the contribution of earnings growth' (from his synopsis of *Private Equity Laid Bare* on LinkedIn, 5 December 2017). • **31.** Lack found that from 1998 to 2010 the titans took a total of $440 billion – 98 per cent of all the internal returns generated – while outside investors took $9 billion, or 2 per cent (see Simon A. Lack, *The Hedge Fund Mirage: The Illusion of Big Money and Why It's Too Good to Be True*, Wiley, 2012). He told me in an interview on 23 June 2017 that he expected returns to outside investors had deteriorated since then, due to the larger amounts of money chasing assets, pushing up prices. The comparison between 'feeble' hedge funds and private equity returns is mine, not his. Also see Simon Caulkin, 'The Naked Truth about British Management', *Financial Times*, 4 December 2016. Among other things, it says: 'London's prowess in finance has operated as a kind of "resource curse", so that manufacturing weakness is the flip side of finance's strength.' • **32.** The quotes from Lack, Phalippou and the anonymous banker come from my interviews and conversations with them in 2013, mostly in March or April, and with subsequent correspondence with Lack on 23 June 2017. • **33.** One complicating factor here is that some of the biggest buyout funds, like KKR and Blackstone, are listed on the stock market. This gives investors a way to buy directly into the titans, rather than being vulnerable limited partners. • **34.** City & County summarised its buy-and-build strategy in its 2016 accounts (p.1) like this: 'Business integration is fundamental to the Group's buy-and-build strategy … the Group has developed a comprehensive and centralized back-office together with leading market-facing functions including Quality Governance, Finance, IT, Business tendering, Branding, Recruitment and HR.' • **35.** The 2 per cent figure is cited in Appelbaum and Batt, *Private Equity at Work*, p.61.

10 *The March of the Takers*

1. Strathclyde is a former Scottish government administrative zone abolished in 1996. • **2.** The Singapore quote is from Karthik Sankaran, director of global strategy at the Eurasia Group, a political risk advisory and management consulting organisation. Less extremely, London mayor Sadiq Khan has called for more autonomy and tax-raising powers for London, • **3.** According to UK Treasury data, total PFI payments in the Major years totalled £25 million or so; this rose to £155 million in the 1997/8 financial year, Blair's first year in power, then £550 million the next year, then over £1 billion in 2000/1, and around £5 billion by the time he left power. Today annual PFI payments are running at around £10 billion. • **4.** As of 15 July 2018, Strathclyde Limited Partnership, the SPV at the bottom of the corporate stack, had two partners: Strathclyde Limited, as General Partner (GP), and IPP Properties (Strathclyde Limited), as Limited Partner (LP). These entities were formerly owned by the high-octane, now-bankrupt Australian investment firm Babcock & Brown. Both the GP and LP were owned by Fieldsecond Limited, which was owned by IPP PFI Holdings Limited, which was owned by Bootle Derby Holdings Limited, which was owned by IPP Investments Limited Partnership, which had IPP Bond Limited as its GP and IPP Investments UK Limited as its LP. Both the GP and LP were owned by IPP Holdings 1 Limited (formerly International Public Partnerships GP Limited), which in turn was owned by International Public Partnerships GP Limited, which was its GP, while its LP was International Public Partnerships LP. Up until this point, the ultimate controlling party for all these entities was listed as International Public Partnerships (INPP), the Guernsey company; its annual report lists these as investments in unconsolidated subsidiaries. However, International Public Partnerships GP Limited, and all the companies above it, list Amber Infrastructure Group Holdings Limited as the ultimate controlling party. International Public Partnerships GP Limited was owned by Amber Infrastructure Group Limited, which was owned by Amber Infrastructure Holdings Limited, which was owned by Amber Infrastructure Holdings Two Limited, which was owned by Amber Infrastructure Group Holdings Limited, which was owned by: Hunt Amber London 2 Limited (the major shareholder); but also Estera Trust (Jersey) Limited; Ambre Holdings SARL; Michael John Gregory; Orangetone Limited (Owned by Giles Frost, CEO of Amber Infrastructure); Thomas Brendan O'Shaughnessy. The tax rate is drawn from INPP's 2017 annual report: on p.71 it listed a tax payment of £110,000 in 2016 and a tax refund of £2.5 million in 2017, which it described as 'Cash flows received from unconsolidated subsidiary entities in respect of surrender of tax losses.' On p.1 it listed £106.4 million in pre-tax profit in 2017, and £175.3 million in 2016, for a total £281.7 million. Amber Infrastructure Group Holdings' 2017 accounts, especially p.20. • **5.** PFI payments are fixed in advance, and are called the unitary charge. These sums are supposed to be subjected to value-for-money analyses, but as Jeremy Colman, UK assistant auditor general, said in 2002, these value-for-money exercises are 'pseudo-scientific mumbo-jumbo where the financial modeling takes over from thinking … It becomes so complicated that no one, not even the experts, really understands what is going on … If the answer comes out wrong you don't get your project. So the answer doesn't come out wrong very often.' • **6.** For the proportion of PFI expenses being construction costs, see Moritz Liebe and Allyson Pollock, 'The experience of the private finance initiative in the UK's National Health Service', Centre for International Public Health Policy, August 2009. As this explains, the unitary charge paid to PFI consortia has two components, the service charge for running costs and the availability charge for construction costs. It estimated that of the then £70.5 billion in estimated PFI charges, £41.5 billion, or 59 per cent, were for availability charges. However, on 20 June 2018 the Amber website stated that for the police training centre 'project revenues are availability-based and paid by the Scottish Police Authority'. For comparisons of financing costs, see Allyson M. Pollock and Professor David Price, 'PFI and the National Health Service in England', University of London, June 2013. This cites one study that found PFI borrowing rates 2.5–4 per cent higher than government would pay; another found PFI rates at 8 per cent annually, compared to 4.5 per cent for the government; and a House of Commons Treasury Committee concluded that the cost of capital for a typical PFI project at that time was double the long-term government gilt rate. It also cited a parliamentary inquiry in 2001 which found that 'the government could have secured 71 per cent more investment by borrowing on its own account'. • **7.** 'Private Finance and Private Finance 2 Projects: 2016 summary data', UK Treasury, 31 March 2016. The PFI numbers are nominal and include operating costs; the £37 million cost figure is my calculation based on Treasury data, assuming that government had borrowed to pay a private contractor directly to build it, instead of resorting to PFI. These were nominal numbers. (The centre has since been renamed Police Scotland Training Centre.) Documents accessed in July 2017 at Companies House for Strathclyde Limited Partnership, Jermyn Investment Properties, IPPL and REO Limited. Both Jermyn and REO Limited were dissolved via compulsory strike-off in 2013. Also from assorted annual reports from different Babcock & Brown entities. The *Scotsman* reported in 'Police Force halts £2m rent over blunders' (12 May 2003) that annual rental payments were £2 million a year, and that Strathclyde Police were refusing to pay rent on the centre 'after a series of blunders ended up with the roof caving in'. It said Babcock & Brown had accused Balfour Beatty and Strathclyde Police of being at fault. Police Scotland, which absorbed Strathclyde Police, told me via email (14 July 2017 from Vikki Wallace) that 'the dispute was resolved amicably' but they no longer held data on the disputed amounts involved. The calculations are necessarily imprecise because of the running costs. Amyas Morse, head of the National Audit Office, said 'we simply do not have the data' to compare PFI value for money with other forms of delivery. See 'Examination of Witnesses, Amyas Morse and Ed Humpherson', parliament.uk, 3 November 2009. • **8.** In addition to Strathclyde, Careline and Trainline, I also looked at South Lanarkshire Schools (whose SPV is called InspirED Education (South Lanarkshire) PLC, and whose ownership trail links up to Jersey); North Tyneside Quality Homes for Older People (whose SPV is called Solutions 4 North Tyneside, and which traces up to Guernsey); HMP Thameside (Belmarsh West), whose SPV is called BWP Project Services Limited and whose ownership trail traces, via Bristol, up to Jersey. Also Newton Abbott Community Hospital, whose SPV was called Ryhurst (Newton Abbot) Limited and traces up, via Preston, to a limited liability partnership with twenty-three members, all registered to an office address at 12 Charles II Street in central London. You can do these investigations into a PFI deal near you. Google 'Private Finance Initiative and Private Finance 2 projects: summary data', download the spreadsheet, scroll down to a PFI project that interests you, then scroll to the far right to a column called 'SPV name' for that project. Then google 'Companies House Beta', which is the UK corporate registry, and plug the SPV name into the search engine. Click on 'filing history' for that company, look for the latest 'annual return' or 'confirmation statement' and find 'full details of shareholders', usually near the bottom of the form. That will usually supply a new company name. Plug that new name into the search engine, and keep going, all the way up. (Be careful to type the names precisely as they are written at every step.) If the name doesn't appear, then it is probably offshore, so type the name instead into a general search engine and you may well find out where it is incorporated. Sometimes, for a small fee, you can obtain ownership information from a tax haven registry. • **9.** On the $59.4 billion and the $306 billion, see the UK Treasury summary, Private Finance and Private Finance 2 Projects: 2016 summary data, UK Treasury, 31 March 2016. On schools and hospitals being 40–70 per cent more expensive via PFI, and the debt costs, see 'PFI and PFI 2, Report by the Comptroller and Auditor General', HM Treasury, 18 January 2018, especially Figure 3, p.14 and Section 1.19, p.15. Also see Dexter Whitfield, 'The financial commodification of public infrastructure The growth of offshore PFI/PPP secondary market infrastructure funds', Research Report 8, European Services Strategy Unit, October 2016, detailing the role of offshore infrastructure funds and tax payments (I've done my own calculations). On Osborne, see 'We'll bring a new model PFI, says George Osborne', *Guardian*, 15 November 2009.

(The headline misleads: he promised to scrap it as it stood.) • **10.** See Dexter Whitfield, 'PPP Profiteering and Offshoring: New Evidence PPP Equity Database 1998–2016 (UK)', Research Report 10, European Services Strategy Unit, October 2017. The report generally refers to 'PPP/PFI' projects. PFI is a subset of PPP, public–private partnerships (PFI involves all-private financing, where PPP may involve greater government involvement). The particular statistic refers just to PFI. On the taxes, see 'PFI: five firms avoid tax despite £2 billion profits, BBC learns', BBC News, 27 October 2017, citing work by the European Services Strategy Unit. • **11.** See, for example, the Ashburton Learning Village, an educational facility in Croydon, which cost £18–24 million to build under a PFI contract but will see £79 million flowing to an SPV registered at Cannon Street in the City of London, whose ownership chain snakes up through six companies and two limited liability partnerships based either in the City of London, Mayfair or Palace Street, just behind Buckingham Palace, and up to the ultimate owner, HICL Infrastructure Company Limited, based in Guernsey. HICL has many diverse owners, with large stakes held by the investment managers Schroders and Investec Wealth & Investment Limited, retail investors and local authority and corporate pension funds, mostly in the UK (see HICL 2018 annual report, pp.9 and 100), so in this case a good chunk of the dividend flows originating in Croydon will stay in the UK. The £24 million is from Treasury Data, but the architects, penoyreprasad.com, estimated construction costs at £18 million. The SPV is listed by Treasury Data as Ashburton Services Limited. In Note 19 on its 31 March 2017 accounts it lists the ultimate controlling party as 'HICL Infrastructure Company Limited, based in St Peter Port, Guernsey'. Treasury Data lists the equity holder for that school project as 'Barclays Private Equity'; Barclays later sold it off. • **12.** See 'Equity investments in privately financed projects, NAO/HM Treasury, Report by the Comptroller and Auditor General', 10 February 2012. The National Audit Office reported that 90 per cent of the money PFI investors put in comes from banks and bondholders – other people's money. Even then, the remaining average 10 per cent equity stake is financed mostly with OPM, especially when private equity firms are involved. So the money that real warm-blooded investors put at risk is only a fraction of that 10 per cent. PFI investors told the NAO that they don't work on the basis of risks but on pre-defined returns demanded by their investment committees: returns on equity of 12–15 per cent a year – a huge return given the minimal risks – and that over 70 per cent of investors were getting returns higher than this. 'The fact that we only found one occasion when a private developer lost money on a PFI project suggests that very little risk is ever transferred to the private sector' (Andrew

Bowman, Ismail Ertürk, Peter Folkman, Julie Froud, Colin Haslam, Sukhdev Johal, Adam Leaver, Michael Moran, Nick Tsitsianis and Karel Williams, *What a Waste: Outsourcing and How it Goes Wrong*, Manchester University Press, 2015, pp.57 and 60). See also Mazzucato, *The Entrepreneurial State*, on the state's role in supporting innovation and the private sector. • **13.** See Andy Bounds, 'Local councils to see central funding fall 77 per cent by 2020', *Financial Times*, 4 July 2017; and Tom Crewe, 'The Strange Death of Municipal England', *London Review of Books*, 15 December 2016. As this last notes, 'local authorities in the top 20 per cent for rates of health deprivation and disability have had their spending power cut by an average of £205 per head, 12 times the average reduction faced by those in the bottom 20 per cent'. • **14.** The Lazonick quotes come mostly from my Skype interview with him on 7 June 2017. See also Bill Lazonick, 'Stock buybacks: From retain-and-reinvest to downsize-and-distribute', Brookings Center for Effective Management, April 2015; and 'The functions of the Stock Market and the Fallacies of Shareholder Value', Brookings Center for Effective Management, 3 June 2017. Over the period 2004–2013, he said, 454 companies in the S&P 500 Index did $3.4 trillion in stock buybacks, representing 51 per cent of net income. These companies expended an additional 35 per cent of net income on dividends. And buybacks remain in vogue. According to data compiled by Factset for the twelve-month period ending December 2014, S&P 500 companies spent $565 billion on buybacks, up 18 per cent from the previous twelve-month period.' The figure for stock ownership in the US is from Arthur B. Kennickell, 'Ponds and Streams: Wealth and Income in the U.S., 1989 to 2007', Divisions of Research & Statistics and Monetary Affairs, Federal Reserve Board, January 2009, Figure A3c, p.65 (the category is 'Equity', which represents direct and indirect holdings of publicly traded stocks). The figure given for 2007 was that the top 5 per cent owned 63 per cent of the wealth (and the top 10 per cent owned 77 per cent), but allowing for the large and well-publicised rise in wealth inequality since then, two thirds is a reasonable estimate. A more recent paper (Edward N. Wolff, 'Household Wealth Trends in the United States, 1962 to 2016: Has Middle Class Wealth Recovered?', NBER Working Paper 24085, National Bureau of Economic Research, November 2017) estimates that the top 10 per cent own 80 per cent of stock. The 'extraction' figure is $416 billion per year over 2007–2016: this figure refers to net equity issuance – new corporate stock issues minus outstanding stock retired through stock repurchases and through merger and acquisition activity. On the European data, see Mustafa Erdem Sakinç, 'Share Repurchases in Europe: A Value Extraction Analysis', Academic-Industry Research Network, May 2017, pp.10–11. The 150 per cent figure for the UK, which came via email from Sakınç on 5 December 2017, confirmed a media report about his forthcoming research but gave no further details. On 'eating themselves', See Andy Haldane, 'Firms are "almost eating themselves"', interview on BBC *Newsnight*, 25 July 2015, available on YouTube. • **15.** As the arch-monopoliser Warren Buffett put it, 'The ideal business is one that takes no capital, and yet grows.' The Lazonick material is drawn from my two phone interviews with him: one on 23 April 2012, for my *Vanity Fair* article about Mitt Romney, the other on 7 June 2017 for this book. Also see Bill Lazonick, 'Profits without Prosperity', *Harvard Business Review*, September 2014. He describes a shift from the early 1980s, when business schools used to ask, 'How do we create productive companies and create value?' to the modern era when, as he put it, the dominant question is 'How can I take a private company, rip the hell out of it, and get as much money out as possible?' • **16.** In the case of Virgin Trains, a big chunk of the returns flowed out to benefit someone who spends much of his time on Necker Island in the British Virgin Islands tax haven, Richard Branson, who consistently wins polls as Britain's most admired entrepreneur. This business model has penetrated deep into our culture. See also Bowman et al., *What a Waste*, pp.42–5 and 66; and 'The Conceit of Enterprise: train operators and trade narrative, CRESC Response to ATOC's "Growth and Prosperity" report', Centre for Research on Socio-Cultural Change, 4 September 2013. • **17.** See Ian Fraser, 'On the trail of Fred the Shred', *Sunday Herald*, 18 June 2014; and 'Market investigation into payment protection insurance', UK Competition Commission, 29 January 2009, p.6, point 34. • **18.** In her book *World City* (Polity Press, 2007) Doreen Massey talks of 'a neoliberalisation of the regional question', which is based on the belief that regions are like separate actors 'competing' with each other and that market mechanisms ought to sort any imbalances out, and a refusal to look at questions of power, inequality and the colonial relationship between the London-focused hub and the rest. This isn't just a British question. When I lived in South Africa soon after the fall of apartheid, I remember white South Africans talking about the need to 'uplift the blacks' while ignoring the question of where their own wealth and privilege came from. • **19.** 'Ownership of UK quoted shares: 2016', UK Office for National Statistics, Table 3 (p.6) shows that 56 per cent of FTSE 100 quoted shares were beneficially owned by 'rest of the world'. This figure is rising fast, up from 43.4 per cent in 2010 and 30.7 per cent in 1998. Figure 3 (p.10) shows the ratio was around 10–15 per cent in the 1980s, and 5–10 per cent in the 1960s and 1970s. • **20.** See Hannah Aldridge, Theo Barry Born, Adam Tinson and Tom MacInnes, 'London's Poverty Profile 2015', Trust for London, p.7. • **21.** As baby boomer John Kay put it in *Other People's Money*, pp.258–9, not only has his generation avoided armed conflict, but 'we have also been effective in transferring wealth from both past and future generations to ourselves … lucky indeed to have lived through the era of financialisation'. • **22.** For the £240 billion figure, see also 'Government Commercial Contracting: an overview of the NAO's work', National Audit Office, spring 2016. Total spending was £733 billion. See also a round-up of studies cited in 'Public sector outsourcing jumps under coalition', *Financial Times*, 30 April 2015. The Innes quotes are from my discussions and emails with her in September 2017. The Soviet comparison is from Abby Innes, 'First-best-world economic theory and the second-best-world of public sector outsourcing: the reinvention of the Soviet Kombinat by other means', LEQS Paper No. 134/2018, May 2018. For a shorter summary, see Abby Innes, 'Why public sector outsourcing is less efficient than Soviet central planning', LSE blogs, 13 June 2018. • **23.** From my interview with Tom Gash, 3 July 2017. He said that on outsourcing there had been 'a strong degree of continuity' from John Major to Tony Blair, but that Gordon Brown had been less gung-ho about it. On Universal Credit, see 'Labour says universal credit will take 495 years to roll out as costs rise £3bn', *Guardian*, 25 June 2015, in which a government report is quoted estimating that the 'total budgeted whole-life costs' of Universal Credit would be £15.84 billion, compared to an initial £2 billion estimated cost of implementation. • **24.** The Railtrack section is from James Meek, *Private Island*, Verso, 2015, especially pp.64 and 69. • **25.** From data.oecd. org. The measure is GDP per hour worked, measured in US$ (constant prices 2010 and PPPs). The figures for 2017 were: Britain $48,300, France $59,900, Germany $60,400, Belgium $64,600, Sweden $56,900, and Norway $80,400. The United States was $63,300. • **26.** Bowman et al., *What a Waste*, section 1.3. • **27.** I interviewed the arranger on 12 September 2016. He asked to remain anonymous. He said activity had reduced after the financial crisis as governments cracked down and arrangers sometimes acted as independent boutique units, sometimes as units inside banks. Many deals required an offshore or cross-border element to make a structure work. This was, he said, a small rootless global community concentrated in the big financial centres but not tied to any one country. • **28.** From my interview with Leaver on 22 July 2017 and subsequent emails. • **29.** He was a former partner at a City law firm whose clients included an offshore fund registered in Panama run by David Cameron's father, which was exposed in the Panama Papers tax haven scandal. Troup was subsequently appointed to chair the Panama Papers inquiry. • **30.** On HMRC staff cuts, see Chris Stephens, 'HMRC: building our future plan', Hansard, 28 April 2016. The figures are: 105,000 staff in 2005, 58,000 in 2016, and indications that the target is 41,000. The Heaton clip is from a *Private Eye*/BBC *Panorama* investigation available at 'HMRC's David Heaton quits after offering tips on avoiding tax', BBC News, 14 September 2013. See 'Osborne advised using financial loopholes to avoid tax and care costs', *Guardian*, 15 February 2015. • **31.** For an in-depth accounting look at Carillion, see Adam Leaver, 'Outsourcing firms and the paradox of time travel', SPERI blog (Sheffield Political Economy Research Institute), 21 February 2018; Adam Leaver, 'Out of time: The fragile temporality of Carillion's accumulation model', SPERI blog, 17 January 2018; and Adam Leaver, 'Intangible concerns: Goodwill and the risk of pro-cyclicality in corporate America', SPERI blog, 20 June 2018. Annual reports of other outsourcers revealed a pattern. For example, Serco's 2017 annual report showed that nearly all disclosed shareholders were investment funds of some sort, and among other outsourcers a number of the same names come up: Blackrock, UBS, Investec Asset Management Limited, Invesco and UBS. Whether these cross-shareholdings create collusive behaviour at the expense of the taxpayer or not, these firms are likely to require each other to conform to a financial consensus, with the same culture of incentives, which would have similar financialising effects. However, a 2017 paper in the US suggests that anti-competitive effects may be strong. See Germán Gutiérrez and Thomas Philippon, 'Investment-less Growth: An Empirical Investigation', NBER Working Paper 22897, National Bureau of Economic Research, January 2017. On corporate debt as the possible epicentre of the next crisis, also see, 'Where will the next crisis occur? – Buttonwood', *The Economist*, 3 May, 2018. • **32.** The 200 per cent return on capital is from Brooks, *Bean Counters*, p.8. On Carillion and PwC, see the House of Commons report on Carillion, parliament.uk, 16 May 2018, especially points 206 and 212. Brooks on p.7 uses the term 'too few to fail'. On the expected £50 million windfall, see Prem Sikka, 'The role of accountancy firms in Carillion's collapse is bigger than we thought', *Left Foot Forward*, 24 January 2018. • **33.** On the 99 per cent figure, see John Plender, 'The Big Four face the dismembering of accountancy's cosy club', *Financial Times*, 18 May 2018. See also Richard Murphy and Saila Stausholm, 'The Big Four: a study in opacity', GUE/NGL European Parliamentary Group, July 2017 (p.6 for Big Four Revenue data). Also see various works by Prem Sikka, as well as data on big4auditorcarousel.wordpress.com. • **34.** Tamasin Cave, 'More than a lobby: finance in the UK', *Open Democracy*, 26 September 2013. • **35.** On 'policy development' see 'Tax policy and controversy', EY website, accessed 12 July 2017, and 'Who really runs this place? A short report on the Big 4 accountancy firms and their ties to government', Spinwatch, June 2013. The poacher quote is from 'Tax avoidance: the role of large accountancy firms', 44th Report of Session 2012–13, Committee of Public Accounts, House of Commons, 26 April 2013. • **36.** Others at Big Four firms suggested a 50 per cent figure, and the share of what they think they can get away with changes with the political climate. The bad stuff that goes unchallenged represents what tax barrister David Quentin calls risk mining – a steady, unwarranted, hidden transfer of wealth away from ordinary taxpayers to big corporations. See 'Risk mining: what tax avoidance is, and exactly why it's anti-social', Tax Justice Network, 26 August 2014, summarising Quentin's underlying paper. • **37.** 'Tax chiefs hit back at criticism over avoidance', *BBC News*, 31 January 2013. • **38.** Spinwatch put it plainly in 'Who really runs this place?', 17 June 2013: 'The Big Four have captured the British government.' When Hodge criticised the Labour Party leadership for accepting free advice from PwC, for instance – which is, for my money, a form of corruption – she said party leader Ed Miliband called her and subjected her to 'a stream of abuse'. The Hodge quotes come from various Committee of Public Accounts hearings, as well as her chapter 'The Big Four' in her 2016 book *Called To Account: How Corporate Bad Behaviour and Government Waste Combine to Cost Us Millions*, Little, Brown, 2016, pp.108–27. For more in-depth treatment of the accounting profession, see John Dunn and Prem Sikka, 'Auditors: Keeping the Public in the Dark', Association for Accountancy and Business Affairs, 1999; and the more recent 'Tax avoidance: the role of large accountancy firms', 44th Report of Session 2012–13, House of Commons, Committee of Public Accounts, 26 April 2013. See also numerous reports by Richard Brooks for *Private Eye*, as well as his book *The Great Tax Robbery*. I also interviewed Brooks on several occasions. See also 'Calling Time: Why SABMiller Should Stop Dodging Taxes in Africa', Actionaid, April 2012 update; and Atul K. Shah, 'Systemic Regulatory Arbitrage, a case study of KPMG', Suffolk Business School, 2015. I have also discussed these issues with Shah on several occasions from 2015 to 2017. See also sourceglobalresearch.com: 'Big Four Firms', with regular blogs and updates. • **39.** See Kara Scannell, 'Big Four auditors face crackdown on global operations', *Financial Times*, 15 December 2016; Harriet Agnew, 'EY fined over Hellas conflict of interest', *Financial Times*, 16 June 2015; Harriet Agnew, 'Professional Services: Accounting for Change', *Financial Times*, 27 August 2015; and Harriet Agnew, 'Big Four auditors extend reach into consultancy', *Financial Times*, 8 March 2015.

11 *The Evidence Machine*

1. See 'UK think tanks and campaigns rated for funding transparency', Whofundsyou.org, comparison table, undated; 'How transparent are think tanks about who funds them, a survey of 200 think tanks', Transparify,

June 2016; and Emma Barnett, 'Cayman Islands sponsors C4 series', *Campaign*, 17 November 2008. Don McDougall, a Cayman Department of Tourism official, is quoted as saying 'followers of the series present exactly the right profile and demographic of visitors to the islands'. Also see 'DoT remains active in UK', *Cayman Compass*, 24 November 2008; and an interview with Ferguson in Daniel W. Dresner, *The Ideas Industry: How Pessimists, Partisans, and Plutocrats are Transforming the Marketplace of Ideas*, Oxford University Press, 2017, in which he describes his lucrative journey from Oxford professor to public pundit, saying, 'I did it all for the money.' • **2.** Devereux told me in a phone interview in 2015 that about half the centre's funding still comes from corporate donations. Its website in 2017 listed seventy-four past and previous donors including AstraZeneca, BAE Systems, BP, HSBC, Lloyds Banking Group, Daily Mail and General Trust, 3I Group, Barclays, ExxonMobil, Rio Tinto plc, SABMiller, and RBS Group, alongside funding from the Economic and Social Research Council. The centre says it subscribes fully to the Oxford University Donors' Charter, which states that 'it values and safeguards its autonomy and the freedom of inquiry by students and staff, and does not accept gifts when a condition of such acceptance would compromise these fundamental principles'. The centre is part of Oxford University's Saïd Business School, which was set up with a £20 million donation from Wafic Saïd, a Syrian-born billionaire and Conservative Party funder who in the 1980s helped broker the Al-Yamamah deal for the supply of British weapons to Saudi Arabia, Britain's biggest-ever arms contract. Devereux is also research director for the European Tax Policy Forum (ETPF), which, like the Oxford University Centre for Business Taxation, has supported a body of academic research broadly arguing that corporate and capital tax cuts tend to be good for investment, jobs and economic growth, and that much of the 'burden' of corporate taxes falls on workers and consumers – so by implication they are bad taxes because they hurt workers and everyone else. The ETPF says on its website that its role is 'to fund independent research and not to advocate particular positions', and adds, thirteen lines below that 'Sponsorship of ETPF is welcome from large European-based companies ... who have an interest in supporting economic research on tax' (from the 'About' page, accessed on various days in July 2017). The competitiveness agenda and associated C-words jump from the ETPF's reports like grasshoppers in summer. See also James Bennett, 'Profile: Christopher Wales, Brown's buddy at Goldman Sachs', *Accountancy Age*, 8 December 2005. I interviewed Devereux on 10 July 2015. • **3.** As an ETPF research report puts it, 'FDI flows have been analyzed quite frequently because they are conveniently available from countries' balance of payments numbers.' See Johannes Voget, 'The effect of taxes on foreign direct investment: a survey of the empirical evidence', ETPF, undated. This report dedicates approximately 4,500 words to the 'benefits' side of corporate tax cuts, and 54 words to the costs side, as a stray afterthought. • **4.** See 'Funds Consultant Helped Senator Behind Scenes', *Washington Post*, 12 December 1997: 'Senate investigators believe, but can't definitively prove, that the Economic Education Trust is funded by Charles and David Koch and testimony of Meredith O'Rourke.' • **5.** State taxes typically make up nearly a third of all US taxes paid, while federal and local taxes make up around three-fifths and one tenth respectively. Data from Urban/Brookings Tax Policy Center, 2015. These percentages fluctuate quite significantly. • **6.** The quotes come from Laffer speaking at about 5 minutes, 30 seconds, 9:20 and 18:20 on National Public Radio in *Planet Money*, Episode 577: 'The Kansas Experiment', 11 January 2017. For an entertaining account of the Laffer curve, see Jonathan Chait, 'Feast of the Wingnuts', *New Republic*, 10 September 2007. Among many problems is a central contradiction among the true believers: starve-the-beast anti-taxers see tax cuts as reducing the size of government, whereas Lafferites think they will boost government revenues. In *Treasure Islands* I quoted Bob McIntyre of Citizens for Tax Justice, who explained it to me thus, with a twinkle of the eye: 'On Mondays, Wednesdays and Fridays Republicans say that cutting taxes raises revenues. On Tuesdays, Thursdays and Saturdays they say cutting taxes reduces revenues so much that it forces governments to cut back – to starve the beast. And on Sundays they rest.' Peter Fisher of the University of Wisconsin-Madison, a leading US expert on public finance, is one of many who laugh at Laffer's la-la land. 'The guy has a PhD from Stanford and he gives an example of his own curve that doesn't even work,' Fisher said. 'It's quite appalling, the lack of integrity on the part of some of these people (from my telephone interview with him, 22 June 2015). • **7.** For a dispassionate early analysis of the tax cut effects see, for example, 'Lessons for other States from Kansas' Massive Tax Cuts', Center for Policy and Budget Priorities, 27 March 2014, p.2: 'Evidence from other states and academic studies casts further doubt on claims that the tax cuts will cause the state's economy to boom. States that cut taxes the most in the 1990s performed worse, on average, over the course of the next economic cycle than states that were more prudent. The academic literature generally finds that states with lower personal income taxes perform no better economically than their peers.' • **8.** Effective tax rates have fallen by a third since 2000 alone; falling corporate tax rates are widely documented. Long-standing research suggests that corporate tax cuts do attract portfolio flows and profits, with high or moderate 'elasticities'. However, new research has found a crucial qualifier: it is only once serious tax haven levels are reached – 5 per cent tax rates or lower – that companies start to take any interest. See Kimberly Clausing, 'The Effect of Profit Shifting on the Corporate Tax Base', Tax Analysts, 18 February 2016, summarising Tim Dowd, Paul Landefeld and Anne Moore, 'Profit shifting of U.S. multinationals', *Journal of Public Economics* 148:C, 2017, pp.1–13. Her crucial sentence runs: 'They find a nonlinear tax response, with far more responsiveness at lower tax rates than at higher ones. Findings indicate tax semi-elasticities of –4.7 at corporate tax rates of 5 per cent and –0.6 at tax rates of 30 per cent.' For instance, individual US states charge corporate tax rates ranging between 0 and 6 per cent, yet there's still a whole industry dedicated to helping corporations escape even this. See also Alex Cobham and Petr Jansky, 'Global distribution of revenues loss from tax avoidance: re-estimation and country results', UNU-WIDER Working Paper 55.2017; and Ernesto Crivelli, Ruud de Mooij and Michael Keen, 'Base Erosion, Profit Shifting and Developing Countries', IMF Working Paper, May 2015. Re the 'orgy' of tax avoidance, see 'New Book Examines Alternative Approach to Taxing Multinational Companies', International Centre for Tax and Development blog, Alex Cobham 28 February 2017. Figure 3 shows that profit shifting by US multinationals grew from less than 10 per cent of gross profits in 1994 to around 50 per cent by 2012. Also see Annette Alstadsæter, Niels Johannesen and Gabriel Zucman, 'Who owns the wealth in tax havens? Macro evidence and implications for global inequality', Working Paper 23805, NBER, National Bureau of Economic Research, September 2017. A qualifier: the Laffer curve does sometimes work for tiny tax havens like Bermuda, where the business of handling corporate profit shifting can be the largest sector of the economy. • **9.** An example of the UK using the Laffer curve to 'skew and distort' the evidence: in 2012 the government produced estimates designed to show that increasing the top rate of income tax from 45 to 50 pence in the pound in 2010 had raised hardly any revenue and argued it may have actually reduced revenue by stifling 'business', driving rich people overseas and encouraging tax dodging. David Gauke, the financial secretary to the Treasury, added that further reports 'are entirely unnecessary ... The 50p rate was ineffective.' And that was that until John Thompson, an independent statistician, investigated for the Tax Justice Network. He found a classic case of 'policy-based evidence': cherry-picking helpful data while disregarding, even misrepresenting, the other side. For instance, the Treasury had cited a paper by the French economist Thomas Piketty in support of its tax-cut conclusions. Thompson ran the Treasury conclusion past Piketty, who replied, 'It is indeed quite surprising to learn that our paper with Saez and Stantcheva was used in this manner, given that we basically find the opposite.' See the article I authored in collaboration with Thompson, 'UK political parties rely on unsafe top tax rate estimates', Tax Justice Network press release, 21 April 2015; and 'The exchequer effect of the 50 per cent additional rate of income tax', HMRC, March 2012, especially the section 'Laffer Curves' on pp.51–2. See also David Gauke in Hansard Debates, 8 April 2014, Column 188. The reason HMRC would undermine its own tax-raising powers is, as I explained in the last chapter, that it has become so thoroughly infiltrated by accountants and organised money that it has become almost an anti-tax tax authority. For a similar example from the United States, see 'Non-Partisan Congressional Tax Report Debunks Core Conservative Economic Theory – GOP Suppresses Study', *Forbes*, 12 November 2012. • **10.** University of Oxford Financial Statements 2015/16, University of Oxford, 2016: total expenditure was £1.32 billion. Eton College, School Fees 2016/17, www.etoncollege.com, 2017: £12,354 per term, three terms. 'Annual Report and Accounts 2015/16', Financial Conduct Authority, Table 1, p.70. The FCA obtains its income not from government but from fees levied on the firms it regulates. Total spending in 2016 was £550 million. 'HMRC annual report and accounts 2016/2017', p.119, shows 63,000 staff costing £2.4 billion. • **11.** Johnson said this via email to me on 22 May 2017. For a discussion of the Institute for Fiscal Studies in this context, see Simon Wren-Lewis, 'But do the numbers add up?', Mainly Macro blog, 17 May 2017. For the IFS statement on Labour Party policy, see Helen Miller, 'Labour's reversal of corporate tax cuts would raise substantial sums but comes with important trade-offs', Institute for Fiscal Studies, 10 May 2017. It is true that the IFS did mention the revenue costs of tax cuts, but it failed to bring in the many other costs of corporate tax cuts, and failed to weave these into an overall narrative. Instead, its focus on micro issues led it to overemphasise the benefits of corporate tax cuts, while underemphasising the costs. • **12.** See these claims made in Helen Miller, 'What's been happening to corporation tax?', Institute for Fiscal Studies, 10 May 2017, especially the section subtitled 'Corporation tax is ultimately paid by people'. This is obviously slanted against corporate taxes: falling tax revenues are 'not necessarily a concern' and 'a significant share of the burden of corporation tax tends to get shifted to labour', which is untrue. Exploring these assertions, see 'Corporate tax: the great incidence hoax', Tax Justice Network, 25 February 2016, and associated links. On corporate tax cuts shifting the tax burden onto workers, see Grace Blakeley, 'Workers, not shareholders, bear the burden of taxes in the UK. Here's how we can fix this broken system,' *Independent*, 11 March 2018, and her related paper, 'Fair Dues: rebalancing business taxation in the UK', Institute for Public Policy Research, 2018. This last document also makes the point: 'These changes have shifted the burden of taxation away from profitable but low-employment businesses to those with more staff but lower profits.' On the Trump tax cuts, see 'Trump Tax Cut Truths', Americans for Tax Fairness. Summarising public estimates, this is regularly updated: at the time of writing (20 June 2018) corporations had spent 65 times as much – $485 billion versus $7 billion – on buying back their own stock than on workers' bonuses and wage hikes (americansfortaxfairness.org, accessed 25 May 2018). • **13.** By receiving income in corporate form, earnings can be retained in the corporation and deferred until a dividend is paid at the discretion of the recipient. Corporate income can have costs set against it, it can be deferred indefinitely, or it can be received in tax-exempt ways. • **14.** The UK Office for Budget Responsibility estimated that the (mostly National Insurance) losses from the tax cuts would be £3.5 billion a year by 2021/2. Corporate tax revenue losses are harder to quantify because people often keep their earnings inside the corporation and defer their taxes, which often enables them to escape paying it at all. See 'Tax System struggles to cope with the gig economy', *Financial Times*, 24 November 2016. On the cannibalisation of income tax by corporate tax cuts, see Andrew Baker and Richard Murphy, 'Re-framing tax spillover', SPERI (Sheffield Political Economy Research Institute), 14 March 2017. The Institute for Fiscal Studies briefing note, 'The Changing composition of UK tax revenues' (April 2016), says income taxes and National Insurance add up to 45 per cent of total tax revenues, while corporation tax contributes 7 per cent. • **15.** For more on tax cuts fostering rent-seeking, see Paul Krugman, 'Monopoly Rents and Corporate Taxation (Wonkish)', *New York Times*, 31 August 2017, which also makes strong points about the 'incidence' of corporate tax. On tax avoidance rewarding multinationals over domestic firms, see, for instance, Katharina Finke, 'Tax Avoidance of German Multinationals and Implications for Tax Revenue: Evidence from a Propensity Score Matching Approach', Centre for European Economic Research (ZEW), September 2013. See also 'How tax wars may affect UK small and big business', foolsgold.international, 29 June 2015. • **16.** David Gauke, 'Speech to the Tax Journal Conference', 9 November 2011. Gauke's office did not respond to my request for an interview. See Kimberley Clausing, 'The Nature and Practice of Capital Tax Competition', Social Science Research Network, 15 April 2015. 'While aggregate capital stocks are not particularly tax-sensitive across countries, the location of profits across countries is very tax sensitive.' • **17.** See Szu Ping Chan, 'Multinational giants line up for UK tax breaks, *Daily Telegraph*, 3 May 2014. • **18.** The companies I found actually relocating – specifically in response to the Controlled Foreign Companies reforms – were Siemens, Hitachi Rail, Brit Insurance, Proteus Digital Health, Aon, CNH Global, Delphi, Ensco, Fiat Industrial, Informa, Lancashire

Holdings, Liberty Global, Noble Corp., Rowan and WPP. The analysis, which was not published because I decided to incorporate the results into this book instead, is based on replies to my emails to their press offices (four replied) and public statements. Richard Brooks supplied additional input. See Tom Bergin, 'Britain becomes haven for U.S. companies keen to cut tax bills', Reuters, 9 June 2014. On Martin Sorrell, see Patricia Kotnik, Mustafa Erdem Sakinç, Alenka Slavec and Dejan Guduraš, 'Executive compensation in Europe: Realised gains from stock-based pay', isigrowth. eu, May 2017. See also 'WPP plc – Return to the United Kingdom', company statement on wpp.com, 13 November, 2012, which said the scheme 'will not result in any significant changes in the day-to-day conduct of the business of the WPP group'. Although I could not find an explicit distributional analysis of the CFC beneficiaries, my research strongly indicated this. A related reform, however – the UK's 'patent box' reforms to try and attract patent-related activity to the UK, is estimated to have cost £617 million in tax revenues in the 2014/15 tax year, 95 per cent of which flowed to the 305 companies in the sample classified as 'large' companies. See 'R&D tax credit scheme changes see 22 per cent hike in SME claims', *Accountancy Daily*, 17 September 2017. Thanks to Professor Sol Picciotto for the pointer. • **19.** On ActionAid, see 'Collateral damage', ActionAid. On corporate tax cuts and job creation, many such studies exist. See, for example, Andrew Leigh, 'Do firms that pay less company tax create more jobs?' *Economic Analysis and Policy*, Vol. 59, September 2018, pp.25–8. As Nathan M. Jensen, 'Fiscal Policy and the Firm: Do low corporate tax rates attract multinational corporations?', Washington University in St. Louis, 1 January 2007, puts it, 'Tax policy has no discernible impact on FDI flows.' Many papers show this. See 'The Labour Share in G20 Economies', Organisation for Economic Co-operation and Development/International Labour Organization (with contributions from IMF and World Bank) prepared for the G20 Employment Working Group, Antalya, Turkey, 26–27 February 2015, which shows that as capital's share of national income has risen, and labour's share has declined, investment and growth have declined. • **20.** For example, there are timing effects that skew the research, nearly always in the same direction. Growth rates after a recession are statistically faster than usual, and governments tend to cut taxes in recessions to kick-start economies, leading to correlations between tax cuts and growth which falsely suggest that it was the tax cuts that caused the growth. What's more, tax cuts often attract investment within years or even months, while the costs, such as a less well-educated population or crumbling infrastructure due to lower tax revenues, will play out over decades. Studies that measure this tend to underplay the costs of the tax cuts relative to their benefits. Corporate tax research is made more misleading still by the fact that the evidence that policymakers use very often includes mostly old or even ancient data sets. Amid public fury following the global financial crisis, governments have tightened up on corporate profit-shifting games, but the elasticities that economists measure in this arena are not the same as they were decades ago, so tax cuts are less effective now than they were back then. Perhaps the most influential study in this area is Ruud A. de Mooij and Sjef Ederveen, 'Corporate Tax Elasticities: a Reader's Guide to Empirical Findings', Oxford University Centre for Business Taxation Working Paper 08/22, 2008. For its profit-shifting 'semi-elasticity' of –1.2 with respect to the corporate tax rate, it relied on a 2005 study, Ruud A. de Mooij, 'Will Corporate Income Taxation Survive?', *De Economist*, September 2005, Table 3, p.294, and Ruud A. de Mooij and Sjef Ederveen, 'What difference does it make? Understanding the empirical literature on taxation and international capital flows', European Economy – Economic Papers 2008–2015 261, Directorate General Economic and Financial Affairs (DG ECFIN), European Commission, December 2006. The studies they cite have publication dates that range between 1985 and 2004, and the data they use come from earlier years, including the 1970s. See also 'Discussing Discussions around the corporate income tax', phdskat.org blog, 18 August 2016. • **21.** The $3 trillion cash piles figure comes from 'EMEA companies' cash pile climbs to almost EUR1 trillion', Moodys.com, 19 July 2017, and 'US corporate cash pile grows to $1.84 trillion, led by tech sector', Moodys.com, 19 July 2017. • **22.** The expert did not want her name published. She added, via email, that policymakers ranged between people who sought to serve the public and people who wanted to deliver on manifesto commitments and did not want evidence to get in the way – and a spectrum of people in the middle. 'In the main, poliycmakers seek for and use evidence to develop and align the policy narrative that they are working on (the overarching story which shapes the decisions that are subsequently made). This shows why it looks like they pick and choose pieces of evidence that suit them: this is a side-effect of the pressure to align policy narratives so that they're coherent and defensible to critics ... there is a tension between ensuring alignment and making them defensible to critics.' In the words of the US Society for Benefit-Cost Analysis, referring to the US Congressional Budget Office's work 'scoring' government legislation, 'by far the most egregious error regarding CBO's work is the tendency of policymakers to overemphasise seemingly precise cost estimates relative to the many other (but certainly harder to define and quantify) factors that should be considered in policy decisions'. See also Chris Dillow, 'The Tyranny of Metrics: a Review', stumblingandmumbling.typepad.com, 11 April 2018. • **23.** When I asked the expert in evidence-based policymaking what typically prompts bad use of evidence in cases like the HMRC one I described, she replied, 'Someone will think that a graph is a good idea because graphs are good at communicating information. Then someone else will say, "But no, we can't because we don't have the data; what we do have is highly ambiguous," and a second person will say, "Yes, we do, look it's here," and point to something that's probably a bit out of date. By this time, the corporate communications people are involved and they say, "Well what's the message?" And then the senior bods in HMRC will say, "This is the message," because they suffer horribly from confirmation bias, and then they and the corporate communications people build up a head of steam. And then the person who said the data is ambiguous says, "Fuck it, I'm only quite junior and I have a mortgage and will fight another battle, because I've lost this one." And so it goes. Corporate communications people are a real menace, they can't cope with ambiguity.' • **24.** Christoph Böhringer, Thomas F. Rutherford and Wolfgang Wiegard, 'Computable General Equilibrium Analysis: Opening a Black Box', Centre for European Economic Research/ZEW Discussion Paper 03-56, 2003. See also Christoph Böhringer and Thomas F. Rutherford, 'CGE Peer Review of Tax Model', Loch Alpine Economics, Inc., 11 October 11, 2013; and 'HMRC's CGE Model Documentation', December 2013, both linked to 'Computable General Equilibrium (GE) modelling', gov.uk (accessed 12 July 2017). Another climate change expert, Ursula Fuentes of Climate Analytics, told me via email that 'Rutherford and Boehringer are recognised names in the field of climate change' and fairly mainstream. I called Loch Alpine's Rutherford on 14 July 2015. He effectively agreed with my 'garbage' conclusion, saying, 'If you look at the model as something that provides the truth, then you are looking at the wrong thing ... the model is a means of articulating in an explicit fashion what you think the important mechanisms are; and the fact that someone has a bias or a specific objective in the analysis, that doesn't mean the analysis is wrong – it just means you disagree with what the assumptions are.' Which is a fair point. The only journalist I could find who had noticed the Loch Alpine story was John McDermott of the *Financial Times*, who concluded, 'I worry that we have a Panglossian computer at the heart of government that has a big influence over public policy but no one other than a few super-geeks understands how it really works.' See 'Why you should care about dynamic modelling', *Financial Times*, 15 April 2014. • **25.** As Paul Krugman has argued, 'mind-changing empirical work almost always involves not much more than simple correlations' and 'really clear analytical arguments'. The complex stuff full of equations 'turns out, in practice, to be too complicated to persuade'. See 'Mind-Altering Economics', *New York Times*, 13 January 2016. On corporate tax cuts, the mantra has been 'Cut the tax rates and broaden the tax base' – the latter meaning broaden the number of things that get taxed. This has happened, and growth rates have fallen while inequality has risen. For higher-tax countries versus lower-tax countries, see for instance Neil Brooks and Thaddeus Hwong, 'Social Benefits and Economic Costs of Taxation: A Comparison of High- and Low-Tax Countries', Canadian Centre for Policy Alternatives, December 2006. • **26.** Michael Mazerov, 'Academic Research Lacks Consensus on the Impact of State Tax Cuts on Economic Growth: A Reply to the Tax Foundation', Center for Budget and Policy Priorities, 17 June 2013. • **27.** Piper is quoted in *The Kansas Experiment*, US National Public Radio (NPR), *Planet Money*, Episode 577, 11 January 2017. • **28.** And this is a more general rule: the US Internal Revenue Service has estimated that state and local taxes total on average just 1.2 per cent of the typical company's cost of doing business. This figure is from Robert G. Lynch, 'Rethinking Growth Strategies: How State and Local Taxes and Services Affect Economic Development', Economic Policy Institute, 2004, Footnote 6. • **29.** The numerous surveys are summarised by the OECD: 'There is a consensus in the [academic] literature about the main factors affecting (foreign) investment location decisions. The most important ones are market size and real income levels, skill levels in the host economy, the availability of infrastructure and other resource that facilitates efficient specialisation of production, trade policies, and political and macroeconomic stability of the host country. Survey analysis shows that host country taxation and international investment incentives generally play only a limited role in determining the international pattern of FDI.' From 'Tax Incentives for Investment: a Global Perspective, Experiences in Mena and NonMena countries', Organisation for Economic Co-operation and Development, 2008. Perhaps a more striking example comes from none other than Robert Ady, known to some as the godfather of US site relocation experts, who of all people would be expected to lobby hard for lower taxes. He estimated that for manufacturing projects and office projects, taxes only accounted for 4–5 per cent of cost factors. The cost factors for a manufacturing project and an office project were, respectively: labour 36 and 72 per cent; transport 35 and 0 per cent; utilities 17 and 8 per cent, occupancy 8 and 15 per cent; and taxes 4 and 5 per cent. See LeRoy, *The Great American Jobs Scam*, p.52, Table 2.1. See also LeRoy, pp.48–50 for an overview of what diverse businesses want. A longer list of such surveys and evidence is provided in the footnotes to Nicholas Shaxson and Ellie Mae O'Hagan, 'A competitive tax system is a better tax system', Tax Justice Network/New Economics Foundation, April 2013. On Boeing, 'Should it Bother Us that Boeing Says it Needs a Tax Incentive to Make Its Planes Safe?', Citizens for Tax Justice blog, 13 January 2014, referencing Boeing arguments submitted to an IRS hearing on 8 January 2014. I took the ice cream analogy from Jolyon Maugham, and the 'refined sugar' analogy from David Quentin, a UK tax lawyer; see Jolyon Maugham, The UK's Tax Competitiveness, waitingfortax. com, 3 November 2016, and Press Release: The UK Law Commission consultation on the fiduciary duties of investment intermediaries: Response from the Tax Justice Network, taxjustice.net, 24 March 2014. Prepared by David Quentin. • **30.** Warren E. Buffett, 'Stop Coddling the Super-Rich', *New York Times*, 14 August 2011. • **31.** Martin Wolf, 'Taxation, prosperity and productivity', *Financial Times*, 31 May 2012. Separately, Pascal Saint-Amans, head of tax at the Organisation for Economic Co-operation and Development, said, 'For the past thirty years we've been saying don't try to tax capital more because you'll lose it, you'll lose investment. Well this argument is dead, so it's worth revisiting the whole story'; see Adam Creighton, 'A Shrinking World Spurs Calls to Rewrite the Tax Guidebook: The argument against taxing capital income relatively more than wages is losing its force', *Wall Street Journal*, 21 July 2016. • **32.** For example, the data on foreign direct investment is systematically skewed in a pro-tax-cut direction by so-called round-tripping. This happens when investors who want to invest at home send their money offshore, hide their identities through financial secrecy or by diluting it in larger vehicles, then bring the money back home again – maybe piggy-backing on a whizzy private equity investment or other vehicle. By pretending to be foreign, they get tax breaks, secrecy and other benefits that a local investor wouldn't get. So a lot of what gets measured as FDI isn't FDI at all but predatory behaviour by locals stiffing their tax authorities and escaping rules and regulations, but tax haven secrecy makes it impossible to measure. Next, as I mentioned in the last chapter, foreigners own well over half the quoted shares in UK-based companies, so if Britain hands a £16 billion annual tax cut to corporations, at least half of that may flow abroad, and a significant share of the rest is likely to go to tax-exempt people and institutions, who may be able to channel this offshore. It is not clear how these entries on the 'benefit' side of the cost-benefit balance constitute a genuine benefit to Britain. Another question further muddles corporate tax data: who bears the burden or 'incidence' of corporate taxes? Is it the owners or shareholders of corporations? Is it consumers? Is it workers? This question is a hornet's nest of academic claims and counter-claims: corporate-funded think tanks will tell you that corporate taxes make workers suffer, while independent ones will tell you that this is not so. See, for instance, Kimberly Clausing, 'Who pays the Corporate Tax in a Global Economy', *National Tax Journal*, October 2012. Separately, much of the research uses GDP as a benchmark for the effects of corporate tax cuts on growth, which tends to flatter the numbers and elasticities by including profit-shifting; gross national income is often a better measure, particularly for smaller economies like Ireland's. Another issue involves the 'lower bound' question: when interest rates are close to zero, a tax-funded government spending increase ought to boost economic activity, in turn boosting taxes, while a tax cut is unlikely to do so. See, for instance, 'But do the numbers add up?', Oxford professor Simon Wren-Lewis's attack on the Institute for Fiscal Studies in his Mainly Macro blog, 17 May 2017. Furthermore, when it comes to FDI flows in response to corporate tax cuts, a big chunk of recorded profit flows to the financial sector, which will deepen the finance curse and worsen future growth. For further points in this area, see 'Ten Reasons to Defend the Corporate Income Tax', Tax Justice Network, 18 March 2015. • **33.** For example, if large multinationals are sitting on trillion-dollar cash piles that they aren't investing, why would any pro-multinational reform – whether cutting corporate taxes or financial regulations, but also reducing workers' rights or wages, or relaxing environmental rules – suddenly encourage them to start? Such measures may quantifiably boost corporate profits, but in terms of attracting or stimulating real investment, they would be pushing on a string. And it's worse than that, for the same reason I explained earlier. Because these measures take wealth out of the hands of workers and other less wealthy stakeholders in society – stakeholders who generally spend a greater share of any extra wealth that comes their way – this will tend to reduce overall demand, making it *less* likely that corporations will invest, inflicting a second round of damage. These measures will also, for the simple mathematical reasons I outlined above, tend to disproportionately reward the extractors and shareholder-value maniacs, at the expense of the patient, job-creating solid businesses that create thriving economies and societies. • **34.** John Christensen, Nick Shaxson and Duncan Wigan, 'The Finance Curse: Britain and the World Economy', *British Journal of Politics and International Relations* 18:1, 2016, pp.255–69. This was the first published paper on the finance curse, though it builds on and formalises an earlier discussion document which I co-authored with Christensen, entitled 'The Finance Curse: how oversized financial sectors attack democracy and corrupt economies'. • **35.** I described the City of London Corporation in much more detail in my last book, *Treasure Islands*, in the final main chapter. I made a couple of mistakes in that chapter, details of which can be found in the 'Errors and Updates' section of my website treasureislands.org. Most significantly, I noted the City's separateness from the rest of Britain and described this as having an offshore character, which led some readers to believe that it was therefore exempt from UK tax laws and regulations. It isn't. • **36.** See Andrew Baker and Duncan Wigan, 'Constructing and contesting City of London power: NGOs and the emergence of noisier financial politics', *Economy and Society*, 2017. For the early discussions on the formation of TheCityUK, see the Bischoff report – 'UK international financial services – the future: A report from UK based financial services leaders to the Government', HM Treasury, May 2009, especially p.49. See also Christensen et al., 'The Finance Curse: Britain and the World Economy'. The £5 million budget figure comes from TheCityUK's 'Director's Report and Financial Statements for the year ended March 31, 2016'. • **37.** For a more detailed exploration of the costs of oversized finance and why the benefits of the financial sector are smaller than TheCityUK claims, see ibid.; and the earlier Christensen and Shaxson, 'The Finance Curse: how oversized financial centres attack democracies and corrupt economies'. This present book is substantially the fruit of those earlier pieces of work. • **38.** Thorstein Veblen, who once asked a student to assess the value of her church to her in terms of kegs of beer, would have understood the problem very clearly.

Conclusion

1. Osborne was excited not just by the prospect of renminbi trading, but also of City institutions getting more direct access to the Chinese market. As he said in a speech to students at Peking University on 14 October 2013, 'I want Chinese families to have the security that comes from British pensions and insurance and banking services.' • **2.** See Jill Treanor, 'Osborne's open door to Chinese banks prompts MPs' check on City rules', *Guardian*, 16 October 2013 and; Angela Monaghan, 'China will be allowed to buy UK nuclear power stations, George Osborne says', *Guardian*, 17 October 2013. The 'bending rules' aspect was that the Chinese banks would be able to set up branches in London, rather than subsidiaries, which would have been subject to much tougher UK regulatory oversight. Andrew Tyrie, chair of the Treasury Select Committee, wrote to Osborne seeking assurances that he had not put too much pressure on regulators to accept these concessions to China. For a more detailed look at the economics of the deal, see 'Hinkley Point: the "dreadful deal" behind the world's most expensive power plant', Holly Watt, *Guardian* Long Read, 21 December 2017. People who used the term 'open for business' to describe the Hinkley C deal include Josh Hardie, deputy director general of the CBI business lobby group; Greg Clark, the business and energy secretary; David Cameron in 2013; and, perhaps more surprisingly, Justin Bowden, the national secretary for energy at the GMB union. On the 'tens of billions' estimate, see 'Report by the Comptroller and Auditor General, Hinkley Point C', National

Audit Office, 23 June 2017, p.4, estimating £30 billion as the net present value of future top-up payments. Other subsequent estimates have been higher. • **3.** See, for instance, David Shambaugh, 'China's Soft-Power Push: The Search for Respect', *Foreign Affairs*, July/August 2015; Anne-Marie Brady, 'Magic Weapons: China's Political Influence Activities under Xi Jinping', Wilson Center, September 2017; and Jonas Parello-Plesner and Belinda Li, 'The Chinese Communist Party's Foreign Interference Operations: How the U.S. and Other Democracies Should Respond', Hudson Institute, June 2018. • **4.** See James Kynge, Lucy Hornby and Jamil Anderlini, 'Inside China's secret "magic weapon" for worldwide influence', *Financial Times*, 26 October 2017; 'It's the mysterious department behind China's growing influence across the globe. And it's getting bigger', *South China Morning Post*, 21 March 2018; and Parello-Plesner et al., 'The Chinese Communist Party's Foreign Interference Operations'. • **5.** The counterterrorism expert added that he had noticed a significant contrast between UK and US banks, even between the New York versus London offices of the same banks. He said he detected a disdain in London for US laws on money laundering, 'as if they were seen as interrupting business.' He added, referring to my last book, 'When I recommend *Treasure Islands* to other people working on counter threat finance (CTF) … when we talk about [offshore issues and London's role] inevitably people say "this makes so much sense". Everyone has tall stories and anecdotes that fit the pattern. *Treasure Islands* provided a very useful framework for understanding how these pieces of the puzzle fit together.' • **6.** See HSBC Holdings plc, 'Annual report and Accounts 2017'. For geographical profit shares, see the table 'Analysis of reported results by geographical regions: HSBC reported profit/(loss) before tax, and balance sheet data', p.53. For the geographical distribution of employees, see the pie chart on p.24 entitled 'Employees (FTEs) by region'. • **7.** Widely reported. See for instance Rachel Armstrong and Lisa Jucca, 'HSBC keeps headquarters in London, rejects move to Hong Kong', Reuters, 14 February 2016. On Renminbi trading, see 'London ranks first for offshore RMB FX transactions', swift.com, 25 April 2017. Chinese officials have also used the threat of relocating renminbi business to London as a crowbar to put pressure on Luxembourg. • **8.** Rana Foroohar, 'US and China must find ways to control their elites', *Financial Times*, 1 July 2018. • **9.** With a nod to Bill Black, who first alerted me to this scene in *War Games* in the context of global 'competition' on financial regulation and tax. • **10.** I have no links to the Open Markets Institute, other than having interviewed two of their officials, Matt Stoller and Barry Lynn, for this book. • **11.** See, for example, 'Moscow's Gold: Russian Corruption in the UK', Eighth Report of Session 2017–19, House of Commons Foreign Affairs Committee.

Index